普通高等教育汽车类专业系列教材

汽车专业英语读译教程

第 3 版

主　编　梁桂航　宋进桂
副主编　谭德荣　牟爱鹏
参　编　孙德林　李　栋
　　　　周华维　神克常

机械工业出版社

本书分为15个单元(UNIT)，按照学习汽车构造的大致顺序编排了15篇有关汽车基本结构原理的英文课文(TEXT A)。在此基础上，对每个单元的相关内容进行扩展(TEXT B)，并编入与汽车使用、诊断与维修相关的实用性内容(TEXT C)以及电动汽车与自动驾驶汽车等内容。

本书的英文课文涉及汽车的发展史、发动机、底盘和电气电子系统，除了包括传统结构外，还涉及汽油机电子控制燃油喷射（包括汽油直喷）、柴油机燃油喷射系统（含高压共轨喷油系统）、排放控制、可变气门定时、自动变速器(AT)、机械式无级变速器(CVT)、机械式自动变速器(AMT)、双离合变速器(DCT)、防抱死制动系统(ABS)、牵引力控制系统(TCS)、电子稳定性控制系统(ESC)、巡航控制系统(CCS)、安全气囊(SRS)、无人驾驶汽车及电动汽车的开发与设计等。每篇课文后编排有词汇表、课文疑难注释和课后练习题，大部分单元后编排有相关专业术语和翻译技巧。

本书可作为车辆工程、交通运输和汽车服务工程等高校本科专业教材，也可供具有较好英语基础的汽车设计、使用、维修、管理等方面的工程技术人员学习参考。为了方便教学，本书配有全部课文的参考译文、教学课件、习题答案和试题库。选用本书作为教材的教师可在机械工业出版社教育服务网(www.cmpedu.com)注册后免费下载。

客服人员微信：13070116286。

图书在版编目(CIP)数据

汽车专业英语读译教程 / 梁桂航，宋进桂主编. —3版. —北京：机械工业出版社，2022.6
普通高等教育汽车类专业系列教材
ISBN 978-7-111-70749-3

Ⅰ.①汽⋯ Ⅱ.①梁⋯②宋⋯ Ⅲ.①汽车工程—英语—高等学校—教材 Ⅳ.①U46

中国版本图书馆CIP数据核字(2022)第079878号

机械工业出版社（北京市百万庄大街22号 邮政编码100037）
策划编辑：何士娟 责任编辑：何士娟
版式设计：霍永明 责任校对：黄兴伟
封面设计：马精明 责任印制：任维东
北京中兴印刷有限公司印刷
2022年7月第3版第1次印刷
184mm×260mm・19.25印张・473千字
标准书号：ISBN 978-7-111-70749-3
定价：79.90元

电话服务 网络服务
客服电话：010-88361066 机 工 官 网：www.cmpbook.com
　　　　　010-88379833 机 工 官 博：weibo.com/cmp1952
　　　　　010-68326294 金 书 网：www.golden-book.com
封底无防伪标均为盗版 机工教育服务网：www.cmpedu.com

前　言

经过120多年的发展，汽车已经成为一种集机械、电子、通信、新材料等多学科门类技术于一身的、结构极为复杂的现代化工业产物。随着科学技术的发展，汽车继续发生着日新月异的变化。为了能够及时地通过各种信息源了解汽车技术的最新发展现状及动态，促进与世界的交流；为了能够正确使用现代化生产设备和工具，解决生产中的实际问题，作为汽车类专业（交通运输、车辆工程和汽车服务工程专业）的本科学生必须具有一定的阅读和翻译英语汽车专业文献的能力。

近几年，汽车技术快速变化，在进一步提高汽车安全性、降低燃油消耗和废气排放、改善舒适性和方便性的同时，汽车传统的驱动方式正在被电动化所替代，自动驾驶技术日趋成熟。为适应这种变化，本书进行了修订。

本书以巩固汽车专业知识和英语基础，训练和提高对英语汽车专业文献的阅读和翻译能力为根本出发点，结合作者多年的教学与翻译实践的经验，对内容进行了精心选编。课文内容绝大部分直接选自近年出版的英文书刊，为读者提供了最新的信息，并按照介绍汽车结构的一般顺序进行编排，易于掌握。本教材的特点是：内容新颖且可选择性强，方便教学，注重培养读译能力。

本书在保留原来的总体结构的基础上，增加了电动汽车、无人驾驶汽车以及电动汽车开发与设计的内容，充实了免费课程资源。按照学习汽车构造的大致顺序编排了15篇有关汽车基本结构原理的英文课文（TEXT A），并在此基础上，对每个单元的相关内容进行扩展（TEXT B），编入与汽车使用、诊断与维修相关的实用性内容（TEXT C）。本次修订保留了课文疑难注释（Notes To The Text）、相关专业术语（Related Terms）和翻译技巧（Translation Techniques）等内容。

本书的英文课文涉及汽车的发展史、发动机、底盘和电气电子系统，除了包括传统结构外，还涉及汽油机电控燃油喷射（含汽油直喷）、柴油机燃油喷射系统（含高压共轨喷油）、排放控制、可变气门定时、自动变速器（AT）、机械式无级变速器（CVT）、机械式自动变速器（AMT）、双离合变速器（DCT）、防抱死制动系统（ABS）、牵引力控制系统（TCS）、电子稳定性控制系统（ESC）、巡航控制系统（CCS）、安全气囊（SRS）、无人驾驶汽车以及电动汽车的开发与设计等。

本书适用于车辆工程、交通运输和汽车服务工程等高校本科汽车类专业，TEXT A属于汽车类专业通用性内容，TEXT B和TEXT C可供不同专业（或专业方向）选学。本书还适用于具有较好英语基础的汽车设计、使用、维修、管理等方面的工程技术人员学习参考。

为了方便教学，需要全部课文参考译文、教学课件、习题答案和试题库（含参考答案）的教师请登陆机械工业出版社教育服务网下载。

本书特点是内容新颖，图文并茂，理论与应用相结合，课程网络资源丰富等。

在本书的编写和修订过程中，鲁东大学蔚山船舶与海洋工程学院和交通学院给予了极大的支持。这里对所有支持本书出版的单位和个人以及参考文献的作者深表感谢。

参与本书修订的有鲁东大学梁桂航、孙德林、宋进桂，山东理工大学谭德荣，鲁东大学牟爱鹏、李栋、周华维、神克常等。由于编者水平所限，书中可能存在不当或错误，敬请同行专家和读者朋友不吝赐教和批评指正。

编　者
2021 年 9 月

CONTENTS

前言

- **UNIT 1　AUTOMOBILE BASICS** ⋯⋯⋯⋯⋯⋯⋯⋯⋯⋯⋯⋯⋯⋯⋯⋯⋯⋯⋯⋯ 1

　　TEXT A　The Basic Components of an Automobile ⋯⋯⋯⋯⋯⋯⋯⋯⋯ 1
　　TEXT B　Automobile's History ⋯⋯⋯⋯⋯⋯⋯⋯⋯⋯⋯⋯⋯⋯⋯⋯⋯⋯ 7
　　TEXT C　How to Start and Drive Your Car ⋯⋯⋯⋯⋯⋯⋯⋯⋯⋯⋯⋯ 12
　　Related Terms ⋯⋯⋯⋯⋯⋯⋯⋯⋯⋯⋯⋯⋯⋯⋯⋯⋯⋯⋯⋯⋯⋯⋯⋯⋯ 17
　　Translation Techniques（1）——翻译过程与翻译标准 ⋯⋯⋯⋯⋯⋯⋯ 18

- **UNIT 2　ENGINE MECHANICAL** ⋯⋯⋯⋯⋯⋯⋯⋯⋯⋯⋯⋯⋯⋯⋯⋯⋯ 19

　　TEXT A　Operation, Main Components and Classification of the Engine ⋯⋯⋯ 19
　　TEXT B　Valve Systems ⋯⋯⋯⋯⋯⋯⋯⋯⋯⋯⋯⋯⋯⋯⋯⋯⋯⋯⋯⋯ 27
　　TEXT C　Piston and Rod Repair ⋯⋯⋯⋯⋯⋯⋯⋯⋯⋯⋯⋯⋯⋯⋯⋯ 35
　　Related Terms ⋯⋯⋯⋯⋯⋯⋯⋯⋯⋯⋯⋯⋯⋯⋯⋯⋯⋯⋯⋯⋯⋯⋯⋯⋯ 43
　　Translation Techniques（2）——词义选择 ⋯⋯⋯⋯⋯⋯⋯⋯⋯⋯⋯⋯ 45

- **UNIT 3　FUEL INJECTION SYSTEMS** ⋯⋯⋯⋯⋯⋯⋯⋯⋯⋯⋯⋯⋯⋯ 46

　　TEXT A　Electronic Fuel Injection ⋯⋯⋯⋯⋯⋯⋯⋯⋯⋯⋯⋯⋯⋯⋯ 46
　　TEXT B　Functions of the Motronic Systems ⋯⋯⋯⋯⋯⋯⋯⋯⋯⋯⋯ 52
　　TEXT C　Troubleshooting the EFI System ⋯⋯⋯⋯⋯⋯⋯⋯⋯⋯⋯⋯ 58
　　Related Terms ⋯⋯⋯⋯⋯⋯⋯⋯⋯⋯⋯⋯⋯⋯⋯⋯⋯⋯⋯⋯⋯⋯⋯⋯⋯ 63
　　Translation Techniques（3）——词类转换 ⋯⋯⋯⋯⋯⋯⋯⋯⋯⋯⋯⋯ 64

- **UNIT 4　GASOLINE FUEL INJECTION** ⋯⋯⋯⋯⋯⋯⋯⋯⋯⋯⋯⋯⋯⋯ 66

　　TEXT A　Gasoline Direct Injection（GDI）and Throttle-By-Wire ⋯⋯⋯ 66
　　TEXT B　Operation of the Motronic System ⋯⋯⋯⋯⋯⋯⋯⋯⋯⋯⋯ 72
　　TEXT C　Servicing the EFI System ⋯⋯⋯⋯⋯⋯⋯⋯⋯⋯⋯⋯⋯⋯⋯ 79
　　Related Terms ⋯⋯⋯⋯⋯⋯⋯⋯⋯⋯⋯⋯⋯⋯⋯⋯⋯⋯⋯⋯⋯⋯⋯⋯⋯ 86
　　Translation Techniques（4）——句子成分转换 ⋯⋯⋯⋯⋯⋯⋯⋯⋯⋯ 87

UNIT 5 DIESEL FUEL INJECTION ... 89

TEXT A Overview of Conventional Diesel Fuel Injection and
        Common Rail Injection Systems ... 89
TEXT B A New Electronically Controlled Fuel Injection System for Diesel Engines ... 94
TEXT C Turbochargers and Superchargers ... 103
Related Terms ... 109
Translation Techniques (5)——省略 ... 109

UNIT 6 ENGINE ELECTRICAL SYSTEMS ... 111

TEXT A Charging, Starting and Ignition Systems ... 111
TEXT B Direct Ignition Systems and Electronic Triggering Devices ... 118
TEXT C Engine Electrical System Service ... 126
Related Terms ... 133
Translation Techniques (6)——增词 ... 133

UNIT 7 EMISSION CONTROL SYSTEMS ... 135

TEXT A Overview of Emission Control Systems ... 135
TEXT B Three-Way Catalytic Converter and NO_x Catalyst ... 143
TEXT C Diagnosis of Computerized Engine Control Systems ... 148
Related Terms ... 153
Translation Techniques (7)——重复 ... 154

UNIT 8 CLUTCHES, MANUAL TRANSMISSIONS AND DRIVE LINE ... 155

TEXT A Clutches and Manual Transmissions ... 155
TEXT B Drive Line ... 161
TEXT C Troubleshooting the Clutch and Manual Transmission ... 167
Related Terms ... 171
Translation Techniques (8)——倒译 ... 172

UNIT 9 AUTOMATIC TRANSMISSIONS ... 174

TEXT A Automatic Transmission (AT) ... 174
TEXT B Continuously Variable Transmissions, Automated Manual Transmissions
        and Double Clutch Transmissions ... 180

TEXT C　Notes of Automatic Transmission Repair ……………………………… 187
Related Terms ……………………………………………………………………… 189
Translation Techniques（9）——分译与合译 …………………………………… 189

• UNIT 10　BRAKING SYSTEMS ……………………………………………… 190

TEXT A　Basic Braking System and ABS ……………………………………… 190
TEXT B　Traction Control System (TRAC) and Electronic Stability Control (ESC) …… 196
TEXT C　Toyota ABS Diagnosis and Troubleshooting ………………………… 202
Related Terms ……………………………………………………………………… 207
Translation Techniques（10）——数字的增减与倍数 ………………………… 208

• UNIT 11　SUSPENSION AND STEERING SYSTEMS ……………………… 209

TEXT A　Basic Parts and Types of the Suspension and Steering Systems ………… 209
TEXT B　Advanced Suspension Systems ………………………………………… 216
TEXT C　Wheel Alignment ………………………………………………………… 219
Related Terms ……………………………………………………………………… 226
Translation Techniques（11）——被动语态的翻译 …………………………… 226

• UNIT 12　BODY ELECTRICAL SYSTEMS …………………………………… 228

TEXT A　Supplemental Restraint System ………………………………………… 228
TEXT B　Cruise Control System and Remote Keyless-Entry System …………… 235
TEXT C　Electrical Troubleshooting ……………………………………………… 238
Related Terms ……………………………………………………………………… 243
Translation Techniques（12）——长句翻译 …………………………………… 243

• UNIT 13　AUTOMOTIVE COMPUTERS AND COMMUNICATION SYSTEMS … 245

TEXT A　Computers on Modern Vehicles ………………………………………… 245
TEXT B　Automotive Network ……………………………………………………… 249
TEXT C　On-Board Diagnostics (OBD) …………………………………………… 255
Related Terms ……………………………………………………………………… 261
Translation Techniques（13）——翻译技巧应用实例 ………………………… 261

• UNIT 14　ELECTRIC AND AUTONOMOUS VEHICLES …………………… 263

TEXT A　Electric Vehicles ………………………………………………………… 263

TEXT B Autonomous Vehicles 268
TEXT C Toyota Prius Hybrid Drive System 271
Related Terms 277
Translation Techniques (14) ——论文摘要翻译 277

- **UNIT 15 DEVELOPMENT AND DESIGN OF ELECTRIC VEHICLES** 281

TEXT A Development of New Battery Electric Vehicles 281
TEXT B Layout Design of Battery Electric Commercial Vehicles 286
TEXT C Optimal Configuration Selection Principle for Hybrid Drive Systems 289

REFERENCES 296

UNIT 1 AUTOMOBILE BASICS

TEXT A The Basic Components of an Automobile

Today's average car contains more than 15,000 separate, individual parts that must work together. These parts can be grouped into four major categories: engine, body, chassis and electrical equipments.

Engine

The engine acts as the power unit. The internal combustion engine is most common: it obtains its power by burning a liquid fuel inside the engine cylinder. There are two types of engine: gasoline(also called a spark-ignition engine) and diesel(also called a compression-ignition engine). Both engines are called heat engines; the burning fuel generates heat which causes the gas inside the cylinder to increase its pressure and supply power to rotate a shaft connected to the transmission.[1]

All engines have fuel, exhaust, cooling, and lubrication systems. Gasoline engines also have an ignition system. The ignition system supplies the electric spark needed to ignite the air-fuel mixture in the cylinders. When the ignition switch is turned on, current flows from the 12-volt storage battery to the ignition coil. The coil boosts the voltage to produce the strong spark of 20,000V needed to ignite the engine fuel.

The automobile supplies all the electricity it needs through its electrical system. For example, the electrical system supplies electricity for the ignition, horn, lights, heater, and starter. The electricity level is maintained by a charging circuit.

The fuel system stores liquid fuel and delivers it to the engine. The fuel is stored in the tank, which is connected to a fuel pump by a fuel line. The fuel is pumped from the fuel tank through the fuel lines. It is forced through a filter into the carburetor where it is mixed with air, or into the fuel injection system. The fuel is mixed with air to form a combustible mixture in the carburetor, the manifold, or the cylinders themselves.[2]

The cooling system removes excessive heat from the engine. The temperature in engine combustion chambers is about 2,000°F (1,094°C). Since steel melts at around 2,500°F (1,354°C), this heat must be carried away to prevent engine damage. Air and a coolant are used to carry away the heat. The radiator is filled with a coolant. The water pump circulates this coolant through the hollow walls of the engine block and head. Constant circulation of the coolant through the engine and the radiator removes heat from the engine. Heat also is removed by the radiator fan, which draws air through the narrow fins of the radiator. This system also supplies heat to the passenger compartment and the window defrosters.

The lubrication system is important in keeping the engine running smoothly. Motor oil is the lubricant used in the system. The lubrication system has four functions:

1) It cuts down friction by coating moving parts with oil;
2) It produces a seal between the piston rings and the cylinder walls;
3) It carries away sludge, dirt, and acids;
4) It cools the engine by circulating the motor oil.

To keep this system working efficiently, oil filters and motor oil must be changed regularly. All other moving parts in an automobile must also be lubricated.

Body

An automobile body is a sheet metal shell with windows, doors, a hood, and a trunk deck built into it. It provides a protective covering for the engine, passengers, and cargo. The body is designed to keep passengers safe and comfortable. The body styling provides an attractive, colorful, modern appearance for the vehicle. It is streamlined to lessen wind resistance and keep the car from swaying at driving speeds.

A sedan has an enclosed body with a maximum of 4 doors to allow access to the passenger compartment. The design also allows for storage of luggage or other goods. A sedan can also be referred to as a saloon and traditionally has a fixed roof. There are soft-top versions of the same body design except for having 2 doors, and these are commonly referred to as convertibles(Fig. 1-1).

Fig. 1-1　Sedan and convertible

Multi-purpose vans(MPV)can be based on common sedan designs or redesigns so that maximum cargo space is available.

The pick-up carries goods. Usually it has stronger chassis components and suspension than a sedan to support greater gross vehicle mass.

The bodies of commercial vehicles that transport goods are designed for that specific purpose.

Buses and coaches are usually 4-wheel rigid vehicles, but a large number of wheels and axles can be used. Sometimes articulated buses are used to increase capacity. Buses and coaches can be single-deck or double-deck. Buses are commonly used in cities as commuter transports while coaches are more luxurious and used for long distances.

Chassis

The chassis is an assembly of those systems that are the major operating parts of a vehicle. The chassis includes the power train, suspension, steering, and braking systems.

Power Train System

The power train system comprises clutch, transmission, propeller shaft, rear axle and differential, and the driving road wheels.

The clutch or torque converter has the task of disconnecting and connecting the engine's power from and to the driving wheels of the vehicle. This action may be manual or automatic.

The main purpose of the transmission or gearbox is to provide a selection of gear ratios between the engine and driving wheels, so that the vehicle can operate satisfactorily under all driving conditions. Gear selection may be done manually by the driver or automatically by a hydraulic control system.

The function of the propeller(drive)shaft is to transmit the drive from the gearbox to the input shaft of the rear axle and differential assembly. Flexible joints allow the rear axle and wheels to move up and down without affecting operation.

The rear axle and differential unit transmits the engine's rotational power through 90° from propeller shaft to axle shaft to road wheels. A further function is to allow each driving wheel to turn at a different speed; essential when cornering because the outer wheel must turn further than the inside wheel. A third function is to introduce another gear ratio for torque multiplication.

Suspension System

The axles and wheels are isolated from the chassis by a suspension system. The basic job of the suspension system is to absorb the shocks caused by irregular road surfaces that would otherwise be transmitted to the vehicle and its occupants, thus helping to keep the vehicle on a controlled and level course, regardless of road conditions.[3]

Steering System

The steering system, under the control of the driver at the steering wheel, provides the means by which the front wheels are directionally turned. The steering system may be power assisted to reduce the effort required to turn the steering wheel and make the vehicle easier to manoeuvre.

Braking System

The braking system on a vehicle has three main functions. It must be able to reduce the speed of the vehicle, when necessary; it must be able to stop the car in as short a distance as possible; it must be able to hold the vehicle stationary. The braking action is achieved as a result of the friction developed by forcing a stationary surface (the brake lining) into contact with a rotating surface (the drum or disc).

Each wheel has a brake assembly, of either the drum type or the disc type, hydraulically operated when the driver applies the foot brake pedal.

Electrical Equipment

The electrical system supplies electricity for the ignition, horn, lights, heater, and starter, etc. The electricity level is maintained by a charging circuit. This circuit consists of a battery, and an alternator (or generator). The battery stores electricity. The alternator changes the engine's mechanical energy into electrical energy and recharges the battery.

NEW WORDS

component	[kəm'pəunənt]	n.	成分，组成，部件，零件
chassis	['ʃæsi]	n.	底盘
transmission	[trænz'miʃən]	n.	变速器，传动，传动系统，传送，发射
lubrication	[ˌluːbri'keiʃən]	n.	润滑
ignition	[ig'niʃən]	n.	点火，点燃
ignite	[ig'nait]	v.	点火，点燃
boost	[buːst]	v.	升压，推进，增加，增压，提高
filter	['filtə]	n.	滤清器，滤波器，过滤器
carburetor	['kɑːbjuretə]	n.	化油器
combustible	[kəm'bʌstəbl]	a.	易燃的
radiator	['reidieitə]	n.	散热器，冷却器，辐射体
hollow	['hɔləu]	a.	空心的，虚伪的；n. 洞，窟窿，山谷
circulate	['səːkjuleit]	v.	(使)循环，(使)流通
defroster	[ˌdiː'frɔstə]	n.	除冰(或霜)装置
sludge	[slʌdʒ]	n.	软泥，淤泥
hood	[hud]	n.	发动机罩
styling	['stailiŋ]	n.	花[式]样
streamlined	['striːmlaind]	a.	流线型的，现代化的
sedan	[si'dæn]	n.	轿车，轿子
enclosed	[in'kləuzd]	a.	封闭的，密闭的
pick-up	['pikʌp]	n.	拾波器，皮卡(轻型货车)，传感器
gross	[grəus]	a.	总的，毛重的；n. 总额
coach	[kəutʃ]	n.	四轮大马车，长途客车，教练
rigid	['ridʒid]	a.	刚硬的，刚性的，严格的
axle	['æksl]	n.	轮轴，车轴

articulated	[ɑːˈtikjuleitid]	*a.* 铰接(的)，有关节的
capacity	[kəˈpæsiti]	*n.* 容量，生产量，才能，能力
commuter	[kəˈmjuːtə]	*n.* 长期月票使用者，(远距离)上下班往返的人
luxurious	[lʌgˈʒuəriəs]	*a.* 奢侈的，豪华的
suspension	[səsˈpenʃən]	*n.* 悬架，悬浮，悬浮液，暂停，中止，悬而未决
differential	[ˌdifəˈrenʃəl]	*n.* 差速器，微分；*a.* 微分的，差动的
clutch	[klʌtʃ]	*n.* 离合器
hydraulic	[haiˈdrɔːlik]	*a.* 液压的，水压的，水力的
isolate	[ˈaisəleit]	*v.* 隔离，孤立，绝缘，查出(故障)
course	[kɔːs]	*n.* 过程，经过，进程，方针，路线，跑道，课程
manoeuvre	[məˈnuːvə]	= maneuvre *v.* 策划，调动，演习，操纵，机动(动作)；*n.* 策略，调动
drum	[drʌm]	*n.* 鼓，鼓声；*v.* 击鼓
pedal	[ˈpedl]	*n.* 踏板
torque	[tɔːk]	*n.* 转矩，扭矩

PHRASES AND EXPRESSIONS

spark-ignition engine	点燃式发动机
compression-ignition engine	压燃式发动机
storage battery	蓄电池
ignition coil	点火线圈
charging circuit	充电电路
combustion chamber	燃烧室
passenger compartment	乘客室，乘客舱
window defroster	风窗除霜器
motor oil	机油
sheet metal	钢板，金属板
trunk deck	行李箱盖
multi-purpose van (MPV)	多用途厢式车
commercial vehicle	商用汽车
power train	传动系，动力装置
propeller shaft	= drive shaft 传动轴
torque converter	液力变矩器
gear ratio	传动比
flexible joint	柔性接头
axle shaft	半轴
road wheel	车轮
brake lining	制动器摩擦片

NOTES TO THE TEXT

[1] Both engines are called heat engines; the burning fuel generates heat which causes the gas inside the cylinder to increase its pressure and supply power to rotate a shaft connected to the transmission.

在这个长句中，后一个分句对前面分句进行说明。在后一个分句中，which causes…至句末是一个定语从句。本句可以译为："这两种发动机均被称为热机。在热机中，燃料燃烧产生的热能使气缸内的气体压力升高，并提供动力，使一根与变速器相连的轴转动。"

[2] The fuel is mixed with air to form a combustible mixture in the carburetor, the manifold, or the cylinders themselves.

此句中的介词短语 in the carburetor, the manifold, or the cylinders themselves 内有三个并列的介词宾语，说明可燃混合气形成的地点或者在化油器内（化油器式发动机），或者在进气歧管内（进气道燃油喷射发动机），或者在气缸内（缸内直接喷射发动机）。本句可以译为："燃油在化油器内，或者在进气歧管内，或者就在各个气缸内与空气混合，从而形成可燃混合气。"

[3] The basic job of the suspension system is to absorb the shocks caused by irregular road surfaces that would otherwise be transmitted to the vehicle and its occupants, thus helping to keep the vehicle on a controlled and level course, regardless of road conditions.

在本句中，应注意三点：①that would otherwise be transmitted to the vehicle and its occupants 是 shocks 的定语从句；②thus helping…现在分词短语做主句的状语，并非定语从句的构成部分；③to keep the vehicle on a controlled and level course 不定式短语的含义是"使汽车保持在可以控制的、笔直的行驶路线上"。本句可以译为："悬架系统的基本作用是吸收路面不平引起的冲击和振动，使其不会传递给车辆和乘客。这样，不管路况如何，都能使车辆具有可控制的、笔直的行驶路线。"

EXERCISES

Ⅰ. *Answer the following questions:*
1. There are two types of engine. What are they?
2. What are the functions of the lubrication system?
3. What are the components of the power train system?
4. What are the three main functions of the braking system?

Ⅱ. *Translate the following terms into Chinese:*
1. sedan
2. convertible
3. pick-up
4. commercial vehicle
5. bus
6. coach

TEXT B Automobile's History

Overview

Although such attempts were done before consider that one of the first autos was created by Karl Friedrich Benz who was a German automobile engineer. It was a single-cylinder, water-cooled, 958cm^3, 0.75hp (560W) unit, but the whole three-wheeled vehicle, and it was first driven through Mannheim in 1885 by his wife Bertha Benz. Simultaneously Gottlieb Daimler and Wilhelm Maybach in Stuttgart made the motorized vehicle. They also are known as inventors of the first motor bike.

The chronological scale of automobile history is here (British classification). All vehicles are divided into two large classes: Antique (1885 - 1979) and Modern (1980 - present). By its part antique autos are subdivided into four group: Veteran (1885 - 1904), Brass or Edwardian (1905 - 1918), Vintage (1919 - 1930) and Classic (1931 - car over 25 years old). These groups also called eras. In addition in Classic era there are two periods: Pre-war (1931 - 1948) and Post-war (1949 - 1979). Antique period is the most interesting when every year new technologies were being invented step by step, vehicles were becoming faster, cheaper and safer.

First mass automobiles manufacturing for people began in Veteran era. Up to 1900 there were already car producing companies in France and USA. One of the first companies was Parhard et Levassor, formed in 1889, in France. The company was quickly followed by Peugeot two years later. In the United States in 1893 was founded the Duryea Motor Wagon Company, becoming the first American automobile manufacturing company. Moreover Oldsmobile (dominated in this era), Cadillac, Winton and Ford were largest auto-producers of that time.

Next automobile era is called Brass or Edwardian, during this era, development of automotive technology was rapid, that time appeared lots of small manufacturers and majority of sales shifted from the hobbyist and enthusiast to the average user. That time were founded such companies as Chevrolet and Isuzu. Henry Leyland former head of Cadillac began new Lincoln Motor Company. Lots of inventions were done. Electric ignition and the electric self-starter both were invented by Charles Kettering, for the Cadillac Motor Company. Engineers devised independent suspension, and four-wheel brakes. The most vivid models of this era were Ford Model T, Bugatti Type 13, Maxwell AA Runabout and Mercedes Simplex.

The Vintage era changed appearance of automobiles; the most recognizable features came front engine location, instead of middle engine, closed body types of vehicles. Also multi-valve and overhead cam, V8, V12, and even V16 engines were produced. Cars became much more practical, convenient and comfortable during this period. Car heating was introduced, as was the in-car radio. Instead of ordinary brakes were used hydraulically actuated. Power steering was also an innovation of this era. Cadillac presented crash proof windscreen and gear box synchronizer. Examples that could give imagination of this era are: Austin 7, Bugatti Type 35, Ford Model A and Cadillac V-16.

Started just after American's Great Depression Classic era however ended much later. By the 1930s, most of the technologies used in automobiles had been invented; however it was often reinvented again at a later date and credited to someone else. Power window, front wheel drive, independent suspension, turbocharger and many other innovations had been used in that time. During the Second WW although civil auto producing was slowed down; lots of inventions were done in military engineering that later were implemented for peaceful car industry. The marking and outstanding autos of Classic era are: Volkswagen Beetle, Citroen Traction Avant, Oldsmobile 88, Jaguar E-type, Ford Mustang and Porsche 911.

Modern era defined as the 25 years preceding the current year. It was surprising us every day. The hi-tech auto features such as installed computer, hybrid technology, new and composite materials for body and engine, researches of new kinds of fuel (as a fuel cell, hydrogen, solar battery etc), improvement of car design...these all and more became true in modern era. Vehicles became essential part of social life; the price of it could emphasize importance of owner, besides cars became more universal and common. The modern tendencies pick out the hatchback, minivan, and sport utility vehicle (SUV) car types. These are the most popular body-styles now. There are great models among brand's model range and auto producers meaning VW Golf, Honda Accord, Toyota Camry, Ford Taurus and Jeep Grand Cherokee. The auto-industry now is one of largest in the world.

First Automobile

"Benz & Co. Rheinische Gasmotoren-Fabrik" Company was founded in 1885. One of this brand founders, Carl Friedrich Benz, began building automobile with internal-combustion engine. He used chassis with three wheels, equipped with wood spokes and rubber hoop.

The company's first engine was meant for industrial purposes and gave only 120-180rpm-rather few for moving a whole vehicle. Benz's second invention was 4-stroke engine with 950 cubic centimeter capacity, 0.75hp power and 400r/min. The construction of the engine included valves instead of a slider, battery ignition and closed cooling system. In addition the engine was arranged between rear wheels and was given horizontal fly-wheel.

The engine drive was carried out via binary chains. The vehicle weighted 263kg and was able to reach 16km/h of average speed. In 1885 the first automobile in world was ready for start and Benz made the first test trip in it. Afterwards the car would be named "Benzina". Next year "Benz and K" Company took out their first patent for a car with gasoline engine. (On January 29, 1886, Karl Benz received the first patent (DRP No. 37435) for a gas-fueled car.)

Thanks to Parisian Emilio Rodecker, representative of Benz Company in France, the name of Benz Patent Motorwagen became more famous in France than in Germany! One day Berta Benz, the wife of Carl Benz, decided to "popularize" this invention in Germany too. One morning they moved the automobile out of the garage, started the engine and drove it for 90km (54miles) to Phoriheim city, where their grandmother lived. At the end of day Carl received telegram from them, saying "Good Luck in Foriheim!"

In 1888 at the Monace Industrial Exhibition, an improved motorwagen model earned a gold medal. Benz was driving his car throughout Monaco's streets and afterwards got the first driving license in the world in Baden on the 1st August, 1888.

From 1888 to 1893 there were produced 15 vehicles of that successful model. Now you can find the original first Benz car in Unterturkheim museum of Mercedes-Benz, in Stuttgart.

NEW WORDS

motorize	[ˈməutəraiz]	vt. 使机动化，使摩托化
chronological	[ˌkrɔnəˈlɔdʒikəl]	a. 按年代顺序的，编年的
antique	[ænˈtiːk]	n. 古物，古董；a. 古代的，过时的
veteran	[ˈvetərən]	n. 老兵，老手，富有经验的人；a. 老练的，经验丰富的
vintage	[ˈvintidʒ]	a. 古老的，古典的，最佳的；n. 制造时期，葡萄收获期
classic	[ˈklæsik]	a. 第一流的，古典的；n. 杰作，名著，经典
dominate	[ˈdɔmineit]	v. 支配，占优势
hobbyist	[ˈhɔbiist]	n. 沉溺于某种癖好者，嗜某爱好成癖的人
enthusiast	[inˈθjuːziæst]	n. 热心家，狂热者
vivid	[ˈvivid]	a. 生动的，活泼的，鲜明的，逼真的
actuate	[ˈæktjueit]	v. 开动，促使，操纵，控制
crash	[kræʃ]	n. 碰撞，坠毁，撞击声，爆裂声；v. 碰撞，坠落，坠毁，(指商业公司等)破产
synchronizer	[ˈsiŋkrənaizə]	n. 同步装置[器]
imagination	[iˌmædʒiˈneiʃən]	n. 想象，空想，想象的事物，想象力
implement	[ˈimplimənt]	v. 贯彻，实现，执行；n. 工具，器具
preceding	[pri(ː)ˈsiːdiŋ]	a. 在前的，前述的
surprising	[səˈpraiziŋ]	a. 令人惊讶的

hybrid	[ˈhaibrid]	a. 混合的；n. 杂种，混血儿，混合物，混合动力装置
hydrogen	[ˈhaidrədʒən]	n. 氢
hatchback	[ˈhætʃbæk]	n. 有舱门式后背的汽车，溜背式汽车
minivan	[ˈminivæn]	n. 微型厢式车
found	[faund]	v. 建立，创立，创办
spoke	[spəuk]	n. 轮辐
hoop	[hu:p]	n. 箍，铁环
slider	[ˈslaidə]	n. 滑雪者，滑冰者，滑块，滑板
patent	[ˈpeitənt]	n. 专利权，专利品；a. 特许的，专利的；v. 取得……的专利权
representative	[ˌrepriˈzentətiv]	n. 代表，代理；a. 典型的，有代表性的
popularize	[ˈpɔpjuləraiz]	v. 普及
museum	[mju(:)ˈziəm]	n. 博物馆

PHRASES AND EXPRESSIONS

independent suspension	独立悬架
power steering	动力转向
crash proof windscreen	防撞玻璃
power window	电动车窗
composite material	复合材料
fuel cell	燃料电池
sport utility vehicle(SUV)	多功能运动车
driving license	驾驶执照

NOTES TO THE TEXT

课文中的人名、地名、车名、公司名

Karl Friedrich Benz	[人名]	卡尔·弗雷德里奇·本茨
Bertha Benz	[人名]	贝莎·本茨
Gottlieb Daimler	[人名]	哥特里布·戴姆勒
Wilhelm Maybach	[人名]	威廉·梅巴赫
Stuttgart	[地名]	斯图加特
Parhard	[人名]	帕卡德
Duryea	[人名]	杜里埃
Oldsmobile	[车名]	奥兹莫比尔
Cadillac	[车名]	凯迪拉克

Winton	[车名]	温顿
Ford	[公司名]	福特
Chevrolet	[车名]	雪佛兰
Isuzu	[公司名]	五十铃
Henry Leyland	[人名]	亨利·利兰德
Lincoln	[车名]	林肯
Charles Kettering	[人名]	查尔斯·凯特林
Bugatti	[车名]	布加迪
Maxwell	[车名]	麦克斯韦
Mercedes	[人名]	默西迪丝
Austin	[车名]	奥斯丁
Volkswagen Beetle	[车名]	大众·甲壳虫
Citroen Traction Avant	[车名]	雪铁龙·特莱克艾文
Jaguar	[车名]	捷豹
Ford Mustang	[车名]	福特·野马
Porsche 911	[车名]	保时捷911
VW Golf	[车名]	大众·高尔夫
Honda Accord	[车名]	本田·雅阁
Toyota Camry	[车名]	丰田·凯美瑞
Ford Taurus	[车名]	福特·金牛座
Jeep Grand Cherokee	[人名]	吉普·大切诺基
Monaco	[地名]	摩纳哥
Baden	[地名]	巴登
Mercedes-Benz	[公司名]	梅赛德斯-奔驰

EXERCISES

I. Translate the following English names of car makers into Chinese:

1. General Motors Corporation
2. Ford Motor Co.
3. Chrysler Motors Corporation
4. Toyota Motor Corporation
5. Nissan Motor Co. Ltd.
6. Honda Motor Co. Ltd.
7. Mitsubishi Motors Corporation
8. Mercedes-Benz AG
9. BMW AG
10. Volkswagen AG

11. Audi AG
12. Suzuki Motor Corporation
13. Isuzu Motors Ltd.
14. Mazda Motor Corporation
15. Volvo Car Corporation
16. Volvo Bus Corporation
17. Porsche AG

II. Translate the following English names of cars into Chinese:
1. Chevrolet Corvette; Buick Century; Cadillac Deville
2. Ford Mustang; Ford Mondeo; Lincoln Town Car
3. Dodge Caravan; Jeep Grand Cherokee; New Yorker
4. Land Cruiser; Camry; Crown; Lexus
5. Bluebird; Sunny; Infiniti
6. Accord; Acura
7. Pajero; Galant
8. Passat; Golf

TEXT C   How to Start and Drive Your Car

Before starting the engine

1. Check the area around the vehicle before entering it.
2. Adjust seat position, seatback angle, headrest height and steering wheel angle.
3. Adjust inside and outside rear view mirrors.
4. Lock all doors.
5. Fasten seat belts.

How to start the engine

Before Cranking

1. Apply the parking brake firmly.
2. Turn off unnecessary lights and accessories.
3. Manual transmission: Press the clutch pedal to the floor and shift the transmission into neutral. Hold the clutch pedal to the floor until the engine is started.

Automatic transmission: Put the selector lever in "P". If you need to restart the engine while the vehicle is moving, put the selector lever in "N". A starter safety device will prevent the starter from operating if the selector lever is in any drive position.

4. Automatic transmission only: Depress the brake pedal and hold it to the floor until driving off.

Starting The Electronic Fuel Injection Engine

The multipoint electronic fuel injection system/sequential multipoint electronic fuel injection system in your engine automatically controls the proper air-fuel mixture for starting. You can start a cold or hot engine as follow:

1. With your foot off the accelerator pedal, crank the engine by turning the key to "START". Release it when the engine starts.

2. After the engine runs for about 10 seconds, you are ready to drive.

If the temperature is below freezing, let the engine warm up for a few minutes before driving.

NOTICE

Do not crank for more than 15 seconds at a time. This may overheat the starter and wiring systems. Do not race a cold engine. If the engine becomes difficult to start or stalls frequently, have the engine checked immediately.

Pretrip safety check

It is a good idea to review the safety check before starting out on a trip. A few minutes of checking can help ensure safe and pleasant driving. Just a basic familiarity with your vehicle is required and a careful eye![1]

If you make this check in an enclosed garage, make sure there is adequate ventilation. Engine exhaust is poisonous.

Before Starting The Engine

Outside the vehicle

Tires. Check the pressure with a gauge and look carefully for cuts, damage, or excessive wear.

Wheel nuts. Make sure no nuts are missing or loose.

Fluid leaks. After the vehicle has been parked for a while, check underneath for leaking fuel, oil, water, or fluid. (Water dripping from the air conditioner after use is normal)

Wiper blades. Look for wear or cracks.

Lights. Make sure that the headlights, stop lights, tail lights, turn signals and other lights are all working. Check the headlight aim.

Inside the vehicle

Spare tire, jack and wheel nut wrench. Check the tire pressure and make sure you have your jack and wheel nut wrench.

Seat belts. Check that the buckles lock securely. Make sure that the belts are not worn or frayed.

Horn. Does it work?

Instruments and controls. Especially make sure that the warning lights, instrument lights, and defroster are working.

Wipers and washer. Make sure that they both work and that the wipers do not streak.

Brakes. Make sure that the pedal has enough clearance.

Spare fuses. Make sure you have spare fuses. They should cover all the amperage ratings designated on the fuse box lid.

In the engine compartment

Coolant level. Make sure that the coolant level is correct.

Radiator and hoses. Make sure the front of the radiator is clean—not blocked with leaves, dirt, or bugs. Check the hoses for cracks, kinks, rot, and loose connections.

Battery and cables. All the battery cells should be filled to the proper level with distilled water. Look for corroded or loose terminals and a cracked case. Check the cables for good condition and connections.

Wiring. Look for damaged, loose, or disconnected wires.

Brake and clutch fluid levels. Make sure that the brake and clutch fluid levels are correct.

Engine drive belts. Check all belts for fraying, cracks, wear or oiliness. Apply thumb pressure between the pulleys. The deflection of each belt should be within the specified limits.

Fuel lines. Check the lines for leaks or loose connections.

After Starting The Engine

Exhaust system. Look for cracks, holes and loose supports. Listen for any leakage. Have any leaks fixed immediately.

Automatic transmission fluid (ATF). Check the dipstick with the engine idling and the selector lever in "P".

Power steering fluid. With the engine idling, give the steering wheel several end-to-end turns and check the fluid level.

Engine oil level. Stop the engine and check the dipstick with the vehicle parked on a level spot.

While Driving

Instruments. Make sure that the speedometer and gauges are working.

Brakes. At a safe place make sure the brakes do not pull.

Tips for driving in various conditions

- Always slow down in gusty crosswinds. This will allow you much better control.
- Drive slowly onto curbs and, if possible, at a right angle. Avoid driving onto high, sharp-edged objects and other road hazards. Failure to do so can lead to severe tire damage, resulting in tire bursts.

- When parking on a hill, turn the front wheels until they touch the curb so that the vehicle will not roll. Apply the parking brake, and place the transmission in "P" (automatic) or in first or reverse (manual). If necessary, block the wheels.
- Washing your vehicle or driving through deep water may get the brakes wet. To see whether they are wet, check that there is no traffic near you, and then press the pedal lightly. If you do not feel a normal braking force, the brakes are probably wet. To dry them, drive the vehicle cautiously while lightly pressing the brake pedal with the parking brake pulled.

CAUTION

- Before driving off, make sure that the parking brake is fully released and the parking brake reminder light is off.
- Do not leave your vehicle unattended while the engine is running.
- Do not rest your foot on the brake pedal while driving. It can cause dangerous overheating, needless wear, and poor fuel economy.
- To drive down a long or steep hill, reduce your speed and downshift. Remember, if you ride the brakes excessively, they may overheat and not work properly.
- Be careful when accelerating, upshifting, downshifting or braking on a slippery surface. Sudden acceleration or engine braking, could cause the vehicle to spin or skid.
- Do not continue normal driving when the brakes are wet. If they are wet, your vehicle will require a longer stopping distance, and it may pull to one side when the brakes are applied. Also, the parking brake will not hold the vehicle securely.

NOTICE

When driving on wet roads, avoid driving through large amounts of standing water on the road. Large amounts of water entering the engine compartment may cause damage to the engine and/or electrical components.

Winter driving tips

- *Make sure you have ethylene-glycol antifreeze in the radiator.*
- *Do not use alcohol type antifreeze.*
- *Check the condition of the battery and cables.*

Cold temperatures reduce the capacity of any battery, so it must be in top shape to provide enough power for winter starting.

- *Make sure the engine oil viscosity is suitable for the cold weather.*
- *Keep the door locks from freezing.*

Squirt lock de-icer or glycerine into the locks to keep them from freezing. To open a frozen lock, try heating the key before inserting it.

- Use a washer fluid containing an antifreeze solution.

This product is available at dealer and most auto parts stores. Follow the manufacturer's directions for how much to mix with water.

NOTICE

- Do not use engine antifreeze or any other substitute as washer fluid because it may damage the vehicle's paint.
- Do not use parking brake when there is a possibility it could freeze.

When parking, put the transmission into "P" (automatic) or into first or reverse (manual) and block the front wheels. Do not use the parking brake, or snow or water accumulated in and around the parking brake mechanism may freeze the parking brake, making it hard to release.

- Keep ice and snow from accumulating under the fenders.

Ice and snow built up under your fenders can make steering difficult. During bad winter driving, stop and check under the fenders occasionally.

- Depending on where you are driving, we recommend you carry some emergency equipment.

Some of the things you might put in the vehicle are tire chains, window scraper, bag of sand or salt, small shovel, jumper cables, etc.

NEW WORDS

headrest	['hedrest]	n. 头枕
seatback	['siːtbæk]	n. 座椅靠背
fasten	['fɑːsn]	v. 固定，连接，扣紧，抓住
crank	[kræŋk]	v. 起动，摇转；n. 曲柄，曲轴
race	[reis]	v.（使）疾跑，猛转，全速行进
familiarity	[fə,mili'ærəti]	n. 熟悉，精通
ventilation	[,venti'leiʃən]	n. 通风，流通空气
wiper	['waipə]	n. 刮水器，手帕，擦拭者
buckle	['bʌkl]	n. 带扣
fray	[frei]	v. 磨损，擦伤；n.（织物等）磨损处
fuse	[fjuːz]	n. 熔断器，熔丝；v. 熔合
designate	['dezigneit]	v. 指明，指出，指派
dipstick	['dipstik]	n. 油标尺
curb	[kəːb]	n. 路边，路缘(石)
crosswind	['krɔswind]	n. 横风，侧风
hazard	['hæzəd]	n. 危险，冒险
burst	[bəːst]	v. 爆裂，炸破，爆发；n. 突然破裂

unattended	[ˌʌnə'tendid]	*a*. 没人照顾的，未被注意的
ethylene-glycol	['eθili:n'glaikɔl]	*n*. 乙二醇
viscosity	[vis'kɔsiti]	*n*. 黏度，黏性
squirt	[skwə:t]	*v*. 喷出
glycerine	['glisəri:n]	*n*. 甘油，丙三醇
de-icer	[di:'aisə]	*n*. 除冰装置
shovel	['ʃʌvl]	*n*. 铲，铁铲
scraper	['skreipə]	*n*. 刮刀，刮的人，平土机，铲土机

PHRASES AND EXPRESSIONS

rear view mirror	后视镜
selector lever	（自动变速器）变速杆
automatic transmission fluid（ATF）	自动变速器液
power steering fluid	动力转向液
steering wheel	转向盘
parking brake	驻车制动器
reminder light	提示灯，警告灯
pull to one side	跑偏
top shape	最佳状态
antifreeze solution	防冻液
tire chain	轮胎防滑链
jumper cable	（利用另一辆汽车蓄电池进行起动使用的）跨接电缆

NOTES TO THE TEXT

[1] a careful eye!
此短语的意思是"仔细检查"。

Related Terms

passenger car	客车，乘用车
fire engine	消防车
wagon	客货两用车，旅行车
station wagon	旅行车
hatchback car	舱背式轿车
off-road vehicle	越野汽车

Translation Techniques(1)——翻译过程与翻译标准

翻译就是将一种语言文字的意义用另一种语言文字表达出来。翻译过程包括理解和表达两个阶段。

理解阶段是要在辨明词义、弄清语法的基础上，结合已经掌握的知识或原理，准确地把握原文含义。理解是翻译的关键，准确、快速理解原文需要有较好的英语基础和汽车专业基础，同时应具备其他相关的专业知识。理解分为两个步骤：通读全文，领略原文大意；确定词义和语法关系。必要时，这两个过程需穿插反复进行。

表达是运用必要的翻译技巧，将英语用规范的汉语体现出原文的内容与含义。表达的过程主要有三个步骤：初译、核对与润色。初译是在理解的基础上，用合乎汉语习惯的表达方式将原文用汉语表达出来。为了确保正确性，应将译文与原文对照，检查有无疏漏或错误。最后还要对译文进行润色，使译文语句精炼、易懂，可能的情况下应适当运用修辞手段，使语言具有美感。

关于翻译的标准，有多种说法，严复先生提出的"信、达、雅"曾是最受推崇的翻译标准。"信"，即忠实原文，忠实原文的内容含义，忠实原文的风格。"达"是指译文应通顺流畅，易于理解。"雅"是风雅，即译文应有韵味和美感。这三个方面在文学翻译中都很重要，但在科技翻译中，更多的人坚持忠实与通顺的翻译原则。

UNIT 2 ENGINE MECHANICAL

TEXT A Operation, Main Components and Classification of the Engine

The automotive engine is essentially a heat engine. The heat engines used in automobiles are internal combustion engines.

Principle of Operation

The spark-ignition engine is an internal-combustion engine externally supplied in ignition. The gasoline engine is a kind of spark-ignition engines.

The four-stroke-cycle gasoline engine cycle is spread over four piston strokes. The operation strokes are shown in Fig. 2-1.

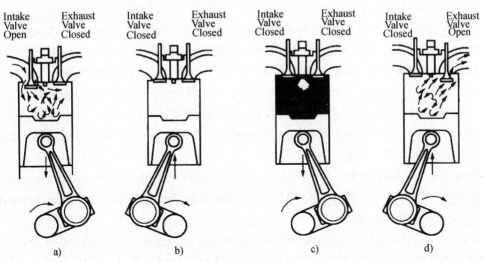

Fig. 2-1 The operation of a four-stroke-cycle gasoline engine
a) Induction b) Compression c) Power d) Exhaust

The first stroke in your engine is called the intake stroke. Instead of opening the intake valve after you have drawn the piston down, you will find it better to open the intake valve as the piston starts down.[1] This allows the air to draw fuel in the entire time the piston is moving down.

Remember, the intake stroke starts with the piston at the top of the cylinder (intake valve open and exhaust valve closed) and stops with the piston at the bottom of its travel.[2]

This requires one-half turn of the crankshaft.

As the crankshaft continues to move, the piston is forced up through the cylinder. If you keep both valves closed, the fuel mixture will be squeezed, or compressed, as the piston reaches the top. This is called the compression stroke. It, too, requires a half turn of the crankshaft.

The compression stroke serves to break up the fuel into even smaller particles. This happens due to the sudden swirling and churning of the mixture as it is compressed.

When the air-fuel mixture is subjected to a sudden sharp compression force, its temperature rises. This increase in temperature makes the mixture easier to ignite and causes it to explode with greater force. As the piston reaches the top of its travel on the compression stroke, it has returned to the proper position to be pushed back down by the explosion.

Remember, the compression stroke starts with the piston at the bottom of the cylinder (both valves closed) and stops with the piston at the top of the cylinder. This requires an additional half turn of the crankshaft.

As the piston reaches the top of the compression stroke, the mixture is broken into tiny particles and heated up. When ignited, it will explode with great force. This is the right time to explode the mixture. A spark plug provides a spark inside the combustion chamber. The spark produced at the plug is formed by the ignition system. This will be discussed in Unit 6.

Just imagine that a hot spark has been provided in the fuel mixture. The mixture will explode and, in turn, force the piston down into the cylinder. This gives the crankshaft a quick and forceful push. This is the power stroke. Both valves must be kept closed during the power stroke or the pressure of the burning fuel will squirt out through the valve ports. Remember, the power stroke starts with the piston at the top of the cylinder (both valves closed) and stops with the piston at the bottom of the cylinder. This requires another half turn of the crankshaft.

When the piston reaches the bottom of the power stroke, the exhaust valve opens. The spinning crankshaft forces the piston up through the cylinder, pushing burned gases out. This is the exhaust stroke.

Remember, the exhaust stroke starts with the piston at the bottom of the cylinder (exhaust valve open and intake valve closed). It stops with the piston at the top of the cylinder. This requires one more half turn of the crankshaft.

If you count the number of half turns in the intake, compression, power, and exhaust strokes, you will find you have a total of four. This gives you two complete turns, or revolutions, of the crankshaft. While the crankshaft is turning around twice, it is receiving power only during one half turn, or one fourth of the time.

As soon as the piston reaches the top of the exhaust stroke, it starts down on another intake, compression, power, and exhaust cycle. This cycle is repeated over and over. Each complete cycle consists of four strokes of the piston, hence the name four-stroke cycle.

Main Engine Components

Engine Block

The engine block serves as a rigid metal foundation for all parts of an engine. It contains the cylinders and supports the crankshaft and camshaft. In older engines, the valve seats, ports, and guides are built into the block. Accessory units and the clutch housing are bolted to it.

Blocks are made of either cast iron or aluminum. The lighter the block(providing it has sufficient strength), the better. The modern thin-wall casting process controls core size and placement much more accurately than the older casting process. This permits casting the block walls much thinner, reducing the weight of the block. Since the block wall thickness is more uniform, block distortion during service is less severe.

Cylinders

The cylinder is a round hole formed in the block. It forms a guide for the piston and acts as a container for taking in, compressing, firing, and exhausting the air-fuel charge. Cylinders have been made of both steel and cast iron. Cast iron is by far the most popular.

When steel cylinders are desired in an aluminum block, they are installed in the form of cylinder sleeves(round, pipe-like liners). These sleeves may be either cast or pressed into the block. Some engines use removable cylinder sleeves. When the cylinder becomes worn, the old sleeves can be pulled out and new sleeves can be pressed in. The sleeves are pressed into oversize cylinder holes. Cylinder sleeves are widely used in heavy-duty truck and industrial engines. Sleeves can also be used to repair a worn or cracked cylinder in a cast iron block.

Pistons

The piston must move down through the cylinder to produce a vacuum to draw a fuel charge into the cylinder. It then travels up in the cylinder and compresses the mixture. When the mixture is fired, the pressure of the expanding gas is transmitted to the top of the piston. This drives the piston back down through the cylinder with great force, transmitting the energy of the expanding gas to the crankshaft. The piston then travels up through the cylinder and exhausts the burned fuel charge.

Pistons are usually made of aluminum. Often, aluminum pistons are tin-plated to allow proper break-in when the engine is started. Aluminum pistons can be forged, but they are more commonly cast. Cast iron is a good material for pistons used in a slow-speed engine. It has excellent wear characteristics and will provide good performance.

Connecting Rods

As the name implies, connecting rods are used to connect pistons to the crankshaft. The upper end of the rod oscillates(swings back and forth), while the lower or big end rotates(turns).

Because there is very little bearing movement in the upper end, the bearing area can be reasonably small. The lower end rotates very fast, and the crankshaft bearing journal turns inside the connecting rod. This rotational speed tends to produce heat and wear. To make the rod wear well, a larger bearing area is required.

The upper end of the rod has a hole through it for the piston pin. The bottom of the large end of the connecting rod must be removed so the rod can be installed on the crankshaft journal. The section that is removed is called the connecting rod cap.

Connecting rods are normally made of alloy steel. They are drop-forged to shape and then machined.

Crankshaft

The engine crankshaft provides a constant turning force to the wheels. It has throws to which connecting rods are attached, and its function is to change the reciprocating motion of the piston to a rotary motion to drive the wheels. Crankshafts are made of alloy steel or cast iron.

The crankshaft is held in position by a series of main bearings. The maximum number of main bearings for a crankshaft is one more than the number of cylinders. It may have fewer main bearings than cylinders. Most engines use precision insert bearings that are constructed like the connecting rod bearings, but are somewhat larger. In addition to supporting the crankshaft, one of the main bearings must control the forward and backward movement.

Flywheel

A heavy flywheel is attached to the rear of the crankshaft with bolts. The function of the flywheel is to smooth out engine speed and keep the crankshaft spinning between power strokes. In some engines, the flywheel also serves as a mounting surface for the clutch. The outer rim of the flywheel has a large ring attached with gear teeth cut into it. The teeth of the starter motor engage these teeth and spin the flywheel to crank the engine. When an automatic transmission is used, the torque converter assembly works with the flywheel.

Camshaft

The camshaft is used to open and close the valves. There is one cam on the camshaft for each valve in the engine. Generally only one camshaft is used in most engines. Newer engines are increasingly equipped with two or more camshafts(Fig. 2-2).

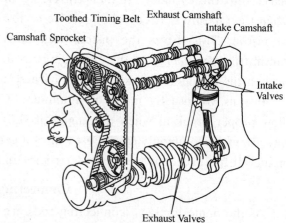

Fig. 2-2 Dual overhead camshaft(DOHC)driven by a toothed drive belt

Valves

Each engine cylinder ordinarily has two valves. However, modern engines often use four valves per cylinder (two intake and two exhaust). A few engines used in smaller vehicles have three or five valves per cylinder: two intake valves and one exhaust valve or three intake valves and two exhaust valves.

Because the head of an exhaust valve operates at temperatures up to 1300°F (704°C), valves are made of heat-resistant metal. In order to prevent burning, the valve must give off heat to the valve seat and to the valve guide. The valve must make good contact with the seat and must run with minimum clearance in the guide.

Valve Lifters

Mechanical valve lifters are usually made of cast iron. The bottom part that contacts the camshaft is hardened. Some lifters are hollow to reduce weight. Most valve trains that contain mechanical lifters have some provision for adjusting clearance. Mechanical valve lifters were used in older engines.

Hydraulic valve lifters perform the same job as mechanical lifters. However, hydraulic lifters are self-adjusting, operate with no lifter-to-rocker arm clearance, and uses engine oil under pressure to operate. Hydraulic lifters are quiet in operation.

Engine Classification

Cycle Classification

Engines are often classified according to cycle. Most internal combustion piston engines use a two- or four-stroke cycle. All modern automobile engines use the four-stroke cycle engine.

The two-stroke cycle engine performs the intake, compression, firing, and exhaust sequence in one revolution of the crankshaft.

Cylinder Classification

The inline engine has its cylinders arranged one after the other in a straight line. They are in a vertical, or near vertical position. Most modern inline engines are four cylinders.

A V-type engine places two banks or rows of cylinders at an angle to each other—generally at 60° or 90°. The V-type engine has several advantages: short length, extra block rigidity, a short crankshaft, and low profile that is conducive to low hood lines. The shorter block permits a reduction in vehicle length with no sacrifice in passenger room.

The horizontal opposed engine is like a V-type engine, except that both banks lie in a horizontal plane. The advantage here is an extremely low overall height, which makes this engine ideally suited to installations where space is limited.

Cooling Classification

As you have learned, engines are either liquid-cooled or air-cooled. Most vehicles use liquid-cooled engines. Air-cooled engines are used in limited numbers on modern vehicles.

Fuel Classification

Automobile engines can use gasoline, diesel fuel, gasohol (mixture of gasoline and alcohol), alcohol, LNG (liquefied natural gas), CNG (compressed natural gas), or LPG (liquefied propane gas). Gasoline powers the majority of vehicles, but diesel fuel is used in some vehicles. Gasohol, LNG, CNG, and LPG are beginning to see wider use. One of the principal differences in these engines is in method of fuel delivery and carburetion. Gasoline, LNG, CNG, and LPG utilize the same basic type of engine, but LNG, CNG, and LPG utilize a slightly different fuel delivery setup. Diesel engines do not use a carburetor or an ignition system.

NEW WORDS

combustion	[kəm'bʌstʃən]	n. 燃烧
stroke	[strəuk]	n. 行程
piston	['pistən]	n. 活塞
cylinder	['silində]	n. 气缸
valve	[vælv]	n. 气门，阀门，阀
exhaust	[ig'zɔ:st]	n. 排气，废气；v. 用尽，耗尽，排气
intake	['inteik]	n. 进气，进（引，吸）入
compression	[kəm'preʃən]	n. 压缩
crankshaft	['kræŋkʃɑ:ft]	n. 曲轴
swirl	[swə:l]	n. 漩涡，涡流，紊流；v. 涡动
churn	[tʃə:n]	v. 搅拌，搅动
foundation	[faun'deiʃən]	n. 基础，基地，基金，机座
camshaft	['kæmʃɑ:ft]	n. 凸轮轴
accessory	[æk'sesəri]	n. 附属品，附件，辅助装置
clutch	[klʌtʃ]	n. 离合器
housing	['hauziŋ]	n. 外壳
bolt	[bəult]	n. 螺栓；v. 用螺栓联接
core	[kɔ:]	n. 芯，核心，铁心，型芯，沙芯，（电缆）芯线
aluminum	[ə'lju:minəm]	= aluminium [ˌælju:'minjəm] n. 铝
liner	['lainə]	n. 衬套，衬里，衬板
oversize	['əuvə'saiz]	n.& a. 加大尺寸
heavy-duty	['hevi'dju:ti]	a. 重型的，重载的
oscillate	['ɔsileit]	v. 振荡，振动，波动，动摇
bearing	['bɛəriŋ]	n. 轴承

journal	[ˈdʒəːnl]	n. 轴颈，杂志
throw	[θrəu]	n. & v. 投掷，扔；n. 投掷距离，偏心距离，摆幅，(pl.)曲柄
attach	[əˈtætʃ]	v. 附着，连接，固定(to)
reciprocating	[riˈsiprəkeitiŋ]	a. 往复的
mount	[maunt]	v. 安装，固定；n. 安装件，支架，机座
rim	[rim]	n. 边缘，轮缘，轮辋，齿圈
heat-resistant	[hiːtriˈzistənt]	a. 耐热的
clearance	[ˈkliərəns]	n. 间隙
lifter	[ˈliftə]	n. 挺杆
harden	[ˈhɑːdn]	v. 硬化，变硬，淬硬
revolution	[ˌrevəˈluːʃən]	n. 转，回转，大变革
inline	[ˈinˈlain]	a. 直列式的，在一条直线上的
bank	[bæŋk]	n. (气缸)列，排，银行
rigidity	[riˈdʒiditi]	n. 刚性
profile	[ˈprəufail]	n. 外形，轮廓
conducive	[kənˈdjuːsiv]	a. 有助于……的，促进……的(to)
sacrifice	[ˈsækrifais]	n. 牺牲(品)，损失；v. 牺牲，放弃
liquefy	[ˈlikwifai]	v. 液化
propane	[ˈprəupein]	n. 丙烷
carburetion	[ˌkɑːbjuˈreʃən]	n. 汽化
carburetor	[ˌkɑːbjuˈretə]	n. 化油器

PHRASES AND EXPRESSIONS

internal combustion engine	内燃机
four-stroke cycle	四冲程循环
spark plug	火花塞
intake stroke	进气行程
power stroke	作功行程
compression stroke	压缩行程
exhaust stroke	排气行程
connecting rod	连杆
automatic transmission	自动变速器
torque converter	液力变矩器
insert bearing	镶入式轴承
valve seat	气门座
valve guide	气门导管

hydraulic valve lifter	液力挺杆
valve train	气门机构，气门组

NOTES TO THE TEXT

[1] Instead of opening the intake valve after you have drawn the piston down, you will find it better to open the intake valve as the piston starts down.

Instead of...的意思是"而不是……""代替着……"。draw...down 的意思是"将……向下移"。better 为副词，意思为"更好""更多""更加"，修饰动词不定式短语 to open the intake valve。本句译为："在活塞下行之后，进气门不只是已经打开，而是随着活塞的下移，开度还在进一步增大。"

[2] Remember, the intake stroke starts with the piston at the top of the cylinder (intake valve open and exhaust valve closed) and stops with the piston at the bottom of its travel.

with 后面的宾语可接现在分词、过去分词、形容词，甚至是副词，with 后面的宾语（名词）与现在分词、过去分词、形容词之间具有"主谓"关系。这时整个 with 短语说明附带情况，或者交代细节。本句译为："记住，进气行程在活塞位于气缸顶部（进气门开启，排气门关闭）时开始，在活塞到达其行程的底部时结束。"

EXERCISES

I. Answer the following questions:

1. What are the four strokes in a four-stroke cycle engine?
2. Using cylinder arrangement, there are three most popular engines in use today. What are they?
3. What are the advantages of a hydraulic lifter?
4. What are the advantages of a V-type engine?

II. Choose the best answer for each of the followings:

1. Crankshafts are usually made of_____.
   A. cast iron   B. stainless steel   C. copper alloy   D. aluminum
2. Connecting rods are usually made of_____.
   A. cast iron   B. stainless steel   C. alloy steel   D. copper
3. Pistons are usually made of_____.
   A. cast iron   B. stainless steel   C. alloy steel   D. aluminum
4. In addition to supporting the crankshaft, one of the main bearings must control the _____ movement.
   A. up and down   B. forward and backward
   C. left and right   D. transverse

TEXT B Valve Systems

Operation of Valve System

You have seen that the intake valve must be opened for the intake stroke, both valves must remain closed during the compression and power strokes, and the exhaust valve opens during the exhaust stroke. The designer must design a device to open and close the valves at the proper times.

The shaft will have an egg-shaped bump called a cam lobe. The cam lobe is machined as an integral part of the shaft. This shaft is called a camshaft.

The distance the valve will be raised, how long it will stay open, and how fast it opens and closes can all be controlled by the height and shape of the lobe. [1]

As you will see later, it is impractical to have the cam lobe contact the end of the valve stem itself. You have placed the camshaft some distance above the end of the valve stem.

When the camshaft is turned, the lobes will not even touch the valve stem. The lifter is installed between the cam lobe and the valve stem. The upper end rides on the lobe and the lower end almost touches the valve stem. The lifter slides up and down in a hole bored in the head metal that separates the valve stem from the camshaft.[2]

You have developed a method of opening and closing the valves. The next problem is how and at what speed to turn the camshafts. Each valve must be open for one stroke. The intake valve is open during the intake stroke and remains closed during the compression, power, and exhaust strokes. This would indicate that the cam lobe must turn fast enough to raise the valve every fourth stroke.

You can see that it takes one complete revolution of the cam lobe for every four strokes of the piston.

Remember that four strokes of the piston require two revolutions of the crankshaft. You can say that for every two revolutions of the crankshaft, the camshaft must turn once. If you are speaking of the speed of the camshaft, you can say that the camshaft must turn at one-half crankshaft speed.

If the crankshaft is turning and the camshaft must turn at one-half crankshaft speed, it seems logical to use the spinning crankshaft to turn the camshaft. One very simple way to drive the camshaft would be by means of gears and a belt. One gear is fastened on the end of the crankshaft, and the other is fastened on the end of the camshaft. The smaller crankshaft gear drives the large camshaft gear through the belt.

If, for instance, the small gear on the crankshaft has 10 teeth and the large gear on the camshaft has 20 teeth, the crankshaft will turn the camshaft at exactly one-half crankshaft speed.

VVT—Toyota's Continuously Variable Valve Timing

The most significant and satisfying changes to the Lexus GS line are in the area of powertrain. In the case of the GS300, Lexus breathes new life into last year's 3.0L inline six, by introducing VVT—continuously variable valve timing system. On the dyno, VVT shows up as only five additional horsepower and 10 lb-ft of torque. But in the car it means fuel economy improvements of 1.6 mpg, smoother idle, California TLEV (transitional low-emissions vehicle) certification and zero-to-60 mph a half second quicker.

Toyota eliminates the compromise of conventional valve timing with the introduction of VVT. By continuously varying intake valve timing (up to 60 crank angle degrees), Toyota optimizes low- to mid-speed torque, improves fuel economy and lowers emissions without having a negative impact on idle.

In essence, the system controls valve overlap, which means it can eliminate it completely for a glass smooth idle, or maximize it to boost volumetric efficiency and reduce pumping losses—this translates into power, economy and cleaner running at all engine speeds.

The heart of the system is the intake cam pulley, which consists of an inner and outer section. The inner portion is fixed to the camshaft and nests inside the belt-driven outer pulley via helical spline gears. An electronically controlled hydraulic piston moves the pulley halves relative to one another, causing the cam portion to rotate within the outer pulley.

This rotation advances or retards intake valve timing. A spool valve reacting to signals from the ECU controls hydraulic pressure.

VTEC—Honda Variable Valve Timing and Lift Electronic Control

By designing a higher valve lift, wider valve-timing, and larger valve diameter, it is possible to obtain a higher volumetric efficiency to cope with higher output engine speeds. The VTEC is used to improve volumetric efficiency from low engine speed to high engine speed. With VTEC, the valve timing and lift can be adjusted at low engine rotation to increase torque and prevent air from being forced back through the intake.

VTEC Layout

In Fig. 2-3 the structure of the VTEC is shown. The engine has one extra cam profile and rocker arm (mid rocker arm) for high engine speed. The cam has 3 different profiles located at the intake and exhaust of each cylinder. The center cam is used exclusively for high speed and the 2 outside cams for low speed.

The rocker arm assembly is composed of a mid rocker arm with primary and secondary rocker arms on each side. Inside the rocker arms are 2 hydraulic pistons, a stopper pin, and a return spring, which make up the change over mechanism.

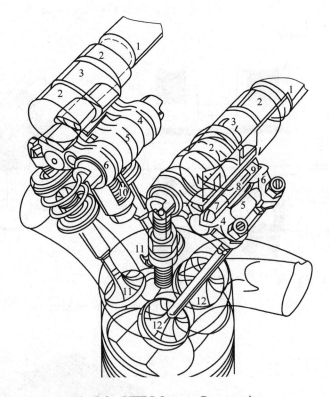

Fig. 2-3 VTEC System Construction
1—Camshaft 2—Cam lobe for low speed range 3—Cam lobe for high speed range
4—Primary rocket arm 5—Mid rocker arm 6—Secondary rocker arm 7—Hydraulic piston A
8—Hydraulic piston B 9—Stopper pin 10—Lost-motion spring 11—Exhaust valve 12—Intake valve

The mid rocker arm has a lost motion spring so that the valve operates smoothly at high speeds and also stops the arm at low speeds.

The whole system is operated by a hydraulic actuator which is controlled by the Engine Control Unit(ECU).

VTEC Operation

Fig. 2-4 shows the VTEC mechanism while operating at low engine speeds. In the low-speed mode the 3 rocker arms are separated and use cams A & B only. At this time the mid rocker arm is in contact with the high speed cam due to the spring force in the lost motion mechanism. It is separated from the primary and secondary rocker arm and thus is not actuating the valves. Fig. 2-5 shows the VTEC mechanism while operating in the high speed mode. During high speed engine operation the 3 rocker arms are connected and move together due to the 2 hydraulic pistons which have moved over due to increased hydraulic pressure.

BMW Variable Camshaft Control(VANOS)

The system consists of hydraulic adjuster, mechanical adjuster and solenoid valve for hydraulic actuation(Fig. 2-6).

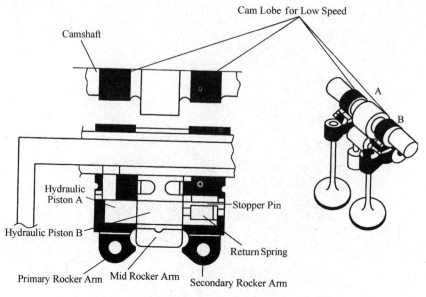

Fig. 2-4 Rocker arm operation (low speed range)

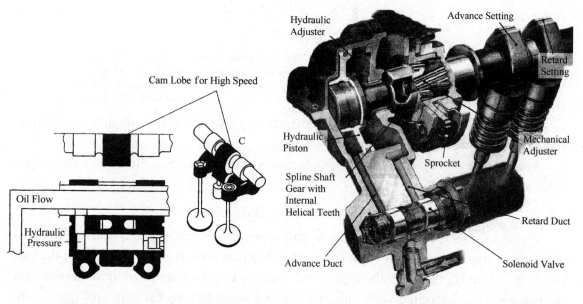

Fig. 2-5 Rocker arm operation (high speed range)　　Fig. 2-6 Design of Camshaft Adjustment

　　This system is similar to Toyota's VVT described above in design and operation. With this system the inlet camshaft is rotated in the opposite direction to the camshaft gear. Depending on the position of the solenoid valve, the hydraulic piston is displaced to the left or right. The axial movement of the hydraulic piston causes camshaft adjust (turn) in the "Advance" or "Retard" direction in the mechanical adjuster by means of the helical teeth (Fig. 2-7). Adjustment can be performed steplessly.

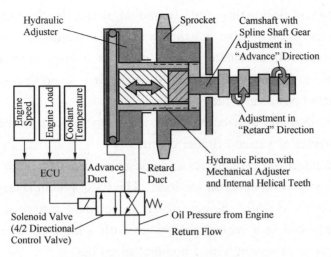

Fig. 2-7 Operation of camshaft adjustment

VaneCam—a Vane-Type Adjuster

Additional adjustment of the exhaust camshaft brings about an increase in torque in the lower to middle speed range as well as in the middle to upper speed range.

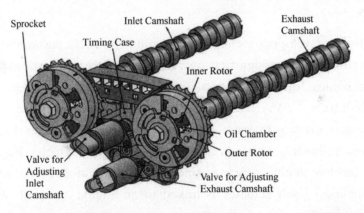

Fig. 2-8 A vane-type adjuster

A vane-type adjuster (VaneCam) is shown in Fig. 2-8. The outer rotor is permanently connected to the sprocket and the inner rotor to the camshaft respectively. The outer rotor and inner rotor can be rotated in opposite directions. The oil pressure in the respective oil chamber is variably controlled by the hydraulic valves. The camshafts are adjusted in this way. The maximum turning angle of the inner rotor to the outer rotor is, for example, 52° CA for the inlet camshaft and 22°CA for the exhaust camshaft.

Electronic Valve Control System

An electronic valve control (EVC) system replaces the mechanical camshaft, controlling each valve with actuators for independent valve timing. The EVC system controls the opening and closing time and lift amount of each intake and exhaust valve with independent actuators on each valve. Changing from a mechanical camshaft driven valve into independently controlled actuator valves provides a huge amount of flexibility in engine control strategy. Vehicles utilizing EVC can realize several benefits including:

1) Increases engine power and fuel economy.
2) Allows centralized and distributed EVC systems to perform at their full potential.
3) Adapts to engines of varied cylinder counts.

With all of the improved efficiencies and consumer benefits, auto manufacturers are eager to get their first EVC systems on the road. The EVC system is targeted to operate in temperatures up to 125℃, while the actuator is targeted to run up to 6,000r/min. The actuator can be controlled in a centralized system with a high-speed multiplex bus(up to 10Mbps)or in a distributed system with a nominal speed bus.

EVC systems must be compact in size, specifically the actuators that must be small enough to fit in the engine space. A vehicle that uses a 42V system is ideal for EVC because it requires high voltage to control the valve actuators, and EVC is targeted for V8 and V12 engines.

Smart Valves

Valeo is actively developing technology for reducing fuel consumption and emissions with an engine cylinder-head design that uses its Smart Valve Actuation(SVA)in place of conventional mechanical operation of engine valves by the cam belt, camshaft, and hydraulic cam followers.[3] SVA is the first of many innovations that Valeo intends to actively develop and market to meet increasing demand for better fuel economy and reduced pollution following its acquisition of Johnson Controls' Engine Electronics Division.[4] In a camless engine, each engine valve is operated by an actuator mounted above the valve guides. Each actuator is linked to an engine-mounted valve control unit that ensures optimal positioning of all valves and performs the power drive function.

By controlling residual gases, minimizing pumping losses, and deactivating cylinders and valves, this technology can reduce fuel consumption and pollutant emissions by 20%. Consumers will benefit from enhanced performance from increases in low-end engine torque. The SVA development program is supported by several car manufacturers and is scheduled for volume production in 2009.

NEW WORDS

bump [bʌmp] n. 撞击,(因撞击而起的)肿块; v. 碰,撞,颠簸
cam [kæm] n. 凸轮

lobe	[ləub]	n. 凸起
integral	[ˈintigrəl]	a. 完整的，整体的，积分的
stem	[stem]	n. 杆，茎
powertrain	[ˈpauətrein]	n. 动力系统，动力装置，传动系统
dyno	[ˈdainəu]	n. = dynamometer 测功机，测力计
breathe	[briːð]	v. 呼吸，发出
certification	[ˌsəːtifiˈkeiʃən]	n. 证明，鉴定，检验证明书
compromise	[ˈkɔmprəmaiz]	v. & n. 妥协，折中
essence	[ˈesns]	n. 基本，本质，实质，精华，要素
pulley	[ˈpuli]	n. 滑轮，带轮
helical	[ˈhelikəl]	a. 螺旋状的
spline	[splain]	n. 花键，方栓
spool	[spuːl]	n. 线轴，卷轴；滑阀；绕圈
mpg		= mile per gallon(英里/加仑)
actuator	[ˈæktjueitə]	n. 执行器，执行元件
strategy	[ˈstrætidʒi]	n. 策略，谋略
flexibility	[ˌfleksəˈbiliti]	n. 灵活性，柔性，适应性
eager	[ˈiːgə]	v. 渴望着，热心于
multiplex	[ˈmʌltipleks]	a. 多元的，多重的，多样的；n. 多路传输，多路通信
nominal	[ˈnɔminl]	a. 名义上的，有名无实的；标定的，额定的；微小的
bus	[bʌs]	n. 总线
innovation	[ˌinəuˈveiʃən]	v. 改进，革新，创新，新发明(技术、方法)
residual	[riˈzidjuəl]	a. 剩余的，残余的

PHRASES AND EXPRESSIONS

cam lobe	凸轮的凸起部分
valve stem	气门杆
variable valve timing(VVT)	可变气门正时
in essence	本质上，实质上
spool valve	滑阀
electronic valve control(EVC)	电子式气门控制
centralized system	集中系统
distributed system	分布系统
camless engine	无凸轮发动机
smart valve	智能气门

NOTES TO THE TEXT

[1] The distance the valve will be raised, how long it will stay open, and how fast it opens and closes can all be controlled by the height and shape of the lobe.

The distance 后面有一个定语从句。本句译为:"气门升起距离的大小、开启持续时间的长短以及开启和关闭速度的快慢全都受凸轮凸起部分的高度和形状的控制。"

[2] The lifter slides up and down in a hole bored in the head metal that separates the valve stem from the camshaft.

句中 that separates...是 lifter 的定语从句。separate...from...是"将……与……隔开"之意。本句译为:"气门挺杆在气缸盖上镗出的孔中上、下移动,它将气门杆与凸轮轴隔开"。

[3] Valeo is actively developing technology for reducing fuel consumption and emissions with an engine cylinder-head design that uses its Smart Valve Actuation(SVA)in place of conventional mechanical operation of engine valves by the cam belt, camshaft, and hydraulic cam followers.

句中 with an engine cylinder-head design 是修饰 reducing 的,而整个 for reducing...介词短语是修饰 technology 的。that uses...一直到句末是一个定语从句,修饰 design。在这个定语从句中,by...介词短语是修饰 mechanical operation 的后置定语。本句可译为:"瓦莱奥(Valeo)公司正在积极开发使用一种气缸盖设计来降低燃油消耗和排放的技术。这种气缸盖技术利用了瓦莱奥公司的智能气门操纵(SVA)机构,来替代使用带传动、凸轮轴和液压气门挺杆的传统的机械式发动机气门操纵机构。"

[4] SVA is the first of many innovations that Valeo intends to actively develop and market to meet increasing demand for better fuel economy and reduced pollution following its acquisition of Johnson Controls' Engine Electronics Division.

句中 that Valeo intends to actively develop and market to meet... pollution 为 innovations(革新项目)的后置定语。Following...一直到句末是分词短语,作状语。本句可译为:"在兼并了江森自控公司的发动机电子器件分公司(Johnson Controls' Engine Electronics Division)之后,瓦莱奥为满足日益增长的提高燃油经济性和降低排放的需求而打算积极开发和销售的多种新技术项目中的第一个就是 SVA。"

EXERCISES

I. Answer the following questions:
1. List the components of the valve system.
2. What are the advantages of a VVT system?
3. What are the advantages of an EVC system?

II. Translate the following terms into Chinese:
1. DOHC
2. top dead center(TDC)

3. bottom dead center(BDC)
4. valve timing
5. timing belt
6. valve spring
7. timing marks
8. push rod
9. rocker arm
10. variable valve timing(VVT)

TEXT C Piston and Rod Repair

This repair procedure requires removal of the cylinder head and oil pan. It is much easier to perform this work with the engine removed from the vehicle and mounted on a stand. These procedures require certain hand tools. A cylinder ridge reamer, a numbered punch set, piston ring expander, snapring tools and piston installation tool (ring compressor) are all necessary for correct piston and rod repair.

Cleaning & Inspection

If the piston is out of specification or otherwise unusable, it must be replaced. If the cylinder is worn or damaged, the engine block must be bored and oversize pistons installed.

1. Remove the piston rings from the piston. The compression rings(top and middle rings) must be removed using a piston ring expander, to prevent breakage and/or scratching the piston.

2. If there is no obvious damage to the piston and the intent is to reuse the piston, clean the ring grooves with a ring groove cleaner, being careful not to cut into the piston metal.

Heavy carbon deposits can be cleaned from the top of the piston with a scraper or wire brush. Do not, however, use a wire wheel on the ring grooves or lands. Clean the oil drain holes in the ring grooves. Clean all remaining dirt, carbon and varnish from the piston with a suitable solvent and a brush. Do not use a caustic solution on aluminum parts.

3. After cleaning, inspect the piston for scuffing, scoring, cracks, pitting or excessive ring groove wear. Replace the piston if obviously worn.

4. If the piston appears serviceable, measure the piston diameter using a micrometer. Measure the piston diameter in the thrust direction, 90 degrees to the piston pin axis, 1-1/4 inch below the top of the piston.

5. Inspect the cylinder bores for taper and out-of-round. The cylinder bores must be measured at 3 levels top to bottom in directions of East-to-West and North-to-South.

Measure the cylinder diameter using a bore gauge, or with a telescope gauge and micrometer. The measurement should be made in the piston thrust direction at the top, middle and bottom of the cylinder. Note: Piston diameter and cylinder measurements should be made with the parts at room temperature, 70°F (21°C).

6. Subtract the piston diameter measurement from the cylinder measurement. This is the piston-to-cylinder wall clearance. If the clearance is excessive or if the cylinder wall is badly scored or scuffed, the cylinder may have to be bored and an oversize piston installed.

7. Verify that the cylinder has a proper cross-hatch pattern. These tiny marks are the result of the honing operation during engine manufacture. They retain engine oil to keep the piston rings from scuffing during engine break-in after overhaul. If little or no cross-hatch is evident, the cylinder may require re-honing if the cylinder is in otherwise good condition or rebore if the cylinder is worn or damaged.

8. If the piston-to-cylinder wall clearance is within specifications, check the ring groove clearance. Roll the piston ring around the ring groove in which it is to be installed and check the clearance with a feeler gauge.[1] Compare the measurement with specification. High points in the ring groove that may cause the ring to bind may be cleaned up carefully with a small flat file. Replace the piston if the ring groove clearance is not within specification.

9. Check the connecting rod for damage or obvious wear. Check for signs of overheating (blue appearance) or fractures and check the bearing bore for out-of-round and taper. A shiny surface on the pin boss side of the piston usually indicates that the connecting rod is bent or the wrist pin hole is not in proper relation to the piston skirt and ring grooves. Abnormal connecting rod bearing wear can be caused by either a bent connecting rod, an improperly machined journal or a tapered connecting rod bore. Twisted connecting rods will not create an easily identifiable wear pattern, but badly twisted rods will disturb the action of the entire piston, rings, and connecting rod assembly and may be the cause of excessive oil consumption.[2]

10. If the piston must be removed from the connecting rod, mark the side of the connecting rod that corresponds with the side of the piston that faces the front of the engine, so the new piston will be installed facing the same direction.[3] Most pistons have an arrow or notch on the top of the piston, indicating that this side should face the front of the engine. If the original piston is to be reinstalled, use paint or a marker to indicate the cylinder number on the piston, so it can be reinstalled on the same connecting rod.

11. The piston pin is a press fit in the connecting rod. If the piston and/or connecting rod must be replaced, the pin must be pressed into the connecting rod using a fixture that will not damage or distort the piston and/or connecting rod. The piston must move freely on the pin after installation.

Ridge Removal & Honing

Ridge Removal

This particular procedure applies to all vehicles. Inspect the upper portions of the cylinder (near the head) for a ridge formed by ring wear. If there is a ridge, it must be removed by first shifting the piston down in the cylinder and then covering the piston top completely with a clean rag. Use a ridge reamer to remove metal at the lip until the cylinder is smooth. If this is not done, the rings will be damaged during removal of the piston.

Honing

Before honing the cylinders, stuff plenty of clean shop towels under the bores and over the crankshaft (if still in the engine) to keep the abrasive materials from entering the crankcase area.

1. The cylinder bore resizing hone equipped with 220 grit stones or equivalent is the best tool for this job.[4] In addition to deglazing, it will reduce taper and out-of-round as well as remove light scuffing, scoring or scratches. Usually a few strokes will clean up a bore and maintain the required limits.

2. Deglazing of the cylinder walls may be done using a cylinder surfacing hone (or equivalent). Use a tool equipped with 280 grit stones if the cylinder is already straight and round. Usually 20-60 strokes, depending on the bore condition will be sufficient to provide a satisfactory surface. Inspect the cylinder walls after each 20 strokes, using a light honing oil available from an automotive parts store.

3. Honing should be done by moving the hone up and down fast enough to get a cross-hatch pattern. When hone marks intersect at 50-60°, the cross-hatch angle is most satisfactory for proper seating of the rings.

4. A controlled hone motor speed between 200-300rpm is necessary to obtain the proper cross-hatch angle. The number of up and down strokes per minute can be regulated to get the desired 50-60° angle. Faster up and down strokes increase the cross-hatch angle.

5. After honing, it will be necessary to clean the block to remove all traces of abrasive.

WARNING: Be sure that all abrasive is removed from the engine parts after honing. It is recommended that a solution of soap and hot water be used with a brush and the parts then thoroughly dried. The bore is considered clean when it can be wiped with a white cloth and the cloth remains clean. Oil the bores after cleaning to prevent rust.

Piston Pin Replacement

The piston pins are press-fit into the piston/connecting rod assemblies. The piston pin must be heated up to an extreme temperature often as high as 1500 °F (815°C) or higher, and then the pin must be pressed into the piston and connecting rod with a special press. Therefore, because of the special machinery and specific skills needed to either remove the old piston pin or to install the new piston pin, the piston, connecting rod and piston pin should be taken to a qualified machine shop.

Piston Ring Replacement

1. Wipe the cylinder bore clean. By hand, gently compress the piston rings to be used in the cylinder, one at a time, and using an inverted piston to keep the ring square to the cylinder bore, push the piston ring down into the cylinder bore.

Using a feeler gauge, check the piston ring gap with the ring positioned at least 0.50 inch(12mm)from the bottom of the cylinder bore. Make sure the measurement is within specifications. A gap that is too tight is more harmful than one that is too loose. If ring end gap is excessively loose, the cylinder is probably worn beyond specification.

2. If the ring end gap is too tight, carefully remove the ring and file the ends squarely with a fine file to obtain the proper clearance.

If the instructions on the ring packaging differ from the following piston ring installation information including ring gap positioning, follow the ring manufacturer's instructions.

3. Install the rings on the piston, lowest ring first. The lowest or bottom groove ring is the oil control ring and is a multi-piece ring set consisting of an upper and lower rail and a center expander ring. These pieces are installed by hand, do not use a piston ring expander tool to install the oil control ring top and bottom rails, install the oil ring expander in the bottom ring groove. This expander goes on easily since it has very little tension. Make sure the ends butt together and do not overlap. Start one end of an oil ring rail ring into the oil ring groove above the expander, hold the end firmly and push down the portion to be installed until it is in position. Finish installing the rail ring by spiraling it the remainder of the way on. Repeat the rail installation with the other(lower)rail ring. Pay attention to the location of the ring gaps in relation to the piston circumference. On the oil ring rails, the gaps must be 180 degrees apart.

4. The upper and intermediate piston rings may have a different cross section. Use care to select the proper ring. Install the piston rings with the manufacturer's identification mark facing UP. The piston ring packaging should contain instructions as to the directions the ring sides should face. The top 2(compression)rings must be installed using a piston ring expander tool. There is a high risk of breaking or distorting the compression rings if they are installed by hand. Spread the intermediate ring carefully with the expander tool and install on the piston. Repeat this step to install the top compression ring using the piston ring expander tool. Stagger the ring end gaps by approximately 120 degrees. The compression ring end gaps must not be aligned, nor should the upper two piston ring gaps align with the oil control ring rail gaps. Staggered ring gaps are important for oil control.

Rod Bearing Replacement

The engine crankshaft and connecting rod bearing clearances can be determined by the use of Plastigage® or a similar product. The following is the recommended procedure for the use of Plastigage®:

1. Rotate the crankshaft until the connecting rod boss to be checked is at the bottom of its stroke.

2. With the connecting rod and the connecting rod bearing cap removed from the crankshaft, remove the oil film from the surface to be checked. Plastigage® is soluble in oil.

3. Place a piece of Plastigage® across the entire width of the bearing shell in the bearing cap approximately 1/4 inch(6.35mm)off center and away from the oil hole.[5] In addition, suspect areas can be checked by placing Plastigage® in the suspect area.

4. Before assembling the rod bearing cap with the Plastigage® in place, the crankshaft must be rotated until the connecting rod being checked starts moving toward the top of the engine. Only then should the cap be assembled and tightened to specifications.[6]

Do not rotate the crankshaft while assembling the cap or the Plastigage® may be smeared, giving inaccurate results.

5. Remove the bearing cap and compare the width of the flattened Plastigage® with the metric scale provided on the package. Locate the band closest to the same width. This band shows the amount of clearance in thousandths of a millimeter. Differences in readings between the ends indicate the amount of taper present. Record all readings taken. Plastigage® generally is accompanied by two scales. One scale is in inches, the other is a metric scale, Plastigage® is available in a variety of clearance ranges. The 0.001-0.003 inch(0.025-0.076mm)is usually the most appropriate for checking engine bearing proper specifications.

NEW WORDS

ridge	[ridʒ]	n. 山脊，屋脊
reamer	[ˈriːmə]	n. 铰刀
punch	[pʌntʃ]	n. 冲压机，冲床，冲子
expander	[ikˈspændə]	n. 扩张器，扩口器，（油环）衬簧
snapring	[ˈsnæpriŋ]	n. 开口环，卡环
scratch	[skrætʃ]	n. 擦伤；v. 擦，抓，划(痕)
intent	[inˈtent]	n. 意向，意图，目的
varnish	[ˈvɑːniʃ]	n. 清漆
solvent	[ˈsɔlvənt]	n. 溶剂；a. 溶解的
caustic	[ˈkɔːstik]	a. 刻薄的，腐蚀性的

英文	音标	释义
scuff	[skʌf]	v. 拖足而行，磨损
score	[skɔː]	v. 擦伤，划痕
crack	[kræk]	n. 裂缝；v. 破裂，爆裂
pit	[pit]	n. 凹坑(处，点，痕)；n. 使成凹痕于，挖坑于
micrometer	[maiˈkrɔmitə]	n. 千分尺
bore	[bɔː]	n. 孔，内径；v. 镗削，镗孔
taper	[ˈteipə]	n. 锥度；v. 逐渐减小
out-of-round	[autəvraund]	a. 椭圆形的，失圆的；n. 失圆
clearance	[ˈkliərəns]	n. 间隙，空隙
cross-hatch	[ˈkrɔshætʃ]	n. 网格状线
lubricate	[ˈluːbrikeit]	v. 润滑，对……进行润滑
hone	[həun]	n. 磨石，珩磨头，珩磨机；v. 珩磨
file	[fail]	n. 文件(夹)，锉刀；v. 用锉刀锉
fracture	[ˈfræktʃə]	v.&n. 破裂
boss	[bɔs]	n. 老板，头子；凸起部，凸台
wrist	[rist]	n. 手腕，腕关节，销轴，耳轴
disturb	[disˈtəːb]	v. 打扰，扰乱
stuff	[stʌf]	n. 原料，填料，织品；v. 装满，塞入
towel	[ˈtauəl]	n. 毛巾，抹布，擦手纸
abrasive	[əˈbreisiv]	a. 研磨的；n. 研磨剂
grit	[grit]	n. 粗沙，沙粒，粒度
deglaze	[diˈgleiz]	v. 使不光滑，拉毛
intersect	[ˌintəˈsekt]	v. 交叉，相交
feeler	[ˈfiːlə]	n. 触须，触角，触针，塞尺
squarely	[ˈskwɛəli]	ad. 直角地，正交地，垂直地，方方正正地
butt	[bʌt]	v. 以头抵触，碰撞
circumference	[səˈkʌmfərəns]	n. 圆周，周围
distort	[disˈtɔːt]	v. 弄歪，扭曲
stagger	[ˈstægə]	v. 摇晃，交错
plastigage®	[ˈplæstigeidʒ]	n. 塑料线间隙规
suspect	[səsˈpekt]	v. 怀疑
smear	[smiə]	v. 诽谤，弄脏
accompany	[əˈkʌmpəni]	v. 伴随，陪伴，陪同
fixture	[ˈfikstʃə]	n. 固定设备，夹具
lip	[lip]	n. 嘴唇，唇缘
qualified	[ˈkwɔlifaid]	a. 有资格的
inverted	[inˈvəːtid]	a. 倒转的，反向的
break-in	[breikin]	n. 磨合，走合，试车，插入
overhaul	[ˌəuvəˈhɔːl]	n. 大修

PHRASES AND EXPRESSIONS

compression ring	压缩环
piston ring	活塞环
ring groove	环槽
carbon deposit	积炭
wire brush	钢丝刷
wire wheel	钢丝轮
piston pin	活塞销
cylinder bore	气缸内孔，气缸直径
bore gauge	孔径量表
telescope gauge	伸缩式内径规
cross-hatch pattern	网格线痕迹
cylinder wall	气缸壁
feeler gauge	塞尺
wrist pin	曲柄销，连杆轴颈
press fit	压入式配合，过盈配合
square to	垂直于……
multi-piece ring set	组合环
end gap	端隙
oil control ring	油环
oil film	油膜
bearing shell	轴瓦
soluble in	可溶于……

NOTES TO THE TEXT

[1] Roll the piston ring around the ring groove in which it is to be installed and check the clearance with a feeler gauge.

in which 后面是一个定语从句，修饰 ring groove，从句中的 it 指代 piston ring。本句译为："将活塞环沿着将要装入的环槽滚动，并用塞尺检查活塞环间隙。"

[2] Twisted connecting rods will not create an easily identifiable wear pattern, but badly twisted rods will disturb the action of the entire piston, rings, and connecting rod assembly and may be the cause of excessive oil consumption.

twisted 是形容词，意为"扭曲的"。按照汉语习惯，需要将其翻译为名词。本句译为："连杆的扭曲所引起的磨损是不容易辨认出来的，但是严重的连杆扭曲将会对整个活塞连杆组件的工作产生不利影响，并会引起过度的机油消耗。"

[3] If the piston must be removed from the connecting rod, mark the side of the connecting rod that corresponds with the side of the piston that faces the front of the engine, so the new piston will be installed facing the same direction.

句中 that corresponds with the side of the piston that faces the front of the engine 是定语从句套定语从句的情况。两个关系代词 that 在定语从句中均作主语，并分别指代它们前面的 side。本句译为："如果必须将活塞从连杆上拆下，应在连杆的一侧做上记号。连杆上做记号的一侧与活塞上朝向发动机前端的一侧相对应。"

[4] The cylinder bore resizing hone equipped with 220 grit stones or equivalent is the best tool for this job.

句中 cylinder bore resizing hone 意为"气缸（尺寸再生）珩磨头"。本句译为："装有粒度为 220 的磨石或类似物的气缸珩磨头是完成这项工作最合适的工具。"

[5] Place a piece of Plastigage® across the entire width of the bearing shell in the bearing cap approximately 1/4 inch(6.35mm) off center and away from the oil hole.

Plastigage® 是商品名，是一种用塑料线测量间隙的测量装置的名称。注意四个介词短语的翻译语序。本句译为："将一段塑料线间隙规沿着轴瓦的宽度方向装入轴承盖内，塑料线间隙规的安装位置应距离中间位置约 1/4 英寸(6.35mm)，并且要离开油道口。"

[6] Only then should the cap be assembled and tightened to specifications.

因为副词 only 开头，而采用倒装结构。本句译为："然后，才能安装连杆盖并将其拧紧到规定力矩。"

EXERCISES

I. *Choose the best answer for each of the followings:*

1. Most pistons have an arrow or notch on the top of the piston, indicating that this side should face_____.
   A. the front of the engine   B. the rear of the engine
   C. the left side of the engine   D. the right side of the engine

2. When hone marks intersect at_____ the cross-hatch angle is most satisfactory for proper seating of the rings.
   A. 30°~40°   B. 40°~50°   C. 50°~60°   D. 60°~70°

3. Using a_____, check the piston ring gap with the ring positioned at least 0.50 inch(12mm) from the bottom of the cylinder bore.
   A. micrometer   B. bore gage   C. telescope gauge   D. feeler gauge

4. The engine crankshaft and connecting rod bearing clearances can be determined by the use of_____.
   A. bore gage   B. Plastigage®   C. telescope gauge   D. feeler gauge

II. *Translate the following paragraphs into Chinese:*

There are several engine types which are identified by the number of cylinders and the way the cylinders are laid out. Motor vehicles will have from 3 to 12 cylinders which are arranged in the engine block in several configurations. In-line engines have their cylinders arranged in a row. 3-,4-,5- and 6- cylinder engines commonly use this arrangement. The "V" arrangement uses two banks of cylinders side-by-side and is commonly used in V-6, V-8, V-10 and V-12 configurations. Flat engines use two opposing banks of cylinders and are less common than the other two designs. They are used in Subaru's and Porsches in 4- and 6-cylinder arrangements as well as in the old VW beetles with 4 cylinders. Flat engines are also used in some Ferrari's with 12 cylinders.

Related Terms

balance shaft	平衡轴
boxer engine	对置式发动机
cam follower	凸轮随动件，气门挺杆，摇臂
cam lobe	凸轮凸起部
chain sprocket	链轮
combustion chamber	燃烧室
compression ratio	压缩比
connecting rod bearing	连杆轴承
crankcase	曲轴箱
crankshaft throw	曲柄销，连杆轴颈
cylinder block	气缸体
cylinder head	气缸盖
cylinder sleeve	气缸套(＝cylinder liner)
cylinder head gasket	气缸垫
detonation	爆燃(＝knock)
dry sleeve	干式气缸套
engine block	发动机气缸体
firing order	点火顺序
flat engine	水平对置式发动机
harmonic balancer	谐波平衡器，谐波减振器
head bolt	缸盖螺栓
horizontal-opposed engine	水平对置式发动机
hydraulic valve lifter	液力式气门挺杆
main bearings	主轴承
mechanical valve lifter	机械式气门挺杆
octane rating	辛烷值(＝octane number)
oil control ring	油环

oil pan	油底壳（sump）
overhead camshaft(OHC)	上置凸轮轴，顶置凸轮轴
pin boss	活塞销凸台，活塞销座
piston skirt	活塞裙部
push rod	推杆
reciprocating motion	往复运动
rocker arm	摇臂
rocker shaft	摇臂轴
roller lifter	滚子式挺杆
rotary engine	转子发动机
rotary motion	旋转运动
square engine	等径程发动机
oversquare engine	短行程（缸径大于行程的）发动机
thrust bearing	推力轴承
timing belt	正时带
timing chain	正时链条
timing mark	正时标记
valve guide	气门导管
valve overlap	气门叠开
valve seat	气门座
valve spring	气门弹簧
valve timing	气门正时
valve train	气门机构，气门组
vibration damper	减振器
wedge chamber	楔形燃烧室
wet sleeve	湿式气缸套
wankel engine	转子发动机（汪克尔发动机）
coolant	冷却液
coolant pump	＝water pump 水泵
radiator	散热器
fan clutch	风扇离合器
thermostat	节温器
expansion tank	膨胀水箱
antifreeze fluid	防冻液
engine oil	机油，发动机润滑油
oil pump	机油泵

Translation Techniques(2)——词义选择

在英语中，一词多类、一词多义的情况极为普遍。在阅读和翻译过程中，如果不能正确判断原文中英语词汇的词类和词义，就不可能正确理解原文句子的含义，更不可能恰当地表达出来。

1. 词类的确定

要确定一个英语单词的正确意义，首先要确定它在句中的词类。确定词类常用的方法是看词尾后缀。例如，一般带有后缀-tion，-ness 的为名词，带有后缀-ful，-less，-al 的为形容词，带有后缀-ize，-en 的为动词，带有后缀-ly，-ward 的为副词。

另外，可以根据单词在句子中的位置和语法关系，来判断其词类。如 control 经常作动词用，但其前面冠有冠词 the 或者 a 时，就作名词用了（控制装置）。

如果有疑问，或者对该词陌生而不能判断其词类，应查阅词典。

2. 词义的确定

词类确定之后，才可确定其正确的含义。另外还可根据上下文和词在句中的搭配关系来确定词义。

例1：

Gasoline powers the majority of vehicles, but diesel fuel is used in some vehicles.

乍一看，power 为一名词，意思为"动力，电源，能量"。但是从整个句子来看，but 前面是一个分句，且 but 前后的两个部分存在呼应关系，故 power 可能作动词用。而且，power 作名词时，后面是不能加 s 的。查词典可知，power 作动词用时，意思为"给……以动力""驱动"。

例2：

The four-stroke-cycle gasoline engine cycle is spread over four piston strokes.

根据 spread 在句子中的位置，该词可能是动词（过去分词形式与原形相同）、名词，也可能是形容词。查词典可知 spread 一词三类，但从 spread 与介词 over 的搭配上（spread M over N 意为"使 M 分布于 N 上"），可以判断 spread 作动词（过去分词）用，从句子意思来看也是合适的。整句译为："四冲程汽油机的一个工作循环包含活塞的四个行程。"

UNIT 3 FUEL INJECTION SYSTEMS

TEXT A Electronic Fuel Injection

Fuel injection systems deliver fuel by forcing it into the incoming air stream(Fig. 3-1). Fuel injection systems actually measure the incoming air and pressurize the fuel to deliver it in precise amounts based directly on that measurement. Because fuel is delivered to the manifold under pressure, the quantity of fuel delivered can be more positively controlled. With this more positive control, fuel delivery can be more easily manipulated to meet the unique demands of extreme operating conditions. This results in greater efficiency over a wider range of operation.

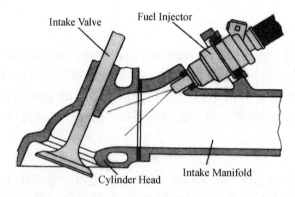

Fig. 3-1 Fuel injector is mounted on the intake manifold

In the electronic injection system, the air-fuel mixture is controlled in one of two ways. The injector may be opened and closed by electrical signals. This is a pulse fuel injection system. In the other type of system, the injector is forced open by fuel pressure. Fuel pressure is controlled by an electronic control device, or by an airflow metering valve, depending on the system. This is the continuous fuel injection system.

Pulse Fuel Injection

In pulse injection systems, the rate of fuel flow through the injectors remains constant. The total amount of fuel delivered is determined by the length of time the injectors are held open. Systems are classified by the type of timing sequence used and the location of the injectors.

Types of Pulse Fuel Injection Systems

The next section will discuss common fuel injection systems which are typical of the pulse systems now in use. The pulse injection system is usually electronically controlled. Although there are a number of design differences between various pulse fuel injection systems, the operating principles are very similar.

The throttle body injection system uses an assembly containing one or two fuel injectors. The assembly is mounted at the entrance to the intake manifold and injects fuel ahead of the throttle valve. These systems are also called single-point injection or central fuel injection.

Multi-point systems, also called multi-port injection systems, deliver fuel at the engine intake ports near the intake valves. This means that the intake manifold delivers only air, in contrast to carburetors or single-point fuel injection systems in which the intake manifold carries the air-fuel mixture.[1] As a result, these systems offer the following advantages:

- greater power by avoiding venturi losses as in a carburetor, and by allowing the use of tuned intake runners for better torque characteristics
- improved driveability by reducing the throttle-change lag which occurs while the fuel travels from the throttle body to the intake ports[2]
- increased fuel economy by avoiding condensation of fuel on interior walls of the intake manifold(manifold wetting)
- simplified turbocharger applications; the turbocharger compressor need only handle air.

Pulse Fuel Injection System Components

The typical pulse system can be broken into three basic parts:
- Air induction system.
- Fuel delivery system.
- Electronic control system(including engine control computer and electronic sensors).

Air induction system

The air induction system consists of an air cleaner assembly, throttle body, and intake manifold. The throttle body section contains the throttle valve, which is opened and closed by the driver to control the amount of air entering the intake manifold.

On throttle body fuel injection systems, the throttle body also contains the fuel injection components as discussed earlier. The intake manifold forms a closed passageway between the throttle body and the cylinder head.

Fuel delivery system

The fuel delivery system(Fig. 3-2)provides the fuel which mixes with the air. Pressure is provided by an electric fuel pump. Some systems use two pumps: a low-pressure fuel pump that delivers fuel to another pump, which develops the pressure.

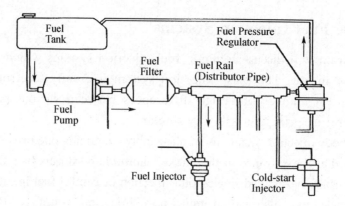

Fig. 3-2 Fuel delivery system

Fuel Pressure Regulators

Pressure in some throttle body fuel injection systems is as low as 7 psi, while some multi-port systems can reach 60 psi(55 kPa to 380 kPa) or more. Injection system pressure is controlled by a pressure regulator. The regulator controls pressure by bleeding excess fuel back into the fuel inlet line or the fuel tank. Pressure regulators on multi-port fuel injection systems are usually connected by a hose to the intake manifold.

Fuel Injectors

The fuel injectors receive fuel from the pump or pumps and spray it into the intake manifold. Injectors can be part of a throttle body, or installed in the intake manifold and connected to the fuel system through a fuel rail. The fuel rail is a rigid piece of steel tubing that feeds fuel to the injectors. Some systems use flexible hoses to connect the injectors to the fuel rail.

Engine control computer

Engine control computers are constructed with many different electronic circuits and components. Size and complexity varies depending upon the system. Modern computers control many other engine systems in addition to the fuel injectors. The computer is usually located in a protected area away from engine vibration and heat, and is connected to the rest of the injection system by means of a sealed wiring harness plug.

The computer receives signals from a number of sensors whenever the engine is running. From this input, the computer evaluates engine fuel needs and adjusts injector pulse width accordingly. Some computers also energize the fuel pump or pumps for 2-5 seconds to pressurize the fuel system before a cold start. Many fuel injection systems do this in place of a cold start valve.

Electronic Sensors

The electronic sensors monitor (check) various engine functions and feed this information to the computer. The number and types of sensors vary with the system.

Oxygen Sensor

The oxygen sensor monitors the amount of oxygen in the engine's exhaust gases. As the oxygen content in the exhaust gases changes, the voltage signal produced by the sensor also changes. The computer uses signals from the oxygen sensor to control the air-fuel mixture. The oxygen sensor is generally mounted in the exhaust manifold. Most electronic fuel injection systems rely on this sensor for much of the engine's operating information.

Engine Speed Sensor

The engine speed sensor monitors engine RPM. Many speed sensors are mounted in the distributor, where they obtain a signal from the rotating distributor shaft. In some cases, the ignition coil or Hall-effect switch provides the signal to the computer. In other systems, the speed sensor is mounted so that it can monitor crankshaft or camshaft rotation.

These speed sensors also indicate the crankshaft and camshaft position so that the computer can open the injector before the intake valve opens. This information is utilized by the computer(along with other sensors input)to help determine injector pulse timing and pulse width.

Throttle Position Sensor

Throttle position is relayed to the computer by the throttle position sensor. Throttle position sensors are installed on the throttle body, and are used to monitor the movement of the throttle valve. They can be resistance types. Resistance sensors contain variable resistance units which send a varying signal to the computer, depending on throttle position.

Manifold Absolute Pressure Sensor

Engine load is transmitted to the computer by means of an intake manifold absolute pressure sensor. The sensor converts manifold vacuum into a small electrical signal. This input allows the computer to increase fuel supply when the engine is under load and needs a richer mixture, and decrease fuel supply when engine load is light.

Barometric Pressure Sensor

Many injection systems have a sensor to measure the pressure of the outside air, usually called atmospheric or barometric pressure. Barometric pressure is compared with manifold vacuum by the computer to more closely monitor engine load. The input of this sensor is important when the vehicle is driven to higher and lower altitudes. This sensor is sometimes combined with the manifold vacuum sensor into a single unit.

Temperature Sensor

Temperature has a great effect on the operation of the fuel injection system. To overcome the tendency of cold fuel to condense into a noncombustible liquid, cold engines must have a richer mixture if they are to run properly. Every injection system has a temperature sensor to measure engine coolant temperature. Many injection systems have an additional sensor to measure the temperature of the incoming air.

Airflow Sensor

Some late model fuel injection systems monitor the amount of air entering the engine by using an airflow sensor. The computer takes this input and compares it with engine RPM and manifold vacuum to determine the amount of fuel to inject. There are three types of airflow sensors, the heated wire, the air valve and the Karmann vortex.

Continuous Injection Systems(CIS)

The continuous systems are sometimes referred to as mechanical or hydro-mechanical, because fuel metering is determined by the mechanical relationship between an airflow sensor and a fuel distributor.

The first continuous systems were distinctly different from EFI systems, since there was no electronic control of basic fuel delivery. The continuous injection family has now grown and spawned more highly developed versions, and electronic control has been a part of almost all CIS fuel injection since 1980.

NEW WORDS

manifold	[ˈmænifəuld]	n.	歧管
manipulate	[məˈnipjuleit]	v.	操纵，控制，支配
venturi	[venˈtuːri]	n.	文丘里管，喉管
driveability	[ˌdraivəˈbiliti]	n.	驾驶性能，操纵性能
lag	[læg]	n.	滞后，惯性，惰性
turbocharger	[ˈtəːbəuˌtʃɑːdʒə]	n.	涡轮增压器，增压器
compressor	[kəmˈpresə]	n.	压气机，压缩机，压缩装置
sensor	[ˈsensə]	n.	传感器
passageway	[ˈpæsidʒwei]	n.	通路
psi			(= pound per square inch)磅力/英寸^2(lbf/in^2)
injector	[inˈdʒektə]	n.	喷油器，注射器
circuit	[ˈsəːkit]	n.	电(气，油，回)路
complexity	[kəmˈpleksiti]	n.	复杂性
plug	[plʌg]	n.	塞子，堵头，插头
energize	[ˈenədʒaiz]	v.	通电，励磁
distributor	[disˈtribjutə]	n.	分配器，分电器
throttle	[ˈθrɔtl]	n.	节气门
relay	[ˈriːlei]	n.	继电器，转播； v. 中继，转播
barometric	[ˌbærəuˈmetrik]	n.	大气压力的
vortex	[ˈvɔːteks]	n.	涡流，涡旋，旋风
distinctly	[disˈtiŋktli]	ad.	显然，清楚地，明明
spawn	[spɔːn]	v.	产卵，繁衍

PHRASES AND EXPRESSIONS

pulse fuel injection	间歇式燃油喷射
continuous fuel injection	连续式燃油喷射
throttle body injection	节气门体喷射
single-point injection	单点喷射
central fuel injection	中央喷射
multi-point(injection) system	多点(喷射)系统
multi-port injection	多点喷射
tuned intake runner	调谐进气管
intake manifold	进气歧管
air induction system	进气系统
fuel delivery system	供油系统
air cleaner	空气滤清器
electric fuel pump	电动燃油泵
pressure regulator	压力调节器
fuel inlet line	进油管
fuel tank	燃油箱
fuel injector	喷油器
fuel rail	燃油分配管，油轨
ignition coil	点火线圈
Hall-effect switch	霍尔效应开关
barometric pressure	大气压力
heated wire	热线式
air valve	空气阀式(＝vane type 叶片式)
Karmann vortex	卡曼涡旋式

NOTES TO THE TEXT

[1] This means that the intake manifold delivers only air, in contrast to carburetors or single-point fuel injection systems in which the intake manifold carries the air-fuel mixture.

that 后面是一个宾语从句，指代 carburetors 和 systems 的关系代词 which 又连接一个定语从句。即 in which the intake manifold carries the air-fuel mixture 是定语从句，修饰 carburetors 和 systems。本句译为："这就意味着进气歧管只需输送空气，而对化油器或者单点燃油喷射系统来说，进气歧管输送的是空气与燃油的混合气。"

[2] improved driveability by reducing the throttle-change lag which occurs while the fuel travels from the throttle body to the intake ports

这是一个名词短语，用来说明多点燃油喷射系统的优点之一。which occurs while the fuel travels from the throttle body to the intake ports 是修饰 lag 的定语从句，其中 while...

是该定语从句中的状语从句。本句译为"由于燃油从节气门体运动到进气道期间所存在的节气门响应滞后现象得到了缓解，因此，改善了车辆的驾驶性"。

EXERCISES

I. Answer the following questions:
1. What are the two kinds of electronic gasoline injection systems?
2. What are the advantages of the multi-port injection systems?
3. What are the three basic parts of the typical pulse fuel injection system?

II. Translate the following paragraphs into Chinese:
1. The pulsed systems are sometimes referred to as "Electronic Fuel Injection" (EFI), and these are the systems that most people think of when you say "fuel injection". There are several Bosch variations of pulsed systems, but their basic functions are the same.

2. In all of the pulsed systems, incoming air is measured by a sensor which puts out an electronic signal proportional to air flow. An electronic control unit (ECU), responding to the signals from the air-flow sensor and other sensors, meters fuel to the engine by way of electrically-operated solenoid valve injectors.

TEXT B   Functions of the Motronic Systems

In simple terms, Motronic is an engine-management system with a single control unit for control of ignition timing as well as fuel injection. Many of the sensors important for fuel injection are also needed for ignition-system control, so the integration of the two systems can accomplish many things:

- Integrated control of fuel injection and ignition can manage the engine better than control of either one alone. That is, timing is sometimes dependent on the air-fuel ratio, and vice versa; also, emissions can be reduced by coordinated control.
- Engine control can be based on actual needs of each engine model based on large amounts of engine-test data during different operating conditions stored in the Motronic Read Only Memory (ROM).[1]
- Many additional operating functions can be provided. Important from the standpoint of service are the adaptive functions, and the self-diagnostics for troubleshooting.
- Motronic advantages are better driveability and fuel efficiency, and reduced emissions. More specific benefits:
  a. fuel savings achieved from best combination of mixture and timing
  b. dependable starting, cold or hot
  c. stable idling at reduced rpm
  d. relative freedom from maintenance
  e. good torque characteristics, allowing longer gear ratios

Ignition Timing Control

I'm talking here about more than electronic ignition—the systems that have replaced the points and condensers of yesterday. I'm talking about microcomputer control of ignition advance angle for every plug firing, or at most, every two plug firings. The millisecond response time of electronic ignition advance control is far faster than the traditional mechanical flyweight/vacuum advance systems.

In a mechanical system (and that includes electronic ignition), as rpm increases, centrifugal weights advance timing. Changing load (manifold pressure) can further change timing advance with a vacuum diaphragm. As rpm increases, there is less dwell time for the coil to charge when perhaps the engine needs more spark energy.

Traditional curves for distributor timing show the limited control of timing advance possible. A timing point that is proper for one combination of rpm and load is probably wrong for other combinations of centrifugal weight position and vacuum diaphragm action. Once the vacuum control or the centrifugal weights reach their limits, advance control is fixed. Mechanical timing has been patched with more vacuum hoses, temperature and delay valves, and other servicing headaches; it's still a compromise. Even at its best, this control fails far short of the precise and rapid timing needed by today's cars.

In Motronic systems, however, the control unit processes a number of inputs, and then adjusts timing for all conditions based on its internal data map.

Timing Data "Maps"

To determine precise timing-advance requirements, each family of engines is tested to learn the best timing for each condition of speed, load, and other variables in heat and cold, on the dynamometer and in the mountains. The goal is to find the timing for best power & economy, all the while meeting emission limits.

The result of these tests is a series of data "maps", as shown in Fig. 3-3. Literally thousands of data points from these tests are stored in the computer memory of the

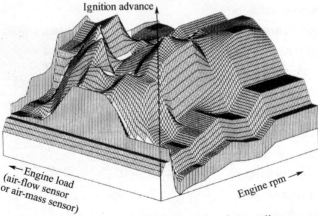

Fig. 3-3 Ignition advance map shows electronic timing control according to engine load and speed.
The maps are symbolic of thousands of data points stored in control unit memory.

Motronic control unit ROM(Read Only Memory) for readout during engine operation. As you may know, a ROM cannot be changed. For any combination of engine load and rpm, the control unit can supply the best ignition timing. For example, for an rpm-input signal of 2000 rpm, at a load signaled by the air-flow sensor, the computer would look up the timing advance angle, let's say it should be 22 degrees BTDC.

But control is even more precise. Suppose the rpm were 2050, and the memory contained only data points for 2000 and 2100; then the computer would look up both 2000 = 22 degrees BTDC, and 2100 = 24 degrees BTDC, and interpolate. It would calculate an advance for the 50 rpm difference between 2000 and 2050, and would output timing of 23 degrees BTDC.

In the control unit, timing is computed so fast that Motronic can adjust timing for every firing of each spark plug!

Distributor

Because it does not control timing or signal rpm, the Motronic distributor's only job is to distribute the secondary, that is, to send the control-unit-timed spark to the proper cylinder.

While timing and dwell were formerly dependent on each other, Motronic memory provides separate dwell-angle data, based on battery voltage and rpm. Later, we'll see how timing and dwell control improve starting and other variations, but here are the principles.

Dwell-Angle Control

As engine rpm increases on mechanical advance systems, there is less dwell time for the coil to charge between firings, resulting in a fall-off of coil voltage. In Motronic systems, dwell angle is electronically controlled so the coil receives the proper current at the time of plug firing. The higher battery voltage, the less dwell angle needed. On the other hand, as rpm increases, more dwell angle is needed for the time to charge the coil. By controlling dwell angle, the coil is charged properly for each ignition firing, no more, no less. The objective is to provide the required secondary power at the plug at the moment of firing with minimum losses in the ignition output transistor and the coil.

To reach the nominal value of primary current at the moment of firing, the dwell angle is changed according to the battery voltage as shown in Fig. 3-4. When battery voltage is lower, dwell time is increased. In effect, the dwell control answers the question: "When should the primary circuit be closed for the optimum time for the coil primary current to rise to proper value at moment of

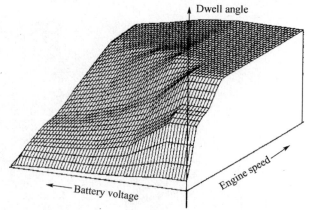

Fig. 3-4 Dwell angle is controlled for battery voltage and engine speed, according to memory map in control unit.

opening primary circuit?" In addition, the control unit output stage limits current so that if, due to rapid engine speed changes as in acceleration, current reaches the nominal value before the ignition point, current is held constant.

So engine speed and battery voltage are inputs to the control unit. From dwell-angle data in the ROM, control unit output is the dwell, or charge-time control, that conserves energy and prevents overheating the coil. Also, if the rpm signal indicates less than 30rpm, as when the engine stops or the key is left on with the engine stopped, primary cut-off prevents coil overheating. Now that you understand the basics of Motronic ignition control.

Control Unit

Motronic systems make extensive use of other data maps stored in ROM for many of the control unit functions, including:
- fuel injection
- lambda closed-loop control
- warm-up
- acceleration
- ignition timing
- dwell angle
- EGR
- idle-speed control

Lambda Memory Map

The main map in the control unit is a set of lambda memory-points used to determine the desired air-fuel ratio for the fuel injection pulses. The lambda memory map, shown in Fig. 3-5, is derived from lab and road tests, and modified for the requirements of the vehicle and the country where it will operate:
- at part load, maximum economy and minimum emissions
- at wide-open throttle, maximum torque while avoiding knocking
- at idle, maximum smoothness
- during throttle opening, maximum driveability

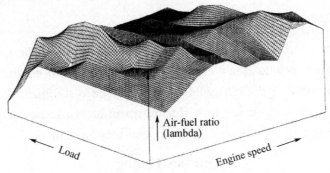

Fig. 3-5 Lambda"map"establishes lambda, or air-fuel ratio for each load/speed point

Air quantity and the requirements for control of injected fuel can vary due to many factors such as manifold-pressure variations resulting from individual piston pumping, and intake-valve opening/closing.[2] Idling manifold absolute pressure can vary by 5kPa from an average 42, over more than 10% plus or minus.[3] For this and other variations, the lambda map insures the best possible adjustment of the air-fuel ratio as corrected by inputs that control fuel injection, and without affecting other operating points. Air flow and rpm set up basic pulse time.

Sequential Fuel Injection

Sequential injection means delivering fuel separately from each injector in sequence—in firing order. With an increase in computing power, and an increased demand for idle smoothness and reduced emissions, Bosch Motronic ML.3 can provide sequential injection. Each injector is timed to cut off just before the intake valve opens. During acceleration, the ECU can deliver additional enriching pulses, cylinder by cylinder for the rapidly changing conditions.

In spite of its increased cost, you'll see more pulsed Motronic sequential injection because:
- each individual injector pulse can be much longer than simultaneous injection, as long as 720° crankshaft rotation
- less intake valve opening, permitting lower idle speeds
- less variation between cylinders in air-fuel ratio for smoother idle and reduced emissions
- injector fuel-rail pressure is more constant because only one injector opens at a time, meaning smoother operation
- improved acceleration enrichment because it can be applied to the "next cylinder"
- soft rpm limitation by reducing fuel flow cylinder by cylinder

Some people think "sequential" means injecting the fuel just as the intake valve opens, but it is not that simple. Depending on the engine, the injection may be timed before the valve opens. It is all based on the desired stratification in the manifold, swirl effects in the cylinder, emissions, and other considerations.

Idle Speed Control

Most Motronics control idle rpm by a combination of the idle-speed stabilizer and ignition timing. Inputs include rpm, closed-throttle signal, and engine temperature. The control unit sends on-off, or digital signals to the idle-speed stabilizer. Early Motronics use the auxiliary air vane to increase air flow during warm-up. In these, cold-engine idle rpm is increased according to temperature; it is an open-loop system.

Ignition Timing

Even before the idle-stabilizer acts on air flow, Motronic idle rpm is first stabilized by changing ignition timing. If idle rpm falls, the control unit advances ignition timing to increase rpm. On the other hand, if rpm rises, it retards timing to cut back rpm. Ignition timing handles small rpm changes, handles them in milliseconds. The idle-speed stabilizer handles larger changes and takes a bit longer.

NEW WORDS

coordinate	[kəuˈɔːdineit]	v. 调整，整理
model	[ˈmɔdl]	n. 模型，车型；v. 模拟
troubleshoot	[ˈtrʌblʃuːt]	v. 排除故障，查找故障
condenser	[kənˈdensə]	n. 冷凝器，电容器
patch	[pætʃ]	v. 修补，补缀
interpolate	[inˈtəːpəuleit]	v. 窜改
fall-off	[ˈfɔːlɔf]	n. 衰退，减少，逐渐下降
conserve	[kənˈsəːv]	v. 保存，保藏，守恒

PHRASES AND EXPRESSIONS

dwell time	保压时间，停留时间，触点闭合时间
short of	缺乏，缺少，不够……（标准）
at the moment of	在……一刻，当……时
idle-speed control	怠速控制
derived from	由……得来，来源于
all the while	一直，始终
lambda closed-loop control	氧闭环控制
idle-speed stabilizer	怠速稳定器

NOTES TO THE TEXT

[1] Engine control can be based on actual needs of each engine model based on large amounts of engine-test data during different operating conditions stored in the Motronic Read Only Memory(ROM).

based on 是"以……为基础""根据""基于"之意。句中有两个 based on，但在句子中充当的成分却不同。①based on 是谓语的一部分，②based on large amounts of engine-test data 是分词短语，during...介词短语作状语，stored...分词短语作 data 的后置定语。本句可译为："根据 Motronic 系统的只读存储器(ROM)中所存储的大量试验数据，就能够按照每个发动机机型的实际需要，对发动机进行控制。Motronic 系统的只读存储器(ROM)中所存储的这些试验数据是在发动机不同工况期间通过试验得到的。"

[2] Air quantity and the requirements for control of injected fuel can vary due to many

factors such as manifold-pressure variations resulting from individual piston pumping, and intake-valve opening/closing.

due to 意思为"归因于……""由于……所引起"。pumping 与 opening/closing 并列，均为动名词。本句可译为："各个活塞的泵吸作用以及进气门的开、闭动作引起了进气歧管的压力波动，像这种压力波动之类的诸多因素都将导致空气量和喷油量的控制要求发生变化。"

[3] Idling manifold absolute pressure can vary by 5kPa from an average 42, over more than 10% plus or minus.

当句子中有表示增减意义的动词或分词出现时，by 后面的数值表示净增减的数。介词 from 此处表示"距离""离开""间隔"之意。所以句中 vary by 5kPa from an average 42 意思为"偏离平均值 42kPa 的变动量达 5kPa"。本句可译为："怠速时的进气歧管压力会偏离平均值 42kPa，变动量达 5kPa，即上、下变动 10%以上。"

EXERCISES

I. *Answer the following questions:*

1. What are the Motronic systems?
2. What are the benefits of the Motronic systems?
3. What are the benefits of the sequential fuel injection?

II. *Translate the following sentences into Chinese:*

1. In a mechanical system(and that includes electronic ignition), as rpm increases, centrifugal weights advance timing.

2. Mechanical timing has been patched with more vacuum hoses, temperature and delay valves, and other servicing headaches.

3. In Motronic systems, however, the control unit processes a number of inputs, and then adjusts timing for all conditions based on its internal data map.

4. By controlling dwell angle, the coil is charged properly for each ignition firing, no more, no less.

5. Some people think "sequential" means injecting the fuel just as the intake valve opens, but it is not that simple.

6. Most Motronics control idle rpm by a combination of the idle-speed stabilizer and ignition timing.

TEXT C Troubleshooting the EFI System

The basic function of the fuel injection system is to supply and meter the correct amount of fuel to the engine in proportion to the amount of air being drawn into the engine to achieve the optimum air-fuel mixture. Any problem with electrical connections, air intake sensing, or fuel supply will cause poor running.

Any troubleshooting should begin with simple and easy checks of the tightness of system wiring and the integrity of the air intake system. Proceed from there to more involved troubleshooting.

Generally, fuel injection problems fall into one of four symptom categories: cold start, cold running, warm running, and hot start. Warm running is the most basic condition. Before troubleshooting a condition in any other category, make sure that the system is working well and is properly adjusted for warm running.

To simplify troubleshooting, concentrate on the sensors and components that adapt fuel metering for a particular condition. For example, if the engine will not start when cold, the components responsible for cold start enrichment are most likely at fault, and should be tested first.

Engine Condition

The fuel injection system is set to operate on an engine that is in good operating condition. Because the fuel injection system is often the "new item", some people waste time checking it when the trouble may be with basic engine operation. It is a good idea to use the car manufacturer's shop manual to perform a tune-up, and to check the following systems before tackling the fuel injection system.

1. Ignition system. Check timing, including advance and retard control, ignition components and spark quality.

2. Electrical system. Check battery condition and connections, and alternator and voltage regulator.

3. Air intake system. Check the air filter, PCV and crankcase connections, and the evaporative emission connections. A loose oil-filler cap or dipstick can lean the mixture by admitting extra air to the intake manifold through the PCV valve. The vapor canister can enrich the mixture by admitting fuel vapors into the intake manifold through the canister purge valve.

4. Fuel system. A clogged filter may reduce fuel flow. A faulty fuel filler cap or tank vent valve may create gas tank vacuum and reduce fuel flow. Be sure the car has fuel in the tank.

5. Mechanical operation. Check grade and condition of crankcase oil, compression, valve timing, and the exhaust system.

Electrical System

Whenever working on the wiring, take care to avoid bending any pins or connectors. Use flat pin probes if possible. Inserting the probes of a voltmeter or ohmmeter too far into a wiring connector may spread the contacts and create a new problem.

Relay Set and System Power

A faulty relay set may prevent the fuel pump from operating, or prevent power from reaching the control unit. Remove the connector from the relay set, and with the ignition on, check for voltage at the terminals of the connector. If there is voltage, then the relay set is probably faulty, but check the continuity of the wiring to the pump and control unit.

Wiring Harness, Connections and Grounds

Strange as it may sound, the components of pulsed systems usually give less trouble than the wiring harnesses and connectors that link them. Even small amounts of corrosion or oxidation at the connector terminals can interfere with the small milliamp currents that signal the system to operate. This problem is compounded by the several ground paths provided to insure reliable operation. More than one owner of a "bad" control unit or component has paid for replacement when the problem was in the wiring. In many cases, cleaning connectors and grounds may solve fuel injection problems.

Identify all wiring connectors and ground locations using the shop manual. The ground locations should be secure and free from corrosion or grease and oil. With the ignition off, disconnect the wiring connectors, including the control unit connector, and also check them for corrosion or dirt. Simply disconnecting and reconnecting the connectors will clean up the contacts, but you can also use a contact cleaner designed for electronic components.

Don't forget to check for breaks or shorts in the wiring harness. A fuel injector or temperature sensor may be good, but the wiring to the control unit may be faulty. You can check this using an ohmmeter. With the ignition off, disconnect the control unit connector and test for continuity between the component terminals and the corresponding terminals at the control unit connector. A reading of zero ohms or very close to it indicates that the wiring is fine.

Some electrical tests of the components can be combined with tests of the wiring harness by removing the control unit connector and then testing between the two pins that lead to a component.[1]

Intake Air Leakage

Another likely cause of trouble in pulsed systems is air leaks between the air-flow sensor and the intake valves. These leaks are often called "false air" because it is air that has not been measured by the air-flow sensor. As a result, the control unit may not provide fuel to burn with the excess air, leading to a lean condition and driveability or emission problems. These are often indicated by hesitation when the engine is cold, or surging at idle. Note that on systems with adaptive control false air is rarely a problem unless the leak is very large.

False Air Checks

If you suspect the air intake leak, there are many possible sources. The soft rubber ductwork can crack and split with age and under-hood heat. Check clamps for tightness. Don't forget the vacuum hoses to the brake booster, the fuel pressure regulator, the evaporative fuel control system, and other places, such as vacuum diaphragms in the heater system inside the car. Check the intake manifold connection to the cylinder head, fuel injector seals, the auxiliary air valve, and the EGR valve, if fitted. Check openings to the crankcase, such as the dipstick, PCV valve, and oil-filler cap for air-tight fits. Check anything downstream of the air-flow sensor that could leak air into the system.

Check for leaks by pressurizing the intake system with air and then spraying a leak detector on the suspected area. An air hose inserted into the fitting for the auxiliary air valve or the idle speed stabilizer can be used to apply low pressure; only about 0.3 bar(5 psi)is needed. A spray bottle of soapy water can serve as a leak detector. Block the throttle so that it's open. Any bubbles will indicate a leak. Also listen for the sound of escaping air. You may have to plug the air-flow sensor intake and the exhaust tailpipe to hold enough pressure in the system.

NOTE

On systems with an air-mass sensor, it is necessary to block the sensor inlet to hold any pressure in the system. A styrofoam coffee cup clamped in the air-mass sensor inlet makes a handy temporary plug.

An alternate leak-detection method involves squirting solvent around suspected leak locations with the engine idling. An rpm increase indicates a leak. Be sure to use an approved solvent with a high-temperature flashpoint. You can also use propane, which tends to be drawn in better than solvent.

Remember though, if the engine has an idle-speed stabilizer, it will ask any rpm increase. If you can sample CO in the exhaust ahead of the catalytic converter, look for CO increase some seconds after applying the solvent as an indication of an air leak.

To correct a leak, start by tightening clamps; you might have to replace the hose or ducting, or replace a gasket. Remember, it's the small intake air leaks that cause trouble, where the engine runs, but poorly.[2] If there's a big air leak, the engine probably won't run at all.

NEW WORDS

tightness	['taitnis]	n.	坚固，紧密
integrity	[in'tegriti]	n.	完整性
concentrate	['kɔnsəntreit]	v.	集中
tune-up	['tjuːnʌp]	n.	调整
tackle	['tækl]	v.	捉住，从事，对
dipstick	['dipstik]	n.	机油尺
PCV			曲轴箱强制通风
canister	['kænistə]	n.	罐
purge	[pəːdʒ]	n. & v.	排污，排空，清除

clog	[klɔg]	v. 堵塞，妨碍；n. 障碍（物）
faulty	[ˈfɔːlti]	a. 报废的，无用的，出故障的
vent	[vent]	v. 通风
crankcase	[ˈkræŋkkeis]	n. 曲轴箱
probe	[prəub]	n. 探索，探针，探头，取样器
meter	[ˈmiːtə]	v. 计量，测量
proceed	[prəˈsiːd]	v. (着手，继续)进行
symptom	[ˈsimptəm]	n. 症状，征兆
continuity	[ˌkɔntiˈnjuiti]	n. 连通，连续性
leakage	[ˈliːkidʒ]	n. 泄漏
hesitation	[ˌheziˈteiʃən]	n. 迟缓，断续工作
surge	[səːdʒ]	n. (发动机)喘振，波动，颤抖
clamp	[klæmp]	n. 夹(具，板，子)，夹紧装置；卡箍(子)
diaphragm	[ˈdaiəfræm]	n. 膜片
soapy	[ˈsəupi]	a. 圆滑的，滑腻的
squirt	[ˈskwəːt]	v. 喷出
gasket	[ˈgæskit]	n. 衬垫
styrofoam	[ˈstairəfəum]	n. 聚苯乙烯泡沫(塑料)

PHRASES AND EXPRESSIONS

vapor canister	蒸气罐
canister purge valve	炭罐排污阀，炭罐清空阀
false air	从窑炉各处缝隙吸入(炉内)的空气
vacuum hose	真空软管
brake booster	制动助力器
leak detector	检漏器，检漏剂
start by + ing	打……开始，(一)开始就(做)
strange as it may sound	听[说]起来也许奇怪

NOTES TO THE TEXT

[1] Some electrical tests of the components can be combined with tests of the wiring harness by removing the control unit connector and then testing between the two pins that lead to a component.

combine with 的意思是"与……相结合"。removing… 和 testing… 并列，均为动名词。that lead to a component 为一个定语从句，关系代词 that 指代 pins。本句可译为："拆下控制单元的连接器，然后在通往一个部件的两个端子之间进行测试，这样便可将部件的电学测试与线束的测试结合在一起进行。"

[2] Remember, it's the small intake air leaks that cause trouble, where the engine runs, but poorly.

it's...that 是一种强调句型。关系副词 where 引导一个非限定性定语从句，修饰 trouble。本句也可译为："记住，正是这种轻微的空气泄漏，导致了发动机出现运转乏力的故障。"

EXERCISES

I. Answer the following questions:
1. What does the term "false air" mean? How do you check it?
2. How do you correct an air leak?

II. Translate the following paragraphs into Chinese:

1. Electronic Fuel Injection(EFI) system check

Check the ground wire connections for tightness. Loose electrical connectors and poor grounds can cause many problems that resemble more serious malfunctions. Check to see that the battery is fully charged, as the control unit and sensors depend on an accurate supply voltage in order to properly meter the fuel. Check the air filter element—a dirty or partially blocked filter will severely impede performance and economy. If a blown fuse is found, replace it and see if it blows again, if it does, search for a grounded wire in the harness related to the system.

Check the air intake duct from the air cleaner housing to the intake manifold for leaks, which will result in an excessively lean mixture. Also check the condition of the vacuum hoses connected to the intake manifold.

2. Injector check

With the engine running, place a stethoscope against each injector, one at a time, and listen for a clicking sound, indicating operation, if you don't have an automotive stethoscope you can use a long screwdriver; just place the tip of the screwdriver against the injector body and press your ear against the handle.

If there is a problem with an injector, purchase a special injector test light ("noid" light) and install it into the injector electrical connector. Start the engine and make sure that each injector connector flashes the noid light. This will test for the proper voltage signal to the injector.

Related Terms

fuel injection	燃油喷射
direct fuel injection	直接燃油喷射
indirect fuel injection	间接燃油喷射
mechanical fuel injection	机械控制燃油喷射

electronic fuel injection(EFI)	电子控制燃油喷射
stoichiometric ratio	理想配比的空燃比,理论空燃比
pulse width	脉冲宽度
cold start valve	冷起动阀
oxygen sensor(O_2S)	氧传感器(O_2S)
heated oxygen sensor(HO_2S)	加热型氧传感器(HO_2S)
engine speed sensor	发动机转速传感器
throttle position sensor(TPS)	节气门位置传感器(TPS)
manifold vacuum sensor	进气歧管真空传感器
manifold absolute pressure(MAP)sensor	进气歧管绝对压力(MAP)传感器
barometric pressure sensor	大气压力传感器
mass airflow sensor(MAF)	质量空气流量计
intake air temperature(IAT)sensor	进气温度传感器
speed density	速度密度
octane number	辛烷值

Translation Techniques(3)——词类转换

由于英语与汉语的表达习惯不同,在翻译过程中,经常需要将英语中的某一词类翻译成汉语中的另一词类,这就是词类转换。

1. 转译成动词

将英语中的分词、不定式、动名词和具有动作含义的动词派生的名词、形容词和副词等翻译成汉语中的动词,甚至是谓语。

例1:

As a result, these systems offer the following advantages:

- <u>greater</u> power by avoiding venturi losses as in a carburetor, and by allowing the use of tuned intake runners for better torque characteristics
- <u>increased</u> fuel economy by avoiding condensation of fuel on interior walls of the intake manifold(manifold wetting)

因此,这些系统具有下列优点:

- 由于消除了化油器的喉管节流损失,以及利用调谐进气管而获得了更好的转矩特性,而<u>提高了</u>功率。(形容词转译成动词)
- 由于避免了燃油蒸气在进气歧管内壁上冷凝(进气歧管湿润),<u>提高了</u>燃油经济性。(动词派生的形容词转译成动词)

例2:

Engine <u>control</u> can be based on actual needs of each engine model based on large amounts of engine-test data stored in the Motronic Read Only Memory(ROM).

根据Motronic系统中存储的大量的发动机试验数据,就能够按照每个发动机机型的实

际需要，对发动机进行控制。（含有动作意味的名词转译成动词）

例3：

The shorter block permits a reduction in vehicle length with no sacrifice in passenger room.

气缸体的缩短可减小汽车的长度，而不会影响容纳乘客的车内空间。（动词派生的名词转译成动词）

例4：

The maps are symbolic of thousands of data points stored in control unit memory.

这些（点火提前）控制图代表着在控制单元存储器内存储的数千个数据点。（形容词转译成动词）

例5：

As soon as the piston reaches the top of the exhaust stroke, it starts down on another intake, compression, power, and exhaust cycle.

活塞一到达排气行程的顶端，它便开始向下运动，进入另一个进气、压缩、做功和排气的工作循环。（副词转译成动词）

2. 转译成名词

主要有这样几种情况：将被动语态中的动词转译成名词，将形容词转译成名词，将部分名词派生的动词以及名词转用的动词转译成名词，将副词转译成名词。

例6：

In the electronic injection system, the air-fuel mixture is controlled in one of two ways.

在电子控制燃油喷射系统中，空气-燃油混合气的控制有两种方式。（被动语态中的谓语动词转译成名词）

例7：

A faulty fuel tank vent valve may create gas tank vacuum and reduce fuel flow.

燃油箱通风阀的失效会使燃油箱内形成真空，从而减小燃油流量。（形容词转译成名词）

3. 转译成形容词

有些形容词派生的名词可以转译成形容词。

例8：

Any troubleshooting should begin with simple and easy checks of the tightness of system wiring and the integrity of the air intake system.

排除任何故障都应从一些简单易行的检查项目开始，如系统线路连接是否松动和进气系统是否完好。（形容词派生的名词转译成形容词）

UNIT 4   GASOLINE FUEL INJECTION

TEXT A   Gasoline Direct Injection(GDI) and Throttle-By-Wire

Gasoline Direct Injection

Conventional gasoline engines are designed to use an electronic fuel injection system, replacing the traditional mechanical carburetion system. Multi-point injection (MPI), where the fuel is injected through each intake port, is currently one of the most widely used systems. [1]Although MPI provides a drastic improvement in response and combustion quality, it is still limited due to fuel and air mixing prior to entering the cylinder.

To further increase response time and combustion efficiency, while lowering fuel consumption and increasing output, systems may use direct injection. Gasoline direct injection engines are engineered to inject the gasoline directly into the cylinder in a manner similar to diesel direct injection engines.

Direct injection is designed to allow greater control and precision, resulting in better fuel economy. This is accomplished by enabling combustion of an ultra-lean mixture under many operating conditions. Direct injection is also designed to allow higher compression ratios, delivering higher performance with lower fuel consumption. Currently, direct injection gasoline engines are being deployed throughout the world in passenger cars.

Mitsubishi GDI

Mitsubishi Motors is aiming to achieve both low fuel consumption and high output. MMC is a world forerunner in the development of direct cylinder injection gasoline engines, known as "GDI", which were first introduced in the 1996 Galant. [2]GDI supplies fuel directly to the inside of the cylinder.

A variety of air-fuel mixtures can be created according to changes in the fuel injection timing. Using methods and technologies unique to Mitsubishi, the GDI engine provides both lower fuel consumption and higher output. This seemingly contradictory and difficult feat is achieved with the use of two combustion modes. Put it another way, injection timings change to match engine load.

Ultra-lean Combustion Mode

Under most normal driving conditions, up to speeds of 120 km/h, the Mitsubishi GDI engine operates in ultra-lean combustion mode, resulting in less fuel consumption. In this mode, fuel injection occurs at the latter stage of the compression stroke and ignition occurs at an ultra-lean air-fuel ratio of 30—40(35—55, including EGR).

Superior Output Mode

When the GDI engine is operating with higher loads or at higher speeds, fuel injection takes place during the intake stroke. This optimizes combustion by ensuring a homogeneous, cooler air-fuel mixture which minimizes the possibility of engine knocking.

These two modes are represented in Fig. 4-1. The piston of the GDI engine is shown in Fig. 4-2.

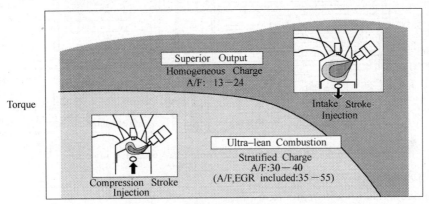

Fig. 4-1 Two combustion modes of the GDI

In addition, the GDI-CVT introduced in the 2000 Lancer significantly reduces energy loss by integrated control that makes the most of GDI characteristics.[3] High-precision torque control and large range for low fuel consumption as well as the CVT characteristics of quick and continuous control of the large gear change ratios enable top class level fuel economy and an exceptionally smooth ride.[4]

Fig. 4-2 A piston of Mitsubishi GDI engine

Bosch MED-Motronic

MED-Motronic(D = direct injection) is a Motronic system which is derived from ME-Motronic and adapted to the particular conditions and requirements of direct injection(Fig. 4-3).

The following operating modes can be used with MED-Motronic gasoline direct injection:
- Stratified-charge operation
- Homogeneous-charge operation
- Homogeneous lean operation

67

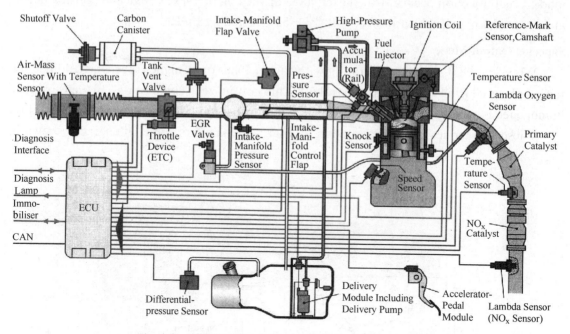

Fig. 4-3 BOSCH MED-Motronic gasoline direct injection

- Homogeneous stratified operation
- Homogeneous knock-protection mode
- Stratified-catalyst-heating operation

These operating modes are matched to each other so as to provide optimal mixture formation and combustion in every operating state. The control system must ensure that during vehicle operation neither power nor torque jumps are perceptible when switching from one operating state to another.

Stratified-charge operation. Stratified-charge operation is possible in the lower torque and speed range up to approx. 3,000 rpm. Here the fuel is injected during the compression stroke into the combustion chamber shortly before the moment of ignition. Because of the short time period until it ignites, the fuel cannot mix uniformly with the air in the combustion chamber.

The fuel is transported in a cloud to the spark plug by an air swirl prevailing in the combustion chamber(Fig. 4-4). Inside the mixture cloud the mixture ratio is approx. 0.95—1. Outside the cloud the mixture is very lean. A large amount of exhaust gas is recirculated into the combustion chamber in order to reduce the creation of NO_x by the altogether lean mixture.

Since the throttle valve is fully open during stratified-charge operation, the torque is generated during stratified-charge operation by quality regulation.

If the torque demand were to become too high in this operating state, the increased injection would cause particles to form. Excessively high speeds give rise to turbulences in the combustion chamber, which no longer permit a steady mixture cloud of $\lambda = 1$. Consequences: faulty combustion, misfiring.

Homogeneous-charge operation. At high torque or high speed the engine is operated with a homogeneous mixture of $\lambda = 1$ or, to achieve maximum power, of $\lambda < 1$. For this purpose, the start of injection is moved to the induction stroke (Fig. 4-5). The period of time thus available until the fuel-air mixture ignites allows the fuel to mix thoroughly with the inducted air and spread uniformly within the combustion chamber. In homogeneous-charge operation the torque is generated by quantity regulation. In other words, the quantity of inducted air is regulated by the throttle valve. Mixture formation and combustion take place accordingly as in manifold injection.

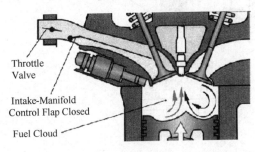 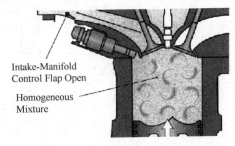

Fig. 4-4 Stratified-charge operation   Fig. 4-5 Homogeneous-charge operation

Homogeneous lean operation. The engine can be operated with a homogeneous lean mixture in a transition range between stratified- and homogeneous-charge operations. With operation at $1 < \lambda < 1.2$, fuel consumption is reduced in comparison with homogeneous-charge operation at $\lambda = 1$.

Homogeneous stratified operation. In this operating mode a homogeneous lean mixture is formed in the combustion chamber by advanced injection (approx. 75% of the fuel) in the induction stroke. A second injection takes place in the compression stroke (double injection), which creates a zone of richer mixture in the area around the spark plug.

This mixture is highly flammable and ensures complete combustion in the combustion chamber. This operating mode is chosen so that the torque can be better set during the changeover from homogeneous- to stratified-charge operation.

Homogeneous knock-protection mode. Thanks to double injection at full load it is possible to dispense with retarding the moment of ignition in order to avoid knocking. Charge stratification prevents the dangerous phenomenon of fuel auto-ignition.

Stratified catalyst-heating operation. Another form of double injection allows the catalyst to be quickly heated. A lean mixture is formed here as in stratified-charge operation. After the fuel has ignited, fuel is injected once again during the power stroke.

This share of fuel burns very late and heats up the exhaust-system branch intensively.

Electronic Throttle—Throttle-By-Wire

Some of the newest Motronic systems have an electronic throttle (also known as a throttle-by-wire system). The electronic throttle has no mechanical link between the accelerator pedal and the throttle valve. Instead, as shown in Fig. 4-6, an accelerator sensor picks up your movement or position of the accelerator pedal. It signals the control unit about pedal movement, and the control unit signals the servomotor on the throttle shaft to open. The electronic throttle(Bosch calls it EGAS)may sound like something none of us needs, but it has many benefits.

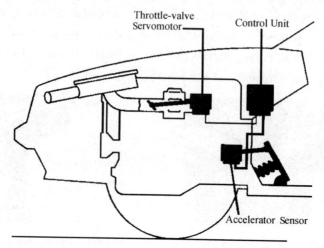

Fig. 4-6 Electronic throttle sends accelerator signal to Motronic control unit, DC motor moves throttle valve, modified by engine temperature, idle rpm, and maximum rpm

The throttle opening signal may be modified according to engine rpm and engine temperature. It can provide simplified cruise control. It can also control minimum rpm, replacing the idle-speed stabilizer, and control maximum rpm, replacing the alternate injector cut-out.

But there's more. For traction control, the electronic throttle links with the ABS(Anti-lock Braking System). The same wheel-speed sensors of ABS also feed the ASR(Anti-Slip Regulator).

When any driving wheel starts to slip, a slight brake application prevents that wheel from slipping so much that the differential delivers no power to the other driving wheel. If both driving wheels show signs of slipping, the electronic throttle cuts back power for maximum traction. Traction control gives the car the max acceleration the tires can deliver to the road. If laying down tire smoke is your thing, avoid ASR. But for making the fastest take off, you cannot beat it.

Can you trust the electronic throttle? Will it provide unintended acceleration? The system checks its safety circuits before start-off, and reports defects to the driver. If a defect is found, a limp-home circuit may disable some of the functions, but it will allow you to get to the house or the shop. It may well be more reliable than some cable actuated throttles.

NEW WORDS

drastic   ['dræstik]   a. 激烈的，猛烈的
GDI   = gasoline direct injection(汽油直接喷射)
forerunner ['fɔːrʌnə] n. 先驱(者)，先锋，祖先

CVT		= continuously variable transmission（无级变速器）
characteristics	[ˌkærɪktəˈrɪstɪk]	n. 特性（曲线）
stratify	[ˈstrætɪfaɪ]	v. 使成层
homogeneous	[ˌhɔməˈdʒiːnjəs]	a. 相似的，均匀的
crossover	[ˈkrɔsˌəuvə]	n. 跨越，交叉，交叠，穿过
throttle-by-wire	[ˈθrʌtl-bai-ˈwaiə]	n. 线控节气门
servomotor	[ˈsəːvəuˌməutə]	n. 伺服电动机，辅助电动机，伺服传动装置
ASR		= anti-slip regulator 或 acceleration slip regulation 防滑调节装置
ABS		= anti-lock braking system 防抱死制动系统
takeoff	[ˈteikɔːf]	n. 起飞，开始
beat	[biːt]	n. 敲打，拍子；v. 打，打败
trust	[trʌst]	v.& n. 信任，信赖
limp-home	[limpˈhəum]	n. 跛行回家

PHRASES AND EXPRESSIONS

fuel consumption	燃油消耗
quality regulation	质调节
quantity regulation	量调节
dispense with	拼弃
driving wheel	驱动轮
cruise control	巡航控制
traction control	牵引控制
lay down	设计，制定，主张

NOTES TO THE TEXT

[1] Multi-point injection(MPI), where the fuel is injected through each intake port, is currently one of the most widely used systems.

where... 引导定语从句。本句可译为："目前，将燃油喷入每个进气道的多点燃油喷射（MPI）系统是应用最广泛的系统之一。"

[2] MMC is a world forerunner in the development of direct cylinder injection gasoline engines, known as "GDI", which were first introduced in the 1996 Galant.

MMC 是 Mitsubishi Motors Corporation 的缩写。known as "GDI"是 engines 的后置定语。Galant 是三菱汽车公司的车名，现译为"戈兰特"。本句可译为："在缸内直接喷射汽油机的开发方面，三菱汽车公司是世界上的先驱者，该公司 GDI 直喷汽油机最早安装在1996款戈兰特轿车上。"

[3] In addition, the GDI-CVT introduced in the 2000 Lancer significantly reduces energy loss by integrated control that makes the most of GDI characteristics.

CVT 是 continuously variable transmission（无级变速器）的缩写。GDI-CVT 是指将 GDI 发动机与 CVT 组合一体的动力总成。Lancer 是三菱公司的车名，可译为"兰瑟"。that makes... 是修饰 control 的定语从句。make the most of... 等于 make the best of...，意思为"充分利用"。本句可译为："另外，2000 款兰瑟轿车上采用的 GDI-CVT 动力总成通过采用能充分利用 GDI 特性的集中控制方式，大大降低了能量损失。"

[4] High-precision torque control and large range for low fuel consumption as well as the CVT characteristics of quick and continuous control of the large gear change ratios enable top class level fuel economy and an exceptionally smooth ride.

理解与翻译该句的关键是弄清语法结构，即找到谓语。本句的谓语是 enable。ride 的意思为"行驶平顺性""乘坐舒适性"。本句可译为："极其精密的转矩控制和宽广的低油耗转速范围，以及 CVT 大传动比的快速、连续控制的特性，使实现最高水平的燃油经济性和特别平滑的行驶平顺性成为可能。"

EXERCISES

I. *Answer the following questions:*

1. What are the advantages of gasoline direct injection?
2. Who is a world forerunner in the development of direct cylinder injection gasoline engines?
3. What are the advantages of electronic throttle?
4. What are the main parts of an electronic throttle system?

II. *Translate the following sentences into Chinese:*

1. Gasoline direct injection engines are engineered to inject the gasoline directly into the cylinder in a manner similar to diesel direct injection engines.

2. A variety of air-fuel mixtures can be created according to changes in the fuel injection timing.

3. At high torque or high speed the engine is operated with a homogeneous mixture of $\lambda = 1$ or, to achieve maximum power, of $\lambda < 1$. For this purpose, the start of injection is moved to the induction stroke.

4. Stratified-charge operation is possible in the lower torque and speed range up to approx. 3,000 rpm. Here the fuel is injected during the compression stroke into the combustion chamber shortly before the moment of ignition.

TEXT B Operation of the Motronic System

In this section, let's look at operating conditions to see how Motronic controls injection and ignition as well as idle-speed bypass air for good engine management.[1]

Starting

Start Control, Fuel

In most Motronics, start enrichment is provided by the port injectors rather than the separate start injector/thermo-time switch. For start control, the important inputs are rpm and engine temperature. The control unit monitors cranking rpm, and also the number of revolutions since the time cranking began. [2] The injection pulses may be longer than normal.

But at low engine temperatures, the control unit may deliver instead several shorter injection pulses per revolution to improve starting. Remember, these are 10 millisecond pulses in a pulse period, or crankshaft revolution time of 200ms. To prevent flooding, fuel quantity will cut back after a measured number of revolutions, or after the engine has reached a cranking rpm that is temperature related, for example 200—300 rpm.

Start Control, Ignition Timing

With a cold engine at low cranking speeds, timing will be controlled near TDC. For normal cranking rpm, a large advance in timing might fire too early, damaging the starter. Further, starting would be difficult if not impossible. With a cold engine at higher cranking rpm, however, timing will be advanced for better starting.

For hot starts, or high intake air temperatures, timing will be retarded because a hot cylinder can fire easier while the piston is rising at cranking rpm. Retarded timing prevents knocking that can occur in high-compression engines, and may be masked by the starter sound.

Start Control, Air

As in L-Jetronic, the idle-speed stabilizer is normally driven open more by increased dwell signals to provide extra bypass air for cold starting.

Post-Start

Post-start—the 5-30 seconds when you want the engine to keep running after you release the key from CRANK—is affected by engine temperature as well as a timer in the control unit. Colder engines get more fuel injected. Also, colder engines get more timing advance. Based on the start-up temperature, and the time since start, post-start enrichment is gradually reduced. The idle-speed stabilizer maintains rpm.

Warm-Up

During warm up, the most important input, besides engine load and rpm for basic pulse time, is engine temperature. The control unit includes a ROM map of warm-up characteristics to apply a correction factor based on load and engine speed, greater at low loads and rpm than at high loads and rpms (Fig. 4-7). [3] Control unit outputs include injection pulses for the proper mixture, ignition timing for driveability (advance under part-load acceleration, retard on deceleration to reduce HC emissions), and idle stabilization to help keep the engine running at idle.

Remember, during warm-up, the temperature of the lambda sensor is important. Unheated lambda sensors can be heated faster by changing ignition timing. Motronic retards timing to cause a hotter exhaust. That heats the oxygen sensor much quicker and also heats the catalytic converter faster for more efficiency.

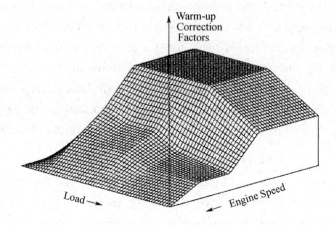

Fig. 4-7　Warm-up correction factors

Closed-Loop Operation

Based on the inputs of a warm engine, and oxygen-sensor voltage when hot, the system normally operates closed-loop. The oxygen sensor fine-tunes the fuel-injection delivery for proper air-fuel ratios.

For every combination of inputs, the control unit looks in its memory for the best timing, the best dwell angle, the best lambda, or air-fuel ratio[4]. On the basis of engine temperature, Motronic controls ignition timing with independent calibrations for starting, idling, deceleration, and acceleration, both part-load and full-load or WOT(Wide Open Throttle). For example, control of timing advance at idle reduces the need for idle fuel enrichment.

Part-Throttle Acceleration

Just as in L-Jetronic, the overswing signal of the air-flow sensor increases fuel delivery, compensated by temperature. For air-mass sensors, the rate of increase of the voltage signals acceleration. During part-throttle acceleration, the normal pulse for steady cruise increases for just about one second while you open the throttle. Then the pulse cuts back even as the engine picks up speed; this saves fuel and reduces emissions.

In addition, ignition timing can be retarded to avoid the brief acceleration knock that could occur for the first few cycles of engine acceleration. Ignition timing control also reduces the formation of NO_x, which is normal with acceleration.

Rate of ignition timing change is also controlled:

- to avoid knocking, the control unit allows fast change
- to reduce jerk during transition, the control unit normally changes ignition advance gradually

Full-Load Acceleration

Full-load enrichment is signaled by the throttle switch. As long as the throttle is full-open, longer injection pulses will be delivered for enrichment. Rich mixtures reduce the tendency to knock. This enrichment is based solely on rpm, and programmed from engine tests. The air-flow signal is ignored.

At the same time as rpm and throttle position control full-load injection enrichment, air temperature and engine temperature supply inputs to control the advance of ignition timing for best acceleration without approaching knock. [5] For engines without knock sensors, timing advance is based on engine test data stored in the timing map. The engine can operate close to the ignition-advance limit, developing maximum torque over the entire rpm range with least chance of knocking based on three factors:

1) the timing curve can be programmed specifically for each engine operating point
2) the system operates with narrow tolerances and freedom from mechanical wear
3) timing is compensated according to engine temperature and intake-air temperature

In some turbocharged cars, a second air-temperature sensor is mounted in the manifold downstream of the turbo or the intercooler to sense the temperature of the air entering the engine. This is a special fast-response sensor overriding the first air-temperature sensor to handle the quick changes in temperature that can occur during full-throttle acceleration.

Knock Control

Programmed timing accuracy, even with compensations, can be improved by a knock-sensor system that causes timing to advance to just before the point where knock could damage the engine. With a knock sensor controlling timing advance in a separate closed-loop system, power output can be maximized without endangering the engine.

Some engines, particularly turbocharged engines, include knock sensors to pick up vibrations from the engine at the first signs of knock. Some systems use two control traits, mounted inside the passenger compartment, one for Motronic, and a related knock control regulator, called KLR. Knock-sensing inputs help both control units to work together. The first and fastest output changes the timing. If the engine is turbocharged, the second output controls the boost. In the Motronic known as ML3, knock sensing and engine management are combined in one control unit.

When the engine knocks, it vibrates with characteristic frequencies of 5-10 kilohertz together with corresponding harmonics. These vibrations must be sorted from other engine vibrations in a recognition circuit in the control unit. The Motronic control unit has accurate information on crankshaft position and firing order so it is possible to determine which cylinder is knocking (one cylinder usually knocks before the others). Further, circuits operate with such speed that ignition timing can be retarded only for the knocking cylinder, and advanced for the firing of the next cylinder. Each knock signal can modify timing in milliseconds. When ignition retard eliminates the knock, timing is advanced slowly in steps to the original value or until knocking again occurs.

On turbocharged engines, if knock continues for seconds, boost control reduces manifold pressure. Knock control permits more boost, and higher compression ratios for greater power. Automatically, it tends to adjust for the octane-rating of the fuel being burned.

With precise control of ignition timing and turbo boost, engines can be designed with higher compression ratios for greater power output. On all engines, the knocking limits depend on many factors:

- intake air temperature
- engine temperature
- engine deposits
- combustion-chamber form
- mixture composition, A/F ratio, and stratification
- fuel quality
- air density

For years, drivers have known that using higher-octane fuel did not add to engine power unless ignition timing was adjusted at the distributor to take advantage of the improved anti-knock index. Now, with knock sensors and closed-loop ignition-advance control, power output can depend on the anti-knock index of the fuel being burned. It is not unusual to see engine power specifications include the anti-knock index of the fuel to be used.[6]

RPM Limitation

If the rpm signal is greater than max-allowable rpm stored in the computer memory, the control-unit signals a cutback of the fuel-injection quantity. A scope set to read four pulses for simultaneous injection for four cylinders shows the limitation cutback of every other pulse, one pulse every other crankshaft revolution. If you press the engine into the rpm-limitation range, you will feel a surge as the limitation of fuel injection cuts in and out.

Coasting Cut-off

Signals of rpm, closed throttle, and engine temperature control coasting cut-off of injection. On the scope during coastdown, the single-injection pattern looks blank except for the TDC pulse. No fuel is being injected. As rpm approaches idle speed, the normal pulse will show again. If the engine is colder, normal fuel injection returns at some higher rpm, to prevent stalling. Motronic adds one refinement: as fuel-delivery resumes, perhaps as the driver resumes speed, ignition timing is gradually advanced to smooth the transition from fuel cut-off to cruise or acceleration.

NEW WORDS

flood	[flʌd]	v.	充满，淹没，溢出；n. 洪水
compensate	[ˈkɔmpenseit]	v.	补偿，偿还
formation	[fɔːˈmeiʃən]	n.	形成，形成量
turbocharge	[ˈtəːbəutʃɑːdʒ]	v.	用涡轮增压
turbo	[ˈtəːbəu]	n.	涡轮增压，涡轮增压器
intercooler	[ˌintəˈkuːlə]	n.	中间冷却器，中冷器
sense	[sens]	v.	理解，感到，感受，检测
override	[ˌəuvəˈraid]	v.	超过(越)，越过，压倒，占优势
overswing	[ˈəuvəswiŋ]	v.	摆动过大
lambda	[ˈlæmdə]	n.	λ值，过量空气系数，氧传感器
endanger	[inˈdeindʒə]	v.	危及
trait	[treit]	n.	特性，显著的特点
harmonics	[hɑːˈmɔniks]	n.	谐波[音]，谐波分量
recognition	[ˌrekəgˈniʃ(ə)n]	n.	承认，赏识，赞誉
modify	[ˈmɔdifai]	v.	更改，修改
stratification	[ˌstrætifiˈkeiʃən]	n.	成层，分层
cutback	[ˈkʌtbæk]	n.	减少
scope	[skəup]	n.	范围，领域，见识，示波器，指示器
simultaneous	[ˌsiməlˈteinjəs]	a.	同时的，同时发生的，同步的
coast	[kəust]	v.	滑行，滑翔，沿海岸航行；n. 海岸，沿岸
cut-off	[ˈkʌtɔf]	n.	切断，关闭，停车
coastdown	[ˈkəustdaun]	n.	降低，下降，滑行
blank	[blæŋk]	ad.	空白的，空着的；n. 空白
stall	[stɔːl]	v.	失速，熄火，(速度不够)停车[停止转动]
refinement	[riˈfainmənt]	n.	精致，文雅，精巧
resume	[riˈzjuːm]	v.	恢复，重新开始

PHRASES AND EXPRESSIONS

port injector	进气道喷油器
start injector	起动喷油器，冷起动喷油器
thermo-time switch	温控定时开关
turbocharged car	涡轮增压轿车
air-fuel ratio	空燃比
knock sensor	爆燃传感器
passenger compartment	乘客舱，乘员室

knock control regulator	爆燃控制调节器
be sorted from	与……分开，从……拣出
scope set	示波器
anti-knock index	抗爆指数

NOTES TO THE TEXT

［1］In this section, let's look at operating conditions to see how Motronic controls injection and ignition as well as idle-speed bypass air for good engine management.

句中 how... 至句末是不定式 to see 的宾语从句。本句可译为："在这一部分中，我们可通过考察 Motronic 系统的工作情况来理解 Motronic 系统是怎样控制喷油、点火和怠速旁通系统，以便获取理想的发动机管理效果。"

［2］The control unit monitors cranking rpm, and also the number of revolutions since the time cranking began.

句中 cranking began 是 time 的定语从句，since the time cranking began 的意思是"从起动开始以后"。本句可译为："控制单元监视着起动转速，还监视着从起动开始以后的转动圈数。"

［3］The control unit includes a ROM map of warm-up characteristics to apply a correction factor based on load and engine speed, greater at low load and rpm than at high load and rpm (Fig. 4-7).

句中 greater at low loads and rpm than at high loads and rpm 为形容词短语作定语，修饰 factor，但由于 factor 的修饰成分多而长，因此该短语可以单独译出。本句可译为："控制单元的 ROM 内存有一个暖机特性曲线图，从而能够根据发动机转速和负荷采用不同的校正系数，此校正系数在发动机低速低负荷时要比高速高负荷时大（见图 4-7）。"

［4］For every combination of inputs, the control unit looks in its memory for the best timing, the best dwell angle, the best lambda, or air-fuel ratio.

句中 air-fuel ratio 是 lambda 的同位语。本句可译为："对于每一种输入信号组合，控制单元均能在其存储器内找到最佳的定时、最佳的闭合角、最佳的 λ 值即空燃比。"

［5］At the same time as rpm and throttle position control full-load injection enrichment, air temperature and engine temperature supply inputs to control the advance of ignition timing for best acceleration without approaching knock.

句中 supply inputs 是主句的谓语和宾语，原意为"提供输入信号"，意译为"利用……信号"意思更清楚。全句可译为："同时，像转速和节气门位置信号用来控制全负荷加浓喷油量一样，空气温度和发动机温度信号用来控制点火提前角的大小，以便获得最好的加速性，又不会达到爆燃的程度。"

［6］It is not unusual to see engine power specifications include the anti-knock index of the fuel to be used.

不定式 to see 后面是一个宾语从句。本句可译为："看到发动机的功率参数中包含所用燃料的抗爆指数是很平常的事。"

EXERCISES

I. Translate the following sentences into Chinese:

1. With precise control of ignition timing and turbo boost, engines can be designed with higher compression ratios for greater power output.
2. For start control, the important inputs are rpm and engine temperature.
3. With a cold engine at low cranking speeds, timing will be controlled near TDC.
4. A scope set to read four pulses for simultaneous injection for four cylinders shows the limitation cutback of every other pulse, one pulse every other crankshaft revolution.

II. Translate the following paragraphs into Chinese:

1. Control of idle speed contributes to fuel economy and reduced emissions. Using many of the same variables already input to the ECU, the control unit adjusts idle rpm by varying the amount of air bypassing the throttle valve, as well as varying the ignition timing.
2. Other engine-management functions may be included in the control unit functions. For example, some Motronic systems control the opening and closing of the fuel-vapor charcoal canister purge valve.

TEXT C   Servicing the EFI System

If problems with the fuel system are suspected, begin testing by making sure that the pump runs when the ignition is turned on. If not, check the wiring and relay set and make sure the relay is receiving the signal indicating the engine is turning over.[1] On some models this comes from the air-flow sensor, on others it comes from the ignition system. Continue to check basic system pressures, fuel delivery, and operation of the fuel injectors.

All of the pressure tests and many other tests of the fuel injection system, as well as component service and replacement, require either one or all of the following procedures: the relieving of fuel pressure, the installation of a pressure gauge, and the operation of the fuel pump without running the engine.

Pressure Tests

Fuel pressure which is too high may richen the air-fuel mixture, while fuel pressure too low may lean the mixture. The following procedures test for basic system pressures, as well as for causes of incorrect pressures. For the tests, relieve system pressure and install a pressure gauge.

System Pressure

There are two parts to testing system pressure in order to check pressure regulator function. In the first part, with the engine idling, the gauge should typically read about 2 bar (29 psi). Check your shop manual for the correct specifications for your model. Many specifications may read 2.5 bar (36 psi), with a tolerance from 2.3 to 2.7—but remember, that's when testing with the pump running with the engine off. Here, the test checks regulation of fuel pressure by the fuel pressure regulator.

For the second part of the test, with the engine still idling disconnect the vacuum line to the intake manifold and close it off. Because the pressure regulator senses higher barometric air pressure than manifold pressure, fuel pressure should rise to about 2.5 bar (36 psi). This most likely is what your shop manual specifies.

Pressures that are too low or too high indicate a problem either with the pressure regulator or with fuel delivery. Check the pressure regulator first as described below, before checking fuel delivery.

Checking Fuel Pressure Regulator

If system pressure tests do not show the 0.5 bar pressure drop with the vacuum line connected, check the vacuum line for leaks. If the line is sound the regulator is faulty.

If system pressure is low in both parts of the test, the regulator could be returning too much fuel or the fuel pump may not be delivering properly. You can pinpoint the problem by pinching off the return line. Do this slowly to avoid a sudden pressure surge that could ruin the gauge. If the gauge shows 4 bar (59 psi) or above, the fuel pump relief valve is working, so the regulator is faulty. If the pressure did not rise, there is a problem with fuel delivery.

If system pressures are too high, temporarily remove the fuel pressure regulator return line. Attach a short hose to the pressure regulator outlet and direct it into an unbreakable container. Run the system pressure test again. If pressures are now correct, then the fuel return line is blocked. If pressures still high, the regulator is faulty.

Residual Pressure Test

With the fuel pressure gauge installed, run the engine or fuel pump briefly to build up system pressure, then shut off the engine. After 20 minutes, pressure in the system should not have fallen below 1 bar (14.5 psi).

If it has, there are many possible sources of leaks that could reduce pressure. Check all fuel line connections for leaks. Make sure the fuel injectors and cold start valve are not leaking. Test the fuel pump check valve by running the engine and then shutting it off. Immediately clamp shut the supply line from the fuel pump. If the pressure drops below specification, then the pressure regulator is faulty. If the pressure is now within specification, then the fuel pump check valve is faulty.

Fuel Delivery

For the fuel system to deliver sufficient fuel to the injectors, the fuel lines must be clear of blockages and the fuel pump must be able to pump a specified volume of fuel. The fuel delivery tests assume that the fuel pressure regulator has been tested and is working properly.

Checking Fuel Delivery

To check fuel delivery, disconnect the return line from the fuel pressure regulator. Run the pump without running the engine and catch fuel in an unbreakable container. Be sure the container is large enough. Most manufacturers specify a delivery of one liter in 30 seconds or less, but check your manual. You can either deliver fuel to the specified measure, shut off the pump and check the time, or run the pump for the specified time period and see how much has been delivered.

If delivery is not to specification, replace the fuel filter, and blow compressed air through the supply line to be sure it is open. Check the fuel pump as described below. Whatever you repair or replace, recheck fuel pump delivery, even if a new pump is installed.

Checking Fuel Pump

You can check the fuel pump for voltage and ground. With the pump running, you should see close to 12 volts at the positive terminal. The negative terminal should show a good ground, zero resistance. If not, clean the terminals and check the wiring. If voltage supply and ground are fine, but delivery volume is still low, the pump must be replaced.

Fuel Injectors

There are a number of methods to test check the operation of the fuel injectors. In addition to those listed here, don't forget to check the wiring to the control unit. Also note that while the injectors may appear to be operating correctly, even a small amount of injector clogging can affect engine performance.

Vibration Test

A quick method is to check for injector vibration—indicating that they are opening and closing—while the engine is idling. If they're too hot to touch with your fingertips, use a mechanic's stethoscope or a screwdriver. You should hear a buzzing or clicking sound. No vibration, or a different pitch of vibration in one versus the others, indicates a bad injector or harness connection. Interchange connectors with an injector on the same circuit from the control unit (check your wiring diagrams). If the same injector is still faulty, then replace the injector; if the injector now works, check the wiring.

RPM Drop Test

With the engine idling, check rpm drop as you disconnect the injector connectors, one at a time. For example, if you read 860 rpm with all four injectors operating then you disconnect an injector, look for a drop to about 770 rpm, and a return to normal when you reconnect it. If there's no rpm drop, either the injector or its wiring is faulty. If possible, replace the injector first to narrow the cause.

If the engine has an idle speed stabilizer, the rpm drop may not be noticeable unless you freeze the idle speed at a fixed rpm before the test. Depending on the car, this can be done by grounding the appropriate test connector, or on other cars by simply pulling the idle speed stabilizer wiring connector.[2]

Injector Leak Tests

Fuel injector leaks can occur at the seams around the body of the fuel injector and bleed off fuel pressure, causing hot-start problems. Clean off the injector and look closely for seepage. The injectors usually leak most when they are cold.

The injector pintles should also be checked for leakage. Remove the injectors and the fuel rail with the injectors still attached. Run the fuel pump without running the engine to build up fuel pressure. If any of the injectors leak at the rate of more than two drops per minute, the injector may be clogged. Clean the injectors as described below. If that does not help, replace the injector.

Electrical Tests

Remove the harness connector from each injector and use an ohmmeter to test the resistance across the injector terminals. The resistance depends on whether there is a separate set of series resistors in the system or not. Check your manual for the correct specifications. If the resistance is incorrect, replace the injector.

On models with an additional set of series resistors in the fuel injection wiring harness, the resistance of each series resistor should be from 5 to 7 ohms. With the ignition on, there should be from 11 to 12.5 volts.

Fuel Injector Clogging

A clogged fuel injector can be indicated by rough idle, a stumble or hesitation during acceleration, or a failed emissions test. Fuel injector clogging is caused by a build up of carbon and other deposits on the injector pintle. This reduces the flow of gasoline through the injectors and results in a poor spray pattern.

Causes of Clogging

Clogging is the result of the combination of a number of factors:
- high underhood temperatures on smaller cars
- fuel being metered at the tip of the injector
- short driving cycles followed by hot-soak periods
- low-detergent fuels with a high carbon content and low hydrogen content

The worst clogging seems to occur with driving cycles where the car is driven for at least 15 minutes, ensuring full warm-up, then parking for about 45 minutes or more. While the engine runs, the injector tips are cooled by the fuel flow. After shut-down the engine acts as a heat sink and temperatures climb, particularly at the valves and manifolds. Injector-tip temperature climbs equally high and the small amount of fuel that is in the tip of the injector breaks down and causes the deposit. Considering the small quantities of fuel that the injector meters, and the tiny orifice of the injector tip, it doesn't take much to restrict the flow.

Normally, one injector clogs before the others, reducing its delivery so that the cylinder runs lean. The lambda sensor compensates by enriching the mixture for all cylinders, which is in turn too rich for the cylinders with unclogged injectors. The result is a rough idle. The engine will most likely fail an emission test, and will send you to the gas pump more often, because it can lose as much as 25% fuel economy.

Solving the Clogging Problem

The first step towards solving the problem of fuel injector clogging is to determine whether one or more injectors is indeed clogged. The injector leak test described above gives one indication of a possible clogged injector. There are also a number of tests that any good repair shop can perform. One is called a pressure-balance test, where each injector is triggered with a fixed pulse and the pressure drop in the system is measured. If one has a greater pressure drop, it's most likely clogged.

The tendency to form injector deposits varies considerably depending on the fuel. Many cases of injector clogging can be cured by using premium fuels where manufacturers advertise more detergent additive. Most regular unleaded fuels probably have enough detergent to keep unclogged injectors clean, but they won't dissolve deposits on clogged injectors.

Air-Flow Measurement

These simple checks cover both types of air-flow measurement, the vane-type air-flow sensor and hot-wire air-mass sensor. The air-flow sensor is not serviceable. If the vane movement is not smooth, or if any of the electrical test values are incorrect, the sensor must be replaced.

The air-mass sensor is not serviceable. If it fails any of the tests below, check for a faulty wiring connector or wiring before replacing the sensor.

Voltage Input

Peel back the protective boot on the air-mass sensor wiring connector. Check the voltage input to the sensor at the proper pin of the connector. Check your shop manual for the correct terminal. With the ignition on, or with the main relay terminal grounded, your meter should read 12 volts.

Voltage Output

Place the probe on the correct terminal for voltage output. With the engine running at normal operating temperature, the voltmeter typically should read 2.12 volts at 760 rpm, and increase to 2.83 volts at 3520 rpm. Changes are more important than the actual numbers.

Burn-off Sequence

With the voltmeter still checking output voltage, rev the engine up to 3000 rpm, then let it return to idle and turn off the engine. After approximately four seconds, the control system should send the one-second burn-off signal, visible as a voltage reading on the voltmeter.

Visual Inspection

If the voltage readings are incorrect, check the wiring connector. Make sure that it's secure, and that the plug is not twisted and putting stress on the wiring harness.

If there's still a problem, remove the sensor and check the wire screens. Replace any broken screens, and check the hot wire for breakage. When you first look inside, you may think the air-mass sensor doesn't have any hot wire. But move it around until the wire is visible against the background. The fine wire is not easy to see.

NEW WORDS

relieve	[ri'li:v]	v. 释放，减压
pinpoint	['pin,pɔint]	v. 查明
ruin	['ru:in]	v. & n. 毁灭，崩溃
unbreakable	[ˌʌn'breikəb(ə)l]	a. 不能破损的，牢不可破的
terminal	['tə:min(ə)l]	n. 接线端，终端
stethoscope	['steθəskəup]	n. 听诊器; v. 用听诊器诊断
buzz	[bʌz]	v. 发出嗡嗡声
pitch	[pitʃ]	n. 间距，节距，螺距，音调
ohmmeter	['əumˌmi:tə]	n. 欧姆表
sink	[siŋk]	n. 洗涤槽
stumble	['stʌmb(ə)l]	v. 绊倒，蹒跚，踌躇
detergent	[di'tə:dʒənt]	n. 清洁剂
restrict	[ris'trikt]	v. 限制，约束，限定，保密
cure	[kjuə]	v. & n. 治疗，治愈
advertise	['ædvətaiz]	v. 做广告，登广告
dissolve	[di'zɔlv]	v. 溶解，解散
serviceable	['sə:visəbl]	a. 可维修的
peel	[pi:l]	v. 剥皮，脱皮，剥落; n. 果皮，嫩树皮
rev	[rev]	v. 加速转动，增加转速(up)
burn-off	['bə:nɔf]	n. 烧穿，降碳，自净
twist	[twist]	v. 扭曲，缠绕，编制，拧

PHRASES AND EXPRESSIONS

pressure gauge	压力表
relief valve	安全阀
pinch off	夹断，夹紧
check valve	单向阀
(be) clear of	没有……，清除了……
heat sink	散热片，散热装置
gas pump	汽油泵，(加油站)汽油加油塔
premium fuel	优质燃料，高级燃料
vane-type air-flow sensor	叶片式空气流量计
hot-wire air-mass sensor	热线式空气流量计

NOTES TO THE TEXT

[1] If not, check the wiring and relay set and make sure the relay is receiving the signal indicating the engine is turning over.

句中 make sure 的意思是"查明""弄明白"，其后接宾语从句。短语 indicating the engine is turning over 是分词短语，作后置定语。而此 indicating…短语中的 the engine is turning over 是分词 indicating 的宾语从句。本句可译为："否则，应检查线路和继电器，并弄清继电器能否接收到表明发动机将要运转的信号。"

[2] Depending on the car, this can be done by grounding the appropriate test connector, or on other cars by simply pulling the idle speed stabilizer wiring connector.

句子主语 this 指代上句中的 freeze the idle speed at a fixed rpm(将急速转速冻结在一个固定值上)。pulling 意思为"拔下"。本句可译为："根据车型的不同，这一点可以通过将适当的检查插接器搭铁的方法来实现，或者在另外的车型上，只需简单地拔开怠速稳定器线束插接器即可。"

EXERCISES

I. Answer the following questions:
1. There are several methods of testing fuel system pressure. What are they?
2. What are the causes of clogging injectors?
3. Describe how to solve the injector clogging problem.

II. Translate the following terms into Chinese:
1. pressure gauge
2. shop manual
3. barometric air pressure

4. residual pressure
5. blockage
6. fuel filter
7. seepage
8. leakage
9. clogging
10. harness connector
11. burn-off signal
12. wiring harness

Related Terms

drill bit	钻头
reamer	铰刀
hacksaw	钢锯
vise	台钳，虎钳
pliers	钳子
screwdriver	螺钉旋具
wrench	扳手
box-end wrench	梅花扳手
impact wrench	冲击扳手
open-end wrench	开口扳手
torque wrench	扭力扳手
socket	套筒
hex key	六角扳手
ratchet	棘轮手柄
puller	拉器
micrometer	千分尺
calipers	卡尺，卡钳，内径规
dividers	分规
dial indicator	百分表
dial caliper	带刻度盘游标卡尺
feeler gauge	塞尺
scan tool	扫描诊断仪，解码器
test light	试灯
ohmmeter	欧姆表
voltmeter	电压表
ammeter	电流表

multimeter	万用表
tachometer	转速表
compression gauge	气缸压力表
vacuum gauge	真空表
oil pressure gauge	机油压力表
fuel pressure gauge	燃油压力表
wire wheel	钢丝轮
scraper	刮刀
hand-operated vacuum pump	手动真空泵
hand tool	手工具
power tool	动力工具

Translation Techniques(4)——句子成分转换

在英译汉时，除了遇到词类转换的情况外，还会遇到这样一种情况：将英语句子中的某个成分转译成汉译句中的另一种成分，这就是英译汉时的句子成分转换。恰当而灵活地运用句子成分转换，能使译文更加流畅和规范。

句子成分的转换主要有以下几种情况：

1. 将主语转换成其他成分

主语→宾语——在被动语态中，可将英语句子中的主语转译成汉译句中的宾语。

主语→谓语——一些有动作意义的名词作主语可以译为谓语。

主语→定语——常用于英语中主语和宾语关系密切的句子中。

例1：

One is called a pressure-balance test, where each injector is triggered with a fixed pulse and the pressure drop in the system is measured.

一个检测项目叫作压力平衡试验。在该检测项目中，用固定脉冲触发每个喷油器，同时测量系统的压力降。（在 where... 的定语从句中，主语转换成宾语）

例2：

Engine control can be based on actual needs of each engine model based on large amounts of engine-test data stored in the Motronic Read Only Memory(ROM).

根据 Motronic 系统中存储的大量的发动机试验数据，就能够按照每个发动机机型的实际需要，对发动机进行控制。（主语转译成谓语动词）

例3：

Lean-burn engines are known for their characteristic high levels of NO_x emissions.

人们知道，NO_x 排放值高是稀燃发动机的特有的缺点。（主语转换成定语）

2. 将谓语转换成其他成分

谓语→主语——有些并不真正表示动作的动词，如 act 等，可在汉译句中转换成主语。

例4：

After shut-down the engine acts as a heat sink and temperatures climb, particularly at the valves and manifolds.

关机之后，发动机的作用就像一个散热器，从而使发动机各处（特别是气门和进气歧管）的温度上升。

3. 将表语转换为其他成分

表语→主语——在英语的主-系-表结构句型中，有时将主语与表语颠倒翻译。

有时，表语可转换成谓语，或者转换成定语。

例5：

During warm up, the most important input, besides engine load and rpm for basic pulse time, is engine temperature.

在暖机期间，除了确定基本喷油脉冲宽度所用的发动机负荷和转速外，发动机温度是最重要的输入。（表语转换成主语）

例6：

Changes are more important than the actual numbers.

比实际（电压）值更重要的是这些（电压）值的变动情况。（表语转换成定语）

4. 其他转换

在翻译中，有时还可能存在将宾语转换成主语，将定语转换成谓语，将状语转换成主语、定语等情况。

总之，了解句子成分转换的翻译技巧，将有助于译作锦上添花。翻译人员具有了一定的专业知识和语言文字修饰技巧，在正确理解原文的基础上，对句子成分转换的恰当运用将是顺其自然的事。句子成分转换不要刻意追求，生搬硬套。

UNIT 5 DIESEL FUEL INJECTION

TEXT A Overview of Conventional Diesel Fuel Injection and Common Rail Injection Systems

Conventional Fuel Injection System

Typical diesel fuel injection system components include the fuel tank, fuel pump, fuel filter, injection pump, injectors, and the necessary fuel lines(Fig. 5-1).

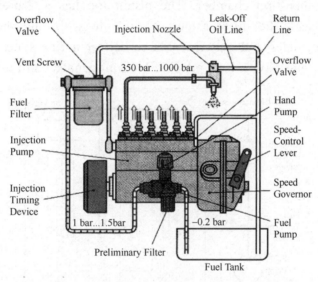

Fig. 5-1 A conventional diesel fuel injection system

Fuel Filter. Diesel fuel must be kept clean to avoid injector system trouble. Very small particles are enough to clog injector nozzles. Diesel fuel systems typically use one or more filters to trap dirt and other deposits.

Injection Pump. Due to the high compression(around 22∶1) used in diesel engines, the diesel injection pump must be capable of producing high pressures. There are a number of injection pump designs. The most commonly used automobile and light truck diesel injection pumps are classified as inline or distributor.

The inline injection pump uses a separate cylinder-plunger-cam unit for each cylinder. These units are contained in a straight row in a common housing.

In the distributor injection pump, a single double-plunger type pump serves all injector outlets. A single delivery valve is located in the rotor.

Injector. There are many different injector designs, but all are a variation of two basic types—inward opening and outward opening. Diesel spray patterns will vary depending upon engine design.

Glow Plug and Intake Air Heaters. To aid in igniting the compressed air-fuel mixture during cold starting, diesel engines use glow plugs and intake air heaters. The glow plug is an electrically operated device that protrudes into the precombustion chamber. On later engines, the glow plugs are turned on and off automatically. Intake air heaters warm the air as it passes through on its way to the intake manifold. The heater element is a wire mesh that is electrically heated. The computer energizes the heater element before cranking.

Common Rail Injection System

Newer diesel engines are equipped with **common rail injection** systems(Fig. 5-2 and Fig. 5-3). Common rail systems are direct injection(DI) systems. The injectors' nozzles are placed inside the combustion chamber. The piston top has a depression where initial combustion takes place. The injector must be able to withstand the temperature and pressure inside the cylinder and must be able to deliver a fine spray of fuel into those conditions. These systems have a high pressure fuel rail connected to individual injectors.

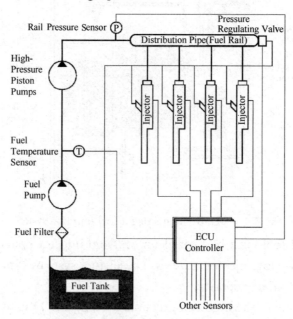

Fig. 5-2 Common rail(CR) system

The injectors are controlled by a computer that attempts to match injector operation to the operating conditions of the engine.

The injector facilitates precise control of the start of injection and injected fuel quantity as well as pre- and post-injection.

Injector closed(rest state). The fuel flows through the fuel-inlet passage into the valve control chamber and to the injection-nozzle pressure shoulder.

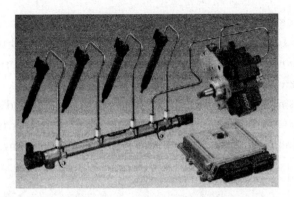

Fig. 5-3　BOSCH third generation common rail system with piezoelectric injectors

The discharge throttle is closed by the valve ball. The pressure above the valve control plunger in the valve control chamber generates a force which is greater than the opposing force which acts on the nozzleneedle pressure shoulder.[1] The nozzle needle thus remains closed, regardless of the rail pressure applied at the injector(see Fig. 5-4).

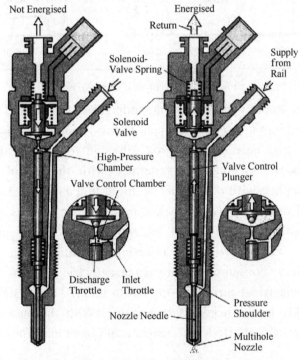

Fig. 5-4　Solenoid-type injector

Injector opens(start of injection). When the solenoid valve is actuated by the ECU, the armature is attracted, as a result of which the valve ball opens the discharge throttle. Now more fuel flows through the discharge throttle than through the inlet throttle. This causes a drop in pressure in the valve control chamber. Now the nozzle needle is raised by the force acting on its pressure shoulder. The nozzle needle opens and fuel is injected(Fig. 5-4).

Injector closes(end of injection). When the solenoid valve is no longer supplied with power by the FCU, the valve spring forces the valve ball onto its seat. As a result, the discharge throttle is closed and the fuel pressure builds up again abruptly in the valve control chamber. The force acting on the valve control plunger and the force of the nozzle spring acting from above exceed the force on the nozzle needle pressure shoulder acting from below. The nozzle needle closes.

Pre-and post-injection(Fig. 5-5). The solenoid valve is only supplied with power for a brief period in order to inject small quantities of fuel. The nozzle needle is raised slightly. The fuel injector opens briefly and in the process does not open the entire opening cross-section.

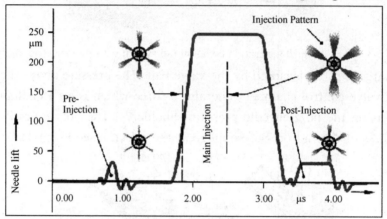

Fig. 5-5 Rate-of-discharge curve

Injector activation. Rapidly switching solenoid valves are required in order to be able to subdivide fuel injection into up to three sequences(pre-, main and post-injection). This can only be achieved with high currents of approx. 20A and voltages of approx. 100V.

This so-called "booster voltage" is generated with the aid of induction when the solenoid valves are supplied with power and is stored in a capacitor in the ECU.

Newer diesel fuel injectors rely on stacked piezoelectric crystals rather than solenoids. In the future, the solenoid valves will be replaced by faster piezo actuators. This piezoelectric injector will allow more injection operations per power stroke with simultaneously low energy consumption. In the piezoelectric injector, Piezoelectric-crystals quickly expand when electrical current is applied to them. The crystals allow the injectors to respond very quickly to the needs of the engine. With this new-style injector, diesel engines are quieter, more fuel efficient, cleaner, and have more power.

NEW WORDS

particle	[ˈpɑːtikl]	n. 微粒,颗粒
clog	[klɔg]	v. & n. 阻塞,堵塞
nozzle	[ˈnɔzl]	n. 喷嘴
trap	[træp]	n. 圈套,陷阱,捕集器
plunger	[ˈplʌndʒə]	n. 柱塞,活塞
variation	[ˌveəriˈeiʃən]	n. 变化,变更,变种,变调

protrude	[prə'truːd]	v.	突出，伸入
solenoid	['səulinɔid]	n.	螺线管，电磁线圈[铁，阀，开关]
energize	['enədʒaiz]	v.	供给……能量，通电，励磁
depression	[di'preʃən]	n.	消沉，萧条；低气压，凹陷，凹坑
stack	[stæk]	n.	堆，一堆；v. 堆叠
piezoelectric	[paiˌiːzəui'lektrik]	a.	压电的

PHRASES AND EXPRESSIONS

fuel tank	燃油箱
fuel pump	燃油泵
fuel filter	燃油滤清器
injection pump	喷油泵
fuel line	燃油管
light truck	轻型货车
inline injection pump	直列式喷油泵
distributor injection pump	分配式喷油泵
delivery valve	出油阀
spray pattern	喷注形状
glow plug	预热塞
intake air heater	进气加热器
precombustion chamber	预燃室
fuel rail	油轨
pressure shoulder	承压锥面
solenoid-type injector	电磁式喷油器
piezoelectric injector	压电式喷油器

NOTES TO THE TEXT

[1] …generates a force which is greater than the opposing force which acts on the nozzleneedle pressure shoulder.

句中的两个 which 均修饰前面的 force，这是一个从句中套有从句的结构。本句可译为：
"(阀控柱塞上方的阀控油腔内的压力)形成一个向下的作用力，这个作用力比加在喷嘴针阀承压推面上的向上的作用力要大。"

EXERCISES

I. Answer the following questions:

1. What are the basic parts of the diesel injection system?
2. What are the two types of injection pumps?

3. What are the advantages of the common rail injection system with piezoelectric injectors?

II. Translate the following terms into Chinese:
1. precombustion chamber
2. fuel pump
3. injection pump
4. inline injection pump
5. distributor type injection pump
6. governor
7. injector nozzle
8. glow plug
9. intake air heater
10. fuel rail
11. solenoidtype injector
12. piezoelectric injector

TEXT B A New Electronically Controlled Fuel Injection System for Diesel Engines

The most important subjects for fuel injection system in the face of ever severer diesel engine emissions regulations are to reduce emissions while improving the principal performances(in terms of higher output, reduced fuel consumption and noise). In view of the above situation, a fuel injection system must satisfy the following requirements:

(1)High pressure capability

(2)Enhanced functions—control of injection pressure and rate, besides control of injection quantity and timing.

A new-concept fuel injection system which is suitable for electronic control and capable of controlling injection quantity, timing, rate and pressure individually as well as realizing high pressure has been developed.[1] The system was named ECD-U2 as the unit injector of the second generation.

The ECD-U2 system has not only excellent injection characteristics but also the following advantages for the engine on which the system is to be installed:

(1)Excellent mountability because no extra camshaft is required for the engine.

(2)Engine pump drive components can be designed with ease and noise is reduced because both mean and peak pump drive torque are lower than those of an in-line pump.

(3)The system can be serviced in the same manner as those of conventional in-line pumps.

(4)The system is adaptable to various engines only with a slight modification of the nozzle holder design.

Scheme of ECD-U2 System

The ECD-U2 system comprises high pressure supply pump, common-rail, injectors and ECU and sensors to control these components (Fig. 5-6 and 5-7).

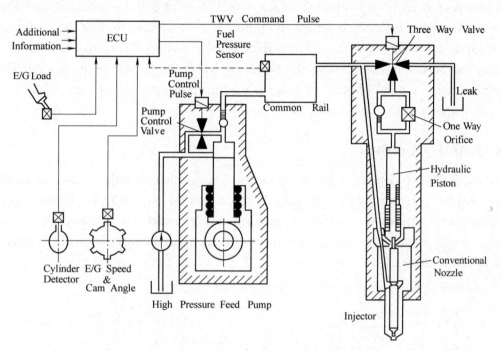

Fig. 5-6　System schematic diagram of ECD-U2

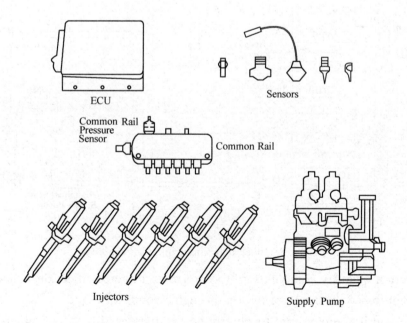

Fig. 5-7　Whole system overview

Common-rail pressure is controlled by varying fuel discharge of the high pressure supply pump with a pump control valve (PCV). Common-rail pressure is detected by a high pressure sensor installed on the rail, and controlled to the predetermined value depending on engine load and speed namely the feedback control of common-rail pressure.

Common-rail pressure is applied to the nozzle side of injector as usual and also the back side of nozzle. Injection quantity and timing is varied by controlling the back pressure of the nozzle by means of a three-way valve (TWV). Injection quantity is controlled by changing the pulse width applied to the three-way valve. Injection timing is controlled by changing timing of pulse applied to the TWV. Injection rate can be controlled in three different shapes, delta, boot and pilot.

Fuel Quantity Control

In the ECD-U2 system, injection quantity is controlled by pulse width, commanded on the injector actuator, which in turn is controlled by the ECU computing optimum injection quantity depending on the engine operating conditions as detected by various sensors.[2] Fig. 5-8 shows the block diagram of the injection quantity control. Computation is conducted in the ECU in two stages:

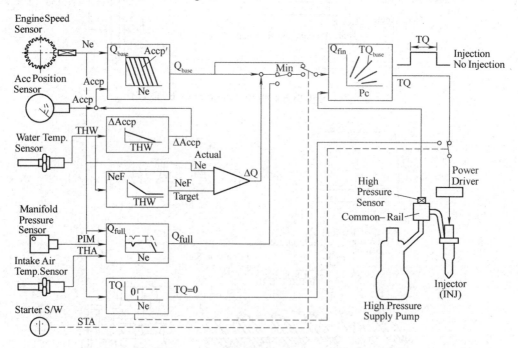

Fig. 5-8 Block diagram of injection quantity

- "Injection quantity computation" to determine targeted injection quantity for each injection based on the information of engine condition, and
- "Pulse width computation" to determine the pulse width to be commanded on the actuator to realize the targeted injection quantity determined.

Injection quantity computation follows the conventional method of electronically controlled governor, that is, base governing pattern Q_{BASE} ($Q_{BASE} = f(Ne, ACCP)$) and maximum allowable injection quantity Q_{FULL} ($Q_{FULL} = f(Ne, PIM, THA)$) are respectively map-retrieved, and the lesser value is selected to obtain final injection quantity Q_{FIN}. Features of the electronic control are fully utilized to ensure that both Q_{BASE} and Q_{FULL} are programmable freely and in flexible patterns. Needless to say, the system is capable of realizing, without adding any hardware but only with a relevant program change (software), additional functions such as fuel delivery increase at cold condition depending on coolant temperature and feedback control of engine idle speed so called ISC control.[3]

Pulse width computation is inherent to the ECD-U2 system. The ECD-U2 system being a perfect "time-pressure metering system", injection quantity is uniquely governed by the relation $Q = f(T_Q, Pc)$, which means that pulse width T_Q can easily be map-retrieved by Q_{FIN} and common-rail pressure Pc immediately before injection.

Eventually, the three-way valve in the injector is energized for a time width T_Q by means of the power driver, and injection quantity corresponding to Q_{FIN} is obtained.

As described above, the ECD-U2 system is an unparalleled injection quantity control system featuring better freedom of control of injection quantity than that existing electronically controlled fuel injection systems, and further, control response capable of detecting the latest engine conditions for every and each injection in principle for reflecting them in the control of injection quantity on a real time basis.

Injector Control

The three-way valve, shown in Fig. 5-9, is lifted when impressed with command pulses from the ECU, and relieves the high pressure fuel, which is filled on top of the command piston of the injector (in other words the back pressure side of the nozzle), to the fuel return passage. At this time, pressure immediately below the three-way valve quickly drops from the common-rail pressure to atmospheric pressure, while pressure of command chamber, downstream of one-way orifice, gradually drops according to the orifice restriction. Thanks to these orifice effects, the nozzle needle movement will have a gradual rise which is suitable for combustion, with the result that so-called delta type injection rate pattern is obtained (Fig. 5-10).

As specified time T_Q elapses, the three-way valve is deenergized, and returns to its original position. At this time, command chamber is impressed with common-rail pressure instantly (The one-way orifice does not work in the direction of pressure rise). With this, the nozzle is closed rapidly so that the sharp cut of injection is achieved.

The operation is described below (Fig. 5-9):

When coil is not energized, outer valve comes down by the force of spring, and inner valve goes up by the hydraulic pressure applied from port (1).

With this, seat A is open and ports (1) and (2) are interconnected, that is, common-rail pressure is introduced from port (1) to command chamber (2).

When coil is energized, outer valve being electromagnetically attracted, it moves up until seat A is closed. Inner valve is already moved up by the hydraulic force applied from port(1).

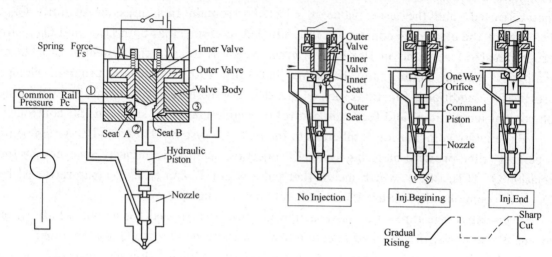

Fig. 5-9 Structure of TWV   Fig. 5-10 Injector operation

As a result, seat A is closed and seat B is opened. Ports(2) and (3) are interconnected, and fuel in command chamber(2) is relieved to leak passage(3).

Injection Timing Control

With the ECD-U2 system, injection timing is freely controlled by the timing (time) of pulses sent to the TWV in the injector.

In injection timing control, the following two-stage computation is conducted in the ECU, in like manner as the injection quantity control:

"θ_{FIN} computation" to determine final injection start time θ_{FIN} ($\alpha°$BTDC) on the basis of various sensor signals, and "T_C computation" to determine start time T_C for energization of pulses to be sent to TWV to realize θ_{FIN}.

θ_{BASE} is basic injection timing determined by engine speed Ne and load Q_{FIN}. Final injection timing θ_{FIN} is then determined after corrections made with intake pressure, water temperature correction at cold, and others. Since θ_{FIN} is a value of crank angle dimension ($\alpha°$BTDC), it is then converted into time T_T according to engine speed. Further, time elapse T_C from 30° BTDC signals (reference for time count) is obtained to output pulses to the injector.

Different from injection quantity control, injection timing control involves conversion of crank angle to time, and is subject to influence of the ever changing engine speed, making it necessary to ensure a certain level of pulse numbers for the engine speed sensor. To ensure accurate injection timing control in consideration of the transient mode, the ECD-U2 system incorporates an engine speed (crank angle) sensor which generates pulses for every 15° crank angle.

Injection Rate Control

Control of injection rate pattern is a very effective means for ensuring compatibility of improved output and fuel consumption and reduced emissions and noise.

With the ECD-U2 system, various injection rate pattern controls are available as shown below.

(1) Delta type: pattern of gradual rise and sharp cut.
(2) Pilot type: pattern where a pilot injection of a small quantity is performed before main injection.
(3) Boot type: pattern where the pilot injection is integral with main injection to form a shape like the tee of a boot.

Delta Shape Injection Rate

Delta shape injection rate is realized by restricting pressure reduction in the command chamber behind the nozzle using a one-way orifice. By restricting the one-way orifice, initial lift of the needle is restrained; injection rate of a better gradual rise obtained (see Fig. 5-10); and, in all cases, the end of injection cuts sharp.

Optimum injection rate pattern for engine combustion will be obtainable by selecting orifice diameter and common-rail pressure.

Pilot Injection

Needless to say, pilot injection (Fig. 5-11) achieved by providing a small pilot pulse before the main injection pulse, and driving the three-way valve twice per injection. As a result of improved response of the three-way valve, and various hardware improvements for the purpose of restricting hydraulic pulsation at various points, a very good pilot injection of quantity as small as 1mm/st and interval between pilot and main injections as short as 0.1ms has been realized.

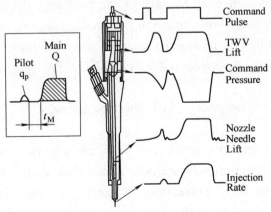

Fig. 5-11 Pilot injection

Boot Shaped Injection Rate

Boot shape injection rate is achieved by temporarily stopping the nozzle needle at a certain pre-lift point. Fig. 5-12 shows the structure and operation of an injector for boot type. Instead of a one-way orifice used in ordinary injectors, a boot valve is installed immediately below the TWV. Gap between the boot valve and command piston serves as the adjustable pre-lift. When the three-way valve is energized, high pressure at the center of boot valve is relieved to the return and the nozzle opens by the amount equivalent to pre-lift. The pre-lift state is maintained until residual high pressure around the periphery of boot valve is reduced via the orifice of the boot valve. The nozzle is then lifted all the way to reach the maximum injection rate condition. In short, various boot patterns are obtainable by the conformance of "amount of pre-lift" and "diameter of boot orifice."

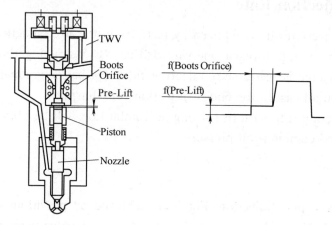

Fig. 5-12 Structure and operation of injector for boot shaped rate

Injection Pressure Control

The ECD-U2 system features free control of injection pressure. Injection pressure, or common-rail pressure, is controlled by varying the discharge quantity of the high pressure supply pump through feedback from common-rail pressure sensor. The high pressure supply pump is precisely controlled by timing the solenoid valve closing.

Two-stage computation is conducted in the ECU, just like in the case of injection quantity control, etc.

"P_{FIN} computation" to determine final injection pressure P_{FIN} on the basis of various sensor signals.

"T_F computation" to determine start time T_F to energize pulse to PCV to realize P_{FIN}.

P_{FIN} is the targeted injection pressure determined from engine speed Ne and load Q_{FIN}. It is finally determined after correction in terms of water temperature. Feedback correction amount is obtained from the difference between control target pressure P_{FIN} and actual common-rail pressure Pc detected by high pressure sensor.

Command value T_F is obtained by referring to the energization start time. Next, pulses are output to the pump control solenoid valve after time lapse T_F supplied from cylinder identifying signals, which serve as the reference for time counting.

At the start up of the system, the pressure that serves as the base for system operation must be generated in the first place. For this reason, a different mode is selected and used as a control algorithm. This mode is used for the time period when the reference cylinder identifying signals are not detected due to very low speed. The valve is repeatedly opened and closed at a fixed frequency, being asynchronous with engine revolution. Values of the valve opening and closing periods are so selected as to realize the largest possible discharge rate on the average.

Pressurized fuel supply by the high pressure supply pump is nearly synchronous with the injection timing of the injector, with the result that temporary excess or shortage of consumption and supply is not generated. For this reason, common-rail pressure remains stable without an accumulator provided. In addition, control of discharge rate of the supply pump is carried out for each injection, and accordingly, high precision and high response can be obtained.

Because consumption and supply are precisely balanced as mentioned above, the system can reduce loss to a great extent as compared with other systems designed to discharge surplus through a relief valve.

NEW WORDS

mountability	[ˌmauntəˈbiliti]	n. 可安装性
modification	[ˌmɔdifiˈkeiʃən]	n. 更改，修改，修正
holder	[ˈhəuldə]	n. 支架
common-rail	[ˈkɔmənreil]	n. 共轨
pilot	[ˈpailət]	n. 飞行员，领航员；v. 导航，领航 a. 先导的，引导的
relevant	[ˈrelivənt]	a. 有关的，相应的
unparalleled	[ʌnˈpærəleld]	a. 无比的，无双的，空前的
passage	[ˈpæsidʒ]	n. 通过，通道，通路
elapse	[iˈlæps]	v. (时间)过去，消逝
compatibility	[kəmˌpætəˈbiliti]	n. 可兼容性，适应性，互换性
tee	[tiː]	n. T形物
pre-lift	[priˈlift]	n. 预升程
periphery	[pəˈrifəri]	n. 外围
conformance	[kənˈfɔːməns]	n. 一致性，适应性
surplus	[ˈsəpləs]	n. 过剩，剩余，余量，顺差；a. 过剩的

PHRASES AND EXPRESSIONS

unit injector	泵喷嘴，组合式喷射器
with ease	轻而易举地，容易地
supply pump	供油泵
feedback control	反馈控制
three-way valve(TWV)	三通阀
injection rate	喷油率，喷油速率
needless to say	不用说
power driver	电源驱动器
on... basis	=on the basis of... 根据，以……为基础，以……为条件
in principle	大体上，基本上
impress M with N	使 M 注意[感觉]到 N，使 M 对 N 有印象
command piston	指令活塞
crank angle	曲轴转角
pilot injection	预喷射
boot valve	靴阀
discharge quantity	泄油量
relief valve	卸压阀，减压阀，调压阀
in consideration of	由于，考虑到

NOTES TO THE TEXT

[1] A new-concept fuel injection system which is suitable for electronic control and capable of controlling injection quantity, timing, rate and pressure individually as well as realizing high pressure has been developed.

句中 which is suitable for... and capable of controlling... as well as realizing high pressure 是个定语从句。在这个从句中 suitable for 与 capable of 并列作表语，controlling 与 realizing 并列，均为 of 的宾语。本句可以译为："一种适合于采用电子控制，能够对喷油量、喷油定时、喷油速率和喷油压力进行单独控制，并实现高压要求的新概念燃油喷射系统已经研制成功。"

[2] In the ECD-U2 system, injection quantity is controlled by pulse width, commanded on the injector actuator, which in turn is controlled by the ECU computing optimum injection quantity depending on the engine operating conditions as detected by various sensors.

句中 commanded on the injector actuator 短语是 pulse width 的后置定语。which... 到句末是一个修饰 injector actuator 的非限制性定语从句，在该从句中，computing... 短语是

ECU 的后置定语，depending on... 短语作状语，修饰 computing。本句可以译为："在 ECD-U2 系统中，喷油量受加给喷油器执行器的脉冲宽度信号的控制，而喷油器执行器又受 ECU 的控制，ECU 按照由各种传感器监测的发动机工作条件，计算出最佳喷油量。"

[3] Needless to say, the system is capable of realizing, without adding any hardware but only with a relevant program change (software), additional functions such as fuel delivery increase at cold condition depending on coolant temperature and feedback control of engine idle speed so called ISC control.

本句可译为："不用说，该系统能够实现像在低温条件下根据冷却液温度增加喷油量，以及发动机怠速反馈控制（即所谓的 ISC 控制）这样的一些附加功能，而做到这些，只需对系统的相关程序（软件）进行调整，无须增加任何硬件。"

EXERCISES

I. *Answer the following questions:*
1. List the basic parts of the ECD-U2 system.
2. What are the advantages of the ECD-U2 system?
3. With the ECD-U2 system, various injection rate pattern controls are available. What are they?

II. *Translate the following terms into Chinese:*
1. fuel consumption
2. emissions regulation
3. injection rate
4. common-rail
5. pulse width
6. command chamber
7. targeted injection quantity
8. one-way orifice

TEXT C Turbochargers and Superchargers

The purpose of superchargers and turbochargers is to force more of the air-fuel mixture into the engine cylinders. This extra air and fuel results in more power output. Turbochargers are a type of supercharger that is driven by the engine exhaust. Superchargers are driven by a belt or chain from the engine crankshaft.

Turbochargers

A turbocharger is installed on some engines to increase the engine's power output. The power generated by the internal combustion engine is directly related to the amount of air that is compressed in the cylinders. By pressurizing the intake mixture before it enters the cylinder, more air and fuel molecules can be packed into the combustion chamber.

The turbocharger relies on the rapid expansion of hot exhaust gases exiting the cylinder to spin turbine blades. A typical turbocharger consists of a turbine(or hot wheel), shaft, compressor (or cold wheel), turbine housing, compressor housing, and center housing and rotating assembly. A waste gate manages turbo output by controlling the amount of exhaust gas that is allowed to enter the turbine housing. Turbo boost is the positive pressure increase created by a turbocharger. Most turbochargers are lubricated by pressurized and filtered engine oil that is line-fed to the unit's oil inlet.[1]

The turbocharger is normally located close to the exhaust manifold. An exhaust pipe runs between the exhaust manifold and the turbine housing to carry the exhaust flow to the turbine wheel. Another pipe connects the compressor housing intake to a throttle plate assembly.

Inside the turbocharger, the turbine wheel(hot wheel) is attached via a shaft to the intake compressor wheel(cold wheel). Each wheel is encased in its own spiral-shaped housing that serves to control and direct the flow of exhaust and intake gases. The shaft that joins the two wheels rides on bearings.

The air compressing process typically starts when the engine's speed is above 2000rpm. The force of the exhaust flow is directed through a nozzle against the side of the turbine wheel. As the hot gases hit the turbine wheel causing it to spin, the specially curved turbine fins direct the air toward the center of the housing where it exits.[2] This action creates a flow called a vortex. Once the turbine starts to spin, the compressor wheel (shaped like a turbine wheel in reverse)also starts to spin. This causes air to be drawn into the center where it is caught by the whirling blades of the compressor and thrown outward by centrifugal force. From there the air exits under pressure through the remainder of the induction system on its way to the cylinder.

Air is typically drawn into the cylinders by the difference in pressure between the atmosphere and engine vacuum. A turbocharger, however, is capable of pressurizing the intake charge above normal atmospheric pressure. Turbo boost is the term used to describe the positive pressure increase created by a turbocharger. For example, 10psi of boost means the air is being fed into the engine at 24.7psi(14.7psi atmospheric plus 10 pounds of boost).

Turbochargers allow an engine to burn more fuel and air by packing more into the existing cylinders. The typical boost provided by a turbocharger is 6 to 8 pounds per square inch(psi). Since normal atmospheric pressure is 14.7psi at sea level, you can see that you are getting about 50 percent more air into the engine. Therefore, you would expect to get 50 percent more power. It's not perfectly efficient, so you might get a 30- to 40-percent improvement instead.

One cause of the inefficiency comes from the fact that the power to spin the turbine is not free. Having a turbine in the exhaust flow increases the restriction in the exhaust. This means that on the exhaust stroke, the engine has to push against a higher back-pressure. This subtracts a little bit of power from the cylinders that are firing at the same time.

A turbocharger helps at high altitudes, where the air is less dense. Normal engines will experience reduced power at high altitudes because for each stroke of the piston, the engine will get a smaller mass of air. A turbocharged engine may also have reduced power, but the reduction will be less dramatic because the thinner air is easier for the turbocharger to pump.

Older cars with carburetors automatically increase the fuel rate to match the increased airflow going into the cylinders. Modern cars with fuel injection will also do this to a point. The fuel-injection system relies on oxygen sensors in the exhaust to determine if the air-to-fuel ratio is correct, so these systems will automatically increase the fuel flow if a turbo is added.

If a turbocharger with too much boost is added to a fuel-injected car, the system may not provide enough fuel—either the software programmed into the controller will not allow it, or the pump and injectors are not capable of supplying it. In this case, other modifications will have to be made to get the maximum benefit from the turbocharger.

Turbochargers use the exhaust gases to drive a turbine wheel. It is connected to the compressor wheel by a shaft (Fig. 5-13). Shaft speeds may approach 150,000 RPM. In order to handle speeds of up to 150,000rpm, the turbine shaft has to be supported very carefully. Most bearings would explode at speeds like this, so most turbochargers use a fluid bearing. This type of bearing supports the shaft on a thin layer of oil that is constantly pumped around the shaft. This serves two purposes: It cools the shaft and some of the other turbocharger parts, and it allows the shaft to spin without much friction.

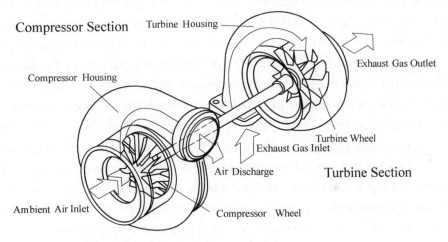

Fig. 5-13 Operation of turbocharger

Some turbocharged engines are equipped with an intercooler that is designed to cool the compressed air from the turbocharger. Retarding spark timing is an often used method of controlling detonation on turbocharged engine systems. Most systems use knock-sensing devices to retard timing only when detonation is detected. Some systems use an electronic control unit to operate the waste gate control valve through sensor signals.

Turbocharger Boost Control

If turbocharger boost pressure(pressure delivered to the intake manifold)becomes too high, it can cause detonation and other engine damage. Boost pressure is controlled by a waste gate. The waste gate controls the engine exhaust gas flow.

The waste gate is operated mechanically or by a vacuum diaphragm, which will move when the intake manifold pressure rises above a set level. When the pressure exceeds this level, the diaphragm opens the waste gate. When the waste gate is open, exhaust gas is permitted to bypass the turbine wheel. This causes the wheel to slow down, reducing the turbocharger boost pressure to a more suitable level.

Due to the increased air-fuel mixture delivered to the engine(with a corresponding increase in pressure), it is essential that the engine compression be lower than that of a non-supercharged engine. Modern supercharged and turbocharged engines have electronic controls which can adjust the ignition timing to prevent detonation.

Turbocharger Service

To inspect a turbocharger, start the engine and listen to the sound the turbo system makes. As a technician becomes more familiar with this characteristic sound, it will be easier to identify an air leak between the compressor outlet and engine or an exhaust leak between engine and turbo by the presence of a higher pitched sound. If the turbo sound cycles or changes in intensity, the likely causes are a plugged air cleaner or loose material in the compressor inlet ducts or dirt buildup on the compressor wheel and housing.

After listening, check the air cleaner and remove the duct from the air cleaner to turbo and look for dirt build up or damage from foreign objects. Check for loose clamps on the compressor outlet connections and check the engine intake system for loose bolts or leaking gaskets. Then disconnect the exhaust pipe and look for restrictions or loose material. Examine the exhaust system for cracks, loose nuts, or blown gaskets. Rotate the turbo shaft assembly. Does it rotate freely? Are there signs of rubbing or wheel impact damage?

Check for exhaust leaks in the turbine housing and related pipe connections. If exhaust gas is escaping before it reaches the turbine wheel, turbocharger effectiveness is reduced. Check for intake system leaks. If there is a leak in the intake system before the compressor housing, dirt may enter the turbocharger and damage the compressor or turbine wheel blades. When a leak is present in the intake system between the compressor wheel housing and the cylinders, turbocharger pressure is reduced.

Visually inspect all hoses, gaskets, and tubing for proper fit, damage, and wear. Check the low pressure, or air cleaner, side of the intake system for vacuum leaks. Check all turbocharger mounting bolts for looseness. A rattling noise may be caused by loose turbocharger mounting bolts. Some whirring noise is normal when the turbocharger shaft is spinning at high speed. Excessive internal turbocharger noise may be caused by too much shaft end play, which allows the blades to strike the housings.

On the pressure side of the system you can check for leaks by using soapy water. After applying the soap mixture, look for bubbles to pinpoint the source of the leak. Inspect the waste gate diaphragm linkage for looseness and binding, and check the hose from the waste gate diaphragm to the intake manifold for cracks, kinks, and restrictions. Also, check the coolant hoses and oil line connected to the turbocharger for leaks.

Excessive blue smoke in the exhaust gas indicates worn turbocharger seals. The technician must remember that worn valve guide seals or piston rings also cause oil consumption and blue smoke in the exhaust. When oil leakage is noted at the turbine end of the turbocharger, always check the oil drain tube and engine crankcase breathers for restrictions. If sludge is found in the crankcase, the engine's oil and filter must be changed.

Leakage in the exhaust system upstream from the turbine housing will also affect turbo operation. If exhaust gases are allowed to escape prior to entering the turbine housing, the reduced temperature and pressure will cause a proportionate reduction in boost and an accompanying loss of power.

If the turbocharger's boost is controlled by the engine computer, a diagnostic trouble code(DTC)is stored in the PCM memory if a fault is present in the boost control solenoid or solenoid-to-PCM wiring.

Superchargers

A supercharger assembly consists of a drive belt, drive and driven gears and a centrifugal compressor wheel. The belt drives the gear and compressor wheel. The compressor wheel pumps air into the engine. Superchargers are installed on top of the intake manifold on V-type engines, and on the side of inline engines.

Supercharger speed is dependent on engine speed and is most efficient at higher engine speeds. Another type of supercharger is a positive displacement vane type and works like a vane oil pump. Its operational speed is also dependent on engine speed.

NEW WORDS

supercharger	[ˈsjuːpətʃɑːdʒə]	n. 机械增压器，增压器
encase	[inˈkeis]	v. 装入，包住，围
spiral-shaped	[ˈspaiər(ə)l-ʃeipt]	a. 螺旋形的
curve	[kəːv]	n. 曲线，特性曲线，弯曲［道］
fin	[fin]	n. 薄片，肋，冷却散热片
whirl	[hwəːl]	v.& n. 旋转，回转，涡流［动］

remainder	[rei'meində]	n. 剩余物；a. 剩余的
intensity	[in'tensiti]	n. 强烈，剧烈，强度
rattling	['rætliŋ]	ad. 极佳，非常；a. 咔嗒咔嗒的
whir	[hwə:]	v. 飞快地旋转，呼呼地转
proportionate	[prə'pɔ:ʃənət]	v. 成比例；a. 成比例的

PHRASES AND EXPRESSIONS

waste gate	旁通阀
turbo boost	涡轮增压器增压压力
fluid bearing	液体轴承
positive displacement vane type	叶片容积式
direct... against...	将……对准……

NOTES TO THE TEXT

[1] Most turbochargers are lubricated by pressurized and filtered engine oil that is line-fed to the unit's oil inlet.

句中 that is line-fed to the unit's oil inlet 是一个定语从句，其谓语是 is line-fed。名词 line 与动词 feed 的过去分词 fed 构成合成动词。本句可以译为："大多数涡轮增压器通过具有一定压力并经过过滤的发动机润滑油进行润滑，这些润滑油是用油管输送到增压器进油口的。"

[2] As the hot gases hit the turbine wheel causing it to spin, the specially curved turbine fins direct the air toward the center of the housing where it exits.

句末 where it exits 是修饰 housing 的定语从句。本句可以译为："在高温废气冲击涡轮并使涡轮旋转的同时，经过特种弯曲成型的涡轮叶片又将废气引向蜗壳的中部，然后废气由此排出涡轮增压器。"

EXERCISES

Ⅰ. *Answer the following questions:*

1. List the components of a typical turbocharger.
2. What is the purpose of the waste gate for turbocharger?

Ⅱ. *Translate the following paragraphs into Chinese:*

At exhaust-gas turbocharging, the exhaust-gas energy which would has been lost is used to drive a turbine. This turbine drives a compressor which aspirates the combustion air and supplies it pre-compressed to the engine. In this way, more fuel can be supplied to the larger air mass and the engine power is increased. A positive effect is also exerted on the combustion process.

The necessity of reducing consumption and the tightening of noxious emissions legislation at the end of the eighties added more weight to the trend towards highly charged engines in the commercial vehicle as well as the passenger car sector. With the aid of the turbocharger, it was possible to considerably increase the efficiency of the engines and simultaneously reduce noxious emissions.

Related Terms

fuel rail	油轨
solenoid winding	电磁阀线圈
spring pressure	弹簧压力
auxiliary air regulator	辅助空气调节器
manifold vacuum sensor	进气歧管压力传感器
barometric pressure	大气压力
airflow sensor	空气流量计
speed density	速度密度
fuel distributor	燃油分配器
diesel fuel injection	柴油机燃油喷射
prechamber	预燃室
cetane number	十六烷值
in-line injection pump	直列式喷油泵
control rack	控制齿条
distributor injection pump	分配式燃油泵
fuel shutoff valve	燃油切断阀
viscosity compensator valve	黏度补偿阀
intake air heater	进气加热器
boost pressure	增压压力
common-rail injection	共轨喷射
unit pump	单体泵

Translation Techniques(5)——省略

在英译汉时,英文原文中的某些词可以省略不译,这就是省译或者叫作减词。省译运用得当,可以使译文简练。

1. 冠词的省译

例1:

A supercharger assembly consists of a drive belt, drive and driven gears and a centrifugal compressor wheel. 该句可以译为:"机械增压器总成是由传动带、主动与从动齿轮和离心式

压气机叶轮所组成。"(省译不定冠词)

例 2：

The bottom of the plunger is connected, by means of a flange, to.... 该句可以译为："柱塞的底部通过凸缘与……相连。"(省译定冠词)

2. 介词的省译

例 3：

In view of the above situation, a fuel injection system... 该句可以译为："考虑到上述情况，燃油喷射系统……。"

例 4：

At this time, pressure immediately below the three-way valve quickly drops... 该句可以译为："这时，紧靠三通阀下面的压力迅速下降……"。

表示时间的介词译在句末，一般不能省略；表示地点的介词位于动词之后，不能省略。

3. 代词的省译

例 5：

When coil is energized, outer valve being electromagnetically attracted, it moves up until seat A is closed. 本句可以译为："线圈通电时，外阀受到电磁吸力作用，而向上移动，直至阀座 A 关闭为止。"

4. 连词的省译

例 6：

As the camshaft rotates, each of the plungers is moved up and down in their cylinders. 该句可译为："当凸轮轴旋转时，每个柱塞在它们各自的泵腔中上下来回运动。"

另外，有的动词、同位语，均可根据实际需要加以省略。

5. 同位语的省译

当英文中的同位语是本位语(说明同位语的词)的别名，而在汉语中两者的译名又是相同的，即汉语中无相应的别名时，该同位语只能省略。

例 7：

This mechanism consists of a ball bearing normally referred to as a throw-out bearing or release bearing. 句中 release bearing 是 throw-out bearing 的同位语，都是"离合器分离轴承"，所以，翻译时 or release bearing 只能省略。本句可以译为："该机构有一个通常称为分离轴承的球轴承。"

UNIT 6   ENGINE ELECTRICAL SYSTEMS

TEXT A   Charging, Starting and Ignition Systems

Charging System

The charging system uses the rotation of the engine to create electricity. The electricity recharges the battery and provides power to operate various vehicle electrical systems. The modern charging system consists of the alternator and regulator.

Alternator

The alternator is a belt-driven, electromagnetic device. After the engine is started, the alternator produces electricity to meet the needs of the vehicle and to keep the battery charged. The modern vehicle contains many circuits that place a heavy load on the electrical system. Since many vehicles are used in stop-and-go city driving, this makes it difficult to maintain the battery in a fully charged state. Therefore, the alternator must be extremely efficient at all speeds.

At idle, when the rotor is turning relatively slowly, the alternator can keep up with the demands of the vehicle electrical system. At normal vehicle speeds, the alternator can produce much more voltage and current than needed. To protect the alternator and the rest of the electrical system from damage, a means of reducing the output must be found.

Voltage Regulator

To reduce alternator output, a voltage regulator is used. The voltage regulator controls the alternator output by adjusting the amount of current reaching the rotor. This controls the strength of the magnetic field passing through the stator windings. The regulator controls the field strength by reading voltage output from the alternator. If output voltage becomes too high, the regulator reduces field strength. If the output voltage drops, the regulator increases field strength.

Electromechanical Voltage Regulator

Older voltage regulators use contact points that are operated by electromagnetic coils. These were called electromechanical voltage regulators.

Electronic Voltage Regulator(EVR)

All vehicles made within the last 15 years use an electronic voltage regulator. The electronic voltage regulator uses power transistors, integrated circuits, diodes, and other solid state parts to control alternator output. The electronic voltage regulator eliminates contact points and moving parts that can stick, oxidize, or wear. Some electronic regulators are remotely mounted. However, electronic voltage regulators are reliable, durable, and small enough to be incorporated into the alternator itself.

Built-in Electronic Regulator Operation

A common charging system circuit with a built-in regulator is illustrated in Fig. 6-1. A small amount of current passes from the stator through the diode trio to the regulator. This equalizes the voltage on either side of the indicator light, putting it out, and tries to ground through resistor R6.

When the stator voltage reaches a certain level, voltage going to ground through resistor R3 will increase to the point that it will cause Zener diode D1 to conduct. Forward-biased (voltage applied in direction causing current flow) transistor TR2 conducts and transistor TR3 is reverse-biased off. This turns transistor TR1 off. The field current and system voltage immediately decrease with TR1 off.

When system voltage decreases, voltage through R3 decreases and D1 stops conducting. This causes transistor TR2 to become reverse-biased off and transistors TR1 and TR3 forward-biased on. Output voltage and field current will increase. This cycle is repeated thousands of times per second, holding alternator voltage output to a preset level.

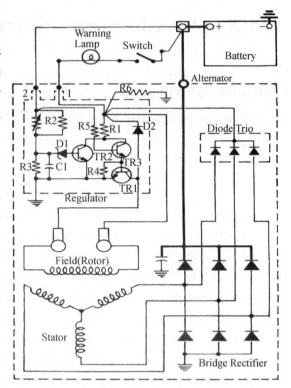

Fig. 6-1 A charging system circuit with a built-in regulator

Sudden voltage change across R3 is prevented by capacitor C1, and excessive back current through TR1 at high temperature is prevented by R4. TR1 is protected by D2 that prevents a high induced voltage in the field winding when TR1 is off. Voltage control temperature correction is provided by a thermistor(resistance decreases as temperature increases).

Computer-Controlled Voltage Regulation

Most vehicles today have several electronic control units(ECUs)or powertrain control modules(PCM)that control the engine and other systems. ECU can also be used to control voltage to the field winding, which eliminates the need for a separate regulator. The disadvantage of this system is that if the portion of the ECU that controls voltage regulation becomes defective, the entire ECU must be replaced.[1]

Starting System

To start an internal combustion engine, it must be cranked (rotated by an outside source). Small two-stroke engines are often cranked by pulling a rope which causes the internal engine parts to revolve. The first automobiles used a hand crank rod for starting. However, this method was dangerous and impractical. A method was soon developed to start the engine by using an electric starting motor, or starter. The starter is mounted on the transmission housing and operates a small gear that can be meshed with a large ring gear attached to the flywheel. To energize the starter, the driver turns the ignition switch to Start, which completes an electrical circuit to the starter.[2] When the starter motor armature begins to turn, the starter gear moves out and engages the ring gear, which spins the crankshaft. When the engine starts, the driver breaks the starter electrical circuit by releasing the ignition key switch. This causes the starter gear to move out of mesh with the ring gear.[3]

Ignition System

The purpose of the ignition system is to create a spark that will ignite the fuel-air mixture in the cylinder of an engine. It must do this at exactly the right instant and do it at the rate of up to several thousand times per minute for each cylinder in the engine. If the timing of that spark is off by a small fraction of a second, the engine will run poorly or not run at all.

The ignition system sends an extremely high voltage to the spark plug in each cylinder when the piston is at the top of its compression stroke. The tip of each spark plug contains a gap that the voltage must jump across in order to reach ground. That is where the spark occurs.

The voltage that is available to the spark plug is somewhere between 20,000 volts and 50,000 volts or better. The job of the ignition system is to produce that high voltage from a 12-volt source and get it to each cylinder in a specific order, at exactly the right time.

The ignition system has two tasks to perform. First, it must create a voltage high enough (20,000+ volts) to arc across the gap of a spark plug, thus creating a spark strong enough to ignite the air/fuel mixture for combustion. Second, it must control the timing of the spark so that it occurs at the exact right time and send it to the correct cylinder.

The ignition system is divided into two sections, the primary circuit and the secondary circuit. The low voltage primary circuit operates at battery voltage (12 to 14.5 volts) and is responsible for generating the signal to fire the spark plug at the exact right time and sending that signal to the ignition coil. The ignition coil is the component that converts the 12-volt signal into the high 20,000+ volts charge. Once the voltage is stepped up, it goes to the secondary circuit which then directs the charge to the correct spark plug at the right time.

The basic principle of the electrical spark ignition system has not changed for over 75 years. What has changed is the method by which the spark is created and how it is distributed.

Three Types of Ignition Systems

Currently, there are three distinct types of ignition systems. The mechanical (conventional) ignition system was used prior to 1975. It was mechanical and electrical and used no electronics. By understanding these early systems, it will be easier to understand the new electronic and computer controlled ignition systems, so don't skip over it. The electronic ignition system started finding its way to production vehicles during the early 1970s and became popular when better control and improved reliability became important with the advent of emission controls. Finally, the distributorless ignition system became available in the mid 1980s. This system was always computer controlled and contained no moving parts, so reliability was greatly improved. Most of these systems required no maintenance except replacing the spark plugs at intervals from 60,000 to over 100,000 miles.

The Mechanical Ignition System

The distributor is the nerve center of the mechanical ignition system and has two tasks to perform. First, it is responsible for triggering the ignition coil to generate a spark at the precise instant. Second, the distributor is responsible for directing that spark to the proper cylinder. The circuit that powers the ignition system is simple and straight forward (Fig. 6-2). When you insert the key in the ignition switch and turn the key to the Run position, you are sending current from the battery through a wire directly to the positive (+) side of the ignition coil. Inside the coil is a series of copper windings that loop around the coil over a hundred times before exiting out the negative (−) side of the coil. From there, a wire takes this current over to the distributor and is connected to a special on/off switch, called the points. When the points are closed, this current goes directly to ground. When current flows from the ignition switch, through the windings in the coil, then to ground, it builds a strong magnetic field inside the coil.

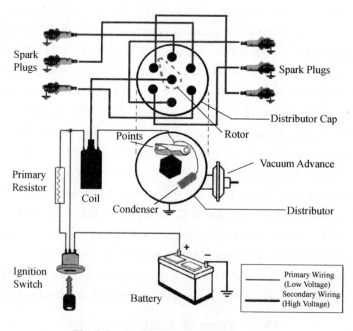

Fig. 6-2 A conventional ignition system

The points are made up of a fixed contact point that is fastened to a plate inside the distributor, and a movable contact point mounted on the end of a spring loaded arm. The movable point rides on a 4-,6-,or 8-lobe cam(depending on the number of cylinders in the engine) that is mounted on a rotating shaft inside the distributor. This distributor cam rotates in time with the engine, making one complete revolution for every two revolutions of the engine. As it rotates, the cam pushes the points open and closed. Every time the points open, the flow of current is interrupted through the coil, thereby collapsing the magnetic field and releasing a high voltage surge through the secondary coil windings. This voltage surge goes out the top of the coil and through the high-tension coil wire.

Now, we have the voltage necessary to fire the spark plug, but we still have to get it to the correct cylinder. The coil wire goes from the coil directly to the center of the distributor cap. Under the cap is a rotor that is mounted on top of the rotating shaft. The rotor has a metal strip on the top that is in constant contact with the center terminal of the distributor cap. It receives the high voltage surge from the coil wire and sends it to the other end of the rotor which rotates past each spark plug terminal inside the cap.[4] As the rotor turns on the shaft, it sends the voltage to the correct spark plug wire, which in turn sends it to the spark plug. The voltage enters the spark plug at the terminal at the top and travels down the core until it reaches the tip. It then jumps across the gap at the tip of the spark plug, creating a spark suitable to ignite the fuel-air mixture inside that cylinder.

The Electronic Ignition System

In the electronic ignition(EI) system, the points and condenser were replaced by electronics. On these systems, there were several methods used to replace the points and condenser in order to trigger the coil to fire. One method used a metal wheel with teeth, usually one for each cylinder. This is called an armature or reluctor. A magnetic pick up coil senses when a tooth passes and sends a signal to the control module to fire the coil.

Other systems used an electric eye with a shutter wheel to send a signal to the electronics that it was time to trigger the coil to fire. These systems still need to have the initial timing adjusted by rotating the distributor housing.

The advantage of this system, aside from the fact that it is maintenance free, is that the control module can handle much higher primary voltage than the mechanical points. Voltage can even be stepped up before sending it to the coil, so the coil can create a much hotter spark, on the order of 50,000 volts instead of 20,000 volts that is common with the mechanical systems. These systems only have a single wire from the ignition switch to the coil since a primary resistor is no longer needed.

On some vehicles, this control module was mounted inside the distributor where the points used to be mounted. On other designs, the control module was mounted outside the distributor with external wiring to connect it to the pickup coil. On many General Motors engines, the control module was inside the distributor and the coil was mounted on top of the distributor for a one piece unitized ignition system. GM called it High Energy Ignition or HEI for short.

The higher voltage that these systems provided allows the use of a much wider gap on the spark plugs for a longer, fatter spark. This larger spark also allows a leaner mixture for better fuel economy and still insures a smooth running engine.

The early electronic systems had limited or no computing power, so timing still had to be set manually and there was still a centrifugal and vacuum advance built into the distributor.

On some of the later systems, the inside of the distributor is empty and all triggering is performed by a sensor that watches a notched wheel connected to either the crankshaft or the camshaft. These devices are called crankshaft position sensor or camshaft position sensor. In these systems, the job of the distributor is solely to distribute the spark to the correct cylinder through the distributor cap and rotor. The computer handles the timing and any timing advance necessary for the smooth running of the engine.

The Distributorless Ignition System

Newer automobiles have evolved from a mechanical system(distributor) to a completely solid state electronic system with no moving parts. These systems are completely controlled by the on-board computer. In place of the distributor, there are multiple coils that each serves one or two spark plugs. A typical 6-cylinder engine has 3 coils that are mounted together in a coil "pack". A spark plug wire comes out of each side of the individual coil and goes to the appropriate spark plug. The coil fires both spark plugs at the same time. One spark plug fires on the compression stroke, igniting the fuel-air mixture to produce power, while the other spark plug fires on the exhaust stroke and does nothing. On some vehicles, there is an individual coil for each cylinder mounted directly on top of the spark plug. This design completely eliminates the high tension spark plug wires for even better reliability. Most of these systems use spark plugs that are designed to last over 100,000 miles, which cuts down on maintenance costs.

NEW WORDS

electromagnetic	[i‚lektrəumæg'netik]	a.	电磁的
trio	['tri:əu]	n.	三件一套，三个一组，三重唱
forward-biased	['fɔ:wəd'baiəst]	a.	正向偏压的
reverse-biased	[ri'və:s'baiəst]	a.	反向偏压[偏置]的
capacitor	[kə'pæsitə]	n.	电容器
thermistor	[θə:'mistə]	n.	热敏电阻
rope	[rəup]	n.	绳，索，绳索；v. 围起
armature	['ɑ:mətjuə]	n.	电枢
collaps	[kə'læps]	v.& n.	倒塌，塌陷，消失，减弱
high-tension	['hai'tenʃən]	a.	高(电)压的
reluctor	[ri'lʌktə]	n.	磁阻轮
centrifugal	[sen'trifjugəl]	a.	离心的
advent	['ædvənt]	n.	出现，到来，来临

PHRASES AND EXPRESSIONS

charging system	充电系统
keep up with	跟上，不落后于
magnetic field	磁场
field strength	磁场强度
contact point	触点
power transistor	功率晶体管
integrated circuit	集成电路
solid state	固态
diode trio	二极管三件组合
starting motor	起动机
transmission housing	变速器壳
be responsible for	（应）对……负责，是造成……的（主要）原因，决定着，导致
with the advent of	随着……的出现（到来）
in time with	与……合拍（同期）
in(constant)contact with	（始终）与……保持接触
pickup coil	传感线圈
electric eye	电眼，光电池
shutter wheel	遮光轮
initial timing	初始点火正时
vacuum advance	真空式点火提前角调节装置
distributorless ignition system	无分电器点火系统

NOTES TO THE TEXT

[1] The disadvantage of this system is that if the portion of the ECU that controls voltage regulation becomes defective, the entire ECU must be replaced.

句中 if the portion of…,… must be replaced 是一个表语从句。该表语从句中的 that controls voltage regulation 是一个定语从句，其先行词为 portion。本句可译为："该系统的缺点是如果 ECU 中控制电压调节的部分电路发生故障，就必须更换整个 ECU。"

[2] To energize the starter, the driver turns the ignition switch to Start, which completes an electrical circuit to the starter.

本句中的第二个 to 是介词。which… 是一个非限制性定语从句，which 指代 the driver turns the ignition switch to Start 这一动作。本句可译为："为了给起动机通电，驾驶员应将点火开关转到 Start 位置，这样便可接通起动机的电路。"

[3] This causes the starter gear to move out of mesh with the ring gear.

句中短语 out of mesh with 的意思是"脱离与……的啮合"。本句可译为："这就引起了起动机小齿轮的移动，从而脱离与齿圈的啮合。"

[4] It receives the high voltage surge from the coil wire and sends it to the other end of the rotor which rotates past each spark plug terminal inside the cap.

理解此句应注意三点：前后两个 it 分别指代 distributor 和 the high voltage surge；sends 是并列谓语；which rotates... 是修饰 rotor 的定语从句。本句可译为："分电器接收来自点火线圈高压线送来的高电压并将其送到分火头的另一端，分火头在分电器盖内旋转并从通往各个火花塞的旁电极旁边经过。"

EXERCISES

Ⅰ. *Answer the following questions:*
1. What are the purposes of a charging system?
2. What are the two types of voltage regulators?
3. What are the three types of ignition systems?
4. What are the advantages of electronic ignition system?
5. What are the advantages of distributorless ignition system?

Ⅱ. *Translate the following paragraphs into Chinese:*

The primary ignition circuit operates on battery voltage with the ignition switch on and the engine stopped, or charging system voltage with the engine running. The following components are in the primary ignition circuit: ignition switch, ballast resistor, primary coil winding, electronic control unit(ECU)and pickup coil.

The secondary ignition circuit operates on a very high induced voltage from the secondary coil winding. The following components are part of the secondary circuit: secondary coil winding, coil secondary(high tension)wire, distributor cap, rotor, spark plug wires and spark plugs.

TEXT B Direct Ignition Systems and Electronic Triggering Devices

Direct Ignition Systems

Some engines use a distributorless ignition system that eliminates the need for spark plug wires. The direct ignition system(DIS)utilizes a coil tower that is installed onto a cover plate and plug boots that fit directly onto the spark plugs. The ignition module and coils are installed under the coil tower. The spark is transmitted to the plug boots through secondary conductors located in the tower. This system operates using the same principles as the distributorless ignition system.

Electronic Ignition Systems with Coils Connected Directly to the Spark Plugs

These EI systems have the same reluctor ring and magnetic sensor as other electronic ignition(EI) systems. However, on these EI systems, the spark plug wires are eliminated and the coil secondary terminals are connected directly to the spark plugs. Since the spark plug wires are eliminated, the chance of high-voltage leaks is reduced. The coil module and coils are mounted under a plate that is positioned between the cam covers on top of the engine(Fig. 6-3). Each coil is connected to a pair of spark plugs, and the spark plug pairs are 1-4 and 2-3. Since the coil module contacts the mounting plate, this plate acts as a heat shield. The mounting plate must be grounded to the engine to provide ignition operation. Remote spark plug wires may be connected between the spark plugs and the coil secondary terminals for test purposes, but the coil mounting cover must be grounded with a jumper wire during this test procedure.

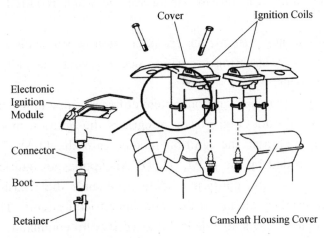

Fig. 6-3 Ignition systems with coils connected directly to the spark plugs

The operation and electrical connections(Fig. 6-4) for these EI systems are similar to the EI system explained previously. The PCM reduces the spark advance for a few milliseconds during transmission shifting to lower the engine torque load on the transmission clutches.

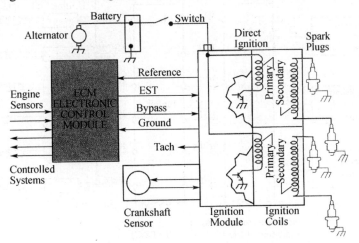

Fig. 6-4 A distributorless ignition system circuit

Independent Ignition System(Coil-On-Plug or Coil-Near-Plug)

The independent ignition system is also known as a coil-on-plug system or coil-near-plug and uses one coil for each cylinder. The independent ignition system mounts an ignition coil as an assembly directly to a spark plug or near the spark plug with a very short secondary ignition wire.

The coil on plug design allows for increased coil saturation time between cylinder firing. Coil saturation time is the period when current flows through the primary windings, increasing the magnetic field generated, and thereby increasing the secondary voltage when required.[1] Misfires are more likely to occur under higher engine speeds and increased load conditions. The ability to increase firing voltage when required lowers the risk of intermittent misfires.

On a typical coil-on-plug system, the crank position sensor sends a signal to the PCM. The PCM then determines the firing order and decides what the individual spark timing should be for each cylinder.[2]

The coil on plug independent ignition system either uses one ignition module to control the primary circuit of all coils(Fig. 6-5) or integrates the ignition module into each coil assembly(Fig. 6-6) or integrates the ignition module into the PCM(CHRYSLER). The ignition module is controlled by the PCM. The PCM supplies an ignition timing signal to the ignition module. Next, the ignition module commands the transistors in the driver circuit to turn on the primary circuit in the independent coil circuit. The ignition module sends a confirmation signal back to the PCM to verify the command. The coil assembly uses a high-voltage diode in the secondary circuit(Fig. 6-7) for rapid cutoff of the secondary ignition voltage. If the ignition module is not integrated into the coil assembly, both the primary and secondary circuits may be checked using a conventional digital ohmmeter for circuit integrity.

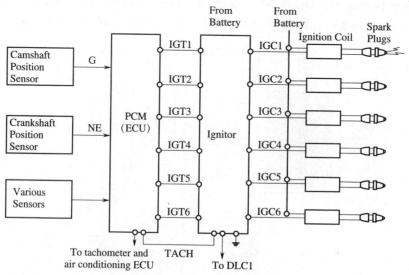

Fig. 6-5 An independent ignition system that uses one ignition module to control the primary circuit of all coils

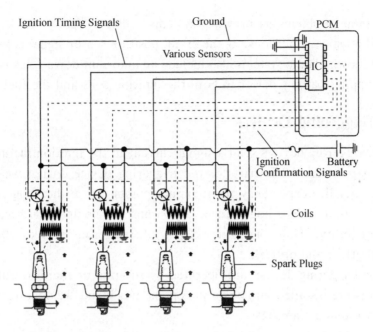

Fig. 6-6 A independent ignition system that integrates the ignition module into each coil assembly

Always compare readings to manufacturer specifications. It is generally recommended to swap coils when testing for a faulty ignition coil since all coils are the same on the engine.

The independent ignition system with integrated ignition modules into each coil assembly typically uses four wires connected to the primary side of the assembly (Fig. 6-6). The four wires consist of battery positive, ground, ignition timing signal, and ignition confirmation signal. The PCM uses the ignition confirmation signal to determine if a coil is not operating. The primary circuits of these coils cannot be tested with an ohmmeter.

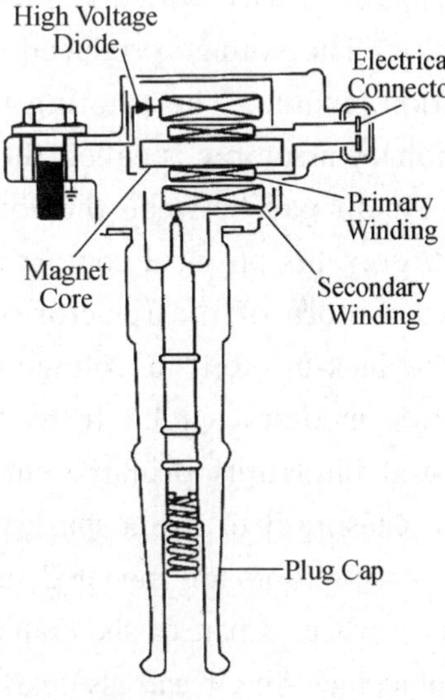

Some engines do not have the physical space to integrate the coil-on-plug design. In these situations, manufacturers have placed the individual coil assemblies as close to the spark plugs as possible, typically on top of the valve cover, and integrated short plug wires from each of the coils to their respective spark plugs.

Fig. 6-7 The coil assembly uses a high-voltage diode in the secondary circuit

The independent ignition system offers greater reliability and a lower incidence of cylinder misfires compared to past ignition systems. The coil-on-plug system eliminates the spark plug wires, which have been a common source of shorts in the past.[3] The independent ignition system has become the preferred ignition system by most vehicle manufacturers.

The coil-on-plug system, sometimes referred to as a coil-over-plug ignition system, is subject to the same problems as previous systems, such as faulty spark plugs, misfire, hard start, and no-start conditions. If the crank position sensor signal is lost, the ignition system will shut down. Some systems also include an auto shut down relay controlled by the PCM, which supplies battery power to both the ignition coils and the fuel injectors.[4]

Electronic Triggering Devices

Electronic triggering devices send a signal current to the ignition module, which then breaks the primary circuit. The parts of the triggering device do not wear, which gives them a much longer life expectancy than contact points. Since the triggering device does not wear, engine timing does not change. This improves engine performance, emissions output, and reliability. There are three types of triggering devices currently in use: magnetic, Hall effect and optical.

Most of the triggering devices are operated by rotation of the distributor shaft. Some triggering devices are installed into or on the engine block and are operated by the rotation of the crankshaft and/or camshaft.

Magnetic Pickup

The magnetic pickup shown in Fig. 6-8 is mounted in the distributor and reacts to distributor speed, which is one half of crankshaft speed. This sensor generates alternating current. The voltage produced is small(about 250 millivolts), but can be read easily by the ignition module. The rotating tooth assembly is called a reluctor, or trigger wheel. The stationary assembly is called the pickup coil or stator.

An air gap between the rotating and stationary teeth prevents physical contact and eliminates wear. When a tooth of the reluctor aligns with the tooth of the pick-up coil, a voltage signal is sent to the ignition module, which turns the power transistor off and interrupts primary current to the ignition coil, causing it to fire a spark plug.

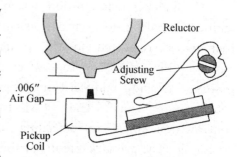

Fig. 6-8　A magnetic crankshaft position sensor

Some sensors are mounted near the crankshaft. A reluctor wheel is part of the crankshaft and is placed at its midpoint. An air gap also exists between this sensor and the reluctor. When the sensor is in the middle of each slot, the transistor is turned off and interrupts current flow to the ignition coil, causing a spark plug to fire. The air gap is critical on all magnetic sensors and must be set to specifications.

Hall-Effect Switch

The Hall-effect switch can be mounted in the distributor or at the crankshaft, Fig. 6-9. The Hall-effect sensor is a thin wafer of semiconductor material with voltage applied to it constantly. A magnet is located opposite the sensor. There is an air gap between the sensor and magnet (Fig. 6-9a).

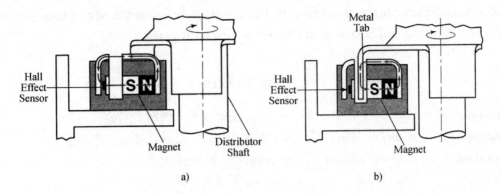

Fig. 6-9　A Hall-effect switch

The magnetic field acts on the sensor until a metal tab, usually called a shutter, is placed between the sensor and magnet (Fig. 6-9b). This metal tab does not touch the magnet or sensor. When contact between the magnetic field and sensor is interrupted, it causes its output voltage to be reduced. This signals the ignition module to turn the power transistor off. This interrupts primary current to the ignition coil, causing it to fire.

Optical Sensor

The optical sensor is usually located in the distributor, as shown in Fig. 6-10a. The rotor plate, Fig. 6-10b, has many slits in it through which light passes from the light emitting diode (LED) to the photo sensitive diode (light receiving).[5] As the rotor plate turns, it interrupts the light beam from the LED to the photo diode. When the photo diode does not detect light, it sends a voltage signal to the ignition module, causing it to fire the coil. The coil fires, the spark exits one terminal, travels through the plug wire to fire the plug, and returns to the other coil terminal through the engine block, the other spark plug, and the other plug wire. In effect, the coil fires both spark plugs at the same time, see Fig. 6-4.

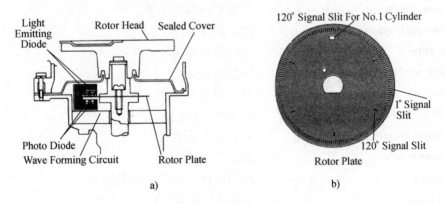

Fig. 6-10　A optical crankshaft position sensor

The coil wires are arranged so that the coil fires one plug on the top of the compression stroke and the other plug on the top of the exhaust stroke. The plug firing on the top of the exhaust stroke has no effect on the operation of the engine and is often called a waste spark. Since it takes very little voltage to jump the spark plug gap on the exhaust stroke, the coil is powerful enough to fire both plugs.

NEW WORDS

coil-on-plug		*a*. 点火线圈位于火花塞上方的
saturation	[ˌsætʃəˈreiʃən]	*n*. 饱和(状态)，浸润，浸透，饱和度
intermittent	[ˌintə(:)ˈmitənt]	*a*. 间歇的，断断续续的
misfire	[ˌmisˈfaiə]	*v*.& *n*. 不发火，缺火
confirmation	[ˌkɔnfəˈmeiʃən]	*n*. 证实，确认，批准
verify	[ˈverifai]	*v*. 检验，校验，查证，核实
command	[kəˈmɑːnd]	*n*. 命令，掌握，司令部；*v*. 命令，指挥，支配
recommend	[ˌrekəˈmend]	*vt*. 推荐，介绍，劝告，使受欢迎
swap	[swɔp]	*v*. 交换；*n*. 交换
expectancy	[iksˈpektənsi]	*n*. 期待，期望
wafer	[ˈweifə]	*n*. 晶片，圆片，薄饼
tab	[tæb]	*n*. 标签，制表符，短小凸出部
shutter	[ˈʃʌtə]	*n*. 关闭者，百叶窗，快门
slit	[slit]	*n*. 裂缝，狭长切口；*v*. 切开，撕裂

PHRASES AND EXPRESSIONS

heat shield	隔热板
mounting plate	安装板
jumper wire	跨接线
transmission clutch	变速器换档离合器
independent ignition system	独立点火系统
saturation time	(磁)饱和时间
intermittent misfire	断续性缺火
firing order	点火顺序
compare M to N	将 M 与 N 比较
crank position sensor	曲轴位置传感器
auto shut down relay	自动关闭继电器
life expectancy	预期寿命，预计使用期限
magnetic pickup	电磁式传感器
trigger wheel	触发轮
air gap	气隙
reluctor wheel	磁阻轮
Hall-effect switch	霍尔效应开关

optical sensor	光电式传感器
rotor plate	遮光板
light emitting diode	发光二极管
photo sensitive diode	光电二极管，光敏二极管
photo diode	光电二极管

NOTES TO THE TEXT

[1] Coil saturation time is the period when current flows through the primary windings, increasing the magnetic field generated, and thereby increasing the secondary voltage when required.

句中有两个 when。第一个 when 是关系副词，引导一个定语从句，修饰 period。在这个定语从句中，有两个并列的现在分词短语 increasing...，作定语从句的状语。第二个 when 是从属连词，其后的 it is required 中的 it is 被省略，也就是说 when required 是一个修饰两个 increasing 的状语从句。本句可译为："线圈的磁饱和时间是指电流持续流经初级线圈，从而在需要时可增加所产生的磁场强度，因而也就增加了次级电压的时间。"也可以意译为："线圈的磁饱和时间是指电流流经初级线圈的持续时间。在需要时，增加磁饱和时间可增加所产生的磁场强度，因而也就增加了次级电压。"

[2] The PCM then determines the firing order and decides what the individual spark timing should be for each cylinder.

句中 what... 是 decides 的宾语从句。可以译为："……并且确定每个气缸的点火正时。"

[3] The coil-on-plug system eliminates the spark plug wires, which have been a common source of shorts in the past.

句中 which have been... 是一个非限制性定语从句，其先行词为 spark plug wires。short 在此处作名词用，意思为"短路故障"。本句可译为："点火线圈位于火花塞上方的点火系统省去了火花塞高压线，过去，这里经常出现短路故障。"

[4] Some systems also include an auto shut down relay controlled by the PCM, which supplies battery power to both the ignition coils and the fuel injectors.

句中 which supplies…是一个非限制性定语从句，其先行词为 relay。本句可译为："有些系统还采用了一个由 PCM 控制的、既要为点火线圈又要为喷油器提供蓄电池电压的自动切断继电器。"

[5] The rotor plate, Fig. 6-10b, has many slits in it through which light passes from the light emitting diode(LED)to the photo sensitive diode(light receiving).

句中 through which... 是一个定语从句，which 指代 slits。注意定语从句中的介词搭配，将定语从句还原为正常语序，即 light passes through slits from... to...，更容易理解。故本句可译为："遮光盘(见图 6-10b)上有许多槽缝，来自发光二极管的光线穿过这些槽缝才能到达光电二极管(接受光照)。"

EXERCISES

I. Answer the following questions:

1. Describe the purposes of electronic triggering devices.
2. What are the three types of electronic triggering devices?
3. What are the advantages of direct ignition system?
4. What is independent ignition system?
5. Describe the advantages of independent ignition system?
6. What are the stationary and rotating assemblies of the three types of electronic triggering devices, respectively?

II. Choose the best answer for each of the following:

1. The primary job of the ignition coil is _____.
   Ⓐ to reduce primary voltage
   Ⓑ to reduce secondary voltage
   Ⓒ to convert low voltage into high voltage
   Ⓓ to convert high voltage into low voltage
2. A high-voltage diode is used in the secondary circuit of the coil assembly for _____.
   Ⓐ rapid build-up of the primary ignition voltage
   Ⓑ rapid cutoff of the primary ignition voltage
   Ⓒ rapid build-up of the secondary ignition voltage
   Ⓓ rapid cutoff of the secondary ignition voltage
3. The optical sensor is usually located _____.
   Ⓐ in the distributor   Ⓑ in the fuel pressure regulator
   Ⓒ in the ignition coil   Ⓓ on the ignition module
4. In an independent ignition system with ignition modules integrated into each coil assembly, the PCM uses the ignition confirmation signal to determine _____.
   Ⓐ if a coil is not operating
   Ⓑ if a spark plug is faulty
   Ⓒ if the crankshaft position sensor is not operating
   Ⓓ if the optical sensor is not operating

TEXT C Engine Electrical System Service

Battery Check and Charging

Warning: Certain precautions must be followed when checking and servicing the battery. Hydrogen gas, which is highly flammable, is always present in the battery cells, so keep lighted tobacco and all other open flames and sparks away from the battery. The electrolyte inside the battery is actually dilute sulfuric acid, which will cause injury if splashed on your skin or in your eyes. It will also ruin clothes and painted surfaces. When removing the battery cables, always detach the negative cable first and hook it up last.

A routine preventive maintenance program for the battery in your vehicle is the only way to ensure quick and reliable starts. But before performing any battery maintenance, make sure that you have the proper equipment necessary to work safely around the battery.

There are also several precautions that should be taken whenever battery maintenance is performed. Before servicing the battery, always turn the engine and all accessories off and disconnect the cable from the negative terminal of the battery.

The battery produces hydrogen gas, which is both flammable and explosive. Never create a spark, smoke or light a match around the battery. Always charge the battery in a ventilated area.

Electrolyte contains poisonous and corrosive sulfuric acid. Do not allow it to get in your eyes, on your skin or your clothes. Never ingest it. Wear protective safety glasses when working near the battery. Keep children away from the battery.

Note the external condition of the battery. If the positive terminal and cable clamp on your vehicle's battery is equipped with a rubber protector, make sure that it's not torn or damaged. It should completely cover the terminal. Look for any corroded or loose connections, cracks in the case or cover or loose hold-down clamps. Also check the entire length of each cable for cracks and frayed conductors.

If corrosion, which looks like white, fluffy deposit is evident, particularly around the terminals, the battery should be removed for cleaning.[1] Loosen the cable clamp bolts with a wrench, being careful to remove the ground cable first, and slide them off the terminals.[2] Then disconnect the hold-down clamp bolt and nut, remove the clamp and lift the battery from the engine compartment.

Warning: When batteries are being charged, hydrogen gas, which is very explosive and flammable, is produced. Do not smoke or allow open flames near a charging or a recently charged battery. Wear eye protection when near the battery during charging. Also, make sure the charger is unplugged before connecting or disconnecting the battery from the charger.

Slow-rate charging is the best way to restore a battery that's discharged to the point where it will not start the engine.[3] It's also a good way to maintain the battery charge in a vehicle that's only driven a few miles between starts. Maintaining the battery charge is particularly important in the winter when the battery must work harder to start the engine and electrical accessories that drain the battery are in greater use.[4]

It's best to use a one or two-amp battery charger (sometimes called a "trickle" charger). They are the safest and put the least strain on the battery. They are also the least expensive. For a faster charge, you can use a higher amperage charger, but don't use one rated more than 1/10th the amp/hour rating of the battery. Rapid boost charges that claim to restore the power of the battery in one to two hours are hardest on the battery and can damage batteries not in good condition. This type of charging should only be used in emergency situations.

The average time necessary to charge a battery should be listed in the instructions that come with the charger. As a general rule, a trickle charger will charge a battery in 12 to 16 hours.

Charging System Check

If a malfunction occurs in the charging circuit, do not immediately assume that the alternator is causing the problem. First check the following items:

- The battery cables where they connect to the battery. Make sure the connections are clean and tight.
- The battery electrolyte specific gravity. If it is low, charge the battery.
- Check the external alternator wiring and connections.
- Check the drive belt condition and tension.
- Check the alternator mounting bolts for tightness.
- Run the engine and check the alternator for abnormal noise.

Using a voltmeter, check the battery voltage with the engine off. It should be approximately 12-volts. Start the engine and check the battery voltage again. It should now be approximately 14 to 15-volts. If the indicated voltage reading is less or more than the specified charging voltage, replace the voltage regulator. If replacing the regulator fails to restore the voltage to the specified range, the problem may be within the alternator.

Due to the special equipment necessary to test or service the alternator, it is recommended that if a fault is suspected the vehicle be taken to a dealer or a shop with the proper equipment.

Some models are equipped with an ammeter on the instrument panel that indicates charge or discharge current passing in or out of the battery. With all electrical equipment switched ON, and the engine idling, the gauge needle may show a discharge condition. At fast idle or normal driving speeds the needle should stay on the charge side of the gauge, with the charged state of the battery determining just how far over (the lower the battery state of charge, the farther the needle should swing toward the charge side).[5]

Some models are equipped with a voltmeter on the instrument panel that indicates battery voltage with the key on and engine off, and alternator output when the engine is running. The charge light on the instrument panel illuminates with the key on and engine not running, and should go out when the engine runs. If the gauge does not show a charge when it should or the alternator light (if equipped) remains on, there is a fault in the system. Before inspecting the brushes or replacing the alternator, the battery condition, alternator belt tension and electrical cable connections should be checked.

In-Vehicle Starting System Check

If the starter motor doesn't turn at all when the switch is operated, make sure the shift lever is in Neutral or Park. Make sure the battery is charged and that all cables at the battery and starter relay/solenoid terminals are secure.

If the starter motor spins but the engine doesn't turn over, then the drive assembly in the starter motor is slipping and the starter motor must be replaced. If, when the switch is actuated, the starter motor doesn't operate at all but the starter relay/solenoid operates (clicks), then the problem lies with either the battery, the starter relay/solenoid contacts or the starter motor connections.[6]

If the starter relay/solenoid doesn't click when the ignition switch is actuated, either the starter relay/solenoid circuit is open or the relay/solenoid itself is defective. Check the starter relay/solenoid circuit or replace the relay or solenoid.

To check the starter relay/solenoid circuit, remove the push on connector from the relay/solenoid wire. Make sure that the connection is clean and secure and the relay bracket is grounded. If the connections are good, check the operation of the relay/solenoid with a jumper wire. To do this, place the transmission in Park. Remove the push-on connector from the relay/solenoid. Connect a jumper wire between the battery positive terminal and the exposed terminal on the relay/solenoid. If the starter motor now operates, the starter relay/solenoid is okay. The problem is in the ignition switch, neutral start switch or in the starting circuit wiring(look for open or loose connections).

If the starter motor still doesn't operate, replace the starter relay/solenoid. If the starter motor cranks the engine at an abnormally slow speed, first make sure the battery is fully charged and all terminal connections are clean and tight. Also check the connections at the starter relay/solenoid and battery ground. Eyelet terminals should not be easily rotated by hand. Also check for a short to ground. If the engine is partially seized, or has the wrong viscosity oil in it, it will crank slowly.

Ignition System Check

Warning: Because of the high voltage generated by the ignition system, extreme care should be taken whenever an operation is performed involving ignition components. This not only includes the igniter(electronic ignition), coil, distributor and spark plug wires, but related components such as spark plug connectors, tachometer and other test equipment.

Electronic Distributorless Ignition(EDIS)system

If the engine turns over but won't start, disconnect the spark plug lead from any spark plug and attach it to a calibrated ignition tester(available at most auto parts stores).

Connect the clip on the tester to a bolt or metal bracket on the engine, crank the engine and watch the end of the tester to see if bright blue, well-defined sparks occur.

If sparks occur, sufficient voltage is reaching the spark plug to fire it(repeat the check at the remaining plug wires to verify that all the ignition coils and wires are functioning). However, the plugs themselves may be fouled, so remove and check them or install new ones.

If no spark or intermittent spark occurs, check for battery voltage to the ignition coil. Check for a bad spark plug wire by swapping wires. Check the coils and EDIS ignition module.

Alternative Method(All Ignition Systems)

Note: If you're unable to obtain a calibrated ignition tester, the following method will allow you to determine if the ignition system has spark, but it won't tell you if there's enough voltage produced to actually initiate combustion in the cylinders.

Remove the wire from one of the spark plugs. Using an insulated tool, hold the wire about 1/4-inch from a good ground and have an assistant crank the engine.

If bright blue, well-defined sparks occur, sufficient voltage is reaching the plug to fire it. However, the plug(s) may be fouled, so remove and check them or install new ones.

If there's no spark, check the remaining wires in the same manner. A few sparks followed by no spark is the same condition as no spark at all. If no sparks occur, remove the distributor cap and check the cap and rotor. If moisture is present, dry out the cap and rotor, then reinstall the cap and repeat the spark test.

If there's still no spark, disconnect the secondary coil wire from the distributor cap, hold it about 1/4-inch from a good engine ground and crank the engine again.

If no sparks occur, check the primary(small)wire connections at the coil to make sure they're clean and tight. If sparks now occur, the distributor cap and rotor(DuraSpark Ⅱ and TFI-Ⅳ[7] systems only), plug wire(s) or spark plug(s)(or all of them) may be defective.

If there's still no spark, the coil-to-cap wire may be bad(check the resistance with an ohmmeter and compare it to the specifications). If a known good wire doesn't make any difference in the test results, the ignition coil, module or other internal components may be defective.

NEW WORDS

ruin	[ˈruːin]	v.(使)破产，堕落，毁灭；n. 毁灭，崩溃，废墟，遗迹
detach	[diˈtætʃ]	v. 分开，分离，分遣，派遣(军队)
corrosive	[kəˈrəusiv]	a. 腐蚀的，腐蚀性的
ingest	[inˈdʒest]	v. 摄取，咽下，吸收
tear	[tiə]	v. 撕破
fluffy	[ˈflʌfi]	a. 松软的，蓬松的，绒状的

strain	[strein]		n. 过度的疲劳，紧张，张力，应变；v. 扭伤，损伤，拉紧
malfunction	[mæl'fʌŋkʃən]		n. 失效，故障
ammeter	['æmitə]		n. 电流表
illuminate	[i'lu:mineit]		v. 照明
tension	['tenʃən]		n. 张力，拉力，电压
eyelet	['ailit]		n. 眼孔，孔眼，小孔，针眼
seize	[si:z]		v. 抓住，逮住，夺取
well-defined	['weldi'faind]		a. 定义明确的，明确的，轮廓分明的
foul	[faul]		n. 脏污的，污浊的；v. 弄脏，变污
swap	[swɔp]		v. 交换，交流

PHRASES AND EXPRESSIONS

sulfuric acid	= sulphuric acid 硫酸
safety glasses	安全眼镜
cable clamp	蓄电池接线夹
hold-down clamp	固定夹
engine compartment	发动机室
eye protection	面罩
slow-rate charging	低速充电
as a general rule	根据一般经验
trickle charger	微电流充电器
specific gravity	比重
instrument panel	仪表板
shift lever	变速杆
starter relay	起动继电器

NOTES TO THE TEXT

[1] If corrosion, which looks like white, fluffy deposit is evident, particularly around the terminals, the battery should be removed for cleaning.

句中 corrosion 原义为"腐蚀"，可以引申为"腐蚀产物"。which looks like white 是（主语 corrosion 的）非限制性定语从句，修饰 corrosion，fluffy deposits 是 corrosion 的同位语。本句可译为："特别是在极桩周围，如果明显存在白色绒状的腐蚀产物，那么就应该将蓄电池拆下，拿去清洗。"

[2] Loosen the cable clamp bolts with a wrench, being careful to remove the ground cable first, and slide them off the terminals.

本句中短语 being careful to remove... 是一个分词短语，作状语，说明 loosen（旋松）的方法。本句可译为："用一把扳手，先将电缆线夹螺钉旋松，然后再将它们从极桩上滑出。

应首先拆下搭铁电缆。"

[3] Slow-rate charging is the best way to restore a battery that's discharged to the point where it will not start the engine.

句中 that's discharged to the point where it will not start the engine 是一个修饰 battery 的定语从句，该从句中包含一个由 where 引导的、修饰 point 的定语从句。本句可译为："对于已经因过度放电而不能起动发动机的蓄电池来说，低速充电是恢复其正常状态的最好方法。"

[4] Maintaining the battery charge is particularly important in the winter when the battery must work harder to start the engine and electrical accessories that drain the battery are in greater use.

句中的 when... 到句末是两个并列的定语从句，用于修饰 winter。后一个定语从句的主语 electrical accessories 又带有定语从句。本句可译以为："在冬季，发动机起动比较困难，并且消耗蓄电池电能的附件用电也更多，因此，保持蓄电池处于充足电状态就显得特别重要。"

[5] At fast idle or normal driving speeds the needle should stay on the charge side of the gauge, with the charged state of the battery determining just how far over(the lower the battery state of charge, the farther the needle should swing toward the charge side).

句中的 with... 短语属于"with + 名词 + 分词（或介词）"的结构，此结构中的名词与分词（或介词）之间有逻辑上的主谓关系，可以作为原因、结果或者辅助说明单独译成一句。短语中的分词 determining 还带有宾语从句（省略 the needle is）。本句可译为："在急速和正常行车速度时，指针应该停留在电流表的充电侧。蓄电池的荷电状态决定了指针摆幅的大小（蓄电池荷电越少，指针向着充电侧的摆幅就越大）。"

[6] If, when the switch is actuated, the starter motor doesn't operate at all but the starter relay/solenoid operates(clicks), then the problem lies with either the battery, the starter relay/solenoid contacts or the starter motor connections.

句中 when the switch is actuated 是 if 从句的时间状语从句。本句可译为："如果操纵开关时，起动机根本不运转，但是起动继电器或起动电磁开关动作（发出"咔嗒"声），那么，问题或者在蓄电池、起动继电器/电磁开关，或者在起动机的导线连接。"

[7] DuraSpark Ⅱ 和 TFI-Ⅳ 是福特汽车上装用的两种电子点火系统。DuraSpark Ⅰ、DuraSparkⅡ 和 DuraSparkⅢ 三种型号均为采用霍尔效应开关和固定的辛烷值调节装置的分电器式电子点火系统，其中 DuraSparkⅢ 是一种点火控制模块单独安装的计算机控制点火系统。TFI 是"厚膜集成"(Thick Film Integrated)的缩写，第五代厚膜集成(TFI-Ⅳ)点火系统是将点火控制模块装入分电器内的计算机控制分电器式点火系统。另外，福特的新车型上采用了计算机控制无分电器式点火系统(EDIS-Electronic Distributorless Ignition System)。

EXERCISES

I. Answer the following questions:

1. What is the best way to restore a battery that's discharged to the point where it will not start the engine?

2. Which items are first checked, if a malfunction occurs in the charging circuit?
3. Which method will allow you to determine if the ignition system has spark?

Ⅱ. *Translate the following terms into English:*
1. 起动机电磁开关_____。
2. 点火模块_____。
3. 低速充电_____。
4. 蓄电池电压_____。
5. 正极桩_____。
6. 维护_____。

Related Terms

battery cell	单体电池
lead-acid battery	铅酸蓄电池
maintenanle free battery	免维护蓄电池
hydrometer	比重计
overrunning clutch	超越离合器
centrifugal advance mechanism	离心式点火提前角调节装置
vacuum advance mechanism	真空式点火提前角调节装置
timing light	正时灯
ignition timing	点火正时

Translation Techniques(6)——增词

英语和汉语在表达方式上有不同之处，在英译汉时，为了使译文意义明确而通顺，常常需要增添一些词。

1. 数词、冠词和可数名词的复数形式的增词译法

在翻译数词时，常常需要加上量词，见例1。不定冠词在翻译时有时也需要加上"个""只""辆""台"等量词，见例2。名词的复数形式的增词译法见例3。

例1：
The distributor has <u>two</u> tasks to perform.
分电器有<u>两个</u>任务需要完成。

例2：
When <u>a</u> tooth of the reluctor aligns with the tooth of the pick-up coil, <u>a</u> voltage signal is sent to the ignition module.
当磁阻轮的<u>一个</u>齿与传感线圈的齿对正时，就将<u>一个</u>电压信号送给点火模块。

例3：
In pulse injection systems, the rate of fuel flow through the <u>injectors</u> remains constant.

在脉冲式燃油喷射系统中,流过各个喷油器的燃油流量始终保持不变。

2. 利用增词译法使抽象名词的含义具体化

有一些由动词或形容词派生的抽象名词,可以增添适当的名词,使其表达的意义更具体明确,见例4。

例4:

If corrosion, which looks like white, fluffy deposits is evident, particularly around the terminals, the battery should be removed for cleaning.

特别是在极桩周围,如果明显存在白色绒状的腐蚀产物(corrosion 的含义是"腐蚀"),那么就应该将蓄电池拆下,拿去清洗。

3. 增加原文省略的部分

有时按照汉语的习惯,对英文中省略的部分,在翻译时必须翻译出来,才能使汉语意义完整,见例5。

例5:

When ignited, it will explode with great force.

混合气点燃后,就会产生爆炸性燃烧,形成巨大的推动力。(原文中 when ignited 为一个省略了 it is 的从句,it 指代前一句中的主语 mixture)。

4. 增加表达时态的词语

与汉语不同,英语常用到动词形式变化或者加助动词。因此在将英文翻译成汉语时,有时必须有意将英文的时态表达出来,才能使译文意义更加清楚。

例6:

The mechanical ignition system was used prior to 1975. It was mechanical and electrical and used no electronics.

1975年之前,使用机械式点火系统。那时候,机械点火系统只采用机械装置和电气装置,并不采用电子装置。

例7:

On some vehicles, this control module was mounted inside the distributor where the points used to be mounted.

在某些汽车上,这种控制模块曾经安装在向来装有触点的分电器的内部。

5. 增加带有强调、突出表达某一意义的词语

例8:

The best service information in the world is useless if the technician cannot readily retrieve the information.

如果技师不会快速地检索信息的话,那么,即使世界上最好的维修信息,也都是没有用的。

UNIT 7   EMISSION CONTROL SYSTEMS

TEXT A   Overview of Emission Control Systems

To minimize pollution from incompletely burned and evaporating gases and to maintain good driveability and fuel economy, a number of emission control systems are used on all vehicles. They include positive crankcase ventilation(PCV)system, evaporative emission control(EVAP) system, exhaust gas recirculation(EGR) system, air injection (AIR)system and three-way catalytic converter(TWC)system.

PCV System

The purpose of the positive crankcase ventilation(PCV)system is to take the vapors produced in the crankcase and piston blow-by, and redirect them into the air/fuel intake system to be burned during combustion. These vapors dilute the air/fuel mixture, they have to be carefully controlled and metered so as not to affect the performance of the engine. This is the job of the positive crankcase ventilation(PCV)valve. At idle, when the air/fuel mixture is very critical, just a little of the vapors are allowed in to the intake system. At high speed when the mixture is less critical and the pressures in the engine are greater, more of the vapors are allowed in to the intake system.[1] When the valve or the system is clogged, vapors will back up into the air filter housing or at worst, the excess pressure will push past seals and create engine oil leaks.[2] If the wrong valve is used or the system has air leaks, the engine will idle rough, or at worst engine oil will be sucked out of the engine.

EGR System

Exhaust gas recirculation(EGR) systems reduce the amount of oxides of nitrogen produced during the combustion process. The EGR system dilutes the air/fuel mixture with controlled amounts of exhaust gas. Since exhaust gas does not burn, this reduces the peak combustion temperatures. At lower combustion temperatures, very little of the nitrogen in the air will combine with oxygen to form NO_x. Most of the nitrogen is simply carried out with the exhaust gases. For driveability, it is desirable to have the EGR valve opening(and the amount of gas flow)proportional to the throttle opening. Driveability is also improved by shutting off the EGR when the engine is started up cold, at idle, and at full throttle. Since the NO_x control requirements vary on different engines, there are several different systems with various controls to provide these functions.

EGR Valves

Most of these systems use a vacuum-operated EGR valve to regulate the exhaust gas flow into the intake manifold(Fig. 7-1 and Fig. 7-2). Exhaust crossover passages under the intake manifold channel the exhaust gas to the valve. (Some in-line engines route the exhaust gas to the valve through an external tube.) Typical mounting of the EGR valve is either on a plate under the carburetor or directly on the manifold.

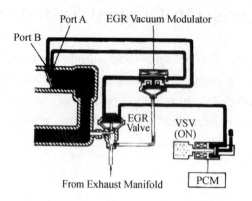
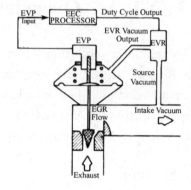

Fig. 7-1 A vacuum-operated EGR system   Fig. 7-2 An electronic EGR system

The EGR valve is a vacuum-operated, flow control valve. Opening the EGR valve by control vacuum at the diaphragm, allows exhaust gases to flow through the valve and into the intake manifold. Here, the exhaust gas mixes with the air/fuel mixture. The effect is to dilute or lean out the mixture, so that it still burns completely but with a reduction in combustion chamber temperatures.

Many different controls have been used to insure that the system works when it should. Ideally the EGR system should operate when the engine reaches operating temperature and/or when the engine is operating under conditions other than idle or wide-open throttle.

There are also various designs of EGR valves. The positive back pressure EGR valve has a bleed port and valve positioned in the center of the diaphragm. A light spring holds this bleed valve open, and an exhaust passage is connected from the lower end of the tapered valve through the stem to the bleed valve. When the engine is running, exhaust pressure is applied to the bleed valve. At low engine speeds, exhaust pressure is not high enough to close the bleed valve. If control vacuum is supplied to the diaphragm chamber, the vacuum is bled off through the bleed port, and the valve remains closed.

As engine and vehicle speed increase, the exhaust pressure also increases. At a preset throttle opening, the exhaust pressure closes the EGR valve bleed port. When control vacuum is supplied to the diaphragm, the diaphragm and valve are lifted upward, and the valve is open. If vacuum from an external source is supplied to a positive back pressure EGR valve with the engine not running, the valve will not open, because the vacuum is bled off through the bleed port.

In a negative back pressure EGR valve, a normally closed bleed port is positioned in the center of the diaphragm. An exhaust passage is connected from the lower end of the tapered valve through the stem to the bleed valve. When the engine is running at lower speeds, there is a high-pressure pulse in the exhaust system. However, between these high-pressure pulses there are low-pressure pulses. As the engine speed increases, more cylinder firings occur in a given time, and the high-pressure pulses become closer together in the exhaust system.

At lower engine and vehicle speeds, the negative pulses in the exhaust system hold the bleed valve open. When the engine and vehicle speed increase to a preset value, the negative exhaust pressure pulses decrease, and the bleed valve closes. Under this condition, the EGR valve is opened. When vacuum from an external source is supplied to a negative back pressure EGR valve with the engine not running, the bleed port is closed, and the vacuum should open the valve.

A digital EGR valve contains up to three electric solenoids that are operated directly by the PCM. Each solenoid contains a movable plunger with a tapered tip that seats in an orifice. When any solenoid is energized, the plunger is lifted and exhaust gas is allowed to recirculate through the orifice into the intake manifold. The solenoids and orifices are different sizes. The PCM can operate one, two, or three solenoids to supply the amount of exhaust recirculation required to provide optimum control of NO_x emissions.

The linear EGR valve contains a single electric solenoid that is operated by the PCM. A tapered pintle is positioned on the end of the solenoid plunger (Fig. 7-2). When the solenoid is energized, the plunger and tapered valve are lifted, and exhaust gas is allowed to recirculate into the intake manifold. The EGR valve contains an EGR valve position or lift sensor, which is a linear potentiometer. The signal from this sensor varies from approximately 1V with the EGR valve closed to 4.5V with the valve wide open.

The PCM pulses the EGR solenoid winding on and off with a pulse width modulation principle to provide accurate control of the plunger and EGR flow. The EGR valve position(EVP) sensor acts as a feedback signal to the PCM to inform the PCM if the commanded valve position was achieved.

Internal Exhaust Gas Recirculation (EGR)

EGR reduces the levels of oxides of nitrogen(nitric oxide NO, and small quantities of nitrogen dioxide NO_2, collectively referred to as NO_x)in engine exhaust gases at part load. The aim of an internal EGR system is to control the recirculation of exhaust gas without the use of external pipework on the engine.

In a conventional plenum throttled engine, at part throttle there is a pressure differential between the inlet and exhaust ports. Towards the end of the exhaust stroke on a four-stroke engine, the inlet valve opens and a period follows when inlet and exhaust valves are open simultaneously. During this valve overlap period, the inlet port depression causes residual exhaust gas in the combustion chamber to flow back into the inlet port. The resultant pressure drop in the combustion chamber causes gases in the exhaust port to flow back into the combustion chamber. These residual exhaust gases dilute the incoming air/fuel charge.

This dilution of the charge reduces the peak combustion temperatures and pressures, which reduces the amount of NO_x in the exhaust gases. Excess dilution can lead to incomplete or unstable combustion which results in an increase in hydrocarbon (HC) levels. The optimum amount of dilution varies with engine speed and load. Conventionally, the dilution requirements for optimized running conditions are achieved by using an external EGR system which recirculates metered quantities of exhaust gas by external pipes and a control valve.

Evaporative Control System

Gasoline evaporates quite easily. In the past these evaporative emissions were vented into the atmosphere. 20% of all HC emissions from the automobile are from the gas tank. In 1970 legislation was passed, prohibiting venting of gas tank fumes into the atmosphere. An evaporative control system was developed to eliminate this source of pollution. The function of the fuel evaporative control system is to trap and store evaporative emissions from the gas tank and carburetor. A charcoal canister is used to trap the fuel vapors. The fuel vapors adhere to the charcoal, until the engine is started, and engine vacuum can be used to draw the vapors into the engine, so that they can be burned along with the fuel/air mixture. This system requires the use of a sealed gas tank filler cap. This cap is so important to the operation of the system that a test of the cap is now being integrated into many state emission inspection programs. Pre-1970 cars released fuel vapors into the atmosphere through the use of a vented gas cap. Today with the use of sealed caps, redesigned gas tanks are used. The tank has to have the space for the vapors to collect so that they can then be vented to the charcoal canister. A purge valve is used to control the vapor flow into the engine. The purge valve is operated by engine vacuum. One common problem with this system is that the purge valve goes bad and engine vacuum draws fuel directly into the intake system.[3] This enriches the fuel mixture and will foul the spark plugs. Most charcoal canisters have a filter that should be replaced periodically. This system should be checked when fuel mileage drops.

In some engines, the powertrain control module(PCM)allows intake manifold vacuum to draw vapors into the combustion chambers during certain operating conditions. All of these engines use a duty cycle purge system. The PCM controls the vapor flow by operating the duty cycle EVAP purge solenoid(Fig. 7-3).

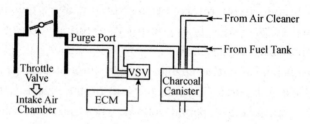

Fig. 7-3　An ECM-controlled EVAP system

Air Injection

Since no internal combustion engine is 100% efficient, there will always be some unburned fuel in the exhaust. This increases hydrocarbon emissions. To eliminate this source of emissions an air injection system was created. Combustion requires fuel, oxygen and heat. Without any one of the three, combustion cannot occur. Inside the exhaust manifold there is sufficient heat to support combustion, if we introduce some oxygen that any unburned fuel will ignite. This combustion will not produce any power, but it will reduce excessive hydrocarbon emissions. Unlike in the combustion chamber, this combustion is uncontrolled, so if the fuel content of the exhaust is excessive, explosions, which sound like popping, will occur. There are times when under normal conditions, such as deceleration, when the fuel content is excessive.[4] Under these conditions we would want to shut off the air injection system. This is accomplished through the use of a diverter valve, which instead of shutting the air pump off, diverts the air away from the exhaust manifold. Since all of this is done after the combustion process is complete, this is one emission control that has no effect on engine performance.

Later versions of the air injection system are under ECM control(Fig. 7-4). When the

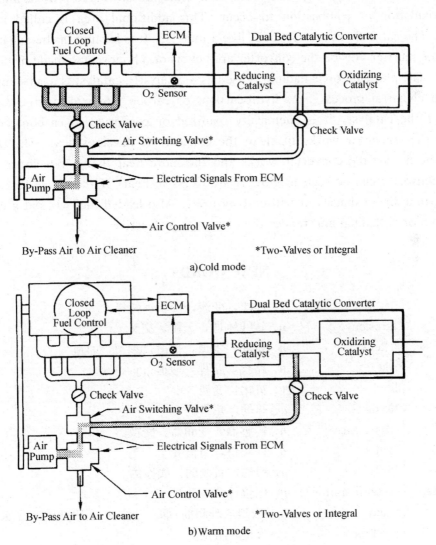

Fig. 7-4 Air management system operation

engine is cold, the ECM energizes a control solenoid. This allows air to flow to an air switching valve. The air switching valve is energized to direct air to the exhaust ports.

On a warm engine, or in "closed loop" mode, the ECM de-energizes the air switching valve, directing air between the beds of the catalytic converter. This provides extra oxygen for the oxidizing catalyst to decrease HC and CO levels, while keeping oxygen levels low in the first bed of the converter. This enables the reducing catalyst to effectively decrease the levels of oxides of nitrogen(NO_x).

Catalytic Converter

Automotive emissions are controlled in three ways. One is to promote more complete combustion so that there are fewer by-products. The second is to reintroduce excessive hydrocarbons back into the engine for combustion and the third is to provide an additional area for oxidation or combustion to occur. This additional area is called a catalytic converter. The catalytic converter looks like a muffler. It is located in the exhaust system ahead of the muffler. Inside the converter are pellets or a honeycomb made of platinum or palladium. The platinum or palladium is used as a catalyst(a catalyst is a substance used to speed up a chemical process). As hydrocarbons or carbon monoxide in the exhaust are passed over the catalyst, it is chemically oxidized or converted to carbon dioxide and water. As the converter works to clean the exhaust, it develops heat. The dirtier the exhaust, the harder the converter works and the more heat that is developed. In some cases the converter can be seen to glow from excessive heat. If the converter works this hard to clean a dirty exhaust, it will destroy itself. Also leaded fuel will put a coating on the platinum or palladium and render the converter ineffective.

NEW WORDS

dilute	[daiˈljuːt]	v.	冲淡，变淡，变弱，稀释
crossover	[ˈkrɔsˌəuvə]	n.	转线轨道，天桥，交叉
channel	[ˈtʃænl]	n.	海峡，水道，信道，频道，通道
route	[ruːt]	n.	路线，路程，通道；v. 发送
lean(out)	[liːn]	v.	贫化，变瘦
thermal	[ˈθəːməl]	a.	热的，热量的
transducer	[trænzˈdjuːsə]	n.	传感器，变频器，变换器
orifice	[ˈɔrifis]	n.	孔，口，节流孔
linear	[ˈliniə]	a.	线的，直线的，线性的
potentiometer	[pəˌtenʃiˈɔmitə]	n.	电位计，电势计
fume	[fjuːm]	n.	(浓烈或难闻的)烟，气体；v. 用烟熏，冒烟，发怒
prohibit	[prəˈhibit]	v.	禁止，阻止
adhere	[ədˈhiə]	v.	黏附，胶着，坚持

pop	[pɔp]	n. 砰的一声，爆裂声，流行乐曲，流行艺术
		a. 流行的，热门的，通俗的
		v. 发出爆裂声，爆开，射击，突然出现
diverter	[dai'və:tə]	n. 分流器，换向器，分流阀
divert	[di'və:t]	v. 转移，转向
catalytic	[ˌkætə'litik]	a. 催化的
muffler	['mʌflə]	n. 消声器
pellet	['pelit]	n. 小球
honeycomb	['hʌnikəum]	n. 蜂房，蜂巢
platinum	['plætinəm]	n. 白金，铂
palladium	[pə'leidiəm]	n. 钯
catalyst	['kætəlist]	n. 催化剂
render	['rendə]	v. 致使，表演，实施

PHRASES AND EXPRESSIONS

at worst	在最坏的情况下
throttle opening	节气门开度
EGR valve	废气再循环阀
wide-open throttle	节气门全开（简写为 WOT）
back pressure	背压
bleed port	通气孔
tapered tip	锥形端
EGR valve position (EVP) sensor	EGR 阀位置（EVP）传感器
pulse width modulation	脉宽调制
charcoal canister	活性炭
along with	与……一道（同时），以及，除……之外（还）
purge valve	清污阀
diverter valve	分流阀
air pump	空气泵
catalytic converter	催化转化器
air injection	空气喷射

NOTES TO THE TEXT

[1] At high speed when the mixture is less critical and the pressures in the engine are greater, more of the vapors are allowed in to the intake system.

句中 when... 是修饰 high speed 的后置定语从句。本句可译为："在高速时，混合气的浓度不太重要，而发动机内的压力也已经提高，因此，可以让更多的蒸气进入进气系统。"

［2］When the valve or the system is clogged, vapors will back up into the air filter housing or at worst, the excess pressure will push past seals and create engine oil leaks.

句中的 valve 是指"PCV 阀", push past seals 的意思为"穿过密封件"。本句可以译为："当 PCV 阀或系统堵塞时，蒸气将倒流回空气滤清器内，甚至更糟的是，过高的压力会破坏密封件，导致机油泄漏。"

［3］One common problem with this system is that the purge valve goes bad and engine vacuum draws fuel directly into the intake system.

句中 that...是一个表语从句。goes bad 的意思为"损坏"。本句可译为："该系统最常见的故障是清污阀损坏和发动机的真空作用使燃油被直接吸入进气系统。"

［4］There are times when under normal conditions, such as deceleration, when the fuel content is excessive.

句中 there are times when...的意思是"有时常会……"。句中的后一个 when……是修饰 normal conditions 的定语从句。本句可以译为："有时，在正常情况下（如减速），废气中的燃油含量也会过高。"

EXERCISES

I. Answer the following questions:

1. What is the purpose of the positive crankcase ventilation(PCV)system?
2. What happens if the wrong PCV valve is used or the system has air leaks?
3. Which system was developed to eliminate HC emissions from gas tank?
4. What are the two types of EGR valves operated by PCM?

II. Translate the following paragraphs into Chinese:

All vehicles use a sealed, maintenance free evaporative canister. Fuel tank pressure vents into the canister. The canister temporarily holds the fuel vapors until the intake manifold vacuum draws them into the combustion chamber. The PCM operates the canister through the EVAP purge solenoid. The PCM then purges the canister at the predetermined intervals and engine conditions.

The PCM controls vapor flow by operating the duty cycle EVAP purge solenoid. The duty cycle EVAP purge solenoid regulates the rate of vapor flow from the EVAP canister to the throttle body.

The engine enters closed loop operation after it reaches a specified temperature and the time delay ends. During closed loop operation, the engine computer energizes and de-energizes the solenoid approximately 5-10 times per second, depending upon operating conditions. The engine computer varies the vapor flow rate by changing solenoid pulse width. Pulse width is the amount of time the solenoid energizes. The engine computer adjusts solenoid pulse width based on engine air flow.

TEXT B Three-Way Catalytic Converter and NO_x Catalyst

Three-Way Catalyst

Modern catalytic converters utilize a three-way catalyst ceramic block substrate containing platinum, palladium, and rhodium as the catalyst material. The substrate is a honeycomb of hundreds of passages. These passages in the substrate create a very large surface area. When the catalyst is hot, generally 475—575°F (246—301°C), these elements speed up the chemical reaction that takes place inside the catalytic converter. The temperature at which the catalyst begins to function is referred to as the light-off point of the catalyst; this is the point at which catalyst efficiency exceeds 50 percent. Once the catalyst reaches the light-off point, maximum chemical conversion efficiency in the catalyst can take place. The closer the catalytic converter is located to the exhaust manifold outlet, the faster the light-off point will be achieved.

The three-way catalyst causes a chemical reaction that converts: hydrocarbon (HC) and oxygen(O_2) into carbon dioxide(CO_2) and water vapor(H_2O); carbon monoxide(CO) and oxygen (O_2) into carbon dioxide(CO_2); and oxides of nitrogen (NO_x) and hydrogen (H_2) into nitrogen (N_2) and water vapor. The percentage of these gases that are converted into environmentally friendly gases is referred to as the conversion efficiency of the catalyst. Three way catalysts are most efficient when the air/fuel ratio is maintained at 14.7 : 1, the stoichiometric point.

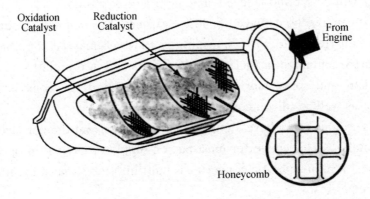

Fig. 7-5 The three-way catalytic converter that contains two separate ceramic substrate blocks

The three-way catalytic converter contains two separate ceramic substrate blocks(Fig. 7-5). The first substrate contains the reducing catalyst, which contains platinum and rhodium to reduce NO_x emissions. When NO_x (NO and NO_2) emissions travel through the first substrate, the nitrogen atom is separated from the oxygen atom freeing both: the nitrogen(N) atom bonds with another nitrogen(N) atom bonded to the substrate to form(N_2).

The oxidation catalyst is the second substrate containing platinum and palladium. The oxidation catalyst burns (oxidizes) hydrocarbon (HC) and carbon monoxide (CO), thereby reducing them into carbon dioxide (CO_2) and water vapor (H_2O).

The catalyst also contains ceria, which is able to store oxygen during lean running conditions as well as when oxygen is created in the reduction catalyst process. It will then release oxygen during rich running conditions, thereby maintaining a chemical balance in the converter. This process allows both reduction and oxidation to occur simultaneously.

Three-way catalysts are most efficient when the air-fuel ratio is maintained at 14.7 : 1, the stoichiometric point. If the air/fuel ratio is leaner than the stoichiometric ratio, the conversion efficiency of NO_x decreases. During periods when the air-fuel mixture ratio is lean or when oxygen content is high and HC levels are low, the catalyst will convert HC, and the left over oxygen will be stored in the catalyst. If the air-fuel ratio is richer than the stoichiometric ratio, the conversion efficiency of HC and CO decreases during periods when the air fuel mixture ratio is rich or when oxygen content is low and HC levels are high, the catalyst will release stored oxygen in order to reduce HC emissions.

A defective catalytic converter will result in excessive emissions of HC, CO and NO_x pollutants. If the OBD-II system detects that emission levels will exceed one and one half times the FTP level, the MIL will be turned on.[1] An engine that is running with an excessively rich or lean air-fuel mixture or one that has a Type A engine misfire will cause severe catalyst overheating (above 2,600 ℉ [1,426℃]), that could damage, even melt, the catalytic converter's monolithic element.[2] This is why one of the OBD-II requirements is to turn on and flash the MIL if a potential catalyst-damaging event has occurred. In addition, DTCs will be set and freeze-frame data will be stored.

The catalyst can also be damaged or lose efficiency by chemical poisoning. Chemiecal poisoning can result from lead (Pb); phosphorus (P) which may be contained in fuel or oil additives; sulfur (S) contained in fuel; zinc (Zn) contained in oil additives; and silicon (Si) from RTV sealant and spray lubricants that have entered the combustion chamber or exhaust system, as well as silicon-contaminated fuel.

Some catalytic converters have an air hose connected from the belt driven air pump to the oxidation catalyst. This converter must have a supply of oxygen to operate efficiently. On some engines, a mini-catalytic converter is built into the exhaust manifold or bolted to the manifold flange.

During oxidation catalyst operation, small amounts of sulfur in the gasoline combine with oxygen in the air to form oxides of sulfur (SO_x). Sulphur dioxide (SO_2) gas is also formed during oxidation converter operation. SO_2 gas is the same gas produced by rotten eggs. Although this gas has an unpleasant smell, it is not considered a major pollutant at present.

The SO_x combines with the water vapor in the converter to form small amounts of sulfuric acid (H_2SO_4). There is some concern among environmental agencies about these small amounts of H_2SO_4 from many vehicles contributing to acid rain.

Catalyst Efficiency Monitor

The OBD-II systems perform a catalyst efficiency monitor to verify the catalysts ability and efficiency to convert HC into H_2O and CO_2. The critical sensors that are part of the system are the pre-catalyst oxygen sensor, which is located upstream of the catalyst, and a post-catalyst oxygen sensor, which is located downstream of the catalyst.[3] If the catalyst is functioning efficiently, the post-catalyst oxygen sensor will have a low switching frequency indicating that the catalyst is either storing oxygen or converting CO and HC emissions. If the catalyst efficiently is low, the post-catalyst oxygen sensor will have a switching frequency that resembles the switching frequency of the pre-catalyst oxygen sensor indicating that the catalyst is unable to store oxygen.[4]

NO_x Storage and Reduction Catalyst for GDI Spark-ignition Engines

In the case of direct-injection spark-ignition engines which are operated in specific operating ranges with charge stratification and $\lambda > 1$, it is not possible for a three-way catalyst to reduce the nitrogen oxides in these load states because of the excess air. In addition to the upstream three-way catalyst, a special NO_x catalyst is deployed as an underfloor catalyst to treat the nitrogen oxides(Fig. 7-6).

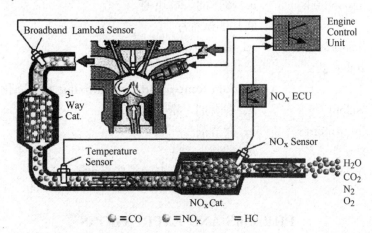

Fig. 7-6 Emission-control system for direct-injection spark-ignition engine at $\lambda > 1$

Design. An intermediate layer(wash-coat) is incorporated on a ceramic substrate. This layer is coated with barium oxide(BaO) or potassium oxide(KO) as the storage material.

Operating principle(Fig. 7-7). NO_x storage: During lean mode the storage materials are able to bind(adsorb) the nitrogen oxides. The NO_x sensor detects when the storage capacity is exhausted. NO_x reduction: Thanks to periodic enrichment(1-5 seconds) the nitrogen oxides are released again and reduced by the noble metal rhodium to nitrogen with the aid of the unburnt exhaust-gas constituents HC and CO.

Operating condition for NO_x absorber. 80%-90% of the nitrogen oxides is reduced at working temperatures between 250°C and 500°C. At temperatures in excess of 500 °C the catalyst is subject

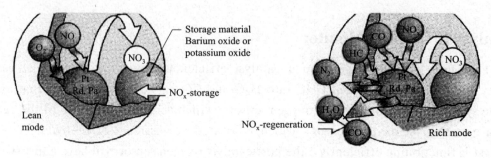

Fig. 7-7　NO$_x$-storage and regeneration

to high-temperature ageing. The exhaust gases must therefore be cooled if necessary, for example via bypass lines. The sulphur content in the fuel should be < 0.050 mg(< 0.050 ppm). Otherwise the storage capacity is significantly reduced("sulphur poisoning").

NEW WORDS

substrate	['sʌbstreit]	n.	基层，底层，载体
rhodium	['rəudjəm]	n.	铑
light-off	['laitɔv]	n.	起燃
ceria	['siəriə]	n.	二氧化铈
monolithic	[ˌmɔnə'liθik]	a.	整体的，单块的
FTP			联邦测试程序
phosphorus	['fɔsfərəs]	n.	磷
zinc	[ziŋk]	n.	锌
RTV			= room temperature vulcanizing 室温固化
sealant	['si:lənt]	n.	密封剂，密封
lubricant	['lu:brikənt]	n.	润滑剂
hose	[həuz]	n.	软管
rotten	['rɔtn]	a.	腐烂的，恶臭的，堕落的

PHRASES AND EXPRESSIONS

three-way catalyst	三元催化转化器
light-off point	起燃点，起燃温度
conversion efficiency	转化效率
reducing catalyst	还原催化剂
oxidation catalyst	氧化催化剂
FTP level	FTP 标准值
mini-catalytic converter	小催化转化器，副催化转化器
external EGR	机外 EGR
internal EGR	机内 EGR

NOTES TO THE TEXT

[1] If the OBD-II system detects that emission levels will exceed one and one half times the FTP level, the MIL will be turn on.

FTP 是 Federal Test Procedure(联邦测试程序)的缩写。Federal Test Procedure 是一种在测功机上通过加载的方法测量过渡工况排放量的测试程序。新车型投放市场前,必须通过该项测试。FTP level 是指"联邦测试程序规定的排放限值"。本句可以译为:"如果第二代车载诊断系统(OBD-II)检测到排放超过美国联邦排放限值的1.5倍,那么故障指示灯(MIL)就会点亮。"

[2] An engine that is running with an excessively rich or lean air-fuel mixture or one that has a Type A engine misfire will cause severe catalyst overheating(above 2,600°F[1,426°C]), that could damage, even melt, the catalytic converter's monolithic element.

句中采用了三个 that,它们均引导了一个定语从句,并在从句中作主语。三个 that...从句的先行词分别是 engine、one(指代 engine)和 overheating。element 是指"要素""基本部分",在这里指催化转化器的"催化剂载体"。本句可以译为:"发动机运转时如果混合气过浓或过稀或者存在 A 型缺火,将导致催化剂严重过热,即温度高于 2600°F(1426°C),从而有可能导致催化转化器的整体式催化剂载体的损坏甚至熔化。"

[3] The critical sensors that are part of the system are the pre-catalyst oxygen sensor, which is located upstream of the catalyst, and a post-catalyst oxygen sensor, which is located downstream of the catalyst.

句中 that 和两个 which 各引导一个定语从句。本句可以译为:"构成该系统的重要传感器有位于催化转化器上游的前氧传感器和位于催化转化器下游的后氧传感器。"

[4] If the catalyst efficiency is low, the post-catalyst oxygen sensor will have a switching frequency that resembles the switching frequency of the pre-catalyst oxygen sensor indicating that the catalyst is unable to store oxygen.

句中 switching frequency 是指传感器输出信号电压高、低变化的转换频率。that resembles...是一个修饰(此 that 前面的)frequency 的定语从句,that the catalyst is...是 indicating 的宾语从句。indicating that the catalyst is unable to store oxygen 是分词短语,是 that resembles...定语从句中的状语。本句可以译为:"如果催化剂效率低,那么,后氧传感器的信号变化频率就会与前氧传感器的信号变化频率相似,也就是说,催化剂失去存储氧的能力。"

EXERCISES

I. Answer the following questions:

1. What is referred to as the conversion efficiency of the catalyst?
2. What are the catalyst materials in the TWC?
3. When are three-way catalysts most efficient?
4. What is the purpose of a catalyst efficiency monitor?
5. Which elements can result in chemical poisoning of catalysts?

II. Put the following paragraphs into Chinese:

1. Operation of a Three-Way Converter

Exhaust gases pass first into the reducing catalyst. Levels of oxides of nitrogen are reduced. There is also some oxidizing of hydrocarbons and carbon monoxide. The air injection system forces air into the passage between the catalyst beds. This adds oxygen to the exhaust gases, allowing a high oxidization heat level.

As the exhaust gases encounter the second oxidizing catalyst, tremendous heat is created and the resultant oxidizing process changes the carbon monoxide and hydrocarbons into water vapor and carbon dioxide.

2. Multiple Converters

Some vehicles have two catalytic converters, in these systems, one converter, which is often quite small, is located very close to the exhaust manifold. The other converter is larger and is located downstream in the exhaust system between the manifold and muffler. Vehicles with V-type engines may have two identical converters(one near each exhaust manifold)instead of a single converter located after the pipes join.

TEXT C Diagnosis of Computerized Engine Control Systems

Interpret scan tool data to determine system condition

A scan tool is a test computer that communicates with the PCM and other onboard computers of a vehicle. The scan tool reads and displays diagnostic information provided by the PCM such as DTCs and system operating data, or parameters.

Data transmitted from the PCM to the scan tool include both digital and analog values. Digital parameters are often called switch parameters, or signals, and are either on or off, high or low, yes or no. An analog parameter provides a signal value with a specific minimum-to-maximum range. These kinds of data include analog voltage readings, speed signals, temperature readings, and frequency ranges.

Every item of data transmitted from the PCM to a scan tool has specific value or signal range described in the vehicle specifications. You must have access to, or knowledge of, these specifications and compare them to the scan tool readings to identify a system fault.

Scan tool readings that identify an open or a short circuit are among the easiest to recognize. If a resistive sensor displays a scan tool reading at or near the 5.0-volt reference voltage on which most such sensors operate, the sensor circuit to the PCM is open.[1] If the scan tool voltage for such a sensor is at or near 0 volt, the circuit is probably grounded.

Scan tool readings of PCM input and output signals reflect values as processed by the PCM. In some systems, a sensor failure will cause the PCM to ignore the signal from the failed sensor and operate on backup values stored in its own memory. In this case, the

PCM may transmit the backup values to the scan tool in place of the failed sensor signal. If any particular scan tool data reading does not make sense in relation to particular problem or symptom, you should test the system component directly with a voltmeter, ohmmeter, oscilloscope, frequency counter, or other test equipment.

OBD-II diagnostic standards require a uniform library of diagnostic trouble codes (DTC)to be used by all carmakers. Additionally, all OBD-II systems must transmit a basic list of 16 data items to a scan tool. Carmakers are free, however, to "enhance" the onboard diagnostic capabilities of their control systems. Many systems provide much more than the minimum OBD-II diagnostic data requirements.

The OBD-II system monitors virtually all emission control systems and components that can affect tailpipe or evaporative emissions. In most cases, malfunctions must be detected before emissions exceed 1.5 times the emission standards. If a system or component exceeds emission thresholds or fails to operate within a manufacturer's specifications, a DTC will be stored and the malfunction indicator light(MIL)will be illuminated within two driving cycles.

The OBD-II system monitors for malfunctions either continuously, regardless of driving mode, or non-continuously, once per drive cycle during specific drive modes.[2] A DTC is stored in the PCM when a malfunction is initially detected. In most cases the MIL is illuminated after two consecutive drive cycles with the malfunction present. Once the MIL is illuminated, three consecutive drive cycles without a malfunction detected are required to extinguish the MIL. The DTC is erased after 40 engine warm-up cycles once the MIL is extinguished.

In addition to specifying and standardizing much of the diagnostics and MIL operation, OBD-II requires the use of standard communication links and messages, standardized DTCs and terminology. Examples of standard diagnostic information are freeze frame data and Inspection Maintenance(IM)Readiness Indicators.

Freeze frame data is stored in the PCM at the point the malfunction is initially detected. Freeze frame data consists of parameters such as engine rpm and load, state of fuel control, spark, and warm-up status. Freeze frame data is stored at the time the first malfunction is detected, however, previously stored conditions will be replaced if a fuel or misfire fault is detected. This data is accessible with the scan tool to assist in repairing the vehicle.

OBD-II Inspection Maintenance (IM) Readiness indicators show whether all of the OBD-II monitors has been completed.

Differentiate between computerized powertrain controls problems and mechanical problems

Any given symptom or driver complaint can be caused by a problem in more than one system. A problem can appear to be based in one system when, in fact, it originates in another. For example, a longer than normal fuel injector pulse width and high long-term fuel trim correction factors are fuel system symptoms, but their causes can lie in several other engine subsystems.[3] A mechanical problem, such as an intake vacuum leak, could be the root cause. On the other hand, an incorrect input signal from a barometric pressure sensor or manifold pressure sensor could cause these unusual fuel control symptoms.

Differentiating between mechanical problems and computer system problems is part of identifying and repairing the root cause of any symptom. As a diagnostic technician, you must look for abnormal test results and isolate the cause of a problem to one system rather than another.

Information is often the key to diagnosing or repairing late-model computer-controlled systems. Diagnostic information will be available both in printed form and in computerized information retrieval systems in the shop or on the Internet. Additionally, many equipment companies provide databases of test procedures and specifications that are built into their test equipment and can be accessed by the technician while performing diagnostics with the equipment.[4] This is an emerging and very useful technology that gives technician information when it is needed. Technical service bulletins (TSBs) are usually high priority information for late-model systems and are included in all of the sources already mentioned. The technician must be aware of what service information is available and how to get the information needed. The best service information in the world is useless if the technician cannot readily retrieve the information.

Intermittent engine control problems will require diagnostic procedures tailored to the conditions present when the problem occurs. This service information needs to be gathered by careful questioning of the vehicle owner so that the technician can perform an effective diagnosis. Heating or cooling affected components could find temperature related faults. Performing wiggle tests and monitoring circuit values can find harness and connection problems. Problems such as these can go undetected if the technician is not provided with accurate service information.

Diagnose no-starting, hard starting, engine misfire, poor driveability, incorrect idle speed, poor idle, hesitation, surging, spark knock, power loss, poor mileage, and emissions problems caused by failures of computerized powertrain controls

The proper operation of computerized powertrain controls is essential for the modern power plant to function correctly. A computer that loses power or ground will not function at all and will cause a no-start condition on any fuel-injected engine. All of the conditions listed above have the potential to be traced back to the computer and its input and output components.

While a failure in the computer-control system is a possible source of these conditions, it should not be considered the problem until basic mechanical and electrical tests have been performed. A manifold absolute pressure sensor (MAP) will not generate a correct signal if the engine is incapable of producing normal manifold vacuum. An out of calibration coolant sensor input can cause hard starting when the engine is both cold and hot, as well as altering fuel delivery enough to cause an emission test failure and poor mileage.[5] A MAP sensor that is out of calibration can cause many different driveability problems on a computer-controlled engine because it is a primary sensor input. Fuel delivery, spark timing, or torque converter clutch lock-up can all be affected by the MAP input. Driveability concerns, such as hard starting, stalling, surging, spark knock, poor mileage, and excessive emissions, can all be traced to an incorrect MAP sensor signal. A problem with the throttle position sensor input may not only cause engine hesitation but may also affect transmission shift points or feel on electronically controlled transmissions.

A failed output actuator, such as an EGR solenoid, may prevent the computer from properly controlling EGR gas flow. The computer may energize the EGR solenoid to allow vacuum to reach the EGR valve while other systems energize the solenoid to block vacuum to the valve. In the first case, if the EGR valve does not receive vacuum, the engine may produce spark knock. In the second case, if the computer cannot limit EGR flow, hesitation, surging, and power loss may be the result. In both cases, understanding system operation is the key to correct diagnosis. A failure inside the computer, such as an open driver transistor for a fuel injector or ignition coil, can cause engine misfire and power loss. Computers may also exhibit intermittent driveability concerns from problems such as solder joint connections that are temperature or vibration sensitive. These types of failures can be very challenging to diagnose and require employing advanced diagnostic procedures, such as circuit monitoring with such tools as labscopes and graphing multimeters.

NEW WORDS

interpret	[in'tə:prit]	v. 判读，翻译，解释，说明
DTC		= diagnostic trouble code 故障码
parameter	[pə'ræmitə]	n. 参数，参量
oscilloscope	[ɔ'siləskəup]	n. 示波器
threshold	['θreʃhəuld]	n. 门限值，阈值，极限
consecutive	[kən'sekjutiv]	a. 连续的
extinguish	[iks'tiŋgwiʃ]	v. 熄灭，灭火
terminology	[ˌtə:mi'nɔlədʒi]	n. 术语，术语学
accessible	[ək'sesəbl]	a. 易接近的，可到达的，易受影响的，可理解的
differentiate	[ˌdifə'renʃieit]	v. 区分，区别
originate	[ə'ridʒineit]	v. 引起，发明，发起，创办，起源（于）
retrieval	[ri'tri:vəl]	n. 检索，取回，恢复，拯救
retrieve	[ri'tri:v]	v. 重新得到，找回，检索
gather	['gæðə]	v.& n. 集合，聚集
wiggle	['wigl]	v.& n.（使）踌躇，摆动
labscope	[læb'skəup]	n. 实验室级示波器

PHRASES AND EXPRESSIONS

access to	进入，访问
knowledge of	了解，知道

resistive sensor	电阻型传感器
reference voltage	参考电压
backup value	备用值
make sense	有意义,有道理,讲得通
data item	数据项
malfunction indicator light(MIL)	故障指示灯
root cause	根本原因,起因
barometric pressure sensor	大气压力传感器
retrieval system	检索系统
be traced back to	追溯到,回溯到
manifold absolute pressure sensor(MAP)	进气歧管绝对压力传感器
graphing multimeter	示波万用表

NOTES TO THE TEXT

[1] If a resistive sensor displays a scan tool reading at or near the 5.0-volt reference voltage on which most such sensors operate, the sensor circuit to the PCM is open.

本句中,on which...引导一个修饰 voltage 的定语从句。本句可译为:"如果扫描诊断仪显示一个电阻型传感器的参考电压为 5.0V 或 5.0V 左右(大多数这样的传感器都用这样的电压来工作),那么,从传感器到 PCM 的电路有断路故障。"

[2] The OBD-Ⅱ system monitors for malfunctions either continuously, regardless of driving mode, or non-continuously, once per drive cycle during specific drive modes.

分析本句时,一是应注意连词 either...or,及其所连接的两个修饰谓语 monitors 的副词 continuously 和 non-continuously,二是应注意 regardless of driving mode 和 once per drive cycle during specific drive modes 两个作状语的短语所起的作用。本句可译为:"OBD-Ⅱ系统故障监测或者是连续不停地进行,即与驾驶模式无关,或者是非连续地进行,即在规定的驾驶模式期间,每个驾驶循环监测一次。"

[3] longer than normal = longer-than-normal 意为"比正常值长的"。

[4] Additionally, many equipment companies provide databases of test procedures and specifications that are built into their test equipment and can be accessed by the technician while performing diagnostics with the equipment.

本句中的 that 引导定语从句,其先行词为 databases。while performing ...在定语从句中作状语。本句可译为:"另外,许多设备公司还将含有检测程序和技术规格的数据库装进它们的检测设备中并提供给客户。当技师用该设备进行诊断操作时,可以访问此数据库。"

[5] An out of calibration coolant sensor input can cause hard starting when the engine is both cold and hot, as well as altering fuel delivery enough to cause an emission test failure and poor mileage.

注意句中的 as well as 连接两个并列的动名词 starting 和 altering。emission test failure 的意思为"排放检测不合格";poor mileage 的意思为"燃油经济性变差"。本句可以译为:

"冷却液温度传感器输入信号失准,会导致发动机在冷态和热态时出现起动困难的现象,还会导致喷油量的变化,从而引起排放检测不合格和燃油经济性变差。"

EXERCISES

I. Answer the following questions:

1. How do we interpret scan tool data to determine system condition?

2. Describe how to differentiate between computerized powertrain controls problems and mechanical problems.

II. Translate the following sentences into Chinese:

1. In some systems, a sensor failure will cause the PCM to ignore the signal from the failed sensor and operate on backup values stored in its own memory.

2. If any particular scan tool data reading does not make sense in relation to particular problem or symptom, you should test the system component directly with a voltmeter, ohmmeter, oscilloscope, frequency counter, or other test equipment.

3. Once the MIL is illuminated, three consecutive drive cycles without a malfunction detected are required to extinguish the MIL.

4. Freeze frame data is stored in the PCM at the point the malfunction is initially detected.

5. Diagnostic information will be available both in printed form and in computerized information retrieval systems in the shop or on the Internet.

6. A MAP sensor that is out of calibration can cause many different driveability problems on a computer-controlled engine because it is a primary sensor input.

Related Terms

exhaust manifold	排气歧管
exhaust pipe	排气管
tail pipe	排气尾管
muffler	消声器
straight-through muffler	直通式消声器
reverse-flow muffler	倒流式消声器
heated oxygen sensor(HO_2S)	加热型氧传感器
thermostatic air cleaner	恒温式空气滤清器
pellet-type converter	颗粒状载体催化转化器
monolith converter	整体式载体催化转化器
secondary air injection	二次空气喷射
DPT	diesel particulate trap(柴油机微粒捕集器)
DPF	diesel particulate filter(柴油机微粒过滤器)

Translation Techniques(7)——重复

在英译汉时，为了将英文的原作者的意思明确表达出来，或者为了修辞的需要，常常需要重复前面的措辞。

1. 将省略的部分重复

例 1：

Digital parameters are often called switch parameters, or signals, and are either on or off, high or low, yes or no.

数字式参数常常叫作开关参数即开关信号，它们或通或断，或高或低，或是或否。（后面将 either 省略）

例 2：

A problem can appear to be based in one system when, in fact, it originates in another.

一种故障看起来可能出现在某一系统中，但是，实际上，故障的起因存在于另一个系统中。（another 后面的 system 省掉了）

2. 将先行词重复

例 3：

The linear EGR valve contains a single electric solenoid that is operated by the PCM.

线性 EGR 阀内仅装有一个电磁阀，这个电磁阀由 PCM 控制。

3. 将代词重复

例 4：

To minimize pollution of the atmosphere from incompletely burned and evaporating gases and to maintain good driveability and fuel economy, a number of emission control systems are used on all vehicles. They include....

为了减轻不完全燃烧和蒸发的气体对大气造成的污染，同时保持良好的运行性能和燃油经济性，所有的汽车上都采用了多种排放控制系统。这些系统有：……。

例 5：

Automotive emissions are controlled in three ways. One is .... The second is ...and the third is....

控制汽车的排放物有三种方法。第一种方法是……；第二种方法是……；第三种方法是……。

4. 将动词重复

例 6：

An out of calibration coolant sensor input can cause hard starting when the engine is both cold and hot, as well as altering fuel delivery enough to cause an emission test failure and poor mileage.

冷却液温度传感器输入信号失准，会导致发动机在冷态和热态时出现起动困难的现象，还会导致喷油量的变化，从而引起排放检测不合格和燃油经济性变差。（句中的 as well as 连接两个并列的动名词 starting 和 altering，它们均为前一个 cause 的宾语。翻译后一个动名词 altering 时，要重复谓语 cause 的含义）

UNIT 8 CLUTCHES, MANUAL TRANSMISSIONS AND DRIVE LINE

TEXT A Clutches and Manual Transmissions

Clutches

The function of the clutch assembly in cars and trucks with manual transmissions or transaxles is to connect or disconnect the flow of power from the engine to the drive line. Although there are many variations in the design of clutches, all work on the same basic principle.

Clutch Purpose

A clutch is a mechanism designed to connect or disconnect power from one working part to another. In a vehicle, the clutch is used to transmit engine power and to disengage the engine and transmission when shifting gears. It also allows the engine to operate when the vehicle is stopped without placing the transmission in neutral(out of gear).

Clutch Construction

The modern clutch is a single plate, dry disc(see Fig. 8-1). It consists of five major parts: flywheel, clutch disc, pressure plate assembly, throw-out bearing, and clutch linkage. Other parts which make up the clutch assembly are the transmission input shaft and clutch housing.

Flywheel

In addition to providing a base for the starter ring gear, the flywheel forms the foundation on which the other clutch parts are attached. The flywheel used with manual transmissions is thick to enable it to absorb a large amount of heat generated by clutch operation.

The clutch side is machined smooth to provide a friction surface. Holes are drilled into the flywheel to provide a means of mounting the clutch assembly. A hole is usually drilled directly into the rear of the crankshaft. This hole allows a bearing to be installed in the center of the flywheel.

The bearing in the center of the flywheel will act as a support for the outboard end of the transmission input shaft. It is referred to as a pilot bearing. The pilot bearing may be either a ball bearing or a bronze bushing.

Dual Mass Flywheel

A dual mass flywheel is sometimes used with diesel engines. To help absorb engine

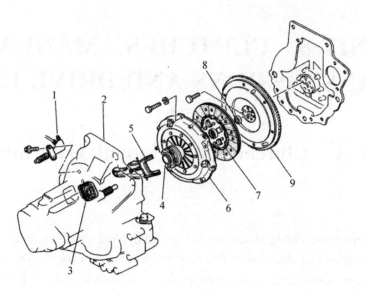

Fig. 8-1 A typical clutch
1—Clutch release cylinder 2—Transaxle 3—Boot 4—Release bearing 5—Clutch release fork
6—Clutch cover 7—Clutch disk 8—Pilot bearing 9—Flywheel

power stroke pulsations, springs mounted inside the flywheel act as a shock absorbing unit when the flywheel sections partially compress, smoothing out the power flow. They also help to reduce stress on the clutch and transmission parts.

Clutch Disc

The clutch disc is round and constructed of thin, high quality steel with a splined (grooved) hub placed in the center. The hub splines engage splines on the transmission input shaft. The clutch disc can move back and forth on the shaft, but when the disc is turned, the shaft must turn also.

Both sides of its outer edge are covered with friction material. It is often made of asbestos or other high temperature material and copper wires either woven or molded together. It is riveted to the disc.

To assist in smooth engagement, the disc outer edges are often split and each piece cupped. The friction material is riveted to these segments. When the disc is compressed, these cupped segments act as a spring-like cushion.

Pressure Plate

The clutch pressure plate is the same in each type of pressure plate assembly. It is made of a thick piece of cast iron for maximum heat absorption. It is round and about the same diameter as the clutch disc. One side of the pressure plate is machined smooth. This side will press the clutch disc facing area against the flywheel. The outer side has various shapes to facilitate attachment of springs and release mechanisms.

Release Lever Operating Mechanism

This mechanism consists of a ball bearing normally referred to as a throw-out bearing or release bearing. This bearing is mounted on a sleeve or collar that slides back and forth on a hub that is an integral part of the transmission front bearing retainer.

The throw-out bearing is filled with grease at the factory and does not need service during its useful life. Another type of throw-out bearing is the graphite type. This bearing employs a ring of graphite to press against a smooth plate fastened to the clutch levers. The throw-out bearing sleeve is moved in and out by a throw-out fork or clutch fork. This fork is usually pivoted on a ball head stud. A return spring pulls the fork away from the pressure plate.

Clutch Operation

The flywheel, clutch cover, release levers, and pressure plate all revolve as a single unit. The transmission input shaft and the clutch disc are splined together, forming another unit.

The only time the clutch disc will turn (vehicle standing still) is when it is pinched between the flywheel and pressure plate. When the release levers draw the pressure plate away from the flywheel, the clutch disc will stand still while everything else continues to revolve. When the pressure plate travels back toward the flywheel, the disc is seized and forced to turn the transmission input shaft(Fig. 8-2).

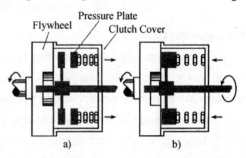

Fig. 8-2 Clutch operation simplified
a)Disengaged b)Engaged

Manual Transmission(M/T)

Transmission Gear Ratios

The modern manual transmission can provide the driver with up to seven forward gear ratios. The reduction gears provide gear ratios of approximately 3.5 : 1(stated as 3.5 to 1) for the lowest gear, to about 1.5 : 1 for the highest. The direct drive gear has a 1 : 1 gear ratio. The overdrive gears have a gear ratio of about 0.7 : 1.

By selecting one of the ratios, it is possible to operate the vehicle under all normal conditions. In addition, torque is multiplied more through the differential gears. Ratios vary from vehicle to vehicle, depending on engine horsepower and vehicle weight. A reverse gear is also used. The reverse ratio is usually about 3 : 1. The five-speed transmission has an overdrive ratio. The overdrive ratio is incorporated into newer transmissions to increase fuel mileage and lower emissions.

Transmission Construction

A typical transmission consists of a case, four shafts, bearings, gears, synchronizers, and a shifting mechanism. Fig. 8-3 shows the relative positions of the four shafts and their gears in the case.

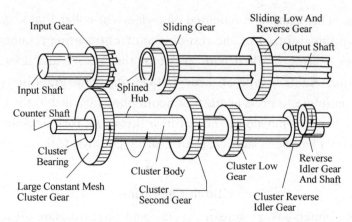

Fig. 8-3　The relative positions of the four shafts in the transmission case

Transmission Case

The transmission case holds the transmission gears, shafts, bearings, and washers. It is bolted to the rear of the engine, or to the clutch housing. Many transmission cases and clutch housings are one-piece units. Most transmission cases are made of cast iron or aluminum and have a separate extension housing, which supports the output shaft. This housing may also contain the speedometer gear. The rear engine mount is usually attached to the extension housing.

Transmission Gear

Transmission gears are made of high quality steel, carefully heat-treated to produce smooth, hard surface gear teeth with a softer, but very tough interior.[1] They are drop-forged(machine hammered into shape)while red-hot. The teeth and other critical areas are cut on precision machinery.

The teeth on transmission gears are cut into spur and helical patterns. The helical gear is superior in that it runs more quietly and is stronger because more tooth area is in contact.[2] Helical gears must be mounted firmly, since there is a tendency for them to slide apart due to the spiral shape. Gear end play in the cluster gear and some other gears and shafts is controlled by the use of bronze and steel thrust washers. These washers are installed on the end of the gear shafts between the moving gears and the stationary transmission case.

There must be some clearance between the gear teeth to allow for lubrication, expansion and possible size irregularity. This clearance is very small(a few thousandths of an inch).

Synchronizing Mechanism

Once the vehicle is in motion, the drive line will turn the output shaft continuously. As a result, the sliding gears will also be turning. When an attempt is made to mesh them with any of the cluster gears(which tend to stop when the clutch is depressed), the gear teeth will be subjected to damaging impact forces. The sound of gear clash when shifting results from the sliding gear teeth literally smashing against the cluster gear.

It is obvious that for one gear to mesh with another quietly and without damage, both gears must be rotating at nearly the same speed. Modern manual transmissions and transaxles have synchronized gears (shown in Fig. 8-4), with special internal clutches to prevent gear clash when shifting. The purpose of the synchronizer is to move ahead of the unit that is to be meshed, seize the other unit, and bring the rotational speed of both units together.[3] Once both units are rotating at the same speed, they may be meshed.

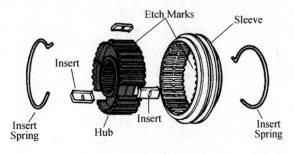

Fig. 8-4 Synchronized gear

NEW WORDS

transaxle	[ˌtrænz'æksl]	n. 变速驱动桥
neutral	['nju:trəl]	a. 中立的，中性的；n. 空档
throw-out	['θrəu'aut]	n. 抛开，断开，次品，分离
bronze	[brɔnz]	n. 青铜，铜像；a. 青铜色的
bushing	['buʃiŋ]	n. 轴衬，衬套，套管
asbestos	[æz'bestəs]	n. 石棉
woven	['wəuvən]	n. 编成的，纺织的
mold	[məuld]	n. 模子，铸型；v. 铸[塑]造，模制
rivet	['rivit]	n. 铆钉；v. 铆接，固定
cup	[kʌp]	n. 杯；v. 使成杯状
segment	['segmənt]	n. 段，节，片，扇形
cushion	['kuʃən]	n. 垫子，软垫，衬垫，缓冲垫[器]
revolve	[ri'vɔlv]	v. (使)旋转，循环出现
pinch	[pintʃ]	v. 夹紧，挤压，节省
seize	[si:z]	v. 挤住，卡住，抓住，逮住，夺取
overdrive	['əuvə'draiv]	n. 超速传动(常缩写为 O/D)
mileage	['mailidʒ]	n. 英里数，里程
drop-forge	['drɔp'fɔ:dʒ]	v. 锤锻，落锤锻造
spur	[spə:]	n. 正齿
washer	['wɔʃə]	n. 垫圈，洗衣机，洗碗机，洗涤器
clash	[klæʃ]	v. (使)发出撞击声，猛撞，冲突
smash	[smæʃ]	v. 碰撞，猛撞
literally	['litərəli]	ad. 照字面意义，逐字地，确确实实地

PHRASES AND EXPRESSIONS

drive line	传动系统
clutch disc	离合器从动盘
pressure plate	离合器压盘
throw-out bearing	分离轴承
release bearing	分离轴承
pilot bearing	导向轴承
ball bearing	球轴承
dual mass flywheel	双质量飞轮
be constructed of	用……制造
splined hub	花键毂
release lever	分离杆
gear ratio	传动比
reduction gear	减速档
direct drive gear	直接档
overdrive gear	超速档
differential gear	差速器
reverse gear	倒档
fuel mileage	燃油经济性
shifting mechanism	换档机构
extension housing	加长壳，后壳
precision machinery	精密机械
end play	轴向间隙
cluster gear	齿轮组，塔齿轮
thrust washer	止推垫片
synchronizing mechanism	同步机构
synchronized gear	同步器，同步机构

NOTES TO THE TEXT

[1] Transmission gears are made of high quality steel, carefully heat-treated to produce smooth, hard surface gear teeth with a softer, but very tough interior.

句中 heat-treated 与 made 并列。本句可以译为："变速器齿轮由优质钢制成，经过精心的热处理，从而使轮齿表面平滑、坚硬，而轮齿内部较软，韧性很好。"

[2] The helical gear is superior in that it runs more quietly and is stronger because more tooth area is in contact.

本句中 that 引导一个介词宾语从句，说明斜齿齿轮优越(superior)的理由。本句可以译为："斜齿齿轮比较优越，原因在于，同时有多个轮齿接触，不仅运转噪声小而且坚固耐用。"

[3] The purpose of the synchronizer is to move ahead of the unit that is to be meshed, seize the other unit, and bring the rotational speed of both units together.

本句 move...、seize...和 bring...是三个并列的动词不定式短语,它们说明连续的三个动作:将一个齿轮(the other unit)移到(move)另一个待啮合的齿轮跟前(ahead of the unit that is to be meshed),保持该齿轮不动,使两个齿轮的转速逼近。the other unit 既是 move,又是 seize 的宾语。本句可以译为:"同步器的作用是先将一个齿轮移到另一个待啮合齿轮的跟前,然后保持该齿轮不动,并使两个齿轮的转速逐步逼近。"

EXERCISES

I. Answer the following questions:
1. Why is the flywheel thick?
2. What are the purposes of the clutches?
3. List the main parts of the manual transmission.
4. List the four shafts of the manual transmission.

II. Translate the following sentences into Chinese:
1. The clutch includes three basic parts: driving member, driven member and operating member.
2. In a coil spring clutch, the pressure plate is backed by a number of coil springs and housed with them in a pressed-steel cover bolted to the flywheel.
3. There are three types of manual transmissions-sliding-mesh, constant-mesh and synchro-mesh transmissions. The synchro-mesh transmission is widely used in today's cars.
4. Modern manual transmissions and transaxles have synchronized gears, with special internal cluthes to prevent gear clash when shifting.

TEXT B　Drive Line

Drive Shaft

The rear-wheel drive shaft is hollow to reduce weight, but has a diameter large enough to give the shaft great strength(Fig. 8-5). Steel, aluminum, and graphite are used in drive shaft construction. Some have a rubber-mounted torsional damper.

A yoke and splined stub (where used) are welded to the ends of a hollow shaft. The shaft must run true and be carefully balanced to avoid vibrations.[1] The drive shaft is often turning at high speeds and can cause great damage if bent, imbalanced, or if there is wear in the flexible joints.

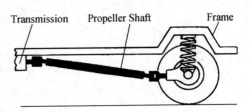

Fig. 8-5　The rear-wheel drive propeller shaft

Universal Joint

The cross and roller universal joint, sometimes called a cardan universal joint, consists of a center cross and two yokes, shown in Fig. 8-6. The yokes are at-tached to the cross through needle bearing assemblies, usually called bearing caps. The bearing caps are retained in the yoke by snap rings, U-bolts, or bolted plates. The bearing cap rollers surround the cross ends. These cross ends are called trunnions. This allows the yokes to swivel on the cross with a minimum amount of friction.

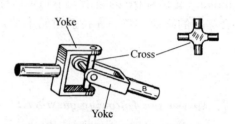

Fig. 8-6 Simple universal joint

Constant Velocity(CV)Joint

CV joints perform the same functions as the universal joint on rear-wheel drive vehicles. CV joints can drive the vehicle and compensate for steering actions while producing less vibration than a universal joint. Fig. 8-7 illustrates one particular front-wheel drive CV joint and shaft assembly.

Front-wheel drive axles are equipped with inboard(inside) and outboard(outside) CV joints. Fig. 8-7 shows one such arrangement. CV joints are used on the front axles of some four-wheel drive vehicles and rear-wheel drive vehicles with independent rear suspensions.

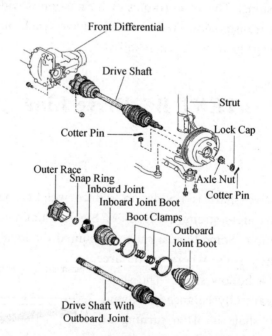

Fig. 8-7 An exploided view of a four-wheel-drive front axle and constant velocity joint

There are two basic CV joint types: tripod and Rzeppa (also called ball and channel) type, both of these are constant velocity designs. The Rzeppa joint is by far the most common.

Tripod Joint

Fig. 8-8 shows the tripod joint. It is composed of three trunnions inside of a three channel housing. Unlike the cross and roller universal joint, the tripod joint trunnions can slide back and forth in the channels as the joint rotates.

This maintains the same drive angle through the joint, allowing power to be transmitted without speed fluctuations. Inboard CV joints are usually tripod joints.

Rzeppa Joint

Fig. 8-9 illustrates the Rzeppa CV joint, which was invented in 1926 by Alfred H. Rzeppa. It consists of a series of balls in a slotted cross and housing assembly. During operation, the balls slide back and forth in the slots as the joint rotates. Since the drive angle through the joint is not subject to fluctuations, power flows smoothly through the joint at any angle. Outboard CV joints are usually Rzeppa joints.

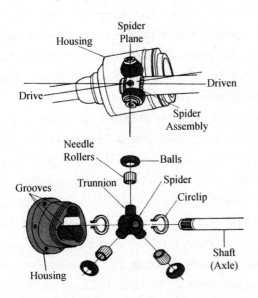

Fig. 8-8 Tripod CV joint

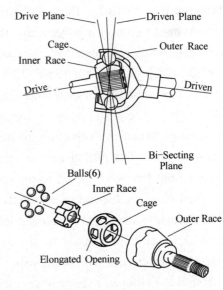

Fig. 8-9 Rzeppa CV joint

Final Drive

The ring and pinion gears are used to transfer the engine power from the drive shaft to the rear wheels. In addition to transferring power, the ring and pinion must cause the power to make a 90° turn between the drive shaft and wheels.

The ring and pinion must also provide the correct axle ratio. The pinion is the smaller driving gear; the ring is always the larger driven gear.

Differential

The rear wheels of a vehicle must turn at different speeds when rounding a corner (outside wheel must roll farther). The rear wheels must also be able to continue driving the vehicle while turning at different speeds. Therefore, it is necessary to use a differential to drive the axles, so both receive power, yet they are free to turn at different speeds when needed.[2]

Differential Operation

The drive shaft turns the ring gear pinion shaft. The pinion gear turns the ring gear which, in turn, revolves the differential case. When the case turns, the differential pinion shaft turns with it. As the differential pinions are mounted on this shaft, they are forced to move with the case. Being meshed with the side gears, the pinions will pull the side gears along with them.

When the vehicle is moving in a straight line, the ring gear is turning the case. The differential pinions and side gears are moving around with the case with no movement between the teeth of the pinions and side gears. The entire movement is like a solid unit.

When turning a corner, the case continues pulling the pinions around on the shaft. As the outer wheel must turn over a larger area, the outer side gear is now moving faster than the inner side gear. The spinning pinions not only pull on both side gears, but also begin to rotate on their shafts while walking in the side gears. This allows them to pull on both side gears, while at the same time, compensating for differences in speed by rotating around their shafts.

When the vehicle is moving in a straight line, the pinion is pulling both gears, but it is not turning. When the vehicle is turning left, the right side gear is moving faster than the left axle gear. The pinion gear is still moving at the same speed. It is still pulling on both gears, but has now started to turn on the pinion shaft. This turning action, added to the forward rotational speed of the shaft, has caused the right-hand side gear to speed up.

The reverse walking effect on the left-hand side gear has caused it to slow down. The differential action adjusts itself to any axle speed variation.[3] If one wheel begins to slip, the axle on firm ground will stand still. The case continues spinning the pinions, but will walk around the stopped axle gear and drive the spinning axle. A limited-slip differential is often used to overcome wheel slip.

Limited-Slip Differentials

To avoid the loss of driving force that occurs when one wheel begins to slip, limited-slip differentials contain internal components that automatically transfer the torque to the wheel that is not slipping. This enables the vehicle to continue its forward motion. This type of differential will provide better traction than the standard differential; it is particularly useful when roads are slippery. It is also valuable by producing faster acceleration in high performance vehicles. A high horsepower engine will often cause one wheel to spin during heavy acceleration if a standard differential is used.

Most limited-slip differentials employ the principle of friction to provide some resistance to normal differential action. Some systems use worm and wheel gears. These are discussed in the following sections.

Clutch Plate Limited-Slip Differential

The clutch plate limited-slip differential, sometimes called a Sure-Grip, Positraction, or Traction-Lok differential, is typical of friction limited-slip differentials. It resembles the standard differential, but with several important additions. The axle side gears are driven by four differential pinions. This requires two separate pinion shafts. The two shafts cross, but are free to move independently of each other. The shaft outer ends are not round, but have two flat surfaces that form a shallow V. These ramp-like surfaces engage similar ramps cut in the differential case.

Torsen® Differential

The Torsen differential (Fig. 8-10), uses worm gears and wheels or spur gears to provide traction under all conditions. The operation of the Torsen differential depends on the fact that the worm gears can turn the wheels easily, but the wheels have a hard time turning the worm gears. This allows the Torsen differential to transmit power to the wheel with the most traction.

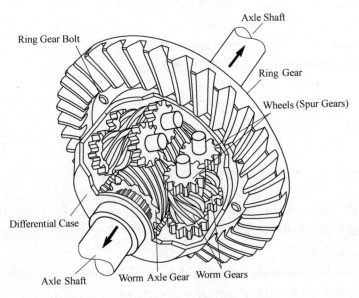

Fig. 8-10 A Torsen®/Gleason No-Spin gear and wheel positive traction differential unit

NEW WORDS

graphite	[ˈgræfait]	n. 石墨
torsional	[ˈtɔːʃənəl]	a. 扭力的，扭转的

trunnion	['trʌniən]	n. 耳轴
tripod	['traipɔd]	n. 三脚架，三脚桌
resemble	[ri'zembl]	v. 像，类似
ramp	[ræmp]	n. 斜坡，坡道，滑道，滑轨

PHRASES AND EXPRESSIONS

drive shaft	传动轴
torsional damper	扭转减振器
flexible joint	柔性接头
cross and roller universal joint	十字轴式万向节
cardan universal joint	十字轴式万向节，万向节
needle bearing	滚针轴承
snap ring	卡环
CV joint	等速万向节
exploded view	分解图
ring gear	齿圈
differential pinion shaft	差速器行星齿轮轴
ring gear pinion shaft	主减速器主动锥齿轮轴
side gear	半轴齿轮
worm and wheel gear	蜗杆蜗轮机构
friction limited-slip differential	摩擦式限滑差速器
worm gear	蜗杆副
spur gear	正齿轮，圆柱齿轮
Torsen differential	托森差速器

NOTES TO THE TEXT

[1] The shaft must run true and be carefully balanced to avoid vibrations.

句中 run 的意思为"运转""试车""试验"。本句可以译为："传动轴必须经过严格的试验和精确的平衡，以防振动。"

[2] Therefore, it is necessary to use a differential to drive the axles, so both receive power, yet they are free to turn at different speeds when needed.

本句中 axles 是指"两根半轴"，both 和 they 均指代 axles。本句可以译为："因此，必须利用差速器来驱动两个半轴。这样，这两根半轴都获得了动力，而在需要时又能以不同的转速自由转动。"

[3] The differential action adjusts itself to any axle speed variation.

句中 adjusts itself to... 的意思是"自行适应于……"。本句可以译为："这种差动作用的程度与半轴速度的变化自行相适应。"

EXERCISES

I. Answer the following questions:
1. There are two basic CV joint types. What are they?
2. What are the purposes of the final drive?
3. List the main parts of a differential.
4. Explain the basic principle of limited-slip differential.

II. Choose the best answer for each of the followings:
1. The cross ends are called_____.
   a. pinions   b. trunnions
   c. studs   d. shafts
2. A front-wheel drive vehicle is equipped with_____.
   a. only one CV joint
   b. two CV joints
   c. one inboard CV joint and one outboard CV joint
   d. four CV joint
3. The differential _____ are splined to the axles.
   a. pinion gears   b. side gears
   c. case   d. pinion shaft
4. A friction clutch plate limited-slip differential will drive the _____ when one wheel begins to slip.
   a. stationary side gears   b. turning side gears
   c. differential case   d. turning pinion gears

TEXT C   Troubleshooting the Clutch and Manual Transmission

Troubleshooting Basic Clutch Problems

Problem	Cause
Excessive clutch noise	Throw-out bearing noises are more audible at the lower end of pedal travel. The usual causes are: ● Riding the clutch ● Too little pedal free-play ● Lack of bearing lubrication A bad clutch shaft pilot bearing will make a high pitched squeal, when the clutch is disengaged and the transmission is in gear or within the first 2″ of pedal travel. The bearing must be replaced.

Problem	Cause
	(Continued)
Excessive clutch noise	Noise from the clutch linkage is a clicking or snapping that can be heard or felt as the pedal is moved completely up or down. This usually requires lubrication. Transmitted engine noises are amplified by the clutch housing and heard in the passenger compartment. They are usually the result of insufficient pedal free-play and can be changed by manipulating the clutch pedal.
Clutch slips (the car does not move as it should when the clutch is engaged)	This is usually most noticeable when pulling away from a standing start. A severe test is to start the engine, apply the brakes, shift into high gear and slowly release the clutch pedal. A healthy clutch will stall the engine. If it slips it may be due to: ● A worn pressure plate or clutch plate ● Oil soaked clutch plate[1] ● Insufficient pedal free-play
Clutch drags or fails to release	The clutch disc and some transmission gears spin briefly after clutch disengagement. Under normal conditions in average temperatures, 3 seconds is maximum spin-time. Failure to release properly can be caused by: ● Too light transmission lubricant or low lubricant level ● Improperly adjusted clutch linkage
Low clutch life	Low clutch life is usually a result of poor driving habits or heavy duty use. Riding the clutch, pulling heavy loads, holding the car on a grade with the clutch instead of the brakes and rapid clutch engagement all contribute to low clutch life.

Troubleshooting the Manual Transmission

Problem	Cause	Solution
Transmission shifts hard	● Clutch adjustment incorrect	● Adjust clutch
	● Clutch linkage or cable binding	● Lubricate or repair as necessary
	● Shift rail binding	● Check for mispositioned selector arm roll pin, loose cover bolts, worn shift rail bores, worn shift rail, distorted oil seal, or extension housing not aligned with case. Repair as necessary.
	● Internal bind in transmission caused by shift forks, selector plates, or synchronizer assemblies	● Remove, disassemble and inspect transmission. Replace worn or damaged components as necessary.
	● Clutch housing misalignment	● Check runout at rear face of clutch housing
	● Incorrect lubricant	● Drain and refill transmission

(Continued)

Problem	Cause	Solution
Transmission shifts hard	• Block rings and/or cone seats worn	• Blocking ring to gear clutch tooth face clearance must be 0.030 inch or greater. If clearance is correct it may still be necessary to inspect blocking rings and cone seats for excessive wear. Repair as necessary.
Gear clash when shifting from one gear to another	• Clutch adjustment incorrect	• Adjust clutch
	• Clutch linkage or cable binding	• Lubricate or repair as necessary
	• Clutch housing misalignment	• Check runout at rear of clutch housing
	• Lubricant level low or incorrect lubricant	• Drain and refill transmission and check for lubricant leaks if level was low. Repair as necessary
	• Gearshift components, or synchronizer assemblies worn or damaged	• Remove, disassemble and inspect transmission. Replace worn or damaged components as necessary.
Transmission noisy	• Lubricant level low or incorrect lubricant	• Drain and refill transmission. If lubricant level was low, check for leaks and repair as necessary.
	• Clutch housing-to-engine, or transmission-to-clutch housing bolts loose	• Check and correct bolt torque as necessary
	• Dirt, chips, foreign material in transmission	• Drain, flush, and refill transmission
	• Gearshift mechanism, transmission gears, or bearing components worn or damaged	• Remove, disassemble and inspect transmission. Replace worn or damaged components as necessary
	• Clutch housing misalignment	• Check run-out at rear face of clutch housing
Jumps out of gear	• Clutch housing misalignment	• Check run-out at rear face of clutch housing
	• Gearshift lever loose	• Check lever for worn fork. Tighten loose attaching bolts.
	• Offset lever nylon insert worn or lever attaching nut loose	• Remove gearshift lever and check for loose offset lever nut or worn insert. Repair or replace as necessary.
	• Gearshift mechanism, shift forks, interlock plate, shift rail, detent plugs, springs or shift cover worn or damaged	• Remove, disassemble and inspect transmission cover assembly. Replace worn or damaged components as necessary.
	• Clutch shaft or roller bearings worn or damaged	• Replace clutch shaft or roller bearings as necessary

169

		(Continued)
Problem	Cause	Solution
Jumps out of gear	● Gear teeth worn or tapered, synchronizer assemblies worn or damaged, excessive end play caused by worn thrust washers or output shaft gears	● Remove, disassemble, and inspect transmission. Replace worn or damaged components as necessary.
	● Pilot bushing worn	● Replace pilot bushing
Will not shift into one gear	● Gearshift selector plates, interlock plate, or selector arm, worn, damaged, or incorrectly assembled	● Remove, disassemble, and inspect transmission cover assembly. Repair or replace components as necessary.
	● Shift rail detent plunger worn, spring broken, or plug loose	● Tighten plug or replace worn or damaged components as necessary
	● Gearshift lever worn or damaged	● Replace gearshift lever
	● Synchronizer sleeves or hubs, damaged or worn	● Remove, disassemble and inspect transmission. Replace worn or damaged components.

NEW WORDS

free-play	[ˈfriːplei]	n. 自由行程
squeal	[skwiːl]	v. 尖叫，抱怨；n. 长而尖的声音
click	[klik]	v. 发出嘀嗒声；n. 嘀嗒声
snap	[snæp]	v. 猛地吸住，使噼啪地响
drag	[dræg]	v. 拖，拖曳，缓慢而费力地行动；n.（离合器）分离迟滞
disassemble	[ˌdisəˈsembl]	v. 分解，拆散
misalignment	[misˈəlainmənt]	n. 未对准
run-out	[ˈrʌnaut]	n. 跳动，偏斜
gearshift	[ˈgiəʃift]	n. 变速，换档
worn	[wɔːn]	a. 用旧的，疲倦的，磨损的
flush	[flʌʃ]	v. 冲洗，使脸红，使激动

PHRASES AND EXPRESSIONS

shift rail	变速轨，拨叉轴
gearshift lever	变速杆
clutch plate	离合器片，离合器从动盘
blocking ring	= block ring（同步器）锁环
cone seat	锥形座

NOTES TO THE TEXT

Oil soaked clutch plate

这里的 oil soaked = oil-soaked 是合成形容词，意思为"浸有机油的"。Oil soaked clutch plate 为一个形容词+名词的短语，作为故障原因，在翻译时，应按照"名词+形容词"的语序译出。

EXERCISES

I. Answer the following questions:
1. What are the causes of basic clutch problems?
2. What are the causes of manual transmission problems?

II. Translate the following paragraphs into Chinese:

1. Inspect the friction surfaces of the clutch plate, pressure plate and flywheel for signs of uneven contact, indicating improper installation or damaged clutch springs. Also look for score marks, burned areas, deep grooves, cracks and other types of wear and damage.

2. Measure the distance from the rivet heads to the lining surface. There should be at least 1/16-inch of lining above the rivet heads.

3. Check the lining for contamination by oil or grease and replace the clutch disc with a new one if any is present. Check the hub for cracks, blue discolored areas, broken springs and contamination by grease or oil.

4. Check the flatness of the pressure plate with a straightedge. Look for signs of overheating, cracks, deep grooves and ridges. The inner end of the diaphragm spring fingers should not show any signs of uneven wear. Replace the pressure plate with a new one if its condition is in doubt.

Related Terms

master cylinder	主缸
slave cylinder	工作缸
clutch linkage	离合器操纵机构
free travel	= free play 自由行程
diaphragm spring	膜片弹簧
first gear	1 档
second gear	2 档
five-speed transmission	5 档变速器
half shaft	= axle shaft 半轴

Translation Techniques(8)——倒译

1. 状语的倒译
(1)后置状语前移
在英语中，经常出现状语(介词短语、分词短语、状语从句等)后置的情况。根据汉语表达习惯，汉译时需要将其移至前面适当位置(例1)或句首(例2)。

例1：

In a vehicle, the clutch is used to transmit engine power and to disengage the engine and transmission when shifting gears.

句中 when shifting gears 修饰动词不定式 to disengage，所以 when shifting gears 翻译到 to disengage 之前。本句可译为："在汽车上，离合器的作用是……，并在换档之前将发动机与变速器分离。"

例2：

Helical gears must be mounted firmly, since there is a tendency for them to slide apart due to the spiral shape.

句中的 since... 是一个原因状语从句，将其译至句首："由于轮齿呈螺旋形的原因，啮合的螺旋齿轮在工作中存在分开的趋势，因此，螺旋齿轮的安装必须牢固可靠。"

(2)几个状语语序的调整
在英语句子中，几个状语的先后排列顺序为先方式状语，再地点状语，最后时间状语。然而，在汉语中，状语语序正好相反，即先时间状语，再地点状语，最后方式状语。因此，汉译时需要调整状语语序(例3、例4)。

例3：

Benz was driving his car throughout Monaco's streets and afterwards got the first driving license in the world in Baden on the 1st August, 1888.

本茨驾驶着他的汽车在摩纳哥的大街上穿行。后来，于1888年8月1日，在巴登(Baden)，本茨取得了世界上最早的驾驶执照。(地点、时间状语的倒译)

例4：

The job of the ignition system is to produce that high voltage from a 12 volt source and get it to each cylinder in a specific order, at exactly the right time.

点火系统的作用是利用12V电源产生这样的高电压，并在适当的时刻、以特定的顺序将高压电分配给各个气缸。(方式、时间状语的倒译)

2. 定语的倒译
(1)将后置定语译为前置定语

例5：

Other parts which make up the clutch assembly are the transmission input shaft and clutch housing.

英译汉时将句中 which make up...定语从句移至 other parts 之前。本句可以译为:"构成离合器总成的其他零件还有变速器输入轴和离合器壳。"

(2)将前置定语倒译

有时将前置定语(特别是分词、形容词)译到被它修饰的名词的后面,此时,同时进行词类转换或句子成分转换。

在本单元课文 C 中,描述离合器故障原因的短语及其译文如下:

A <u>worn</u> pressure plate or clutch plate——离合器压盘或从动盘<u>磨损</u>;
<u>Insufficient</u> pedal free-play——踏板自由行程<u>不足</u>;
<u>Improperly adjusted</u> clutch linkage——离合器操纵机构<u>调整不当</u>。

UNIT 9 AUTOMATIC TRANSMISSIONS

TEXT A Automatic Transmission(AT)

In today's automobile, the automatic transmission is by far the most complicated mechanical component. It is a type of transmission that shifts automatically. Automatic transmission or transaxle has four basic systems—a torque converter, a gear system, a hydraulic system and an electronic system(Fig. 9-1).

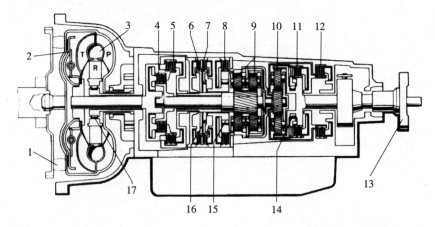

Fig. 9-1 Components of a typical automatic transmission
1—Drive plate 2—Converter lockup clutch 3—Torque converter P. Impeller R. Stator T. Turbine
4—Clutch A 5—Clutch B 6—Clutch C′ 7—Clutch C 8—Clutch D 9—Planetary gear set
10—Planetary gear set, fourth gear 11—Clutch E 12—Clutch F 13—Output 14~17—One-way clutch

Torque Converter

The torque converter replaces the conventional clutch. It has three functions:

1. It allows the engine to idle with the vehicle at a standstill, even with the transmission or transaxle in gear.[1]

2. It allows the transmission or transaxle to shift from range-to-range smoothly, without requiring that the driver close the throttle during the shift.

3. It multiplies engine torque to an increasing extent as vehicle speed drops and throttle opening is increased. This has the effect of making the transmission or transaxle more responsive and reduces the amount of shifting required.

The torque converter is a metal case which is shaped like a sphere that has been flattened on opposite sides, it is bolted to the rear end of the engine's crankshaft.

Generally, the entire metal case rotates at engine speed and serves as the engine's flywheel.

The case contains three sets of blades(Fig. 9-2). One set is attached directly to the case. This set forms the torus or pump. Another set is directly connected to the output shaft, and forms the turbine. The third set is mounted on a hub which, in turn, is mounted on a stationary shaft through a one-way clutch. This third set is known as the stator.

A pump, which is driven by the converter hub at engine speed, keeps the torque converter full of automatic transmission fluid at all times. Fluid flows continuously through the unit to provide cooling.

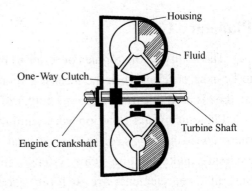

Fig. 9-2 The torque converter housing is rotated by the engine's crankshaft, and turns the impeller. The impeller then spins the turbine, which gives motion to the turbine shaft, driving the gears

Under low speed acceleration, the torque converter functions as follows:

The torus is turning faster than the turbine. It picks up fluid at the center of the converter and, through centrifugal force, slings it outward. Since the outer edge of the converter moves faster than the portions at the center, the fluid picks up speed.

The fluid then enters the outer edge of the turbine blades; it then travels back toward the center of the converter case along the turbine blades. In impinging upon the turbine blades, the fluid loses the energy picked up in the torus.

If the fluid was now returned directly into the torus, both halves of the converter would have to turn at approximately the same speed at all times, and torque input and output would both be the same.

In flowing through the torus and turbine, the fluid picks up two types of flow, or flow in two separate directions. It flows through the turbine blades, and it spins with the engine. The stator, whose blades are stationary when the vehicle is being accelerated at low speeds, converts one type of flow into another.[2] Instead of allowing the fluid to flow straight back into the torus, the stator's curved blades turn the fluid almost 90° toward the direction of rotation of the engine. Thus the fluid does not flow as fast toward the torus, but is already spinning when the torus picks it up. This has the effect of allowing the torus to turn much faster than the turbine. This difference in speed may be compared to the difference in speed between the smaller and larger gears in any gear train. The result is that engine power output is higher, and engine torque is multiplied.

As the speed of the turbine increases, the fluid spins faster and faster in the direction of engine rotation. As a result, the ability of the stator to redirect the fluid flow is reduced. Under cruising conditions, the stator is eventually forced to rotate on its one-way clutch in the direction of engine rotation. Under these conditions, the torque converter begins to behave almost like a solid shaft, with the torus and turbine speeds being almost equal.

Planetary Gear

The ability of the torque converter to multiply engine torque is limited. Also, the unit tends to be more efficient when the turbine is rotating at relatively high speeds. Therefore, a planetary gearbox is used to carry the power output of the turbine to the driveshaft.

Planetary gears function very similarly to conventional transmission gears. However, their construction is different in that three elements make up one gear system, and, in that all three elements are different from one another.[3] The three elements are: an outer gear that is shaped like a hoop, with teeth cut into the inner surface; a sun gear, mounted on a shaft and located at the very center of the outer gear; and a set of four planet gears, held by pins in a ring-like planet carrier, meshing with both the sun gear and the outer gear(Fig. 9-3). Either the outer gear or the sun gear may be held stationary, providing more than one possible torque multiplication factor for each set of gears. Also, if all three gears are forced to rotate at the same speed, the gear set forms, in effect, a solid shaft.

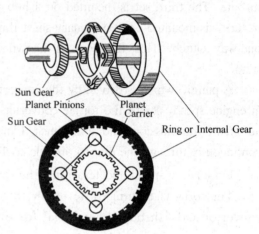

Fig. 9-3 Planetary gears work in a similar fashion to manual transmission gears, but are composed of three parts

Most automatics use the planetary gears to provide various reductions ratios. Bands and clutches are used to hold various portions of the gear sets to the transmission case or transaxle case or to the shaft on which they are mounted.[4] Shifting is accomplished, then, by changing the portion of each planetary gear set which is held to the case or to the shaft.

Hydraulic System

Servos and Accumulators

The servos(Fig. 9-4) are hydraulic pistons and cylinders. They resemble the hydraulic actuators used on many other machines, such as bulldozers. Hydraulic fluid enters the cylinder, under pressure, and forces the piston to move to engage the band or clutches.

The accumulators are used to cushion the engagement of the servos. The automatic transmission or transaxle fluid(ATF) must pass through the accumulator on the way to the servo. The accumulator housing contains a thin piston which is sprung away from the discharge passage of the accumulator. When fluid passes through the accumulator on the way to the servo, it must move the piston against spring pressure, and this action smoothes out the action of the servo.

Hydraulic Control System

The hydraulic pressure used to operate the servos comes from the main oil pump. This fluid is channeled to the various servos through the shift valves. There is generally a manual shift valve which is operated by the selector lever and an automatic shift valve for each automatic upshift the transmission or transaxle provides.

There are two pressures which affect the operation of these valves. One is the governor pressure which is affected by vehicle speed. The other is the modulator pressure which is affected by intake manifold vacuum or throttle position. Governor pressure rises with an increase in vehicle speed, and modulator pressure rises as the throttle is opened wider. By responding to these two pressures, the shift valves cause the upshift points to be delayed with increased throttle opening to make the best use of the engine's power output.

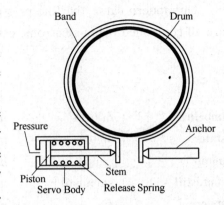

Fig. 9-4 Servos, operated by pressure, are used to apply or release the bands, to either hold the ring gear or allow it to rotate

The modulator also governs the line pressure, used to actuate the servos. In this way, the clutches and bands will be actuated with a force matching the torque output of the engine.

Electronic Control System

Many new transmission or transaxles are electronically controlled(Fig. 9-5). On these units, electrical solenoids are used to better control the hydraulic fluid. Usually, the solenoids are regulated by an electronic control module.

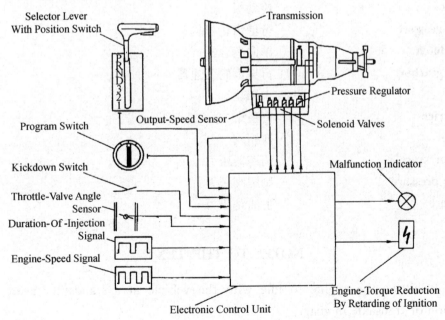

Fig. 9-5 An electronic transmission control system

On modern cars, the line pressure, converter lockup, shift point and shift quality, are all controlled by an electronic control unit.

NEW WORDS

impeller	[im'pelə]	n. 推进者，叶轮，泵轮
stator	['steitə]	n. 定子，导轮
pump	[pʌmp]	n. 泵，泵轮
standstill	['stændstil]	n. 停止，停顿
sphere	[sfiə]	n. 球，球体，圈子，半球
flatten	['flætn]	v. 变平，变单调
torus	['tɔ:rəs]	n. 圆环面，环形，叶轮[植]花托
sling	[sliŋ]	n. 投掷，抛
impinge	[im'pindʒ]	v. 撞击，打击
fashion	['fæʃən]	n. 样子，方式，流行，风尚
servo	['sə:vəu]	n. 伺服，伺服系统
accumulator	[ə'kju:mjuleitə]	n. 蓄能器，蓄压器，集液器，蓄电池
solenoid	['səulinɔid]	n. [电]螺线管

PHRASES AND EXPRESSIONS

drive plate	传动板
planetary gear set	行星齿轮机构
one-way clutch	单向离合器
planetary gearbox	行星齿轮变速器
sun gear	太阳轮
planet carrier	行星架
shift valve	换档阀
governor pressure	调速器压力
modulator pressure	调压阀压力
line pressure	主油路压力

NOTES TO THE TEXT

[1] It allows the engine to idle with the vehicle at a standstill, even with the transmission or transaxle in gear.

句中with、even with后面的名词和介词短语构成"with+主谓关系"的结构，在这里作状语。本句可以译为："在汽车静止的情况下，即使变速器或变速驱动桥挂在档位上，（液力变矩器)也可使发动机怠速运转。"

[2] The stator, whose blades are stationary when the vehicle is being accelerated at low speeds, converts one type of flow into another.

句中 whose... 是一个非限制性定语从句。本句可以译为："当汽车在低速加速时，导轮的叶片固定不动。这样，导轮就将一种液流转变成另一种液流。"

[3] However, their construction is different in that three elements make up one gear system, and, in that all three elements are different from one another.

句中两个 that... 均作介词 in 的宾语从句。本句可以译为："然而，它们的结构的不同在于，三个元件构成了一个齿轮系统，并且这三个元件相互不同。"

[4] Bands and clutches are used to hold various portions of the gear sets to the transmission case or transaxle case or to the shaft on which they are mounted.

句中的"to hold ...to ...or to ..."的意思为"将……固定到……上，或者固定到……上"，后面的两个"to ..."是并列关系。on which 引导的定语从句修饰 shaft。本句可以译为："制动带和离合器用来将齿轮机构的各个部分固定到变速器壳或变速驱动桥壳上或者固定到安装它们(制动带和离合器)的轴上。"

EXERCISES

I. Answer the following questions:

1. List the four basic systems of the automatic transmission.
2. What are the three functions of the torque converter?
3. There are two pressures which affect the operation of the shift valves. What are they?
4. What are the three elements of a planetary gear set?

II. Translate the following paragraphs into Chinese:

The computer uses sensors on the engine and transmission to detect such things as throttle position, vehicle speed, engine speed, engine load, stop light switch position, etc. to control exact shift points as well as how soft or firm the shift should be. Some computerized transmissions even learn your driving style and constantly adapt to it so that every shift is timed precisely when you would need it.

Because of computer controls, sports models are coming out with the ability to take manual control of the transmission as though it were a stick shift, allowing the driver to select gears manually. This is accomplished on some cars by passing the shift lever through a special gate, then tapping it in one direction or the other in order to up-shift or down-shift at will. The computer monitors this activity to make sure that the driver does not select a gear that could overspeed the engine and damage it.

TEXT B Continuously Variable Transmissions, Automated Manual Transmissions and Double Clutch Transmissions

Continuously Variable Transmissions

A continuously variable transmission, or CVT, is a type of automatic transmission that provides more useable power, better fuel economy and a smoother driving experience than a traditional automatic.

History of CVT

Leonardo DaVinci sketched the first CVT in 1490. Dutch automaker DAF first started using CVTs in their cars in the late 1950s; however technology limitations made CVTs unsuitable for engines with more than around 100 horsepower. In the late 1980s and early 1990s, Subaru offered a CVT in their Justy mini-car, while Honda used one in the high-mileage Honda Civic HX of the late 1990s.

Improved CVTs capable of handling more powerful engines were developed in the late 1990s and 2000s, and CVTs can now be found in cars from Nissan, Audi, Honda, Ford, GM, and other automakers.

How CVT Works

There are several types of CVTs. Most cars use a pair of variable-diameter pulleys, each shaped like a pair of opposing cones, with a metal belt or chain running between them. [1]

The primary V-pulley is driven by the planetary gear when the forward- or reverse-gear clutch is engaged. It drives the secondary V-pulley via a pushbelt or a link chain (Fig. 9-6, Fig. 9-7 and Fig. 9-8).

The gear ratios are varied continuously over the entire working range by the primary and secondary V-pulley pairs(variator). Variation of the gear ratio is achieved by axial displacement of a diagonally opposite pulley half in each case. In this way, the effective diameters of the primary and secondary pulleys are continuously varied in opposition, i. e. bigger or smaller. Displacement of the pulley halves is effected by the two pressure-controlled primary and secondary cylinders.

Selector-lever position N(Neutral)*and P*(Park). Both clutches are released. There is no power transmission. In the P position the secondary V-pulley is blocked by the parking lock.

Selector-lever position D (Drive) ***and L*** (Low). The forward-gear clutch is closed and the reverse-gear clutch released. The planet carrier, planet gears, internal gear and sun gear circulate as a single block and drive the secondary V-pulley via the primary V-pulley and pushbelt or link chain. The secondary pulley directs the torque to the output shaft.

The input shaft, primary and secondary V-pulleys and output shaft all rotate in the same direction.

Selector-lever position R (Reverse). The forward-gear clutch is released and the reverse-gear clutch closed. This brakes the internal gear on the transmission housing. The planet-gear pairs driven via the planet carrier reverse the direction of rotation.

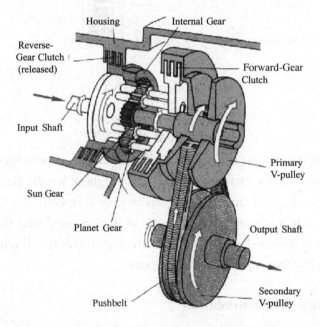

Fig. 9-6 A CVT with pushbelt

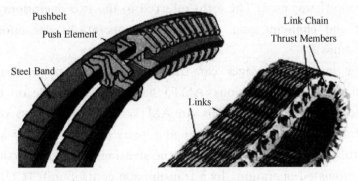

Fig. 9-7 Pushbelt and link chain

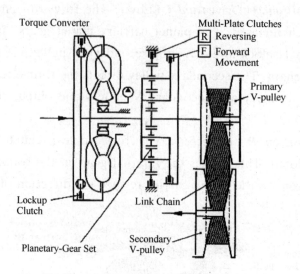

Fig. 9-8 Diagram of CVT

Advantages of the CVT

Engines do not develop constant power at all speeds; they have specific speeds where torque, horsepower and fuel efficiency are at their highest levels. Because there are no gears to tie a given road speed directly to a given engine speed, the CVT can vary the engine speed as needed to access maximum power as well as maximum fuel efficiency. This allows the CVT to provide quicker acceleration than a conventional automatic or manual transmission while delivering superior fuel economy.

Automated Manual Transmissions

Automated Manual Passenger Car Transmissions

When manual transmissions for passenger cars began to be automated, the term "semi-automatic transmission" was used. The term referred to the two operations "Engaging the clutch/moving-off" and "changing gear". One of these operations was automated in semi-automatic transmissions.

Semi-automatic manual passenger car transmissions have never found broad use. (Fully) automated manual transmissions (AMT) have been available on the market for passenger cars since the end of the 1990s. In AMTs, both the process of engaging the master clutch and moving-off as well as changing gears are executed by actuators which receive their control signal via shift paddles on the steering wheel, a gearshift lever or, in the case of fully automated operation, by a transmission control unit (TCU).

Automated manual transmissions combine the high efficiency of manual transmissions with the ease of operation of a fully automatic transmission. The biggest difference to automatic powershift transmissions for the user is the less comfortable gearshifting, which according to the principle of the design is subject to power interruption, as with manual transmissions. Attempts to transfer residual power with oversized synchronizing units and an incomplete opening of the clutch during the shifting process showed positive results in test vehicles, but have not led to series production.

AMTs are further classified as add-on and integrated systems. Add-on systems furnish existing manual systems with built-on actuators. In this way, a basic gear unit can become either a manual transmission or an automated manual transmission. Integrated systems are already designed as automated manual transmissions. They cannot be used as MTs.

Fully Automated Manual Commercial Vehicle Transmissions

Automated manual commercial vehicle transmissions have had top level automation since the end of the 1990s. This level of automation is characterised by an automated moving-off element, automated clutch engagement in gearshifting, automated gear change and data communication between the engine control unit and the transmission control unit. Through this total clutch automation, the clutch pedal can be disposed of entirely, thus allowing for a two-pedal system in commercial vehicles with acceleration and brake pedals. In addition to the automatic mode, a manual mode enables the driver to intervene at any time.

As already discussed in "Automated Manual Passenger Car Transmissions", a distinction is made among the actuating elements between add-on systems for adding onto existing manual transmissions and integrated systems. In the case of integrated systems, the transmission is developed for purely automated implementation. The automation of manual transmissions offers many advantages, the most important of which are:

- a high level of efficiency comparable to a manual transmission;
- improved driving comfort as a result of relieving the driver of engaging the clutch and shifting;
- improved driver alertness in road traffic;
- reduction of life-cycle costs through:
  - decreased clutch wear;
  - decreased fuel consumption through the use of an optimised driving strategy (selection of shift programmes);
- increased protection of components through the prevention of shifting misuse (transmission and clutch protection);
- transmission control without rods and cables by means of a drive selector, which means:
  - reduced noise in the cabin, as there is no mechanical connection between the gearshift lever and the transmission;
  - optimised packaging, as the rod shifting system and the clutch pedal are left out, which means a more simple and cost-effective assembly.

A disadvantage of automated manual transmissions is power interruption, but since the shifting times of modern commercial vehicles are short, this is acceptable for road traffic.

Structure of Automated Manual Commercial Vehicle Transmissions

The automated clutch engagement and the automated gear change are facilitated by the use of different actuating elements(actuators). These are the clutch actuator CA and the transmission actuator TA. Figure 9-9 shows the system structure of an automated manual commercial vehicle transmission.

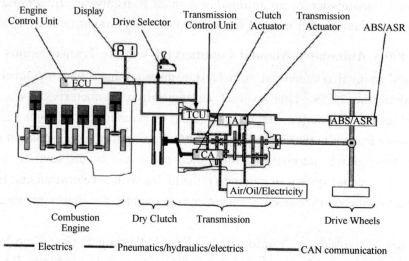

Figure 9-9 System structure of an automated manual transmission

The following types of actuating elements are used in automated manual commercial vehicle transmissions:
- electropneumatic actuators;
- electrohydraulic actuators;
- electromechanical actuators.

Electropneumatic actuators are suited to heavy-duty trucks, as they are equipped with a compressed air system. If no compressed air is present, either an electrohydraulic or an electromechanical system is used, depending on the required properties of the actuating element.

Actual and reference data are exchanged via the data bus(CAN bus) between the engine control unit(ECU) of the diesel engine and the transmission control unit(TCU), as well as connected sub-systems such as the drive selector, the display, the ABS/ASR and the sensors.

Automated manual commercial vehicle transmissions are available on the market as "AS-Troni"(ZF), "eTronic"(ZF), "Telligent EAS" or "PowerShift"(Mercedes-Benz), "Sprintshift"(Mercedes-Benz), "I-Shift/Geartronic"(Volvo), "Opticruise"(Scania) and "SAMT B"(Eaton).

Dual Clutch Transmissions

Dual clutch transmissions(DCT) were already developed in the 1940s. The original intention was to furnish heavy commercial vehicles with technology which provided for driving without power interruption. Serial production was not achieved, however. In the 1980s, Porsche and Audi took up this transmission concept again and developed a dual clutch transmission for racing cars. These transmissions were not suited to serial production because the control quality of the systems was not yet sufficient.

The first DCT for passenger cars went into production in 2003. The goal of this model was to combine the advantages of manual transmissions with those of automatic transmissions. Attributes of manual transmissions are a high level of efficiency, a gear ratio spread which is freely selectable in broad ranges, as well as sportiness, driving dynamics and driving pleasure. Conventional automatic transmissions are characterised by their ease of handling when moving-off thanks to the torque converter and by automatic shifting without power interruption.

The principle of dual clutch transmission is based on the idea of two independent sub-gearboxes each connected to the engine via its own clutch(Figure 9-10). One sub-gearbox contains the odd gears(1, 3, 5...) and the other the even gears(2, 4, 6...). By dividing the gears through the dual clutch, the DCT becomes fully power shiftable. However, the dual clutch is not only implemented in a DCT for shifting; it also serves as a moving-off element.

In actual designs, the two sub-gearboxes are not arranged side-by-side, as in Figure 9-10, but rather one is nested in the other to save space. One of the two gearbox input shafts is used as a hollow shaft.

The basic functioning of dual clutch transmissions will be explained in the following on the example of the upshift from second to third gear. When a situation arises during vehicle operation which requires an upshift from the currently engaged second gear(sub-gearbox 2) to third gear, third gear is engaged in the free sub-gearbox 1. The synchronizing process of the corresponding idler gear is not noticeable to the driver. In virtue of the overlapping of closing clutch C1 and opening clutch C2, the power flow is not interrupted. Once C1 has taken over the torque, the second gear is disengaged in sub-gearbox 2, which is now free, and another gear can be preselected, if necessary. The basic process is the same for both upshifting and downshifting.

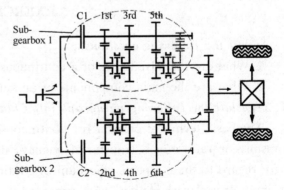

Figure 9-10 Principle of dual clutch transmissions(VW DSG)

NEW WORDS

sketch	[sketʃ]	v.	勾画，绘略图
pushbelt	[ˈpuʃbelt]	n.	推力传动钢带
variator	[ˈvɛərieitə]	n.	变化器，变速传动机构
upshift	[ˈʌpʃift]	n.	升档
downshift	[ˈdaunʃift]	n.	降档

PHRASES AND EXPRESSIONS

continuously variable transmission	无级变速器
automated manual transmission	机械式自动变速器
dual clutch transmission	双离合变速器
call up	召唤，提取
link chain	扁节链

NOTES TO THE TEXT

[1] Though there are several types of CVTs, most cars use a pair of variable-diameter pulleys, each shaped like a pair of opposing cones, with a metal belt or chain running between them.

句中插入了分词独立结构 each shaped like a pair of opposing cones，对 a pair of variable-diameter pulleys(一对可变直径的带轮)进行说明。句末的 them 指代 pulleys，而不是 cones。本句可以译为："CVT有若干种类型。大多数小轿车都使用一对可变直径的带轮，每个带轮的外形就像两个面对面靠在一起的锥体一样。两个带轮之间用金属带或链条连接。"

EXERCISES

I. *Answer the following questions:*
   1. What are the advantages of a continuously variable transmission?
   2. What are the main components of an automated manual transmission?

II. *Translate the following paragraph into Chinese:*

The basic technical criteria for continuously variable transmissions are size, weight, transmission-ratio range, transfer efficiency, noise emissions and installation possibilities. With regard to these aspects, mechanical continuously variable transmissions, in the form of chain-driven transmission, have provided the best results so far.

TEXT C   Notes of Automatic Transmission Repair

Limp-home operation on account of electrical faults. E. g. cable interruptions, solenoid switching valves defective, no sensor signals, gearbox electronics fails. The vehicle can continue to be moved in selector lever position D only in one gear, e. g. 2nd gear, and in R. Safety functions such os selector-lever interlock are if necessary no longer active. On restart, it may not be possible for a selector-lever position to be selected. The faults are stored in self-diagnosis and must be deleted on completion of repairs.

Limp-home operation on account of mechanical-hydraulic faults (gearbox electronics OK). E. g. multi-plate clutch slips due to excessively low pressure build-up, multi-plate clutch worn. This is identified from engine-speed differences if these, for example, are greater than 3%. The last gear to be detected as good remains selected. The reverse gear can be engaged. The selector-lever interlock is active. The fault is reset on restarting. Depending on the manufacturer, these faults are not stored in the ECU's self-diagnosis.

Towing. It is absolutely essential when towing vehicles with automatic gearboxes to follow the manufacturer's instructions to the letter because the fluid pump is not driven. There is therefore insufficient lubrication in the gearbox. The selector lever must be in the N position. In vehicles with electromagnetically actuated parking locks, the parking lock must be mechanically unlocked. Towing speed as a rule 50 km/h; towing distance 50 km.

Fault diagnosis. To be able to carry out safe diagnosis of faults in the automatic gearbox, it is necessary to perform the following checks before removing the gearbox:

- Fluid level. An excessively high fluid level causes over hard gearshifts and possibly leaks. An excessively low fluid level results in an insufficient frictional connection and thus in slipping shifting points. Make sure that the correct ATF oil grade is used for topping up!
- Fluid quality. Burnt-smelling fluid indicates that the multi-plate clutches and/or brake bands are worn.
- Check self-diagnosis with a tester.
- Retrace the upshift and downshift points as a function of selector-lever position, load and driving speed.
- Check the selector-lever setting.
- On older automatic gearboxes—check the throttle-cable adjustment.
- Check the hydraulic pressures.
- If necessary, check the fluid strainer in the shift valve housing for contamination.
- Check the stall speed. Follow the manufacturer's instructions to the letter when carrying out this check. The gearbox is subject to the risk of damage, e. g. leaks, clutch wear, on account of very intensive fluid heating.

NEW WORDS

remove   [riˈmuːv]   v. 移动；搬家；拆卸
retrace   [riˈtreis]   v. 折回[返]，再探查
strainer   [ˈstreinə]   n. 滤网，过滤器
contamination   [kenˌtæmiˈneiʃən]   n. 玷污，污染，污染物

PHRASES AND EXPRESSIONS

to the letter   照字句，严格地，不折不扣地
fluid pump   自动变速器油泵
as a rule   通常
shift valve housing   = valve body 阀体
on account of   由于
stall speed   失速

EXERCISES

I. *Answer the following questions:*

1. What are checks that must be performed before removing the gearbox?
2. How to tow a vehicle with an automatic gearbox ?

II. *Translate the following terms into Chinese:*

1. ATF
2. oil grade
3. selector lever
4. multi-plate clutch
5. selector lever interlock
6. parking lock
7. fluid level
8. fluid quality
9. downshift point
10. throttle cable
11. hydraulic pressure
12. fluid strainer

Related Terms

Simpson geartrain	辛普森行星齿轮机构
compound planetary gearset (Ravigneaux gearset)	复合式行星齿轮机构（拉维纳行星齿轮机构）
electronically controlled transmission(ECT)	电子控制变速器
lockup clutch	（变矩器）锁止离合器
valve body	阀体
pressure regulation solenoid valve	调压电磁阀
shift(control)solenoid valve	换档（控制）电磁阀
lockup(control)solenoid valve	锁止（控制）电磁阀

Translation Techniques(9)——分译与合译

1. 分译

在英译汉时，为使译文含义清楚、语言简练，有时需将原文中的一个单词、一个短语或者一个从句，从句子中拿出来译成一个独立的成分或从句，或者译成一个并列分句。

例1：

The three elements are: an outer gear that is shaped like a hoop, with teeth cut into the inner surface; a sun gear, mounted on a shaft and located at the very center of the outer gear; and a set of four planet gears, held by pins in a ring-like planet carrier, meshing with both the sun gear and the outer gear.

这三个元件是：齿圈、太阳轮和一组（4个）行星齿轮。齿圈呈环形，其内表面上制有轮齿。太阳轮安装在一根轴上，并正好位于齿圈的中心处。行星齿轮靠行星架上的轴销定位，并同时与太阳轮和外齿圈啮合。（这里将从句和分词短语分译成了独立的句子。将定语从句译成单独的句子时，需要将关联词译出。将短语译成句子时，应加上主语。）

2. 合译

合译是将原文的两个或更多的简单句或复合句用一个汉译句来表达的翻译方法。

在定语从句的翻译中也常常采用合译法，即将定语从句译在所修饰的词语之前，此法也叫作前置法。如果定语从句比较短，从句与先行词之间的关系比较紧密，则一般采用合译法。相反，如果定语从句较长，或者从句与先行词之间的关系不够紧密，则采用分译法更好。

例2：

A pump, which is driven by the converter hub at engine speed, keeps the torque converter full of automatic transmission fluid at all times.

在液力变矩器毂的驱动下以发动机转速旋转的油泵使液力变矩器内总是充满自动变速器液。

UNIT 10   BRAKING SYSTEMS

TEXT A   Basic Braking System and ABS

In order to reduce the speed of the vehicle, the brakes have to convert the kinetic energy stored in the vehicle to heat energy. A braking system consists of an energy-supplying device, a control device, a transmission device and the brake.

Today, there are three types of braking systems in use: service braking system, parking braking system and additional retarder braking system. The service braking system and the parking braking system have separate control and transmission devices. The service braking system is normally foot-operated, while the parking braking system is hand-operated.

Basic operating principle of the hydraulic system

Hydraulic systems are used to actuate the brakes of all small cars. The system transports the power required to force the frictional surfaces of the braking system together from the pedal to the individual brake units at each wheel.

The master cylinder consists of a fluid reservoir and a double cylinder and piston assembly. Double type master cylinders are designed to separate the front and rear braking systems hydraulically in case of a leak.

Steel lines carry the brake fluid to a point on the vehicle frame near each of the vehicle's wheels. The fluid is then carried to the calipers and wheel cylinders by flexible tubes in order to allow for suspension and steering movements.

The hydraulic system operates as follows: When at rest, the entire system, from the piston(s) in the master cylinder to those in the wheel cylinders or calipers, is full of brake fluid. Upon application of the brake pedal, fluid trapped in front of the master cylinder piston(s) is forced through the lines to the wheel cylinders. Here, it forces the pistons outward, in the case of drum brakes, and inward toward the disc, in the case of disc brakes. The motion of the pistons is opposed by return springs mounted outside the cylinders in drum brakes, and by spring seals, in disc brakes.

Upon release of the brake pedal, a spring located inside the master cylinder immediately returns the master cylinder pistons to the normal position. The pistons contain check valves and the master cylinder has compensating ports drilled in it. These are uncovered as the pistons reach their normal position. The piston check valves allow fluid to flow toward the wheel cylinders or calipers as the pistons withdraw. Then, as the return springs force the brake pads or shoes into the released position, the excess fluid reservoirs through the compensating ports.

It is during the time the pedal is in the released position that any fluid that has leaked out of the system will be replaced through the compensating ports.[1]

Dual circuit master cylinders employ two pistons, located one behind the other, in the cylinder. The primary piston is actuated directly by mechanical linkage from the brake pedal through the power booster. The secondary piston is actuated by fluid trapped between the two pistons. If a leak develops in front of the secondary piston, it moves forward until it bottoms against the front of the master cylinder, and the fluid trapped between the pistons will operate the rear brakes. If the rear brakes develop a leak, the primary piston will move forward until direct contact with the secondary piston takes place, and it will force the secondary piston to actuate the front brakes. In either case, the brake pedal moves farther when the brakes are applied, and less braking power is available.

Disc brakes

Instead of the traditional expanding brakes that press outward against a circular drum, disc brake systems utilize a disc(rotor) with brake pads positioned on either side of it. Braking effect is achieved in a manner similar to the way you would squeeze a spinning phonograph record between your fingers. The disc(rotor) is a casting with cooling fins between the two braking surfaces. This enables air to circulate between the braking surfaces making them less sensitive to heat buildup and more resistant to fade. Dirt and water do not affect braking action since contaminants are thrown off by the centrifugal action of the rotor or scraped off by the pads. Also, the equal clamping action of the two brake pads tends to ensure uniform, straight line stops. Disc brakes are inherently self-adjusting. There are three general types of disc brake: fixed caliper, floating caliper and sliding caliper.

The fixed caliper design uses two pistons mounted on either side of the rotor(in each side of the caliper). The caliper is mounted rigidly and does not move. The sliding and floating designs are quite similar. In fact, these two types are often lumped together. In both designs, the pad on the inside of the rotor is moved into contact with the rotor by hydraulic force. The caliper, which is not held in a fixed position, moves slightly, bringing the outside pad into contact with the rotor.

Drum brakes

Drum brakes employ two brake shoes mounted on a stationary backing plate. These shoes are positioned inside a circular drum which rotates with the wheel assembly. The shoes are held in place by springs. This allows them to slide toward the drums(when they are applied) while keeping the linings and drums in alignment. The shoes are actuated by a wheel cylinder which is mounted at the top of the backing plate. When the brakes are applied, hydraulic pressure forces the wheel cylinder's actuating links outward. Since these links bear directly against the top of the brake shoes, the tops of the shoes are then forced against the inner side of the drum. This action forces the bottoms of the two shoes to contact the brake drum by rotating the entire assembly slightly (known as servo action). When pressure within the wheel cylinder is relaxed, return springs pull the shoes back away from the drum.

ABS

Stopping a car in a hurry on a slippery road can be very challenging. Anti-lock braking systems(ABS)take a lot of the challenge out of this sometimes nerve-wracking event. In fact, on slippery surfaces, even professional drivers can't stop as quickly without ABS as an average driver can with ABS.

There are four main components in an ABS system: speed sensors, a pump, valves and a controller(Fig. 10-1).

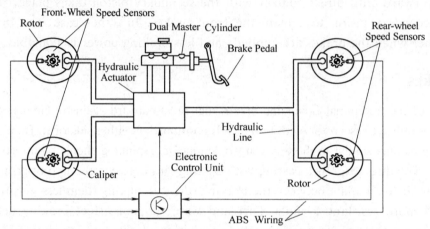

Fig. 10-1 Main components of the anti-lock braking system

Components

Speed Sensors

The speed sensors are located at each wheel and provide the speed reference to the control unit. The speed sensors are permanently magnetized inductive sensors that read pulses from a tooth wheel on each hub. A voltage signal is generated as each tooth passes through the magnetic field. The sensors are replaceable. The tooth wheels are integral with the wheel hubs and are replaced with the complete hub.

Control Unit

The control unit contains all the signal conditioning circuitry and the output circuits. The output circuits control the hydraulic unit to adjust the line pressure to each caliper. The unit is located under the dash panel on the left side, above the glove compartment and in the forward position of the electronic box in the engine compartment. If a problem is sensed, the control

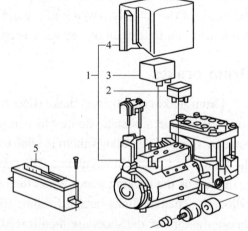

Fig. 10-2 Hydraulic unit of the anti-lock brake system
1—Hydraulic control unit 2—Valve relay
3—Motor relay 4—Cover 5—ABS control unit

unit will light the instrument panel warning lamp.

Pump and Valves

The hydraulic unit (Fig. 10-2), also known as hydraulic actuator, located in the engine compartment contains valves and a pump. The valves have 3 positions: pressure build-up, pressure hold and pressure drop. As the tires locks, the control unit informs the valve to hold the pressure. If the tire remains locked, the control unit will allow the valve to drop the pressure until the tire starts to turn. The control unit will allow the valve to start building pressure to start the cycle over again.

The pump returns the brake fluid taken from the wheel cylinder while the pressure is lowered. The pump is designed to maintain separation of the 2 braking circuits.

During operation of the anti-lock system, a pulsing may be felt at the brake pedal and a clicking heard from the hydraulic unit. This is normal and informs the operator that the ABS is in the functioning mode.

Operating principle

There are many different variations and control algorithms for ABS systems. We will discuss how one of the simpler systems works.

The controller monitors the speed sensors at all times. It is looking for decelerations in the wheel that are out of the ordinary. Right before a wheel locks up, it will experience a rapid deceleration. If left unchecked, the wheel would stop much more quickly than any car could. It might take a car five seconds to stop from 60mph (96.6 kph) under ideal conditions, but a wheel that locks up could stop spinning in less than a second.

The ABS controller knows that such a rapid deceleration is impossible, so it reduces the pressure to that brake until it sees an acceleration, then it increases the pressure until it sees the deceleration again. It can do this very quickly, before the tire can actually significantly change speed. The result is that the tire slows down at the same rate as the car, with the brakes keeping the tires very near the point at which they will start to lock up. [2] This gives the system maximum braking power.

When the ABS system is in operation you will feel a pulsing in the brake pedal; this comes from the rapid opening and closing of the valves. Some ABS systems can cycle up to 15 times per second.

Types of Anti-Lock Brakes

Anti-lock braking systems use different schemes depending on the type of brakes in use. We will refer to them by the number of channels—that is, how many valves that are individually controlled—and the number of speed sensors.

- Four-channel, four-sensor ABS—This is the best scheme. There is a speed sensor on all four wheels and a separate valve for all four wheels. With this setup, the controller monitors each wheel individually to make sure it is achieving maximum braking force.
- Three-channel, three-sensor ABS—This scheme, commonly found on pickup trucks with four-wheel ABS, has a speed sensor and a valve for each of the front wheels, with one

valve and one sensor for both rear wheels. The speed sensor for the rear wheels is located in the rear axle.

This system provides individual control of the front wheels, so they can both achieve maximum braking force. The rear wheels, however, are monitored together; they both have to start to lock up before the ABS will activate on the rear. With this system, it is possible that one of the rear wheels will lock during a stop, reducing brake effectiveness.

- One-channel, one-sensor ABS—This system is commonly found on pickup trucks with rear-wheel ABS. It has one valve, which controls both rear wheels, and one speed sensor, located in the rear axle.

This system operates the same as the rear end of a three-channel system. The rear wheels are monitored together and they both have to start to lock up before the ABS kicks in. In this system it is also possible that one of the rear wheels will lock, reducing brake effectiveness.

This system is easy to identify. Usually there will be one brake line going through a T-fitting to both rear wheels. You can locate the speed sensor by looking for an electrical connection near the differential on the rear-axle housing.

NEW WORDS

kinetic	[kai'netik]	a. (运)动的，动力(学)的
reservoir	['rezəvwɑ:]	n. 水库，蓄水池，储油室
caliper	['kælipə]	n. 卡钳，测径器，制动钳
withdraw	[wið'drɔ:]	v. 缩回，收回，退出
phonograph	['fəunəgrɑ:f]	n. 电唱机，留声机
fade	[feid]	v. (声音等)减弱下去，衰减，枯萎，凋谢
inherently	[in'hiərəntli]	ad. 天性地，固有地
lump	[lʌmp]	v. 使成块状，混在一起
lining	['lainiŋ]	n. 衬里，内层，衬套
relax	[ri'læks]	v. 放松，缓和
nerve-wracking	['nə:vˌrækiŋ]	a. (= nerve-racking)极端令人头疼的，非常伤脑筋的
magnetize	['mægnitaiz]	v. 使磁化，吸引
magnetic	[mæg'netik]	a. 磁的，有磁性的，有吸引力的
deceleration	[di:ˌselə'reiʃən]	n. 减速
algorithm	['ælgəriðəm]	n. [数] 运算法则，算法
scheme	[ski:m]	n. 方案，安排，配置，计划
T-fitting	['ti:fitiŋ]	n. T形管接头

PHRASES AND EXPRESSIONS

service braking	行车制动
parking braking	驻车制动

retarder braking	缓速制动
fluid reservoir	储液室
wheel cylinder	轮缸
master cylinder	主缸
drum brake	鼓式制动器
disc brake	盘式制动器
in a hurry	匆忙
inductive sensor	感应式传感器
magnetic field	磁场
integral with	与……成一体
line pressure	管路压力，主油路压力
dash panel	仪表板
instrument panel	仪表板
hydraulic unit	液压单元
hydraulic actuator	液压执行器

NOTES TO THE TEXT

[1] It is during the time the pedal is in the released position that any fluid that has leaked out of the system will be replaced through the compensating ports.

句中"It is...that..."是一个强调句型，强调时间状语。that has leaked out of the system 是定语从句。本句可以译为："正是在制动踏板进入放松位置的过程中，系统泄漏的任何液体都将通过补偿孔得到补充。"

[2] The result is that the tire slows down at the same rate as the car, with the brakes keeping the tires very near the point at which they will start to lock up.

句中有三点值得注意："that the tire slows down..."是表语从句；"with the brakes keeping..."是一个"with + 名词 + 分词"的独立结构；"at which..."是一个修饰 point 的定语从句。因此本句可以译为："结果是车轮与汽车能以同样的减速度减速，这样，制动器就使车轮始终保持在即将抱死的状态。"

EXERCISES

I . Answer the following questions:

1. List the three types of braking systems in use.
2. There are four main components to an ABS system. What are they?
3. Explain what is meant by a"four-channel and four-sensor ABS".
4. What is the function of the ABS pump?

II . Translate the following paragraph into Chinese:

One of the greatest contributions to automotive safety was the advent of anti-lock braking systems. Anti-lock braking systems(ABS)allow maintaining directional control of the vehicle during braking. While benefits from ABS can be derived(得到，起源)on dry pavement(路面)driving, the most substantial benefits are witnessed(目睹,表明)under adverse traction conditions. Braking systems operate on the principle that motion energy is removed from the vehicle in the form of heat and dissipated.

TEXT B Traction Control System(TRAC) and Electronic Stability Control(ESC)

Traction Control System(TRAC)

The purpose of the traction control system(TCS, or TRAC)(Fig. 10-3)is to prevent wheel spin from occurring due to acceleration. The maximum torque that can be transmitted to the wheels is determined by the coefficient of friction generated between the road and the tires. If torque exceeds that level, the wheels are likely to spin. Conditions for TRAC operation may include: loose gravel, slippery road surfaces, acceleration while cornering and hard acceleration.[1]

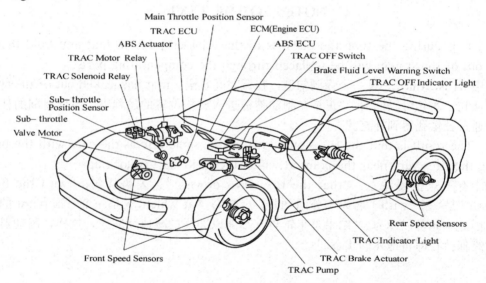

Fig. 10-3 TRAC system components

Once activated, the TRAC system reduces engine torque and rear wheel speed as necessary to bring the vehicle under control. The ABS ECU, TRAC ECU and ECM all work together to provide traction control. ABS speed sensors are monitored by the TRAC ECU which in turn controls a sub-throttle plate and applies the rear brakes. The ECM also retards engine timing while the ABS modulates pressure at the rear brakes.

Components

The TRAC OFF switch is located on the instrument panel above the center console. It allows the driver to activate or deactivate the TRAC system when the switch is depressed. The system defaults to ON when the ignition switch is cycled.

The TRAC OFF indicator light goes on when anyone of the following occurs:
- the TRAC system is deactivated by the TRAC OFF switch;
- a TRAC related problem is detected with the engine;
- an ABS related problem is detected.

The TRAC indicator light indicates when:
- the system is operating;
- a malfunction occurs in the system(it remains illuminated to warn the driver);
- the diagnostic mode is set within the TRAC ECU(the light blinks the trouble code).

Sub-throttle Actuator

The sub-throttle actuator (Fig. 10-4) uses a step motor located between the main throttle valve and air cleaner. It is fitted on the throttle body and controls the position of the sub-throttle valve based on commands made by the TRAC ECU thus controlling the engine output. By controlling the sub-throttle plate, engine management controls engine torque reducing wheel spin.

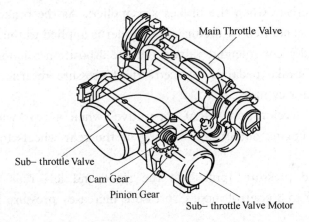

Fig. 10-4　Sub-throttle actuator

Sub-throttle Position Sensor

This sensor is fitted to the sub-throttle valve shaft. It converts the sub-throttle valve opening angle to a voltage signal and sends this signal to the TRAC ECU via the ECM (Engine ECU). The sensor operates in the same way as the main throttle position sensor.

TRAC Pump

The function of the TRAC pump is to generate brake fluid pressure necessary for applying the rear disc brakes when the TRAC system is operating. It draws brake fluid from the master cylinder reservoir, pressurizes and directs it to the TRAC brake actuator.

TRAC Brake Actuator

The TRAC brake actuator consists of two cut solenoid valves and three spring loaded valves which regulate the brake fluid pressure in the right and left rear wheels. The rear wheels are controlled independently through the ABS actuator based on signals from the ABS ECU.

The master cylinder cut solenoid valve opens and closes the hydraulic circuit from the master cylinder or TRAC pump to the ABS actuator. When the TRAC system is operating, it supplies the brake fluid pressure from the TRAC pump to the disc brake cylinders via the ABS actuator. It also prevents the fluid from flowing out of the ABS actuator pump to the master cylinder.

The reservoir cut solenoid valve is located between the return side of the ABS 3-position solenoid and the master cylinder. It returns the fluid from the disc brake cylinders back to the master cylinder reservoir.

The pressure regulator valve controls the brake fluid pressure generated by the TRAC pump.

The relief valve relieves the highest system pressure should a malfunction occur.[2]

The check valve prevents fluid from flowing out of the disc brake cylinder to the TRAC pump.

TRAC Operation

During normal operation(TRAC not activated)all solenoid valves of the TRAC brake actuator remain inactive. when the brakes are applied. As the brake pedal is depressed, brake fluid pressure generated by the master cylinder is applied to the disc brake cylinders, via the master cylinder cut solenoid valve, and the 3-position solenoid valves in the ABS actuator. When the brake pedal is released, fluid pressure returns from the disc brake cylinders to the master cylinder.

During vehicle acceleration (TRAC operative) when a rear wheel slips the TRAC system controls the engine output and braking of the rear wheels to help prevent wheel slippage.

The brake fluid pressure applied to the right and left rear wheels is controlled separately according to 3 control modes: pressure increase, pressure holding and pressure reduction.

Pressure Increase Mode

When a rear wheel starts to slip, just as the accelerator pedal is being depressed:
- All the solenoid valves in the TRAC brake actuator are activated by signals received from the ABS ECU.
- The 3-position solenoid valves in the ABS actuator are engaged in the pressure increase mode(Fig. 10-5).
- The master cylinder cut solenoid valve is activated(ports "A" and "C" open), and brake fluid pressure generated by the TRAC pump is applied to the disc brake cylinders via the master cylinder cut solenoid valve and the 3-position solenoid valves in the ABS actuator.
- The reservoir cut solenoid valve is also activated(open)allowing fluid to flow back to the master cylinder reservoir.
- The TRAC pump discharge pressure is maintained constant by the pressure regulator valve.

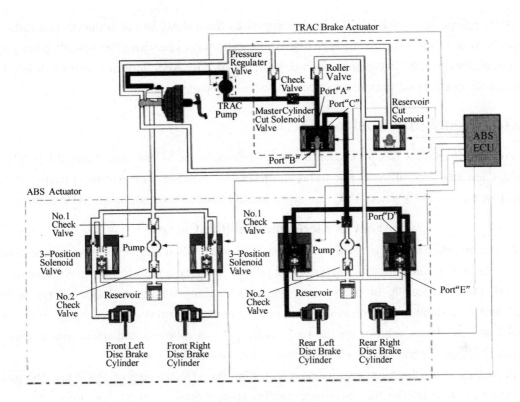

Fig. 10-5 Pressure increase mode

Pressure Holding Mode

When the brake fluid pressure for the rear brake cylinders is increased or decreased as required, the system switches to the holding mode. This mode change is performed by engaging the 3-position solenoid valve in the ABS actuator to the holding mode. This results in blocking the TRAC pump pressure from flowing to the disc brake cylinder through port D.

Pressure Reduction Mode

When decreasing pressure applied to the rear brake cylinders, the ABS ECU engages the 3-position solenoid valve in the ABS actuator to the pressure reduction mode. Fluid pressure applied to the brake cylinder returns to the master cylinder reservoir from the 3-position solenoid valve and reservoir in the ABS actuator to the reservoir cut solenoid valve, thus alleviating the brake fluid pressure.

Wheel Speed Control

The TRAC ECU constantly receives signals from the 4 speed sensors and calculates the speed of each wheel. At the same time, it estimates the vehicle speed based on the speed of the 2 front wheels and sets a target control speed.

When the accelerator pedal is depressed on a slippery road, the rear wheels (driving wheels) begin to slip and the rear wheel speed exceeds the target control speed. The TRAC ECU then sends a close signal to the sub-throttle valve motor.

At the same time, ABS ECU sends a signal to the TRAC brake actuator and causes it to supply brake fluid pressure to rear disc brake cylinders, changing the rear disc brakes in the TRAC mode. The 3-position solenoid valves of the ABS actuator are modulated to control rear brake fluid pressure to prevent wheel slippage.

Electronic Stability Control(ESC)

Automotive safety has taken center stage, especially as SUVs have made the headlines for their tendency to rollover. For today's consumers, however, electronic stability control (ESC) can make a difference. ESC can significantly reduce the risk of an SUV rollover.

What Is Electronic Stability Control?

ESC is an active safety system that uses sensors to detect when a driver is about to lose control of the vehicle and automatically intervenes to provide stability and help the driver stay on the intended course, especially in oversteering and understeering situations. Industry experts have hailed electronic stability control as a milestone in automotive safety, comparing it to seatbelts and airbags. ESC keeps vehicles on the road, helps prevent rollovers and skids, and is thus the easy safety choice for consumers when purchasing a new vehicle.

A number of studies have been conducted testing the effectiveness of ESC, and the global auto safety research verifies that electronic stability control does, in fact, save lives.

Five different studies projected a 30%-35% reduction in single vehicle crashes thanks to ESC.

How ESC Works

It incorporates anti-lock brakes (ABS) and traction control (TCS), which prevent wheel lock when braking and wheel spin when accelerating, and goes a step beyond both systems, acting when lateral forces are at work to further reduce the risk of skidding in all driving situations.

ESC constantly compares the driver's intention with the vehicle's actual behavior by monitoring wheel speeds, steering wheel angle, yaw-rate, lateral acceleration, throttle position and master cylinder pressure.

A central microcomputer analyzes the incoming data. When instability is detected, ESC immediately triggers a response to keep the vehicle on course, automatically braking any of the four wheels and/or adjusting engine torque.

ESC is offered as optional or standard equipment in a wide variety of vehicles from nearly every automaker. It is a safety feature that goes by many names:

- Electronic Stability Program—ESP(Audi, Mercedes, VW)
- Dynamic Stability Control—DSC(BMW, Land Rover, Jaguar)
- StabiliTrak(Buick, Cadillac, Chevrolet, GMC)
- AdvanceTrac(Ford, Lincoln, Mercury)
- Vehicle Dynamics Control—VDC(Subaru, Nissan, Infiniti)

- Vehicle Stability/Skid Control—VSC(Toyota, Lexus)
- Vehicle Stability Assist—VSA(Acura)
- Dynamic Stability Traction Control—DSTC(Volvo)
- Stability Management System(Porsche)
- Active Handling(Chevrolet Corvette)

Despite the proven effectiveness of Electronic Stability Control, only 6% of all vehicles manufactured in the U. S. are equipped with it, compared to more than 30% in Europe.

NEW WORDS

coefficient	[ˌkəuiˈfiʃənt]	n. 系数
gravel	[ˈgrævl]	n. 砂砾,砂砾层
console	[kənˈsəul]	n. 控制台
deactivate	[diːˈæktiveit]	v. 解除,使无效,使不活动
slippage	[ˈslipidʒ]	n. 滑动,滑移
alleviate	[əˈliːvieit]	v. 减轻
headline	[ˈhedlain]	n. 头条新闻
rollover	[ˈrəulˌəuvə]	n. 倾翻
intervene	[ˌintəˈviːn]	v. 干涉,干预,插入,介入
oversteer(ing)	[ˈəuvəstiə(riŋ)]	n. 转向过度
understeer(ing)	[ˈʌndəstiə(riŋ)]	n. 转向不足
hail	[heil]	v.& n. 招呼,欢呼,高呼
yaw-rate	[ˈjɔːˈreit]	n. 横摆速率
default	[diˈfɔːlt]	n.& v. 默认(值)

PHRASES AND EXPRESSIONS

traction control system(TCS)	牵引控制系统(TCS)
sub-throttle plate	副节气门
center console	中央控制台
TRAC brake actuator	TRAC 制动执行器
master cylinder cut solenoid valve	主缸切断电磁阀,主缸隔离电磁阀
pressure regulator valve	调压电磁阀
electronic stability control(ESC)	电子稳定性控制(ESC)
make the headline	成为头条新闻
make a difference	发生影响,起作用,区别对待
active safety system	主动安全系统

NOTES TO THE TEXT

[1] acceleration while cornering and hard acceleration.

转弯时加速和猛烈加速。

[2] The relief valve relieves the highest system pressure should a malfunction occur.

句中的 should a malfunction occur 是一个假设条件从句，省略了 if，将 should 提到从句最前面。本句可以译为："如果发生故障，安全阀会释放掉系统的最高压力。"

EXERCISES

I. Answer the following questions:

1. What is the purpose of a traction control system?
2. What is the purpose of an electronic stability control?
3. List the main parts of a traction control system.
4. List the main parts of electronic stability control.

II. Translate the following phrases into Chinese:

1. traction control system(TCS)
2. electronic stability control(ESC)
3. TRAC brake actuator
4. sub-throttle plate
5. electronic stability program(ESP)

TEXT C   Toyota ABS Diagnosis and Troubleshooting

The ABS ECU has a self-diagnostic system which monitors the input and output circuits. The ABS ECU operates the solenoid valves and the pump motor in sequence in order to check each respective electrical system. This function operates only once each time when the ignition switch is turned ON. On some earlier models it operates when the vehicle is traveling at a speed greater than 4 mph with the stop light (brake light) switch OFF. During this check the operation of the actuator can be heard, however this is normal and does not indicate a malfunction.

Diagnostic Function

When a problem is detected in any of the signal systems, the ECU turns on the ABS warning light in the combination meter to alert the driver that a malfunction has occurred. The code is stored in memory for access at a later time. Diagnostic trouble codes can be read from the Warning light. The ABS ECU will also store the diagnostic trouble codes for any ABS malfunction.

Trouble Code Check

To access the diagnostic trouble codes stored in the ECU, locate the data link connector(DLC1) or (DLC2). Consult the repair manual or the ABS reference card to determine whether the ABS check connector is physically disconnected or the short pin for terminals Wa and Wb is removed.

To access diagnostic codes:
- Disconnect the check connector or remove the short pin in DLC1(Fig. 10-6).
- Jump terminals Tc and E1 of the data link connector(DLC1 or DLC2).
- Turn the ignition switch ON and read the trouble code from the ABS warning light on the combination meter.

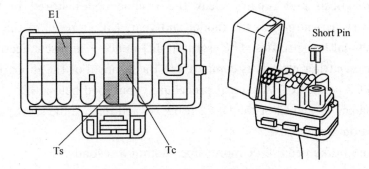

Fig. 10-6 Data link connector(DLC1)

If the computer has not detected a malfunction, the lamp will blink two times per second after a two second pause. When a malfunction has been detected there will be a 4-second pause, then the first digit will begin. The number of times the lamp blinks before a one and a half second pause is the first digit of the code. Next, the number of blinks before the second pause is the second digit of the code. In the example below(Fig. 10-7), the first code is Code 11 and the second code is 21.

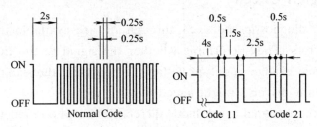

Fig. 10-7 Diagnostic Codes

If there is more than one trouble code, the code with the smallest number will appear first, followed by a pause for 2.5 seconds, then the next code will appear in the same manner as described earlier. Finally, the entire procedure will be repeated after a four second pause.

The trouble code chart in the repair manual identifies each code and reveals the circuit or component which requires further diagnosis. The total number of diagnostic codes may vary between vehicles so it is important to refer to the repair manual for the specific vehicle you are diagnosing.[1]

Circuit Inspection

The repair manual takes the diagnosis several steps further in providing a circuit inspection and inspection procedure for each diagnostic code. It provides a circuit description as well as the parameters under which the code was set for each stored code. A wiring diagram schematic of the electrical circuit is also provided for ready reference.

Diagnostic Trouble Code Clearance

Following diagnosis and repair, clear the trouble codes stored in the ECU. The procedure will vary depending on the model and year. Either refer to the ABS reference card or repair manual for specifics. The essential difference is in disconnecting the actuator check connector on earlier models as compared to the removal of the short pin connector in the DLC1 or DLC2 connector. A typical procedure is outlined below:

- Jump terminals Tc and E1 of the DLC2 or DLC1 and remove the short pin from DLC1.
- Turn ignition switch ON.
- Depress the brake pedal 8 or more times within 3 seconds.
- Check that the warning light shows the normal code.
- Remove the jumper wire and reinstall the short pin.

To ensure that the brake light switch opens and closes each time, allow the brake pedal to return to the full up position each time when clearing codes. If the code does not clear, the ignition switch must be cycled OFF then ON before depressing the brake pedal 8 times in 3 seconds.

Speed Sensor Signal Check

Eight additional diagnostic codes (71 through 78) are available to trouble-shoot the speed sensors and rotors. They determine whether the signal to the ECU is a low output voltage or an abnormal change in output voltage. When using the signal check, make sure that the vehicle is being driven straight ahead.

The ECU is placed in signal check mode differently based on model and year, so again it is important to have the appropriate repair manual available. In some early models, the parking brake in conjunction with the service brake were used to enter this mode.

In most cases, connect terminals Tc and E1 at DLC1 prior to driving the vehicle. To read the code:

- Connect terminals Ts and E1 (Tc and E1 remain connected).
- In earlier models the actuator check connector was disconnected.

ABS Actuator Checker

The actuator operation can be checked using a special service tool called an ABS actuator checker and related sub-harness and overlay sheet where needed. This special service tool can check the operation of the solenoid valves and the pump motor. The actuator is disconnected from the vehicle harness, taking the ECU out of the loop and operated independently by the special service tool.

The ABS actuator checker statically checks the operation of the actuator which includes: the pump, solenoids, and relays. If a normal code is displayed, but symptoms still occur, refer to the problem symptoms chart in the repair manual. The chart indicates when the checker is to be used.

The actuator cannot be disassembled for service. If a malfunction develops with the solenoid valves or pump motor, the entire ABS actuator assembly must be replaced.

Bleeding the ABS hydraulic system does not differ from the bleeding procedure of a conventional brake system except for rear wheel ABS. As fluid is bled, it flows through the solenoids to the wheels. The part of the actuator hydraulic circuit going from the solenoids through the No.1 check valve is sealed to prevent air entry when the ABS is not activated.[2]

If a malfunction occurs in the electrical system to the ECU, current to the actuator from the ECU is turned off. As a result, the brake system operates the same as if the antilock brake system is not operating and normal braking function is assured.

Toyota Diagnostic Tester

Toyota models equipped with a DLC2 connector located under the instrument panel have the capability to read diagnostic codes using the diagnostic tester (Fig. 10-8). In addition, ECU pin voltage values on all ABS ECUs can be read on the tester screen using the vehicle break-out box (Fig. 10-9). The diagnostic tester has a number of components and harnesses which vary, based on the vehicle and ECU being tested. An operator's manual is provided with the tester which describes the test functions and tool set-up. The vehicle break-out box is connected between the vehicle harness and the ECU connectors.

Remember that while diagnosing any electrical system, disconnecting and reconnecting electrical connectors may eliminate a system fault.

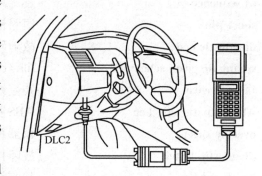

Fig. 10-8 Read diagnostic codes using the diagnostic tester

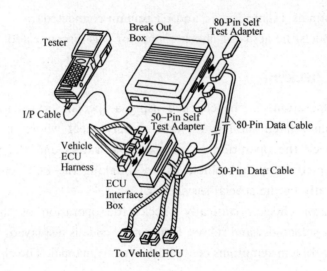

Fig. 10-9 Read ECU pin voltage values on the tester screen using the vehicle break-out box

NEW WORDS

sequence	[ˈsiːkwəns]	n. 次序，顺序，序列
consult	[kənˈsʌlt]	v. 商量，参考，考虑
pause	[pɔːz]	n.& v. 暂停，停顿
reveal	[riˈviːl]	v. 显示，揭示，暴露
clearance	[ˈkliərəns]	n. 清除，间隙，空隙
specific	[spiˈsifik]	n. 细节；a. 特殊的
outline	[ˈautlain]	n. 轮廓，要点，概要；v. 略述

PHRASES AND EXPRESSIONS

in sequence	逐一
short pin	短路销
diagnostic code	故障码
wiring diagram schematic	电路图
jumper wire	跨接线
ABS actuator checker	ABS 执行器检查仪
overlay sheet	仪器覆盖面板
diagnostic tester	故障检测仪
break-out box	检测箱

NOTES TO THE TEXT

[1] The total number of diagnostic codes may vary between vehicles so it is important to refer to the repair manual for the specific vehicle you are diagnosing.

句中 you are diagnosing 是修饰 vehicle 的定语从句。本句可以译为:"故障码的数目因车而异,因此查阅将要诊断的特定车辆的维修手册是很重要的。"

[2] The part of the actuator hydraulic circuit going from the solenoids through the No. 1 check valve is sealed to prevent air entry when the ABS is not activated.

句中"going from...through..."短语是 part 的后置定语。本句可以译为:"ABS 不工作时,执行器液压油路中从电磁阀到 1 号单向阀的油路部分是密闭的,以防进入空气。"

EXERCISES

Ⅰ. Answer the following questions:

1. Describe how to clear the trouble codes stored in the ECU.
2. What is the purpose of an ABS actuator checker?

Ⅱ. Translate the following sentences into Chinese:

1. The ECU is placed in signal check mode differently based on model and year, so again it is important to have the appropriate repair manual available.
2. An operator's manual is provided with the tester which describes the test functions and tool set-up.
3. The ABS actuator checker statically checks the operation of the actuator which includes: the pump, solenoids, and relays.
4. Bleeding the ABS hydraulic system does not differ from the bleeding procedure of a conventional brake system except for rear wheel ABS.

Related Terms

hydraulic control unit(HCU)	液压控制单元
traction assist(TA)	(福特公司的)牵引控制系统
anti-slip regulation(ASR)	防滑控制系统(欧洲对牵引控制系统的称谓)
isolation solenoid valve	(主缸)隔离电磁阀
electronic braking distribution(EBD)	制动力分配电子控制系统

Translation Techniques(10)—— 数字的增减与倍数

1."……数字(或倍数) + 比较级 + than + ……"表示数字或倍数多半是净增减的数（或净增加的倍数或净减到 $\frac{1}{n+1}$）。

2."……倍数 + as + 形容词或副词 + as + ……"表示净增加 $n-1$ 倍数，或减少到 $1/n$（即减少了 $\frac{n-1}{n}$）。

3. "as + 形容词(如 high，many，much 等) + as + 具体数字"表示"高(多)达……(具体数字)"。

例 1：

The trucks feature hydraulic hybrid drivetrain technology claimed to reduce fuel consumption in heavy vehicles by as much as 70%. 这种货车利用液压混合动力技术，从而使重型车辆的燃油消耗下降高达 70%。

4."…… + 动词(或分词)或比较级 + by + 数字或倍数 + ……"句型中，by 后面的数字或倍数为净增减量。

例 2：

This rule permits airbags to be depowered by 20 to 35 percent. 这个法规允许安全气囊的展开力减小 20%~35%。

5."表示增减意义的谓语 + by a factor of + n"表示增加了 $n-1$ 倍或减小 $\frac{n-1}{n}$。

6."表示增减意义的动词或分词 + to + 数字 + ……"表示增加到或减少到某个数字。

例 3：

Moreover, the travel range will be limited to one sixth of the gasoline vehicle even if the tank pressure is increased to as high as 20MPa. 此外，即使将油箱压力提高到 20MPa，运行里程也只能是汽油车辆的六分之一。

7."增减意义的谓语或词组 + 倍数"表示增加了 $n-1$ 倍或减少 $\frac{n-1}{n}$。

例 4：

…if a malfunction is detected by the power-train control module(PCM)that causes the emission levels of the vehicle to exceed one and one half times(50 percent above)the emission standards for the vehicle.

that causes…是该条件从句中 malfunction 的分隔定语从句。该句可以译为："如果动力控制模块(PCM)检测到一个会导致汽车的排放值比该车排放标准值高 0.5 倍的故障时……"

UNIT 11   SUSPENSION AND STEERING SYSTEMS

TEXT A   Basic Parts and Types of the Suspension and Steering Systems

Suspension System

If a vehicle's axles were bolted directly to its frame or body, every rough spot in the road would transmit a jarring force throughout the vehicle. Riding would be uncomfortable, and handling at freeway speeds would be impossible. The fact that the modern vehicle rides and handles well is a direct result of a suspension system.

Even though the tires and wheels must follow the road contour, the body should be influenced as little as possible. [1] The purpose of any suspension system is to allow the body of the vehicle to travel forward with a minimum amount of up-and-down movement. The suspension should also permit the vehicle to make turns without excessive body roll or tire skidding.

Suspension System Components

Vehicle Frame

A vehicle's frame or body must form a rigid structural foundation and provide solid anchorage points for the suspension system. There are two types of vehicle construction in common use today: body-over-frame construction, which uses a separate steel frame to which the body is bolted at various points and unibody construction, in which the body sections serve as structural members. Unibody construction is the most common, but body-over-frame construction is still used on pickup trucks and large cars.

Springs

The springs are the most obvious part of the suspension system. Every vehicle has a spring of some kind between the frame or body and the axles. There are three types of springs in general use today: leaf spring, coil spring, and torsion bar. Two different types of springs can be used on one vehicle. Air springs were once used in place of the other types of springs, but are now obsolete. Many modern vehicles have air-operated suspensions, but they are used to supplement the springs.

Shock Absorbers

When the vehicle is traveling forward on a level surface and the wheels strike a bump, the spring is rapidly compressed(coil springs)or twisted(leaf springs and torsion bars). The spring will attempt to return to its normal loaded length. In so doing, it will rebound, causing the body of the vehicle to be lifted. Since the spring has stored energy, it will rebound past its normal length. The upward movement of the vehicle also assists in rebounding past the spring's normal length.

The weight of the vehicle then pushes the spring down after the spring rebounds. The weight of the vehicle will push the spring down, but since the vehicle is traveling downward, the energy built up by the descending body will push the spring below its normal loaded height. This causes the spring to rebound again. This process, called spring oscillation, gradually diminishes until the vehicle is finally still. Spring oscillation can affect handling and ride quality and must be controlled.

Air Shock Absorbers

Some suspension systems incorporate two adjustable air shock absorbers that are attached to the rear suspension and connected to an air valve with flexible tubing.

Air operated shock absorbers have hydraulic dampening systems which operate in the same manner as those on conventional shocks. In addition, they contain a sealed air chamber, which is acted on by pressure from a height control sensor. Varying the pressure to the air chamber causes the air shock to increase or decrease its length or operating range.

Air pressure is delivered to the air shocks through plastic tubing. The tubing connects the shocks to an air valve. Air pressure for raising the shocks is generally obtained from an outside source, such as a service station compressor, and is admitted through the air valve. To deplete the shocks of unwanted air(lower vehicle curb height), the air valve core is depressed, allowing air to escape.

Control Arms

All vehicles have either control arms or struts to keep the wheel assembly in the proper position. The control arms and struts allow the wheel to move up and down while preventing it from moving in any other direction. The wheel will tend to move in undesirable directions whenever the vehicle is accelerated, braked, or turned. Vehicle suspensions may have control arms only or a combination of control arms and struts.

Types of the Suspension

Front Suspension Systems

Almost all modern front suspension systems are independent. With an independent suspension, each front wheel is free to move up and down with a minimum effect on the other wheel. In an independent suspension system, there is also far less twisting motion imposed on the frame than in a system with a solid axle. Nevertheless, a few off-road, four wheel drive vehicles and large trucks continue to use a solid axle front suspension. The two major types of independent front suspension are the conventional front suspension and the MacPherson strut front suspension.

Conventional Front Suspension

In the conventional front suspension system, one or two control arms are used at each wheel. In most systems, the coil springs are mounted between the vehicle's frame and the lower control arm. In older systems, coil springs are mounted between the upper control arm and vehicle body. In a torsion bar front suspension system, the lower arm moves upward, it twists the torsion bar.

Coil Spring Front Suspension

Fig. 11-1 shows a typical independent front suspension that uses rubber bushing control arm pivots. The top of the coil spring rests in a cup-like spot against the frame(unshown). The bottom of the coil spring is supported by a pad on the lower control arm. The top of each shock absorber is fastened to the frame; the bottom is attached to the lower control arm.

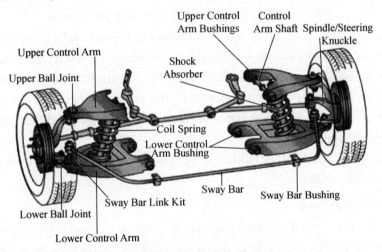

Fig. 11-1 A typical independent front suspension

When the wheel strikes a bump, it is driven upward. This causes arms to pivot upward, compressing the spring and shock. Rubber bumpers limit control arm travel and soften the blow when the limit is reached. For steering, the front wheel steering knuckle pivots on ball joints.

Torsion Bar Front Suspension

A torsion bar is located on each side of the frame in the front of the vehicle. The lower control arm is attached to the free end of the torsion bar. When the wheel is driven upward, the lower control arm moves upward, twisting the long spring steel bar.

MacPherson Strut Front Suspension

Most modern vehicles, especially those with front-wheel drive, use the MacPherson strut front suspension systems(Fig. 11-2). Note that the MacPherson strut contains a coil spring, which is mounted on top of the heavy strut-and-pedestal assembly. Rubber pads at the top and bottom of the coil spring reduce squeaks. The entire MacPherson strut assembly is attached to the steering knuckle at the lower part of the pedestal. The bottom of the MacPherson strut assembly is attached to the single control arm through a ball joint.

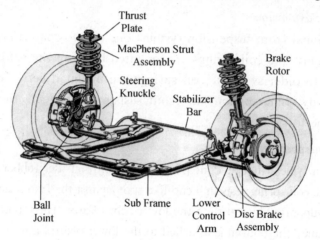

Fig. 11-2 A MacPherson strut front suspension system

The entire strut assembly turns when the wheel is turned. A bearing or thrust plate at the top of the strut assembly allows relative movement between the assembly and the vehicle body. The ball joint allows the strut assembly to turn in relation to the control arm. The strut contains a damper, which operates in the same manner as a conventional shock absorber. Most damper assemblies have a protective cover that keeps dirt and water away from the damper piston rod.

The advantage of the MacPherson strut is its compact design, which allows more room for service on small car bodies.

Solid Axle Front Suspension

The use of the solid axle front suspension(or dependent suspension)is generally confined to trucks and off-road vehicles. This system uses a solid steel dead axle(does not turn with wheels) with a leaf spring at each side. Pivot arrangements between the axle and the wheel spindles allow the wheels to swivel on each end. Any up or down movement of either front wheel causes a vertical tipping effect of both wheels because they share a common axle.

Rear Suspension Systems

Rear suspensions on vehicles with a solid rear axle housing generally utilize coil springs or leaf springs. When the vehicle has an independent rear suspension system, coil springs, MacPherson struts, a single transverse leaf spring, or even torsion bars can be used.

Steering System

The steering system is designed to allow the driver to move the front wheels to the right or left with a minimum of effort and without excessive movement of the steering wheel. Although the driver can move the wheels easily, road shocks are not transmitted to the driver. This absence of road shock transfer is referred to as the nonreversible feature of steering systems.

The basic steering system can be divided into three main assemblies:
- The spindle and steering arm assemblies.
- The linkage assembly connecting the steering arms and steering gear.
- The steering wheel, steering shaft, and steering gear assembly.

Steering Gear

The steering gear is designed to multiply the driver's turning torque so the front wheels may be turned easily. When the parallelogram linkage is used, the torque developed by the driver is multiplied through gears and is then transmitted to the wheel spindle assemblies through the linkage. On the rack-and-pinion steering system, the steering shaft is connected directly to the pinion shaft. Turning the pinion moves the rack section, which moves the linkage. Late-model vehicles use either manual steering gears or power steering gears.

There are three types of the steering gears in use: recirculating ball steering gear, worm-and-roller steering gear and rack-and-pinion steering gear.

Power Steering

Power steering is designed to reduce the effort needed to turn the steering wheel by utilizing hydraulic pressure to bolster (strengthen) the normal torque developed by the steering gear. Power steering systems should ease steering wheel manipulation and, at the same time, offer enough resistance so that the driver can retain some road feel. Power steering is used with both conventional and rack-and-pinion systems (Fig. 11-3).

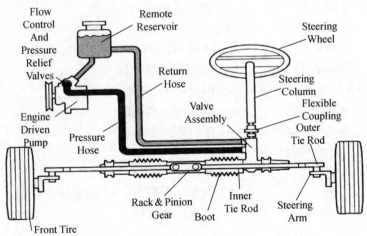

Fig. 11-3 Overall view of a power rack-and-pinion steering assembly

The self-contained steering gear contains the control valve mechanism, the power piston, and the gears. Pressure developed by the unit is applied to the pitman shaft.

The power rack-and-pinion steering system also uses a rotary control valve that directs the hydraulic fluid from the pump to either side of the rack piston. An overall view of this setup is shown in Fig. 11-3. Steering wheel motion is transferred to the pinion. From there, it is sent through the pinion teeth, which are in mesh with the rack teeth. The integral rack piston, which is connected to the rack, changes hydraulic pressure to a linear force(back and forth movement in a straight line). This, in turn, moves the rack in a right or left direction. The force is transmitted by the inner and outer tie rods to the steering knuckles, which, in turn, move the wheels.

NEW WORDS

jarring	['dʒɑ:riŋ]	a. 刺耳的不和谐的； n. 振动、抖动
contour	['kɔntuə]	n. 轮廓，等高线
anchorage	['æŋkəridʒ]	n. 停泊地，抛锚地，固定(支座)
unibody	['ju:ni'bɔdi]	n. 整体式车身
obsolete	['ɔbsəli:t]	a. 荒废的，陈旧的
bump	[bʌmp]	n. 凸起，(曲线)拐点，肿块，撞击
rebound	[ri'baund]	n.& v. 回弹
descend	[di'send]	v. 下来，下降
oscillation	[ˌɔsi'leiʃən]	n. 摆动，振动，振荡
deplete	[di'pli:t]	v. 耗尽，减少，放空
strut	[strʌt]	n. 滑柱，支柱
impose	[im'pəuz]	v. 强加，征税
nevertheless	[ˌnevəðə'les]	ad. 仍然，不过
rest	[rest]	n. 静止，支持物，其余，其他； v. 搁在，保持(状态)
soften	['sɔ(:)fn]	v. (使)变柔软，(使)变柔和
knuckle	['nʌkl]	n. 关节，转向节
pedestal	['pedistl]	n. 底座，基础
squeak	[skwi:k]	n. 尖叫声，吱吱声； v. 发出尖叫声
damper	['dæmpə]	n. 减振器，缓冲器
confine	[kən'fain]	v. 限制； n. 界限，边界
transverse	['trænzvə:s]	a. 横向的，横断的
parallelogram	[ˌpærə'leləgræm]	n. 平行四边形
late-model	['leit'mɔdəl]	a. 新型的
bolster	['bəulstə]	v. 支持，加强； n. 垫子
ease	[i:z]	n. 安逸，不费力； v. 使悠闲，减轻
pitman	['pitmən]	n. 矿工； 连接杆

PHRASES AND EXPRESSIONS

make turns	偏转
steel frame	钢梁车架

leaf spring	叶片弹簧
coil spring	螺旋弹簧
torsion bar	扭杆弹簧
air spring	空气弹簧
ride quality	乘坐平顺性
shock absorber	减振器
curb height	全装备高度
control arm	悬架摆臂
solid axle	整体式车桥
conventional front suspension	传统式前悬架
MacPherson strut front suspension	麦弗逊滑柱式前悬架
rubber bumper	橡胶缓冲垫
steering knuckle	转向节
dependent suspension	非独立悬架
dead axle	从动桥，非驱动桥
steering wheel	转向盘
steering gear	转向器
parallelogram linkage	平行四杆机构
rack-and-pinion steering system	齿轮齿条式转向系统
steering shaft	转向轴
manual steering	人力转向
power steering	动力转向
pitman arm	转向摇臂

NOTES TO THE TEXT

[1] Even though the tires and wheels must follow the road contour, the body should be influenced as little as possible.

句中 follow the road contour 可以翻译成"随着道路的凹凸不平而上下跳动"。全句可译为："尽管轮胎和车轮必须随着道路的凹凸不平而上下跳动，但是车身受到的影响应尽可能小。"

EXERCISES

I. Answer the following questions:

1. What is the purpose of any suspension system?
2. List the main components of a suspension system?
3. What are the two major types of independent front suspensions?
4. What is the advantage of the MacPherson strut?
5. The basic steering system can be divided into three main assemblies. What are they?
6. What are the three types of the steering gears in use?

II. Translate the following sentences into Chinese:

1. The two major types of independent front suspension are the conventional front suspension and the MacPherson strut front suspension.

2. The MacPherson strut contains a coil spring, which is mounted on top of the heavy strut-and-pedestal assembly.

3. The advantage of the MacPherson strut is its compact design, which allows more room for service on small car bodies.

4. When the vehicle has an independent rear suspension system, coil springs, MacPherson struts, a single transverse leaf spring, or even torsion bars can be used.

5. On the rack-and-pinion steering system, the steering shaft is connected directly to the pinion shaft.

6. Power steering systems should ease steering wheel manipulation and, at the same time, offer enough resistance so that the driver can retain some road feel.

TEXT B Advanced Suspension Systems

Automatic Leveling Suspension

Automatic leveling suspension system consists of an air compressor, a compressor relay, an air dryer, an exhaust solenoid, a control module, a height sensor, a pair of air adjustable rear shock absorbers and the air lines and fittings connecting the compressor to the shocks.

The adjustable air shocks used with this system are essentially conventional shock absorbers enclosed in air chambers. A rubber sleeve is attached to the dust tube and to the shock reservoir, creating a flexible chamber which can extend the shocks when air pressure is increased. When air pressure is reduced, the weight of the vehicle collapses the shocks.

As the vehicle is loaded, its weight increases, which lowers the vehicle and causes the height sensor's actuating arm to rotate up. This generates two sensor signals to the control module. After a continuous height sensor signal of 7 to 13 seconds, the control module activates the compressor through a relay. The compressor motor runs and air is sent through the system. As the shock absorbers inflate, the vehicle body moves up toward its former height and the height sensor actuating arm rotates down until the preset trim height is reached. When the body reaches the prescribed height, the control module stops the compressor.

As the vehicle is unloaded, its weight decreases, which raises the vehicle and rotates the height sensor actuating arm down. Again, this generates two sensor signals to the control module. 7 to 13 seconds later, the module activates the vent solenoid. As the body comes down, the height sensor actuating arm rotates up again until the preset trim height is reached. When the sensor arm reaches its original height above the ground, the module turns off the vent solenoid, preventing air from escaping.

Computer-Controlled Air Suspension

Some luxury passenger cars(such as Lincoln Town Car)are equipped with a computer-controlled suspension system that automatically provides height control and soft spring rates to improve ride quality. This system automatically levels the rear of the vehicle and maintains the optimal vehicle attitude whether the vehicle is empty or fully loaded. The automatic air suspension system includes the following components: a compressor/air dryer assembly, a compressor relay, a pair of front air struts with integral height sensors, a pair of rear air springs(Fig. 11-4), a pair of rear shocks, a control module, the air lines, a compressor, a rear height sensor(in the right rear shock absorber), a wiring harness assembly and a compressor cover.

The rear air springs, a pair of cylindrical inflatable bladders, are mounted in the same location as conventional coil springs(they even use the same upper and lower spring seats). Their main advantage over coil springs is that they allow a reduction in spring rate to soften vehicle ride quality.

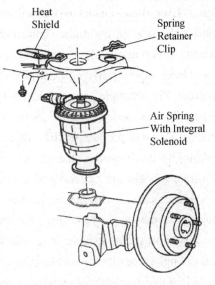

Fig. 11-4 Air spring

A pair of solenoid valves control air flow in and out of the air springs. Vehicle height is monitored and controlled by an electronic control module. A linear height sensor is located in front of the axle. The upper end of the sensor is attached to the frame cross member and the lower end is attached to the left upper suspension arm. If vehicle height is too low(i. e. the vehicle is loaded down), the sensor gets shorter; when the ride height goes up(vehicle is unloaded), the sensor gets longer. Magnets in the lower sliding part of the sensor move up and down in relation to the sensor housing, generating a signal that is sent to the control module through two small Hall effect switches attached to the housing. The movement of these magnets determines whether the air suspension switch is open or closed. At trim(ride) height, the switches are both closed and the control module receives a"trim"signal. If the magnets move up, they open one switch to indicate a"high" condition; if the magnets move down, they open another switch to indicate a "low" condition. When the control module receives a low signal, it energizes the solenoids and activates the compressor, which pumps up the air springs until the correct vehicle height is restored; if the control module receives a high signal(vehicle is emptied), the control module activates the solenoids, which vent air from the air springs until vehicle height is correct again.

Computerized Ride Control Systems

Computerized ride control systems, also called active suspensions, are computer-controlled electronic suspension systems that can adapt to specific driving conditions.

Typical ride control systems contain steering sensors, which monitor the direction and speed of steering wheel rotation; brake sensors, which monitor brake system applications; and an acceleration signal sensor, which monitors the rate of acceleration.[1] A control module receives signals from these sensors and uses them to determine output signals to the actuators. The actuators control the flow of hydraulic fluid to adjustable shock absorbers. Many systems have a mode select switch, which allows the driver to adjust the ride control system.

Under normal driving conditions, a driver can pick the ride best suited for handling and comfort. For example, if a vehicle is being driven on a winding road, the driver can pick a firm setting. In this mode, the ride control module will signal actuators to close valves on the adjustable shocks. This will produce a stiff ride and the vehicle will corner well. If the vehicle is being driven on a highway, however, the driver can switch to a soft mode. In this mode, the valves in the adjustable shocks are opened and a soft, comfortable ride is produced.

Under certain driving conditions, the control module can override the driver's selection. During periods of hard braking, for example, a brake sensor signals the control module to close the valves on the adjustable front shocks or struts. This stiffens front shocks and minimizes front-end diving. Under heavy acceleration, the acceleration sensor signals the control module to stiffen the adjustable rear shocks or strut, preventing rear-end squatting.

NEW WORDS

dryer	[draiə]	n. 干燥剂[器]
collapse	[kə'læps]	n. 倒塌, 崩溃, 失败, 压平, 减弱
prescribe	[pris'kraib]	v. 规定, 指示
bladder	['blædə]	n. 球胆, 软外壳, 气泡
stiffen	['stifn]	v. 使变硬, 使黏稠
dive	[daiv]	v. & n. 潜水, 俯冲
squat	[skwɔt]	v. & n. 蹲坐, 蹲伏

PHRASES AND EXPRESSIONS

automatic leveling suspension	自动调平系统
exhaust solenoid	排气电磁阀
height sensor	高度传感器
trim height	车身调平高度
vent solenoid	排气电磁阀

frame cross member	车架横梁
computerized ride control system	计算机控制悬架系统
active suspension	主动悬架
mode select switch	模式选择开关

NOTES TO THE TEXT

[1] Typical ride control systems contain steering sensors, which monitor the direction and speed of steering wheel rotation; brake sensors, which monitor brake system applications; and an acceleration signal sensor, which monitors the rate of acceleration.

本句中有三个并列宾语：steering sensors，brake sensors，an acceleration signal sensor；翻译时宜采用分译法，即将三个宾语先译出，然后再分别译出各个宾语的定语从句。本句可以译为："典型的乘坐控制系统含有转向传感器、制动传感器和加速信号传感器。转向传感器的作用是检测转向盘的转动方向和转动速度，制动传感器的作用是检测驾驶员是否应用制动系统，加速信号传感器的作用是检测加速度的大小。"

EXERCISES

I. Answer the following questions:

1. List the main parts of an automatic leveling suspension system.
2. List the main parts of a computer-controlled air suspension.
3. List the main parts of a typical ride control system.
4. What is meant by an "active suspension"?

II. Translate the following terms into English:

1. 空气压缩机
2. 空气干燥器
3. 空气弹簧
4. 主动悬架
5. 计算机控制空气悬架
6. 线性高度传感器
7. 可调式空气减振器
8. 控制模块

TEXT C Wheel Alignment

Wheel alignment is the process of measuring and correcting the various angles formed by the front and rear wheels, spindles, and steering arms. Correct alignment is vital. Improper alignment can cause hard steering, pulling to one side, wandering, noise, and rapid tire wear.

Types of Wheel Alignment

Rear-wheel drive vehicles require a two-wheel alignment or front-wheel alignment only. The rear wheels are attached to a solid rear axle assembly which cannot be adjusted, and generally stays in alignment throughout the life of the vehicle.

Today, most front-wheel drive vehicles have provisions for adjusting the rear wheels. In addition, many rear-wheel drive vehicles are equipped with independent rear suspensions, which also must be adjusted. Also, modern solid rear axles and suspension systems are lightweight and can become misaligned. Therefore, the four-wheel alignment, in which the front and rear wheel alignment angles are checked and adjusted, is commonly performed.

Adjustable front wheel settings on most modern vehicles are caster, camber, and toe. Nonadjustable settings are steering axis inclination and toe-out on turns. Rear wheel settings that can be made on many modern vehicles are camber and toe. Modern practice is to check both front and rear wheel alignment. Note that the various alignment angles are all related. A change in one can alter the others.

Alignment Measurement Values

All alignment values, except for toe, are measured in degrees. Toe is measured in fractions of an inch or millimeters.

Caster

Positive caster tends to force the wheels to travel in a straight ahead position. It also assists in recovery(wheels turning back to straight ahead position)after making a turn.

On late model cars, there is often little or no positive caster. Positive caster makes it more difficult to turn the wheels from the straight ahead position than when no caster angle is present.[1]

Another aspect of positive caster is a mild tipping effect when cornering. When making a right turn, the right wheel will cause the steering knuckle to raise slightly, while the left wheel will allow the knuckle to lower, creating the tipping effect. If the left side of the vehicle was allowed to rise during a right turn, it would have an adverse effect on the vehicle's cornering ability.

To ease turning, many cars employ a negative caster angle, which angles the top of the steering knuckle to front of car. This will ease steering while also causing the mild tipping effect needed when cornering.

Camber

Camber is the tilting of the wheel centerline, viewed from the front of the vehicle, away from a true vertical line. Camber angles are usually small, usually no more than 1° positive or negative from zero. An incorrect camber setting will cause pulling and tire wear.

Steering Axis Inclination

The steering knuckle ball joints are closer together at the top than the bottom. The steering axis(view from the front of the car)places the centerline of the steering ball joints closer to the centerline of the wheel. This angle is known as steering axis inclination, or SAI.

When the wheel centerline is to the outside of the center line of the steering axis(where they intersect the road), the wheels tend to toe-out. This is caused by the road-tire resistance pushing back on the spindle, causing it to swivel backward on the ball joints or toe-out. When the centerline of the wheel intersects the road at a point inside of the steering axis centerline intersection, the wheels tend to toe-in(tires are closer together in the front than in the back).

Toe

Toe is the relative positions of the front and rear of a tire in relation to the other tire on the axle. Note that distance at the back of the tires is greater than distance in the front. Rear-wheel drive vehicles are toed in to compensate for the natural tendency of the road-to-tire friction to force the wheels apart.

On some front-wheel drive vehicles, the front tires are toed out. This is done to offset the force created by the drive axles, which tend to pull the tires inward during operation. The toe setting compensates for this and allows the front tires to run parallel to one another while rolling straight down the road.

Toe compensates for the wheel movement tendencies plus any wear or play in the steering linkage. Proper toe will allow the tires to move forward without a scrubbing, scraping action between the tire and road. Excessive toe conditions will cause a rapid tire wear condition called feathering. Toe can also be adjusted on most vehicles to set the steering wheel in the centered position when driving straight ahead.

Toe-Out on Turns

When a car turns a corner, the inner wheel must turn in a shorter radius(smaller circle)than the outer wheel. To allow the inner wheel to cut more sharply, both wheels must be able to toe-out on turns automatically. This essential action is accomplished by bending both steering arms so that they angle slightly toward the center of the vehicle.

Thrust Angle

Aligning all four wheels makes it possible to set the thrust angle to ensure perfect wheel tracking. The thrust angle is an imaginary line at a right angle(90°)to the rear axle. Ideally, the thrust angle should be parallel with the vehicle's centerline. The vehicle should follow this line with no deviation when driving straight ahead. This is known as wheel tracking. If the rear wheels are not tracking correctly, the vehicle will not travel in a straight line unless the front wheels are turned to compensate for the misalignment. This misalignment is often referred to as dog tracking.

Tracking is set by aligning the vehicle's thrust angle with its geometric centerline to obtain perfect tracking. However, factory tolerances, accident damage, and normal wear make perfect tracking rare. Perfect thrust angle alignment is also more difficult on vehicles with front-wheel drive, four-wheel drive, and four-wheel steering. The thrust angle should be aligned as close as possible to the vehicle's geometric centerline. This will reduce tire wear, increase fuel economy, and improve handling.

Front Wheel Alignment Adjustments

On some vehicles, caster is adjusted by moving the lower strut rod in or out(Fig. 11-5). The rod has a threaded section and locknuts to make adjustment easier. Fig. 11-6 illustrates how caster is adjusted on some vehicles with MacPherson strut suspensions by loosening the nuts holding the top of the strut tower and sliding the tower forward or backward. The strut tower mounting holes may be cut or filed out to allow enough movement.

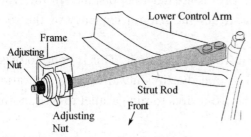

Fig. 11-5 Adjusting caster by moving the lower strut rod in and out by turning adjusting nuts

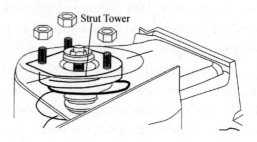

Fig. 11-6 Adjusting front caster by moving the strut tower

Fig. 11-7 shows one common way of changing the camber and caster by loosening the nuts holding the top of the strut tower and sliding the tower in or out. In this design, the rivets holding the top of the strut tower to the body are drilled out or chiseled off and the tower moved to the desired position. Another method uses an egg-shaped washer, sometimes called an eccentric, or eccentric cam, attached to the lower control arm(Fig. 11-8).

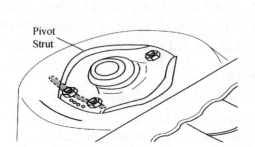

Fig. 11-7 Sliding strut tower in or out to change camber

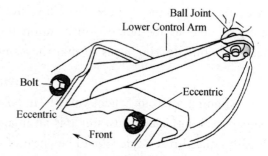

Fig. 11-8 Adjusting camber and/or caster can be adjusted by rotating the eccentrics on the lower control arm

In Fig. 11-9, the camber is adjusted by moving an eccentric located on the top or bottom bolt holding the strut assembly to the spindle. On other designs, camber is adjusted by loosening the strut bolts and pushing or pulling the wheel into position. The strut bolts are then retightened. The strut rod mounting slots may require filing or cutting to allow enough movement to reach the desired camber angle.

On many vehicles, adjusting caster will affect camber and vice versa. For this reason, caster and camber are usually adjusted and checked together. Front toe is set by adjusting the tie rods.

Rear Wheel Alignment Adjustments

Since the rear wheels on most vehicles do not affect steering, the most common effects of improper settings are tire wear and noise. However, if the rear toe is off, it may be difficult to center the steering wheel for straight ahead driving. Note that there is no adjustment for caster on the rear wheels, since this is an alignment angle that affects steering, and is not needed on the rear.

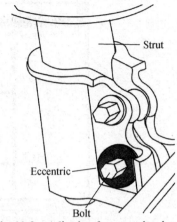

Fig. 11-9 Adjusting front camber by loosing and turning the eccentric

Alignment Equipment

Wheel alignment equipment varies greatly, from simple mechanical gauges to complex electronic devices. Simple camber and caster checking devices, held by magnets to the wheel hub, will allow fairly accurate checking. Toe can be checked by using a trammel bar, or even a tape measure. However, to do an accurate four-wheel alignment on a modern vehicle, more elaborate equipment is needed.

The alignment machine itself should be able to accurately measure all of the alignment angles. Modern alignment machines must be capable of measuring the rear-wheel alignment as well as front-wheel alignment. This necessitates the use of rear wheel sensing devices. The wheel mounted sensing devices used on modern alignment machines are usually referred to as alignment heads.

Many alignment machines use wheel-mounted light beam generators to measure the alignment angles. The latest alignment machines use wheel mounted electronic sensors and

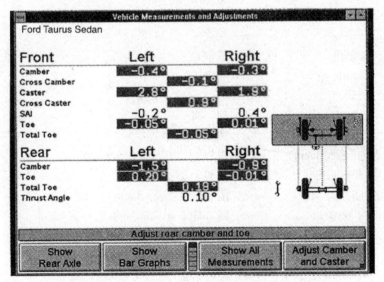

Fig. 11-10 A computer wheel alignment display screen

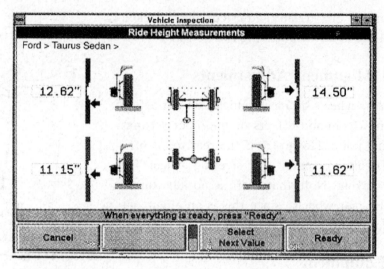

Fig. 11-10　A computer wheel alignment display screen(continued)

a self-contained computer to provide readouts on a screen(Fig. 11-10). There are many manufacturers of alignment equipment. When checking and adjusting wheel alignment, use quality equipment that is in good condition. Wheel alignment is a precision operation; both equipment and techniques must be perfect.

NEW WORDS

wandering	['wɔndəriŋ]	n. 漫游，神志恍惚，离题
provision	[prə'viʃən]	n. 预备，防备，设备，装置
misalign	['misəlain]	v. 不重合，未对准，失准
setting	['setiŋ]	n. 调整位置，设定值，安置，安装
caster	['kɑ:stə]	n. 主销后倾（角）
camber	['kæmbə]	n. 车轮外倾
toe	['təu]	n. 前束
toe-out	['təuaut]	n. 负前束
toe-in	['təuin]	n. 前束
offset	['ɔ:fset]	n.& v. 偏移，抵销
scraping	['skreipiŋ]	n. 刮，擦
scrubbing	['skrʌbiŋ]	n. 洗擦，擦净
imaginary	[i'mædʒinəri]	a. 假想的，想象的，虚构的
deviation	[ˌdi:vi'eiʃən]	n. 背离，偏离
chisel	['tʃizl]	n. 凿子；v. 凿，雕
eccentric	[ik'sentrik]	n. 偏心轮；a. 偏心的
trammel	['træməl]	n. 束缚物，量规
elaborate	[i'læbərət]	a. 精心制作的，完善的，复杂的
necessitate	[ni'sesiteit]	v. 成为必要

PHRASES AND EXPRESSIONS

wheel alignment	车轮定位
steering axis inclination	转向轴线内倾角
toe-out on turns	转弯负前束
tipping effect	侧倾效应
thrust angle	推力角，推力线
wheel tracking	（前轮与后轮）同辙行驶
dog tracking	蛇形行驶
eccentric cam	偏心凸轮
trammel bar	游标前束测量规
alignment machine	车轮定位仪
tape measure	卷[皮]尺
tie rod	横拉杆

NOTES TO THE TEXT

[1] Positive caster makes it more difficult to turn the wheels from the straight ahead position than when no caster angle is present.

句中 it 是形式宾语，实际宾语为 to turn... 短语。本句可以译为："与无主销后倾角相比，采用正的主销后倾角会使车轮转离直线朝前位置更加费力。"

EXERCISES

Ⅰ. Answer the following questions:
   1. What is wheel alignment?
   2. What can improper alignment cause?
   3. What are adjustable front wheel settings on most modern vehicle?
   4. Describe how to adjust caster and camber.

Ⅱ. Translate the following terms into Chinese:
   1. front-wheel alignment
   2. caster
   3. camber
   4. steering axis inclination
   5. toe-in
   6. toe-out

7. toe-out on turns
8. thrust angle
9. egg-shaped washer
10. alignment machine

Related Terms

sprung weight	簧上质量
unsprung weight	簧下质量
stabilizer bar	横向稳定杆
steering arm	转向节臂
relay rod	中间拉杆
wheel rotation	车轮换位
radial tire	子午线轮胎
tie bar	横拉杆
track rod	横拉杆
drag link	直拉杆

Translation Techniques(11)——被动语态的翻译

在科技英语中，被动句应用广泛，约占三分之一，这是科技英语的一个重要特征。而在汉语中多用主动句，因此，在翻译英语汽车文献时，更多地采用将英语被动句翻译成汉语主动句的方法，或者翻译成汉语的特殊结构来回避人们不太习惯的"被"字，个别时候才译成汉语的被动句。

1. 译成汉语的主动句

例1：

Air springs were once used in place of the other types of springs, but are now obsolete.

空气弹簧一度用来代替其他种类的弹簧，但是现在已经时过境迁了。（原文的主语在译文中仍作主语）

例2：

In the conventional front suspension system, one or two control arms are used at each wheel.

在传统式前悬架上，每个车轮使用一个或者两个悬架摆臂。（原文的主语在译文中转译为宾语）

例3：

When the vehicle has an independent rear suspension system, coil springs, MacPherson struts, a single transverse leaf spring, or even torsion bars can be used.

当汽车装有独立后悬架系统时，可以使用螺旋弹簧、麦弗逊滑柱，甚至采用单个横置钢板弹簧。（译成无主语的主动句）

例 4：

Power steering is designed to reduce the effort needed to turn the steering wheel by utilizing hydraulic pressure to bolster (strengthen) the normal torque developed by the steering gear.

动力转向的设计目的是利用液压力来放大由转向器产生的正常力矩，来减小转动转向盘所需的作用力。（被动句的主语转译成定语，谓语转译成主语）

2. 译成汉语的被动句

例 5：

This angle is known as steering axis inclination, or SAI.

这个角被称为转向轴线内倾角（或缩写为 SAI）。

3. 译成汉语的特殊结构

使汉译句中含有"把""使""由""予以""受到"等字或词。

例 6：

Front toe is set by adjusting the tie rods.

前轮前束通过调节横拉杆而得到调整。

UNIT 12 BODY ELECTRICAL SYSTEMS

TEXT A Supplemental Restraint System

System Operation

The supplemental restraint system(SRS)is designed to work in concert with the seat belts to further prevent personal injury during a head-on collision with another object. The SRS utilizes an airbag module, front impact sensors, a clock spring, and a diagnostic module.

With the battery cables connected, the SRS system is energized and monitoring the forward impact sensors and the safing sensor for collision confirmation messages. When the vehicle strikes, or is struck by, another object (such as a tree, wall, another vehicle, etc.), the forward impact sensors and safing sensor send impulses to the diagnostic module, which determines the force and direction of the impact. Based on this information the diagnostic module either deploys or does not deploy the airbag. Inflation happens when there is a collision force equal to running into a brick wall at 10 to 15 miles per hour(16 to 24 km per hour). The airbag's inflation system reacts sodium azide(NaN_3) with potassium nitrate(KNO_3) to produce nitrogen gas(Fig. 12-1). Hot blasts of the nitrogen inflate the airbag.

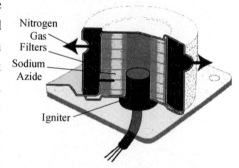

Fig. 12-1 The airbag inflator uses a solid propellant and an igniter

System Components

Control Module

The airbag control module or SRS ECU is one of the most visible parts of the system. It contains the airbag safing sensor and energy reserve capacitor. The module is mounted on the tunnel floor pan forward of the center console. Some safing sensor is located inside the control module. The safing sensor provides confirmation of a crash, but does not determine the severity.

The control module monitors the system to determine the system readiness. The control module will store a sufficient energy to deploy the airbags for only two minutes after the battery has been disconnected. The control module contains on-board diagnostics, and will illuminate the AIR BAG warning lamp on the dash when a fault has occurred. The warning equipment is tested for a few seconds every time the vehicle is started.

Front Impact Sensors

By function, there are 2 types of front impact sensors, forward impact sensors and safing sensors.

The forward sensors are located in various locations forward of the passenger compartment. Some are located inside the fenders, some are on the cowl, some are attached to the support in front of the radiator.

Rear sensors are also known as safing sensors as their function is to determine that a crash has occurred. Rear safing sensors are located in various locations in the passenger compartment depending on the manufacturer. Some are integrated with the control/diagnostic module.

The rear safing sensor must close before the forward sensors to avoid airbag deployment in cases where the impact is not severe enough to cause deployment.[1] When the vehicle is parked with the ignition off deployment is very unlikely because there is no power to the circuits for deployment.

The two front impact sensors provide verification of the direction and severity of the impact. The impact sensors are threshold sensitive switches that complete an electrical circuit when an impact provides a sufficient inertia force to close the switch(Fig. 12-2). The sensors are calibrated for the specific vehicle and react to the severity and direction of the impact.

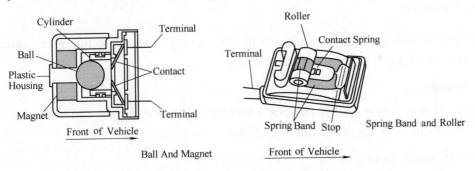

Fig. 12-2 Two types of impact sensors

Clock Spring

The clock spring is mounted on the steering column behind the steering wheel and is used to maintain a continuous electrical circuit between the wiring harness and the driver's airbag module. This assembly consists of a flat ribbon-like electrically conductive tape which winds and unwinds with the steering wheel rotation.[2]

Air Bag Module

The driver's airbag module is located on the steering wheel and is the most visible part of the system. It contains the airbag cushion and its supporting components. The module contains a housing to which the cushion and inflator are attached and sealed.

The driver side inflator assembly is mounted from the back of the module housing. When supplied with the proper electrical signal the inflator assembly will produce a gas and discharge it directly into the cushion. A protective cover is fitted to the front of the driver's air bag module and forms a decorative cover in the center of the steering wheel. The driver's airbag module is mounted directly to the steering wheel.

The passenger's airbag module is located beneath the decorative cover of the instrument panel, facing the passenger seat. The passenger inflator is within the module housing. The module is mounted to the upper and lower instrument panel. A protective cover is fitted into the instrument panel over the way passenger's airbag module. This cover will pivot out of the way and allow the cushion to fully inflate.

Airbag Deactivation

In response to concerns about children—and others, especially smaller people—being killed or seriously injured by malfunctioning or overly powerful airbags, the National Highway Traffic Safety Administration (NHTSA) in 1997 issued a final rule to allow auto manufacturers to use lower-powered airbags. This rule permits airbags to be depowered by 20 to 35 percent. In addition, starting in 1998, repair shops and dealers were allowed to install on/off switches that allow airbags to be deactivated.

Smart Systems

The smart airbag of the future is not just the airbag, but a redesign of the components in the current airbag systems. Features include:

Weight Sensors

This is a new sensor for the passenger seat to classify the weight and to determine what type of occupant is in the seat: adult or child.

Infrared Occupant Detection

This system will use infrared beams (just like in your TV remote control) to detect the distance the passenger is from the airbag and adapt the force of deployment accordingly.

Capacitive Reflective Occupant Sensing

These sensors will be located in the seat backs and in the dash to identify the distance you and/or your passengers are from the dashboard. These sensors will be able to discriminate between a human occupant and inanimate objects like your groceries. This alone will save thousands of dollars in the cases where the driver is the only occupant in the front seat.

Updated Sensors

The updated sensors will have the capabilities of deploying the seatbelt pretensioners faster, so in a crash situation you will be in the best position to benefit from the airbag deployment.

Centralized Electronic Control Unit

The new control units will be able to use all the input from the new sensor technology and thru new software deploy what you need when you need it.

Service Precautions

When working on the SRS or any components which require the removal of the airbag, adhere to all of these precautions to minimize the risks of personal injury or component damage:

- Before attempting to diagnose, remove or install the airbag system components, you must first disconnect and isolate the negative(-)battery cable. Failure to do so could result in accidental deployment and possible personal injury.
- When an undeployed airbag assembly is to be removed from the steering wheel, after disconnecting the negative battery cable, allow the system capacitor to discharge for two minutes (Chrysler) before commencing with the airbag system component removal.
- Replace the airbag system components only with specified replacement parts, or equivalent. Substitute parts may visually appear interchangeable, but internal differences may result in inferior occupant protection.
- The fasteners, screws, and bolts originally used for the SRS have special coatings and are specifically designed for the SRS. They must never be replaced with any substitutes. Anytime a new fastener is needed, replace with the correct fasteners provided in the service package or fasteners listed in the parts books.

Handling a Live Air Bag Module

At no time should any source of electricity be permitted near the inflator on the back of the module.[3] When carrying a live module, the trim cover should be pointed away from the body to minimize injury in the event of accidental deployment. In addition, if the module is placed on a bench or other surface, the plastic trim cover should be face up to minimize movement in case of accidental deployment.

When handling a steering column with an airbag module attached, never place the column on the floor or other surface with the steering wheel or module face down.

Handling a Deployed Air Bag Module

The vehicle interior may contain a very small amount of sodium hydroxide powder, a by-product of airbag deployment. Since this powder can irritate the skin, eyes, nose or throat, be sure to wear safety glasses, rubber gloves and long sleeves during cleanup.

If you find that the cleanup is irritating your skin, run cool water over the affected area. Also, if you experience nasal or throat irritation, exit the vehicle for fresh air until the irritation ceases; if irritation continues, see a physician.

Begin the cleanup by putting tape over the two airbag exhaust vents so that no additional powder will find its way into the vehicle interior. Then remove the airbag and airbag module from the vehicle.

Use a vacuum cleaner to remove any residual powder from the vehicle interior. Work from the outside in so that you avoid kneeling or sitting in an uncleaned area.

Be sure to vacuum the heater and A/C outlets as well. In fact it's a good idea to run the blower on low and to vacuum up any powder expelled from the plenum. You may need to vacuum the interior of the car a second time to recover all of the powder.

Check with the local authorities before disposing of the deployed bag and module in your trash.

After an airbag has been deployed, the airbag module and clock spring must be replaced because they cannot be reused. Other airbag system components should be replaced with new ones if damaged.

Disarming the System

The supplemental restraint system(SRS)system must be disarmed before repair and/or removal of any component in its immediate area including the airbag itself. Failure to do so may cause accidental deployment of the airbag, resulting in unnecessary SRS system repairs and/or personal injury.

1. Disconnect the negative battery cable and isolate the cable using an appropriate insulator(wrap with quality electrical tape).

Always wear safety goggles when working with, or around, the airbag system.

2. Allow the system capacitor to discharge for 2 minutes(CHRYSLER) before starting any repair on any airbag system or related components. This will disable the airbag system.

Arming the System

To arm the SRS, reconnect the negative battery cable. This will automatically enable the airbag system.

NEW WORDS

restraint	[ris'treint]	n.	约束，抑制，制止，克制
head-on	['hedɔn]	a.	正面的
brick	[brik]	n.	砖，砖形物
potassium	[pə'tæsjəm]	n.	钾
sodium	['səudjəm]	n.	钠
azide	['æzaid]	n.	叠氮化物
nitrate	['naitreit]	n.	硝酸盐，硝酸钾

blast	[blɑːst]	n.	一阵(风)，一股(气流)，冲击波
cowl	[kaul]	n.	壳，罩，颈
fender	[ˈfendə]	n.	挡泥板
severity	[siˈveriti]	n.	严重(性)，激烈，严酷程度
ribbon-like	[ˈribənˈlaik]	a.	带状的
inflator	[inˈfleitə(r)]	n.	充气器，充气机，打气筒
decorative	[ˈdekərətiv]	a.	装饰的
overly	[ˈəuvəli]	ad.	过度地，极度地
infrared	[ˌinfrəˈred]	a.	红外线的；n. 红外线
accordingly	[əˈkɔːdiŋli]	ad.	因此，从而，相应地
capacitive	[kəˈpæsitiv]	a.	电容性的
reflective	[riˈflektiv]	a.	反射的
dashboard	[ˈdæʃbɔːd]	n.	仪表板
discriminate	[disˈkrimineit]	v.	区别，区别对待，歧视
inanimate	[inˈænimit]	a.	死气沉沉的，没生命的，单调的
grocery	[ˈgrəusəri]	n.	食品，杂货
updated	[ʌpˈdeitid]	a.	最新的，现代化的
pretensioner	[priːˈtenʃənə]	n.	预紧器
commence	[kəˈmens]	v.	开始，着手
substitute	[ˈsʌbstitjuːt]	v.	代替，替换；n. 代用品，替代品
inferior	[inˈfiəriə]	a.	下等的，差的，自卑的
fastener	[ˈfɑːsnə]	n.	紧固件，接合件，固定器，扣闩
live	[liv]	a.	活的，精力充沛的；v. 活着，生活
hydroxide	[haiˈdrɔksaid]	n.	氢氧化物
irritate	[ˈiriteit]	v.	刺激，激怒，使急躁
nasal	[ˈneizəl]	a.	鼻子的，鼻音的，
vacuum	[ˈvækjuəm]	n.	真空，真空吸尘器；v. 用真空吸尘器打扫
expel	[iksˈpel]	v.	排出，开除，驱逐
plenum	[ˈpliːnəm]	n.	压力通风系统，强制通风；充实，充满
dispose	[disˈpəuz]	v.	处理，处置
trash	[træʃ]	n.	无价值之物，垃圾，废料[物]
wrap	[ræp]	v.& n.	包裹，缠绕

PHRASES AND EXPRESSIONS

supplemental restraint system	乘员约束辅助保护装置(SRS)
in concert with	与……合作
front impact sensor	前碰撞传感器
clock spring	钟弹簧，盘旋电缆

sodium azide	叠氮化钠
potassium nitrate	硝酸钾
energy reserve capacitor	储能电容器
forward sensor	前传感器
safing sensor	保险传感器
over the way	路对面，街对面
out of the way	向旁边，不再挡路，不再碍事
smart airbag	智能气囊
service package	修理包
sodium hydroxide	氢氧化钠
vacuum cleaner	真空吸尘器
local authority	地方当局

NOTES TO THE TEXT

[1] The rear safing sensor must close before the forward sensors to avoid airbag deployment in cases where the impact is not severe enough to cause deployment.

句中的 where... 是一个定语从句。本句可以译为："为了避免在碰撞程度不足以使气囊张开的情况下出现气囊张开的现象，后保险传感器必须在前传感器之前先闭合。"

[2] This assembly consists of a flat ribbon-like electrically conductive tape which winds and unwinds with the steering wheel rotation.

句中的 which... 是一个定语从句，修饰 tape。本句可以译为："这个组件中有一个带状的扁平导电条，在转向盘转动时，这个导电条或卷起或伸展开。"

[3] At no time should any source of electricity be permitted near the inflator on the back of the module.

此句因强调 at no time 短语而将其放在句首，从而采用将 should 移到前面的部分倒装结构。本句可以译为："千万不要将任何电源靠近安全气囊模块背部的充气器。"

EXERCISES

I. Answer the following questions:

1. List the main components of an SRS system.
2. What is the purpose of a safing sensor?
3. How to handle a live airbag module?
4. How to handle a deployed airbag module?

II. Translate the following paragraphs into Chinese:

1. The bag itself is made of a thin, nylon fabric, which is folded into the steering wheel or dashboard or, more recently, the seat or door. The sensor is the device that tells the bag to inflate. A mechanical switch is flipped when there is a mass shift that closes an

electrical contact, telling the sensors that a crash has occurred. The sensors receive information from an accelerometer built into a microchip.

2. When carrying a live airbag, make sure the bag and trim cover are pointed away from the body. In the unlikely event of an accidental deployment, the bag will then deploy with minimal chance of injury. When placing a live airbag on a bench or other surface, always face the bag and trim cover up, away from the surface. This will reduce the motion of the module if it is accidentally deployed.

TEXT B   Cruise Control System and Remote Keyless-Entry System

Cruise Control Systems

Most older cruise control systems were operated by various electromechanical devices. However, the latest cruise control systems are operated by ECUs. Cruise control systems consist of several common components which include vehicle speed sensor, operator controls, control module, and throttle actuator.

Vehicle Speed Sensor

The vehicle speed sensor uses a rotating magnet to generate a small electrical signal. It is usually mounted on the drive shaft or is driven by the transmission or transaxle governor assembly. It sends a speed signal to the control module. The speed sensor may also send a signal to the engine control computer.

Operator Controls and Control Module

The operator controls are used to set the desired speed. Control location varies between manufacturers, but is usually mounted on the turn signal lever. The operator can set the speed, and can also make minor adjustments to speed as necessary.

Another operator control is the brake pedal release switch, usually mounted on the brake pedal bracket. When the driver presses on the brake pedal, the switch sends a signal to the cruise control module to disengage the cruise control. The control module processes the inputs from the controls and speed sensor and produces an output signal to the throttle actuator.

Throttle Actuator

The throttle actuator opens and closes the vehicle throttle to maintain the operator set speed. Throttle actuators can be electric motors directly operated by the control module. In most cases, however, the throttle actuator is a vacuum diaphragm servo connected to a vacuum controller. The module operates the vacuum controller, which in turn operates the vacuum diaphragm.

Remote Keyless-Entry System

With the remote keyless-entry systems that you find on cars today, security is a big issue. If people could easily open other people's cars in a crowded parking lot at the mall, it would be a real problem. And with the proliferation of radio scanners, you also need to prevent people from "capturing" the code that your transmitter sends. Once they have your code, they can simply re-transmit it to open your car.

However, the controller chip in any modern controller uses something called a hopping code or a rolling code to provide security. For example, a system uses a 40-bit rolling code. Forty bits provide 2^{40} (about 1 trillion) possible codes. Here's how it works:

- The transmitter's controller chip has a memory location that holds the current 40-bit code. When you push a button on your key fob, it sends that 40-bit code along with a function code that tells the car what you want to do (lock the doors, unlock the doors, open the trunk, etc.).
- The receiver's controller chip also has a memory location that holds the current 40-bit code. If the receiver gets the 40-bit code it expects, then it performs the requested function. If not, it does nothing.
- Both the transmitter and the receiver use the same pseudo-random number generator. When the transmitter sends a 40-bit code, it uses the pseudo-random number generator to pick a new code, which it stores in memory. On the other end, when the receiver receives a valid code, it uses the same pseudo-random number generator to pick a new one. In this way, the transmitter and the receiver are synchronized. The receiver only opens the door if it receives the code it expects.
- If you are a mile away from your car and accidentally push the button on the transmitter, the transmitter and receiver are no longer synchronized. The receiver solves this problem by accepting any of the next 256 possible valid codes in the pseudo-random number sequence. This way, you could "accidentally" push a button on the transmitter up to 256 times and it would be okay — the receiver would still accept the transmission and perform the requested function. However, if you accidentally push the button 257 times, the receiver will totally ignore your transmitter. It won't work anymore.

So, what do you do if you desynchronize your transmitter by pushing the button on it 300 times, so that the receiver no longer recognizes it? Most cars give you a way to resynchronize. Here is a typical procedure:

- Turn the ignition key on and off eight times in less than 10 seconds. This tells the security system in the car to switch over to programming mode.
- Press a button on all of the transmitters you want the car to recognize. Most cars allow at least four transmitters.
- Switch the ignition off.

Given a 40-bit code, four transmitters and up to 256 levels of look-ahead in the seudo-random number generator to avoid desynchronization, there is a one-in-a-billion chance of your transmitter opening another car's doors. When you take into account the fact that all car manufacturers use different systems and that the newest systems use many more bits, you can see that it is nearly impossible for any given key fob to open any other car door.[1]

You can also see that code capturing will not work with a rolling code transmitter like this. Older garage door transmitters sent the same 8-bit code based on the pattern set on the DIP switches. Someone could capture the code with a radio scanner and easily re-transmit it to open the door. With a rolling code, capturing the transmission is useless. There is no way to predict which random number the transmitter and receiver have chosen to use as the next code, so re-transmitting the captured code has no effect. With trillions of possibilities, there is also no way to scan through all the codes because it would take years to do that.

NEW WORDS

electromechanical	[iˌlektrəumi'kænikəl]	a. 电动机械的，机电的
security	[si'kjuəriti]	n. 安全，保险
crowded	['kraudid]	a. 拥挤的，塞满的
mall	[mɔːl]	n. 商业街，购物商场
proliferation	[prəuˌlifə'reiʃən]	n. 增殖，扩散
capture	['kæptʃə]	n. 捕获，战利品；v. 俘获，捕获，夺取
trillion	['triljən]	num. 万亿
transmitter	[trænz'mitə]	n. 发射器，遥控器
receiver	[ri'siːvə]	n. 接收器，收信机
request	[ri'kwest]	v.& n. 请求，要求
pseudo-random	[ˌpsjuːdəu'rændəm]	a. 伪随机的
look-ahead	['lukə'hed]	a. 超前的，考虑未来的
desynchronization	[diːˌsiŋkrənai'zeiʃən]	n. 去同步化(作用)，失调，同步破坏

PHRASES AND EXPRESSIONS

cruise control system	巡航控制系统
operator control	操作开关
release switch	解除开关
throttle actuator	节气门执行器
remote keyless-entry system	遥控无钥匙进车系统
parking lot	停车场
radio scanner	无线电扫描器
hopping code	跳动码
rolling code	滚动码
memory location	存储单元
key fob	钥匙坠，钥匙饰
function code	功能码

pseudo-random number generator	伪随机数发生器
security system	防盗装置
programming mode	编程模式

NOTES TO THE TEXT

[1] When you take into account the fact that all car manufacturers use different systems and that the newest systems use many more bits, you can see that it is nearly impossible for any given key fob to open any other car door.

句中的 that... and that... 这两个并列的同位语从句较长，如果按照原来的语序翻译，汉译句显得过长，因此将这两个从句单独译出并放在前面。本句可以译为："所有的汽车制造者采用的系统都互不相同，并且最新系统的密码位数也更多。考虑到这一实际情况，你就会明白使用任何一个钥匙饰遥控器来打开其他的任何一辆汽车的车门是几乎不可能的。"

EXERCISES

I. Answer the following questions:

1. List the main parts of the cruise control systems.
2. How does the controller chip in any modern controller works?

II. Translate the phrases and expressions into Chinese:

1. vehicle speed sensor
2. to set the desired speed
3. throttle actuator
4. rolling code
5. controller chip
6. requested function
7. key fob
8. valid code
9. programming mode
10. security system

TEXT C   Electrical Troubleshooting

A typical electrical circuit consists of an electrical component, any switches, relays, motors, fuses, fusible links or circuit breakers related to that component and the wiring and connectors that link the component to both the battery and the chassis. To help you pinpoint an electrical circuit problem, refer to the wiring diagrams of vehicle that is testing. The symbols of wiring diagrams are included at the end of this text.

Before tackling any troublesome electrical circuit, first study the appropriate wiring diagrams to get a complete understanding of what makes up that individual circuit. Trouble spots, for instance, can often be narrowed down by noting if other components related to the circuit are operating properly. If several components or circuits fail at one time, chances are the problem is in a fuse or ground connection, because several circuits are often routed through the same fuse and ground connections.

Electrical problems usually stem from simple causes, such as loose or corroded connections, a blown fuse, a melted fusible link or a failed relay. Visually inspect the condition of all fuses, wires and connections in a problem circuit before troubleshooting the circuit.

If test equipment and instruments are going to be utilized, use the diagrams to plan ahead of time where you will make the necessary connections in order to accurately pinpoint the trouble spot.[1]

The basic tools needed for electrical troubleshooting include a circuit tester or voltmeter(a 12-volt bulb with a set of test leads can also be used), a continuity tester, which includes a bulb, battery and set of test leads, and a jumper wire, preferably with a circuit breaker incorporated, which can be used to bypass electrical components. Before attempting to locate a problem with test instruments, use the wiring diagram to decide where to make the connections.

Voltage Checks

Voltage checks should be performed if a circuit is not functioning properly. Connect one lead of a circuit tester to either the negative battery terminal or a known good ground. Connect the other lead to a connector in the circuit being tested, preferably nearest to the battery or fuse. If the bulb of the tester lights, voltage is present, which means that the part of the circuit between the connector and the battery is problem free.[2] Continue checking the rest of the circuit in the same fashion. When you reach a point at which no voltage is present, the problem lies between that point and the last test point with voltage.

Most of the time the problem can be traced to a loose connection. Note: Keep in mind that some circuits receive voltage only when the ignition key is in the Accessory or Run position.

Finding a Short

One method of finding shorts in a circuit is to remove the fuse and connect a test light or voltmeter in place of the fuse terminals. There should be no voltage present in the circuit. Move the wiring harness from side to side while watching the test light, if the bulb goes on, there is a short to ground somewhere in that area, probably where the insulation has rubbed through.[3] The same test can be performed on each component in the circuit, even a switch.

Ground Check

Perform a ground test to check whether a component is properly grounded. Disconnect the battery and connect one lead of a self-powered test light, known as a continuity tester, to a known good ground. Connect the other lead to the wire or ground connection being tested. If the bulb goes on, the ground is good. If the bulb does not go on, the ground is not good.

Continuity Check

A continuity check is done to determine if there are any breaks in a circuit—if it is passing electricity properly. With the circuit off(no power in the circuit), a self-powered continuity tester can be used to check the circuit. Connect the test leads to both ends of the circuit(or to the"power" end and a good ground), and if the test light comes on the circuit is passing current properly. If the light doesn't come on, there is a break somewhere in the circuit. The same procedure can be used to test a switch, by connecting the continuity tester to the switch terminals. With the switch turned on, the test light should come on.

Finding an Open Circuit

When diagnosing for possible open circuits, it is often difficult to locate them by sight because oxidation or terminal misalignment are hidden by the connectors. Merely wiggling a connector on a sensor or in the wiring harness may correct the open circuit condition. Remember this when an open circuit is indicated when troubleshooting a circuit. Intermittent problems may also be caused by oxidized or loose connections.

Electrical troubleshooting is simple if you keep in mind that all electrical circuits are basically electricity running from the battery, through the wires, switches, relays, fuses and fusible links to each electrical component(light bulb, motor, etc.)and to ground, from which it is passed back to the battery. Any electrical problem is an interruption in the flow of electricity to and from the battery.

	Symbols Used on Wiring Diagrams		
+	Positive		Connector
−	Negative		Male Connector
	Ground		Female Connector
	Fuse		Denotes Wire Continues Elsewhere
	Gang Fuses with Bus Bar		Denotes Wires Goes to One of Two Circuits
	Circuit Breaker		Splice
	Capacitor		Splice Identification
Ω	Ohms		Thermal Element
	Resistor	TIMER	Timer
	Variable Resistor		Multiple Connector
	Series Resistor		Optional Wiring With Wiring Without
	Coil		"Y"Windings
	Step Up Coil	88:88	Digital Readout
	Open Contact		Single Filament Lamp

(continued)

Symbols Used on Wiring Diagrams

Symbol	Name	Symbol	Name
	Closed Contact		Dual Filament Lamp
	Closed Switch		L. E. D—Light Emitting Diode
	Open Switch		Thermistor
	Closed Ganged Switch		Gauge
	Open Ganged Switch		Sensor
	Two Pole Single Throw Switch		Fuel injector
	Pressure Switch	#36	Denotes Wire Goes Through Bulkhead Disconnect
	Solenoid Switch	#19 STRG COLUMN	Denotes Wire Goes Through Steering Column Connector
	Mercury Switch	#14 INST PANEL	Denotes Wire Goes Through instrument Panel Connector
	Diode or Rectifier	#7 ENG	Denotes Wire Goes Through Grommet to Engine Compartment
	Bi-Directional Zener Diode		Denotes Wire Goes Through Grommet
	Motor		Heated Grid Elements
	Armature and Brushes		

NEW WORDS

tackle	['tækl]	n. 处理，对付，解决
troublesome	['trʌblsəm]	a. 棘手的，麻烦的，讨厌的
voltmeter	['vəult‚miːtə(r)]	n. 伏特计，电压表
preferably	['prefərəbli]	ad. 更可取，宁愿，最好
bypass	['baipɑːs]	n. 旁路；v. 设旁路，迂回
interruption	[‚intə'rʌpʃən]	n. 中断，打断

PHRASES AND EXPRESSIONS

fusible link	易熔线
circuit breaker	电路断电器
trouble spot	出故障处
narrow down	减小，变小，变窄
at one time	同时
ahead of time	提前，在原定时间之前
jumper wire	跨接线

most of the time	多半时间
test light	试灯
wiring harness	线束
short to ground	搭铁
self-powered test light	自备电源试灯
continuity tester	连通性检查仪
open circuit	开路，断路
stem from	由……发生[产生，引起]，归因于

NOTES TO THE TEXT

[1] If test equipment and instruments are going to be utilized, use the diagrams to plan ahead of time where you will make the necessary connections in order to accurately pinpoint the trouble spot.

句中 where... 是 plan 的宾语从句。本句可以译为："如果准备使用测试设备与测试仪器的话，应利用电路图提前设计好接线的位置，以便精确地查明故障部位。"

[2] If the bulb of the tester lights, voltage is present, which means that the part of the circuit between the connector and the battery is problem free.

句中 which means... 是一个非限制性定语从句，关系代词 which 指代前面的主句。本句可以译为："如果检测仪的灯泡点亮，表明有电压存在，这就意味着电路中连接器与蓄电池之间的部分是无故障的。"

[3] Move the wiring harness from side to side while watching the test light, if the bulb goes on, there is a short to ground somewhere in that area, probably where the insulation has rubbed through.

句中 where... 是 somewhere 的定语从句。本句可以译为："来回摆动线束，同时观察试灯。如果灯泡点亮，摆动的那个区域在某处存在搭铁故障，大概该处出现了绝缘层磨破的现象。"

EXERCISES

Ⅰ. *Answer the following questions:*

1. Electrical problems usually stem from simple causes. What are they?
2. Describe how to find an open circuit.
3. Describe how to check the circuit continuity.

Ⅱ. *Translate the following terms into Chinese:*

1. continuity
2. open circuit
3. short circuit
4. short to ground
5. jumper wire
6. test light
7. voltmeter
8. thermister

Related Terms

ammeter	电流表
multimeter	万用表
ohmmeter	欧姆表
head light	前照灯
turn signal light	转向信号灯
hazard warning light	危险警告灯
backup light	倒车灯
indicator light	指示灯
coil assembly	(安全气囊)盘旋电缆,时钟弹簧
supplemental inflatable restraint(SIR)	辅助充气保护装置(SIR),(通用汽车公司对安全气囊的称谓)
power window	电动门窗
power door lock	电动门锁
power rear mirror	电动后视镜

Translation Techniques(12)——长句翻译

科技英语文献中较多地采用了修饰语,从而导致了英语中经常出现长句。而在汉语中,则多采用短句。怎样才能将结构严密紧凑的英语长句翻译成层次清晰、脉络分明、语义正确、语气连贯的汉译句呢?下面就简单介绍一下英语长句的翻译步骤和方法。

1. 翻译步骤与方法

1)区分主从,化整为零——找出主句和从句,将长句拆分成几个具有主谓结构的部分。将拆分的若干个主谓结构逐一正确理解或表达出来。

如果没有并列谓语,那么,有几个谓语就有几个主谓结构。

2)合零为整,调整润色——根据主、从句之间的修饰关系,将各个主谓结构的汉译句连接起来。应恰当运用翻译技巧,调整语序和对汉译句进行必要的文字修饰。

2. 实例分析

例1:

The basic tools needed for electrical troubleshooting include a circuit tester or voltmeter(a 12-volt bulb with a set of test leads can also be used), a continuity tester, which includes a bulb, battery and a set of test leads, and a jumper wire, preferably with a circuit breaker incorporated, which can be used to bypass electrical components.

第一步:区分主从,化整为零。

在区分谓语动词和非谓语动词之后,显然可以将整个长句拆分为三个主谓结构和一个介词短语：①The basic tools needed for electrical troubleshooting include... 是主句；②which includes... 是定语从句；③preferably with a circuit breaker incorporated 是一个介词短语作后置定语；④which can be used... 也是一个定语从句。which 指代 jumper wire。

主句中有三个并列宾语，它们中间被修饰成分隔开。将各个主谓结构及短语译成汉语：①电气故障诊断所必需的基本工具有电路检测仪或电压表(有时还可能用到一只12V的灯泡和一套测试线)、连通性检测仪和跨接线；②连通性检测仪包括一只灯泡、蓄电池和一组测试线；③最好内含一只电路断电器；④跨接线用来跨接电器部件。

第二步：合零为整，调整润色。

将各个主谓结构或短语的汉译句组合在一起，并根据修饰关系调整语序或加以文字修饰，并适当运用翻译技巧：将第④部分提到第③部分前面(倒译)。将各个后置定语(短语或从句)提出来分别表述(分译)。最后的汉译句为："电气故障诊断所必需的基本工具有电路检测仪或电压表(有时还可能用到一只12V的灯泡和一套测试线)、连通性检测仪和跨接线。连通性检测仪包括一只灯泡、一个蓄电池和一组测试线。跨接线用来跨接电器部件，其内最好包含有一只电路断电器。"

例2：

Electrical troubleshooting is simple if you keep in mind that all electrical circuits are basically electricity running from the battery, through the wires, switches, relays, fuses and fusible links to each electrical component(light bulb, motor, etc.)and to ground, from which it is passed back to the battery.

第一步：区分主从，化整为零。

显然本句开头就是主句。从谓语动词来看，可以断定 if 后有三个主谓结构，并且根据关联词(修饰关系)可以断定，这三个主谓结构构成了一个从句套从句再套从句的结构。所以可以将整个长句拆分为四个主谓结构：①Electrical troubleshooting is simple 是主句；②if you keep in mind 是一个条件从句；③that all electrical circuits are ... and to ground 是一个宾语从句；④from which ... 是一个定语从句。

将四个主谓结构译成汉语：①电器故障的排除很容易；②如果记住；③所有的电路基本上都是这样的：电流从蓄电池开始，然后流经导线、开关、继电器、熔断器和易熔线到达电气部件(灯泡、电动机等)，再搭铁；④从这里，电流再回到蓄电池。

第二步：合零为整，调整润色。

将四个主谓结构的汉译句组合一起，根据修饰关系调整语序或进行文字修饰，并适当运用翻译技巧：第④部分从属于第③部分且关系密切，这两部分加在一起又很长，所以采用倒译法，将这两部分提到前面，即按照③＋④＋②＋①的顺序进行表述。最后的汉译句为："在所有的电路中，电流基本上都是从蓄电池开始，然后流经导线、开关、继电器、熔断器和易熔线到达电气部件(灯泡、电动机等)，再搭铁，最后再回到蓄电池。如果记住这一点的话，排除电气故障就简单了。"

UNIT 13 AUTOMOTIVE COMPUTERS AND COMMUNICATION SYSTEMS

TEXT A Computers on Modern Vehicles

Almost every vehicle built in the last 10-15 years has at least one on-board computer. There may be up to six different computers on some vehicles. On-board computers control ignition and fuel systems, emission controls, cooling fans, air conditioner compressor, torque converter clutch, and transmission shift points.

Other vehicle computers control the airbags, anti-lock brake and traction control systems, interior air temperature and distribution, suspension and steering systems, and the anti-theft system. Many modern vehicles combine the engine control computer and other vehicle computers into one large microprocessor, which monitors and controls most vehicle functions.

The primary reason for using on-board computers in modern vehicles is to meet fuel economy and emissions regulations. The use of computers allows the ignition, fuel, and emission systems operations to be controlled precisely. The end result is a stoichiometric air-fuel ratio that is as close to 14.7 : 1 as possible.

This air-fuel ratio is necessary for optimum catalytic converter operation as well as good fuel economy and emissions performance. Newer on-board computers also control the torque converter clutch, transmission shift points, and air conditioner operation to increase fuel mileage as well as lower emissions. The computer control system can be divided into three major subsystems: computer, input sensors and output devices.

Computers

A vehicle's on-board computer is normally referred to as an electronic control unit or ECU. The ECU has many different names. A vehicle's ECU may be referred to by one of the following terms:
- controller
- microprocessor
- on-board computer
- engine control computer(ECC)
- engine or electronic control module(ECM)
- powertrain control module(PCM)

These names are the most common and depending on the manufacturer and vehicle system[1], other specific names may be used. ECUs are usually contained in one casing. Most ECUs are located inside the vehicle's interior away from the heat and vibration of the engine compartment, but can be located almost anywhere depending on the vehicle, system, and manufacturer.

A few ECUs are made in two parts, with the processor located in the passenger compartment and the output part under the hood. Whatever their physical locations, all ECUs contain two main sections: the central processing unit and the memory section. The memory section has two separate sections of memory—permanent and temporary.

Central Processing Unit

The central processing unit(CPU) is the section of the electronic control unit that performs calculations and makes decisions. The CPU is sometimes called the controller. The CPU is constructed using one or more integrated circuits, or ICs. Incoming data from the input sensors must go through the CPU, where the data is processed and adjustments made to the output sensors. The ECU must be replaced if the CPU is defective, as it is affixed to the ECU's circuit board.

Permanent Computer Memory

There are four basic types of permanent computer memory, read only memory (ROM), programmable read only memory(PROM), erasable programmable read only memory (EPROM), and electronically erasable programmable read only memory (EEPROM). A program that tells the ECU what to do and when to do it is stored in ROM.

The ROM also contains general information that is used as a standard of operation under various conditions. Once this information is placed in memory, it cannot be modified. The ROM is an integral part of the ECU. If the ROM is defective, the ECU must be replaced. Programmable read only memory(PROM) is a variation of ROM. On some vehicles, the PROM is plugged into the ECU and can be replaced if it is defective or if a revised PROM is needed. This eliminates the expense of replacing the entire ECU. On most newer vehicles, the PROM is permanently affixed to the ECU. The ROM and PROM are nonvolatile memories. This means that information stored in these memories will remain even if the battery is disconnected. The EPROM can be reprogrammed by exposing it to ultraviolet light and then reprogramming it. This can only be done by the manufacturer. The EEPROM can be erased electronically and reprogrammed or "burned in", using either electronic scan tools or computerized diagnostic equipment.

Temporary Computer Memory

The ECU uses random access memory(RAM) as a temporary storage place for data from the sensors. As new information is received from the sensors, it is written over the old information inside the RAM. The ECU constantly receives new signals from the sensors while the engine is running. If no signal or the wrong signal is received by the ECU, a diagnostic trouble code is stored in the RAM.

The RAM is contained inside the ECU. If the RAM is defective, the ECU must be replaced. The RAM has a volatile memory. This means that if the battery, fuse, or the power source at the ECU is disconnected, all data in the RAM will be erased, including any stored trouble codes. Some ECUs use another type of memory called keep alive memory(KAM).

KAM is a memory chip that allows the ECU to maintain normal vehicle performance by compensating for sensor and parts wear. This is sometimes called an adaptive strategy. Any data in KAM is also lost if power to the ECU is disconnected.

Computer Control Operation

Although it is far simpler, the computer control system operates in much the same way as the human nervous system. If you touch a hot engine part, the nerves in your hand send a signal to your brain. Based on the signal, your brain decides that your hand may get burned and tells your arm muscles to pull your hand away from the part.

An ECU receives input data in the form of electrical signals from the sensors(nerves). The ECU(brain) compares the input data to the standards in the ROM. Based on its calculations, the ECU sends commands to the output devices(arm muscles). This process is performed over and over as engine, environmental, and vehicle conditions change.

Open and Closed Loop Operation

When the engine is cold, it cannot provide optimum fuel economy and emissions control. Also, several of the input sensors must warm up to operating temperature before they can provide reliable readings. Therefore, while one or more of the input sensors tells the ECU that the engine is below a certain temperature, the ECU operates in open loop mode. In open loop mode, the ECU controls the air-fuel ratio based on preset information while monitoring the input sensor readings. Some computer control systems also go into open loop mode when the throttle is opened completely, often called wide open throttle mode.

When the input sensors tell the ECU that the engine has warmed up sufficiently, the ECU goes into closed loop mode. In the closed loop mode, the ECU begins processing the information from the input sensors and bases its commands to the output devices on the sensor information. The result is optimum fuel economy and engine performance with minimal emissions output.

Input Sensors

The electronic control unit receives hundreds of input signals every second. These signals are created by input sensors. Each sensor measures one operating condition of the engine or drive train. The sensor then sends an electrical signal that represents the measurement to the ECU. Some sensors produce their own voltage signal and other sensors adjust the voltage sent to it by the ECU. The voltage sent to these sensors by the ECU is called the reference voltage.

The amount of resistance at the sensor determines how much output voltage is sent to the ECU. The ECU then compares its reference voltage to the sensor output voltage. This determines the sensor measurement. Some inputs to the ECU are electrical in nature and do not require a separate sensor to operate them. Examples are the charging system voltage, and voltage to apply the air conditioner clutch.

Output Devices

An electrical unit controlled by the ECU is called an output device. Output devices control the fuel, ignition, emission control, and other parts of the vehicle. Output devices can be solenoids, relays, electric motors, or other electronic devices.

Examples of output devices are the idle speed motor or solenoid, mixture control solenoid, fuel injector, ignition coil, ignition module, EGR system, air injection system, fuel pump relay, and electric fan motor relay.

NEW WORDS

defective	[di'fektiv]	a. 有缺陷的，损坏的，有故障的
affix	[ə'fiks]	v. 使附于，粘贴，使固定
revise	[ri'vaiz]	v. 修订，修正，修改
nonvolatile	['nɔn'vɔlətail]	a. 非易失性的
ultraviolet	[ˌʌltrə'vaiəlit]	a. 紫外线的，紫外的
random	['rændəm]	a. 任意的，随机的；n. 随意，任意
volatile	['vɔlətail]	a. 可变的，易失的，不稳定的

PHRASES AND EXPRESSIONS

fuel mileage	燃油经济性
burn in	烧上，烙上，腐蚀，留下不可磨灭的印象
volatile memory	易失存储器
keep alive memory(KAM)	可保持存储器(KAM)
read only memory(ROM)	只读存储器(ROM)
programmable read only memory(PROM)	可编程只读存储器(PROM)
erasable programmable read only memory (EPROM)	可擦可编程只读存储器(EPROM)
electronically erasable programmable read only memory(EEPROM)	电可擦可编程只读存储器(EEPROM)
over and over	反复
in nature	本质上，实际上

NOTES TO THE TEXT

[1] ... and depending on the manufacturer and vehicle system...

动词词组 depend on 是"依靠""取决于""因……而异"的意思。本句译为："……并且因为制造厂家和车辆系统的不同而不同……"

EXERCISES

I. Answer the following questions:
  1. List the three major subsystems of the computer control system.
  2. List the four basic types of permanent computer memory.

II. Choose the best answer for each of the followings:
  1. Which of the following types of computer memory stores data temporarily?
     A. RAM   B. ROM   C. PROM   D. EPROM
  2. Diagnostic trouble modes are stored in _____?
     A. RAM   B. ROM   C. PROM   D. All of the above
  3. When does the ECU go into open loop mode?
     A. When the engine is at normal temperature.
     B. When the engine is at middle speed.
     C. When the engine is at wide open throttle.
     D. When the engine is at lighter load.
  4. When does the ECU go into closed loop mode?
     A. When the engine has warmed up sufficiently.
     B. When the engine is at middle speed.
     C. When the engine is at middle load.
     D. When the engine is at lighter load.

TEXT B Automotive Network

Data Bus Network

Often, information that is transmitted to and from a control module is in the form of a serial data stream. A serial data stream is a digitized code of ones and zeros that is known as a binary code. Each one or zero in a data stream is referred to as a binary digit, or bit of information. A group of bits form a binary term, or byte. The wire or wires over which serial data is transmitted is referred to as a data bus network. Often, the data bus network is a twisted pair of wires. The twisted pair helps to eliminate the induction of electromagnetic interference (EMF), which could disrupt or cloud the data signal. Any microprocessor that communicates on the data bus network is referred to as a node. A node may only be capable of transmitting (send) information or may have bidirectional capabilities allowing it to both send/receive data on the network.

Control modules (nodes) may be multiplexed on a data bus network allowing them to share information and sensor data between one another. Examples of control modules that may share data on a data bus network include the PCM, body control module (BCM), transmission control module (TCM), instrument panel cluster (IPC) and electronic brake control module (EBCM) to name a few (Fig. 13-1). The data bus network eliminates the need to run hard wire from each sensor to each control module. Instead, the information is shared on the bus network.

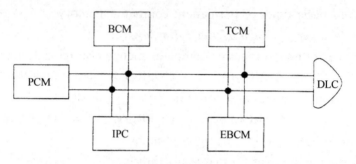

Fig. 13-1 A data bus network used to share information between controllers

The DLC allows the connection of a diagnostic scan tool, which becomes a node on the network with bidirectional data communication.

In general, a twisted pair data bus sends data in a fixed pulse width data stream. Each of the data bits is the same length. Data bits that are strung together (01100101) in this way are referred to as a pulse width modulated (PWM) serial data stream (Fig. 13-2).

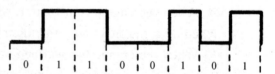

Fig. 13-2 Equal length bits of data strung together form a pulse width modulated (PWM) serial data stream

Controller Area Network

The Controller Area Network (CAN) protocol is the latest serial bus communication network used on OBD systems and offers real-time control. It is expected to be the predominente protocol by 2008. Mercedes Benz first integrated CAN into their engine and transmission control units in 1992, with many other manufacturers integrating CAN into some of their new vehicle platforms in the early 2000s. The CAN protocol has been standardized by the International Standards Organization (ISO) as ISO Standard 11898 for high speed and ISO 11519 for low speed data transfer. The speed of data transmission is expressed in bits per second (bps). The high-speed version can operate at 1 megabit per second (Mbps) and is used for powertrain management systems, and operates in virtually real-time data rate transfer speeds. The low-speed version can operate at 125 kilobits per second (Kbps) and is used for body control modules and passenger comfort features. While the prefix "kilo" usually indicates a multiplier value of 1,000, a kilobyte, in a serial data stream has a value of 1,024 bytes of data. This is the mathematical result of a base two numbering system (ones and zeros) carried to the tenth place. Additionally, a megabyte has a value of 1,048,576 bytes of data, which is one kilobyte (1,024) squared. The CAN system has allowed for improved communication with on-board vehicle systems and is a true multiplexed network.

The Society of Automotive Engineers (SAE) has divided the speed of serial data transfer for automotive applications into three classes. Class A is the slowest transmission rate with speeds less than 10 kbps. Class A networks are used for low-priority data transmission, generally related to non-critical body control module functions such as memory seats. Class B networks are mid-speed range networks with data transmission speeds between 10 kbps and 125 kbps, generally related to less critical devices such as HVAC, advanced lighting systems, and dash clusters. Class C networks have the fastest data transmission rate with speeds up to 1 Mbps. Class C networks are the most expensive to produce and are used for "mission critical" data transmission that flow at "real-time" speeds. Examples of Class C data include fuel control and ABS activation activity. The DLC is also connected to the Class C network for improved on-board diagnostics.

CAN enables the use of enhanced diagnostics and more detailed DTCs. With CAN, a scan tool is capable of communicating directly with sensors, independently of the PCM. The CAN protocol uses smart sensors. Each component contains its own control unit (microprocessor) called a "node". Each node on the network has the ability to communicate over a twisted pair of wires or a single wire called a data bus with all the other nodes on the network (bidirectional communication) without having to go through a central processing unit unlike other multiplexed systems used in the past for data sharing. Every component on the network is independently capable of processing and communicating data over a common transmission line. Nodes transmit information (messages) with an identifier that prioritizes the message. The messages transmitted from a node are a package of data bits, which include a beginning of message signal, component identifier, message (sensor output signal), and an end-of-message signal. Since this is a bidirectional communication network, the control module receiving the data will send a signal back that the information was received. In order for this sophisticated communication protocol to function, the data transmission package must be a set size (number of bits), format, and the information order must be consistent for all devices.

When multiple nodes need to send data to the control module simultaneously, the node will first see if the data bus is busy. The system uses collision detection similar to an

Ethernet system. But, unlike Ethernet, the CAN system can handle high data transmission rates. In essence, the node is looking into traffic to see if a higher priority node should be allowed to pass. Each CAN node on the network will have its own network unique identifier code and nodes may be grouped based on function. The data message is then transmitted with its unique identifying code onto the network. Each node and control module on the network will perform an acceptance test of the transmission to determine if it is relative or not based on its identifier. Relative information is processed, and non-relative information is ignored. The system then segments transmissions based on the priority identifier of the data package. The priority is determined by the unique number of the identifier, with lower-number identifiers having higher priority. This guarantees higher priority node identifier messages access to the network and lower-priority node messages will be automatically retransmitted in the next available bus cycle based on priority.

Since the CAN protocol technology allows for many nodes on one set of wiring, the overall vehicle wiring harness size is greatly reduced. A twisted pair wired network contains a CAN(+) and a CAN(−) wire. The CAN(−) bus is a differential bus system where the data signal from the CAN(+) wire is a mirror image of the CAN(−) network wire(Fig. 13-3). The combination of the twisted pair network wiring, combined with the differential bus data, eliminates the effect of EMI noise on the data transmission. Multiple networks on the vehicle can be linked together by gateways if necessary(Fig. 13-4). Class C high-speed data flows on one network. Class B mid-speed data flows on a second network, while Class A low-speed data flows on a third network. For example, the intake air temperature (IAT) sensor will place its data on the network data bus allowing any control module on the network direct access to the information without the need for one control module(i. e. , BCM) requesting the information from another control module(i. e. , PCM).[1] The body control module(BCM) has direct access to information without having to request it from the PCM.

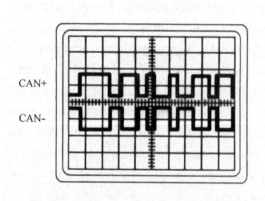

Fig. 13-3 The data signal from the CAN(+) network wire is a mirror image of the CAN(−)

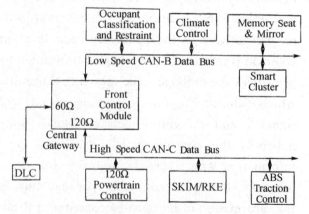

Fig. 13-4 Multiple networks on the vehicle can be linked together by gateways if necessary

In 1996, the EPA specified that all vehicles must be able to transmit generic scan tool data. However, proprietary data and any data other than P0 codes and data steams were free to use any other protocol the manufacturer chose. The CAN PCM will still transmit data to the DLC in SAE's generic scan tool protocol as specified by the EPA for generic scan tool data communication, such as generic DTCs. But, in order to access all the functions available, you will need to have a scan tool that is compatible with CAN if that is the vehicle's network operation system. Unless you have purchased a scan tool since the turn of the century(2000), it will be necessary to upgrade your existing scan tool or replace it with one that is capable of communicating with CAN. The EPA emission regulations for the 2008 model year have specified CAN as the new scan tool communications protocol for all vehicles sold in the United States, providing the repair technician more data for troubleshooting emission failures. With CAN, the industry finally has a single standard for on-board diagnostic communication.

The CAN protocol still allows access to the typical DTC information and data streams, but with enhanced DTC detail. A scan tool is also capable of direct bidirectional communication with a smart sensor or actuator node as well as other control modules on the network. In addition, flash calibration for almost all nodes on the network will become commonplace. A smart sensor is capable of reporting the result of internal voltage drops, opens, grounds, and other self-test features. The network has the ability to take faulty sensor off line and can self-diagnose the difference between a faulty device or circuit.

As discussed earlier, the EPA has required pass-thru flash programming using a standard PC connected to the Internet or by using a data disk beginning in 2003 and required by 2008. The CAN will be the standard communication protocol, and scan tool will be the interface device between the vehicle and the Internet or PC.

NEW WORDS

bit	[bit]	n. （二进制）位，比特
byte	[bait]	n. 字节
twist	[twist]	v. 绞，编织，缠绕，扭曲
interference	[ˌintəˈfiərəns]	n. 干涉，干扰
disrupt	[disˈrʌpt]	v. 使中断，使陷于混乱，破坏
cloud	[klaud]	n. 云；v. 乌云密布，玷污，使黯然，把……弄得朦胧不清
node	[nəud]	n. 节点，网点；结点
bidirectional	[ˌbaidiˈrekʃənl]	a. 双向的
multiplex	[ˈmʌltipleks]	a. 多路传输，多路通信
express	[iksˈpres]	a. 急速的；n. 快车；v. 表达，表示
megabit	[ˈmegəbit]	n. 百万位，兆位
low-priority	[ˈləupraiˈɔriti]	n. 低优先级[次序]

identifier	[aiˈdentifaiə]	n.	标识符，检验人
prioritize	[praiˈɔritaiz]	v.	把……区分优先次序
end-of-message		n.	信息结束，终端信息
format	[ˈfɔːmæt]	n.	格式，形式，版式
consistent	[kənˈsistənt]	a.	一致的，相容的
gateway	[ˈgeitwei]	n.	网关
generic	[dʒiˈnerik]	a.	一般的，普通的，通用的
proprietary	[prəˈpraiətəri]	a.	所有的，私人拥有的
purchase	[ˈpəːtʃəs]	v.& n.	买，购买
commonplace	[ˈkɔmənpleis]	n.	平凡的事，平常话；a. 平凡的
calibration	[ˌkæliˈbreiʃən]	n.	校准，刻度
interface	[ˈintə(ː)ˌfeis]	n.	界面，分界面，接口

PHRASES AND EXPRESSIONS

serial data stream	串行数据流
binary code	二进制(代)码
data bus network	数据总线网络
electromagnetic interference(EMI)	电磁干扰
collision detection	冲突检测
in essence	其实，本质上，大体上
look into	窥视，观察
access to	有权使用，能够使用
twisted pair	双股绞合线，双绞线
mirror image	镜像，映像，反像
data steam	数据流
be compatible with	与……相容[相适应，一致]
model year	年款
smart sensor	智能传感器
interface device	接口设备，接口

NOTES TO THE TEXT

[1] For example, the intake air temperature(IAT) sensor will place its data on the network data bus allowing any control module on the network direct access to the information without the need for one control module (i.e., BCM) requesting the information from another control module(i.e., PCM).

本句虽然是一个简单句，但是后面却跟着两个长长的短语。一个是分词短语 allowing...，另一个是介词短语 without the need for...。介词短语 without the need for 后面是一个"名词+动名词+名词"的具有主谓关系的结构，作 for 的宾语。整个句子可以译为："例如，进气温度(IAT)传感器将它的数据提供给网络的数据总线，从而使网络上的任何一个控制模块都能直接使用该信息，不需要一个控制模块（即车身控制模块）从另一个控制模块（即动力控制模块）那里请求获得信息。"

EXERCISES

I. Answer the following questions:

1. Explain what is meant by a "serial data stream".
2. What is a data bus network?
3. What is a pulse width modulated(PWM) serial data stream?
4. The Society of Automotive Engineers(SAE) has divided the speed of serial data transfer for automotive applications into three classes. What are they?
5. What is a node called?
6. Using the CAN protocol technology, the overall vehicle wiring harness size is greatly reduced. Why?

II. Translate the following paragraphs into Chinese:

1. The twisted pair helps to eliminate the induction of electromagnetic interference (EMF), which could disrupt or cloud the data signal.
2. The data bus network eliminates the need to run hard wire from each sensor to each control module. Instead, the information is shared on the bus network.
3. The Controller Area Network(CAN) protocol is the latest serial bus communication network used on OBD-II systems and offers real-time control.
4. The low-speed version can operate at 125 kilobits per second(Kbps) and is used for body control modules and passenger comfort features.
5. The high-speed version can operate at 1 megabit per second(Mbps) and is used for powertrain management systems, and operates in virtually real-time data rate transfer speeds.
6. With CAN, a scan tool is capable of communicating directly with sensors, independently of the PCM.

TEXT C On-Board Diagnostics(OBD)

First Generation OBD Systems

The first generation OBD systems monitored the fuel metering system and all major engine sensors. The system circuits were monitored for shorts, opens, as well as normal sensor input ranges in some instances. OBD systems were limited in their ability to determine faults outside of these basic parameters.

The malfunction indicator light(MIL) served as an alert to the driver that something was wrong with the system. The light would stay illuminated as long as the fault existed but would go out if the condition was intermittent or corrected itself. Once a MIL came on, the OBD system would generate a DTC and store it in a long-term memory regardless of whether it was generated by a hard fault or intermittent condition. These early systems did not store information on how many drive cycles ago the light was first illuminated or if the condition was intermittent.[1]

These DTCs would be stored in the ECM memory regardless of whether they were a continuous hard fault or a soft(intermittent)fault. DTCs could be cleared by removing power to the ECM. Some of these early systems could be accessed through the use of a scan tool which offered a serial data stream. Other systems offered trouble codes by activating the MIL to flash a sequence to identify the DTC and required the use of pin tests to determine sensor operation. These non-standardized codes(each manufacturer developed its own codes and numbering system) identified the failure condition, and the technician needed to refer to a diagnostic chart or trouble tree and often needed to use a breakout box for pin testing.

While OBD was a good beginning, it had many shortcomings. One of the major shortfalls of the first generation systems was the lack of standardization, in terminology or trouble code identification. Each manufacturer was able to use its own specific terms when naming components and systems. It offered limited system monitoring of air-fuel ratios. There was minimal use of rationality checks on system function. The code retrieval method varied greatly from one manufacturer to another, with little consistency between systems. Fault codes were often limited to current related failures of open and shorted circuits. A limited number of DTC were utilized, and each manufacturer had its own specific code for a failure with no commonality between manufacturers. In addition, the MIL would turn off once the system fault corrected itself. With intermittent faults causing the MIL to intermittently come on and go, some owners leaned to ignore the MIL if no apparent driveability concern was noticed, thus defeating the intended purpose of having an emission-related failure corrected.

There was limited use of serial data stream by manufacturer for scan tool communication, and scan tool access as well as data link connector(DLC)design and location was manufacturer specific. DTC also required manual clearing from memory by removing power to the ECM. Tailpipe testing remains the most reliable method for determining needed repairs of the emission systems on vehicles manufactured prior to the 1996 model year.

Generation Two On-Board Diagnostics

California further refined the emission control regulations for vehicles being sold in the state beginning in 1994, and it was known as generation two on-board diagnostics(OBD-II). The Clean Air Act(CAA)of 1990 required that OBD computer based diagnostics be equipped on vehicles sold in the United States. The Federal Environmental Protection Agency(EPA)followed California's lead and mandated OBD-II's more stringent requirements beginning with the 1996 model year and applying to all gasoline-powered cars and light trucks sold in the United States, both import and domestic.[2] In addition, by 1999, all motor vehicles had to implement OBD standards. The Society of Automotive Engineers(SAE)has defined the standards and recommended practice for the implementation of OBD-II systems.

The CAA also required states to include checks of the OBD system in all mandatory I/M programs. Even with the improvements made on emission systems, vehicles remain a major source of air pollutant accounting for 77 percent of the carbon monoxide production and 44 per cent of NO_x production which contributes to ground-level ozone production and smog.

The objectives of OBD-II are three fold. First, reduce high emission levels that result from the failure of emission related components. Second, detect the failure when it occurs and notify the driver. Third, improve methods for diagnosis and repair of the malfunction. It is no longer necessary to learn new diagnostic systems developed by various manufacturers. The basic premise is to allow the diagnostic technician the ability to diagnose any vehicle with the same diagnostic equipment. Manufacturers will still have the ability to introduce additional diagnostic capabilities of special diagnostic tools to their own system as long as they provide the required OBD-II features.

This system offers many improvements over the earlier OBD systems. The system functions as an on-board diagnostics emissions monitoring system that alerts the driver if a malfunction is detected by the power-train control module(PCM) that causes the emission levels of the vehicle to exceed one and one half times (50 percent above) the emission standards for the vehicle.[3] Malfunctions are often detected before they lead to high emission levels. In addition, OBD-II will enable the MIL in order to protect the catalytic converter from damage.

OBD-II required more standardization among vehicle manufacturers. The SAE set standard features and practices that vehicle manufacturers have to adhere to. These features are:

- Universal OBD 16-pin DLC for all manufacturers, with dedicated pin assignments and location based on SAE Standard J 1962.
- Industry standard communication serial data protocol SAE Standard J1850, ISO 9141-2, and ISO 14230-4 describe the various communication protocols and message formats that a manufacturer may use when developing and implementing the OBD software on a vehicle required for diagnostics, class B data communication network interface.
  - Standard Corporate Protocol(SCP)(Ford)
  - Controller Area Network(CAN)
  - Serial Communications Interface(SCI)(DaimlerChrysler)
- Generic scan tool interface based on SAE Standard J1978. Basic serial data stream and diagnostic test modes on all vehicle makes and models based on SAE standard J1979. A single generic diagnostic scan tool that meets SAE standard J1978 is able to access data and P0XX codes on all OBD-II compliant vehicles. An OBD-II compliant scan tool automatically identifies all information necessary to communicate with the vehicle. The scan tool operator does not need to input information such as vehicle make, model, year, and powertrain information into the diagnostic tool. In addition, the diagnostic scan tool will automatically determine and display:
  - Communication protocol used
  - Diagnostic data parameters

- Freeze-flame data captured when a DTC is set
- DTCs
- Ability to clear DTCs, freeze frame data, and adaptive memory from PCM computer memory
- Results of oxygen sensor monitoring test
- Results of continuous and non-continuous monitors
- Status of OBD-II readiness tests
- Special test supported by vehicle

☐ Vehicle identification number(VIN) must be automatically transmitted to scan tool.

☐ Enhanced diagnostic test modes based on SAE Standard J2190.

☐ Manufacturers are to provide OBD-II electronic service information access and standardized data format as stipulated and regulated by SAE J2008.

☐ Standard DTC designation and list of generic DTCs based on SAE Standard J2012.

☐ Stored trouble code must be erasable from the PCM memory using a standard scan tool.

☐ Set a DTC in memory if a malfunction is detected that causes the emission levels of the vehicle to exceed one and one half times (50 percent above) the emission standards for the vehicle.

☐ Record and store a snapshot of the operating conditions that existed when an emissions fault occurred.

☐ Standardized component names and acronyms related to electronic control systems based on SAE standard J1930.

☐ Monitor virtually all emission related components and systems that may result in increased emission levels should they fail.

With OBD-II systems, it is possible for a vehicle to pass a tailpipe emissions test but fail an OBD test. This is because OBD-II systems monitor sensor and system operations so that they may detect a component malfunction before it leads to excessive emission levels. This is in part due to the catalytic converter's ability to lower tailpipe emission levels. Current systems not only monitor engine control systems, but also evaporative emission system such as gas cap seal failures. The MIL functions as an early warning of an impending emissions failure.

Components and connectors related to OBD-II emission control systems are mandated to last 10 years or 100,000 miles(160,927 kilometers) under EPA Tier 1 standards(1995 and later) and 120,000 miles under EPA Tier 2 standards(2004).

The United States requires that all new vehicles should be certified through the Federal Test Procedure(FTP) which was established in 1972. The FTP sets the maximum emission levels based on federal government regulations and uses a constant volume sampling of exhaust gases.

The FTP is a set of tests conducted by vehicle manufacturers to show that a vehicle model complies with EPA emission standards before the vehicles can be sold in the U.S. The test simulates various driving conditions and driver behavior. The FTP is performed on pre-production prototypes of new vehicle models driven by trained drivers on a test dynamometer simulating real road force conditions. Revisions to the FTP went into effect in 2004 which simulate two more rigorous real-world driving conditions, one provides for the control of emissions during aggressive acceleration, and the other provides for the control of emissions during high-speed driving up to 80 mph(128.75km/h).

It is a federal offense for vehicle owners or repair facilities to tamper with or modify the vehicle-certified configuration to a non-certified configuration. An example of tampering is the installation of a non-certified computer chip or the removal of the catalytic converter and the installation of a straight pipe in the exhaust system.

The CAA also regulated emission system-related warranties on vehicles produced beginning in 1995 and requires an 8-year, 80,000 mile(128,748 kilometers)warranties on the catalytic converter(s) and other major emission-related components(PCM). Other emission-related components are warranted for 24 months, or 24,000 miles (38,624 kilometers). Refer to the vehicle owner's manual for specific warranty periods and components covered. Warranted repairs can only be performed by a facility authorized by the vehicle manufacturer. According to the EPA, if a repair facility is not authorized by the vehicle manufacturer to perform warranty emission repairs, the facility is not obligated to advise the customer that the failed part(s)are covered under a manufacturer's warranty, though ethically the service facility should inform the customer.

NEW WORDS

alert	[ə'lə:t]	n.	警惕，警报
shortcoming	['ʃɔ:tkʌmiŋ]	n.	缺点，短处
shortfall	['ʃɔ:tfɔ:l]	n.	不足，亏空
rationality	[ˌræʃə'næliti]	n.	合理性
retrieval	[ri'tri:vəl]	n.	取回，恢复，挽救，检索
consistency	[kən'sistənsi]	n.	一致性，连贯性
commonality	[ˌkɔmə'næliti]	n.	共性，公共，平民
defeat	[di'fi:t]	n.	击败，战胜，使失效，作废，消除
mandate	['mændeit]	v.	强制执行，托管
practice	['præktis]	n.	实践，实际，惯例，操作规程
define	[di'fain]	v.	详细说明，定义
mandatory	['mændətəri]	a.	命令的，强制的，托管的
notify	['nəutifai]	v.	通报
premise	['premis]	n.	前提
compliant	[kəm'plaiənt]	a.	顺从的，适应的
stipulate	['stipjuleit]	v.	规定，保证
designation	[ˌdezig'neiʃən]	n.	指定，选派，名称，命名
snapshot	['snæpʃɔt]	n.	快照
impend	[im'pend]	v.	悬挂，即将发生
certify	['sə:tifai]	v.	证明，保证，颁发合格证书
revision	[ri'viʒən]	n.	修订(本)，修改，修正

rigorous	['rigərəs]	a.	严格的，严酷的，严峻的
offense	[ə'fens]	n.	犯法[罪]，冒犯，进攻
tamper	['tæmpə]	v.	窜改
authorize	['ɔːθəraiz]	v.	批准，允许，授权
obligate	['ɔbligeit]	v.	使……负义务[责任]
ethically	['eθikəli]	ad.	伦理(学)上，道德上

PHRASES AND EXPRESSIONS

hard fault	硬故障
soft [intermittent] fault	软故障（断续性故障）
pin test	端子测试
rationality check	合理性检测
recommended practice	操作规程建议
continuous monitor	连续监控器
non-continuous monitor	非连续监控器
gas cap	汽油箱盖
constant volume sampling	定容取样
comply with...	照……做
service [repair] facility	维修机构，维修厂家
be obligated to...	有责任去……

NOTES TO THE TEXT

[1] These early systems did not store information on how many drive cycles ago the light was first illuminated or if the condition was intermittent.

句中 on... 和 if... 为 information 的定语从句。本句可以译为："这些早期的系统并不存储从故障指示灯第一次点亮之后已经经过了多少个驾驶循环或者该故障是否为间断性故障这样的一些信息。"

[2] The Federal Environmental Protection Agency (EPA) followed California's lead and mandated OBD-II's more stringent requirements beginning with the 1996 model year and applying to all gasoline-powered cars and light trucks sold in the United States, both import and domestic.

beginning with... 和 applying to... 是两个并列的分词短语，作 requirements 的后置定语。因为较长，将这两个分词短语分译为两个句子。全句可以译为："联邦环境保护局（EPA）在加利福尼亚的超前性的法规（实施）之后，强制实行了更加严格的要求。这些要求从1996年款车型开始执行，并适用于在美国销售的所有汽油机轿车和轻型货车，包括进口和本土车型。"

[3] The system functions as an on-board diagnostics emissions monitoring system that alerts the driver if a malfunction is detected by the power-train control module (PCM) that

causes the emission levels of the vehicle to exceed one and one half times (50 percent above) the emission standards for the vehicle.

此长句中有4个主谓结构(画线为谓语)。其中,that alerts... 是一个定语从句,if a malfunction... 是该定语从句中的条件从句,而 that causes... 又是该条件从句中 malfunction 的分隔定语从句。全句可以译为:"该系统用作一种车载诊断排放检测系统。如果动力控制模块(PCM)检测到一个会导致汽车的排放值超过排放标准1.5倍(超出50%)的故障时,该系统就会通知驾驶员。"

EXERCISES

I. Answer the following questions:
1. What are the shortcomings of first generation OBD systems?
2. The objectives of OBD-II are three fold. What are they?
3. What will be automatically determined and displayed by an OBD-II compliant scan tool?

II. Translate the following paragraph into Chinese:
A single generic diagnostic scan tool that meets SAE standard J1978 is able to access data and P0XX codes on all OBD-II compliant vehicles. An OBD-II compliant scan tool automatically identifies all information necessary to communicate with the vehicle. The scan tool operator does not need to input information such as vehicle make, model, year, and powertrain information into the diagnostic tool.

Related Terms

transmission [transaxle] **control module** (TCM)	变速器[变速驱动桥]控制模块
data list	数据列表,数据流
diagnostic tester	诊断(检测)仪
data monitor	数据检测
active test	主动测试(也叫执行元件检测)

Translation Techniques(13)——翻译技巧应用实例

例1:
The ECU <u>uses</u> random access memory (RAM) as a temporary storage place for data from the sensors. As new information <u>is received</u> from the sensors, it <u>is written</u> over the old information inside the RAM. The ECU constantly <u>receives</u> new signals from the sensors while the engine <u>is running</u>. If no signal or the wrong signal <u>is received</u> by the ECU, a diagnostic trouble code <u>is stored</u> in the RAM.

译文:ECU将随机存取存储器(RAM)用作存储传感器发送来的信息的临时存储场所。

当接收到来自传感器的新的信息时，它就会覆盖 RAM 内部的旧信息。发动机运转时，ECU 不停地接收着来自传感器的新信息。如果 ECU 接收不到信号或者接收到错误信息，在 RAM 中就会存储一个故障码。

分析：原文第二句中有 As 引导状语从句。第三句中 while... 是一个时间状语从句，采用倒译法，将其译到句首。原文第四句中有一个条件从句。原文中有 7 个主谓结构（谓语见下划线），但其中 4 个为被动语态，但在译文中将它们全都译成主动语态。

例 2：

The FTP is a set of tests conducted by vehicle manufacturers to show that a vehicle model complies with EPA emission standards before the vehicles can be sold in the U. S. The test simulates various driving conditions and driver behavior. The FTP is performed on pre-production prototypes of new vehicle models driven by trained drivers on a test dynamometer simulating real road force conditions. Revisions to the FTP went into effect in 2004 which simulate two more rigorous real-world driving conditions, one provides for the control of emissions during aggressive acceleration, and the other provides for the control of emissions during high-speed driving up to 80 mph.

译文：联邦测试程序（FTP）是旨在证明一个车型满足 EPA 排放标准，而由汽车生产厂家在该车型投放美国市场之前所进行的一整套测试项目。FTP 测试要求模拟各种各样的行车条件和各种各样的驾驶员操作风格。测试时，经过专门训练的驾驶员在测功机上驾驶投产前的新车型样车，来模拟真实道路的受力条件。FTP 的修正版于 2004 年生效，（该修正版要求）模拟两个更加严格的真实道路行车条件，一个可以提供急加速期间的排放控制状况，另一个提供最高 80mile/h 的高速行车期间的排放控制状况。

分析：本段英文有 4 个句子，共含有 9 个主谓结构（谓语有下画线）。在第一句中，有 3 个主谓结构，before... 这个从句修饰分词 conducted。第四句中含有 4 个主谓结构，其中 which... 是修饰 revisions 的分隔定语从句。

例 3：

Monitoring of the ignition system is very important as misfiring not only produces more emissions of hydrocarbons, but the unburned fuel can enter the catalytic converter and burn there. This can cause higher than normal temperatures and may damage the catalytic converter.

译文：缺火不仅会产生更多的碳氢化合物排放，而且未燃的燃油也将进入催化转化器并在那里燃烧，这就可能导致催化转化器温度过高而损坏，所以对点火系统进行监控是非常重要的。

分析：有时需要将上下文联系起来，才能更准确地理解和翻译，甚至将段落内的含义综合之后进行表达。本段落中的第二句，是对第一句中的部分内容作补充说明，所以在翻译时，将两句合并一起进行翻译。

UNIT 14   ELECTRIC AND AUTONOMOUS VEHICLES

TEXT A   Electric Vehicles

Classification of Electric Vehicles

Electric vehicles are broadly categorized into four groups based on the electric design of their powertrains, namely battery electric vehicles(BEVs), plug-in hybrid electric vehicles(PHEVs), hybrid electric vehicles(HEVs), and fuel-cell electric vehicles(FCEVs).

• Battery Electric Vehicles(Fig. 14-1). BEVs, also known as pure electric or full electric vehicles, are powered by an electric motor and do not employ an internal combustion engine.[1] The battery of a BEV is charged primarily by the power grid and partially via regenerative braking. Even though air pollution occurs during electricity generation, BEVs do not have tailpipe emissions and, therefore, they are also called zero-emission vehicles. In order to facilitate reasonable driving ranges, the BEVs typically have the largest battery packs compared to other models.

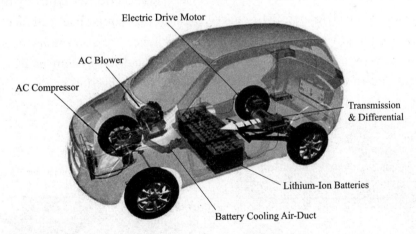

Fig. 14-1   A battery electric vehicle

• Plug-in Hybrid Electric Vehicles. PHEVs employ both an electric motor and an internal combustion engine, which can use gasoline or diesel. Typically, PHEV batteries are smaller than those of BEVs, because the required driving range is mostly supported by internal combustion engines and their combined driving range is higher than that of BEVs. As a result, the main advantage of PHEVs is employing both engines types, which helps the consumers overcome range anxiety[2]. In PHEVs, the electric motor is used mostly in urban environments where driving involves frequent stops. On the other hand, an internal combustion engine is used when the battery is depleted, during intensive cooling or heating, or during rapid acceleration.

• Hybrid Electric Vehicles (Fig. 14-2). HEVs are primarily powered by internal combustion engines, which use conventional fuel sources such as gas and diesel. These vehicles are also equipped with battery packs, which are charged by regenerative braking systems and are mainly used to enhance the fuel efficiency of the vehicle. The first generation of HEVs was presented to the market in 1997, when Toyota introduced the Prius model, and two years later Honda introduced the Insight model.

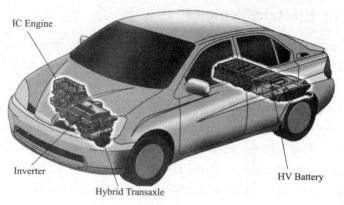

Fig. 14-2 A hybrid electric vehicle

• Fuel-Cell Electric Vehicles (Fig. 14-3). FCEVs use fuel cells, typically hydrogen, to power their onboard electric motors or charge their storage units. Fuel cell electric vehicles (FCEVs) also fall under the all electric vehicle types hence has also similar powertrain like BEV but its energy source is a fuel cell stack. The propulsion system in FCEVs is more efficient than those in the conventional ICEVs (internal combustion engine vehicles), and

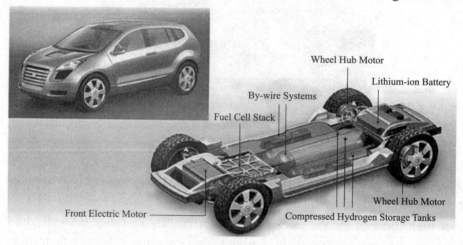

Fig. 14-3 Chevrolet Sequel fuel-cell electric vehicle

they do not emit any pollutants. FCEVs can be fueled within 10 minutes and they can drive up to 300 miles. Over the last few years, a number of car manufacturers and government agencies have supported research and development activities that accelerate fuel-cell technology. Unlike BEVs and PHEVs, the FCEVs do not use power grid to charge their batteries. Also, their onboard batteries are fairly small in size compared to those of BEVs, PHEVs, and HEVs. The disadvantages of FCEVs included having limited networks of hydrogen fueling stations, and the technology being still in its infancy stages.

Classification of Hybrid Drive

According to the layout of the prime movers, hybrid drives of hybrid electric vehicles can be divided into serial hybrid, parallel hybrid and power-split hybrid(also called series-parallel hybrid) drive as follows.

• Serial hybrid drive (Fig. 14-4). In this system, there is no mechanical coupling between internal combustion engine and wheels, a mechanical gearbox is not mandatory, a combustion engine, in conjunction with a generator, functions solely as a electricity producer and two electric machines are necessary.

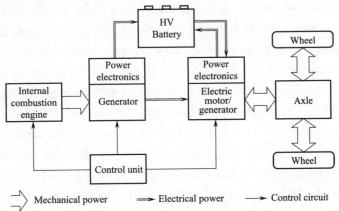

Fig. 14-4 Serial hybrid drive

• Parallel hybrid drive(Fig. 14-5). A mechanical gearbox is required. Both drives are connected to the mechanical gearbox, and only one electric machine is necessary.

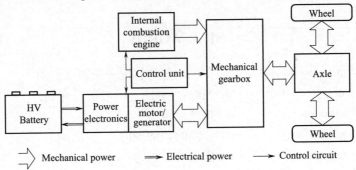

Fig. 14-5 Parallel hybrid drive

• Power-split hybrid drive (Fig. 14-6). The combustion engine power output is split into mechanical and electric paths, and a planetary gear set (summarising gear) is required for the splitting and joining of the mechanical and electric power paths. At least two electric machines are needed.

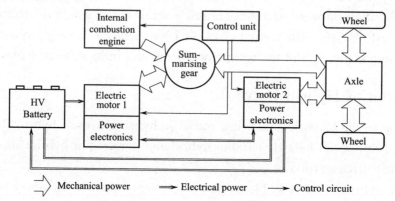

Fig. 14-6　Power-split hybrid drive

PHEV models can also be categorized by their levels of hybridization.

• Mild hybrid. A mild hybrid, also called a micro-hybrid, usually uses a 42-volt electrical motor and battery package (36-volt batteries, 42-volt charging) and is not capable of using the electric motor to propel the vehicle on its own without help from the internal combustion engine. [3] A mild hybrid system has the advantage of costing less, and saves less fuel compared to a full hybrid vehicle. The fuel savings for a mild type of hybrid design is about 8% to 15%.

• Medium hybrid. A medium hybrid uses 144- to 158-volt batteries. Like a mild hybrid, a typical medium hybrid is not capable of propelling the vehicle from a stop using battery power alone. The fuel savings are about 20% to 25% for medium hybrid systems. Examples of a medium hybrid include Honda Accord, Insight and Civic.

• Full hybrid. A full hybrid, also called a strong hybrid, is able to propel the vehicle using the electric motor(s) alone. Each vehicle manufacturer has made its decision on which hybrid type to implement based on its assessment of the market niche for a particular model. The fuel economy savings are about 30% to 50% for full hybrid systems. Examples of a full or strong hybrid include the Ford Escape SUV, Toyota Prius, and Lexus RX400h.

NEW WORDS

categorize	[ˈkætəɡəraiz]	v. 将……分类，把……加以归类
charge	[tʃɑːdʒ]	v. 充电，增压；n. 电荷，充气
tailpipe	[ˈteilpaip]	n. 排气尾管
conventional	[kənˈvenʃənl]	a. 传统的，常规的
propulsion	[prəˈpʌlʃn]	n. 推动力，推进
hybridization	[ˌhaibridaiˈzeiʃn]	n. 杂化，杂混，杂交

PHRASES AND EXPRESSIONS

powertrain	动力总成，传动系统，动力传动系统
battery electric vehicles(BEVs)	纯电动汽车(BEVs)
hybrid electric vehicles(PHEVs)	插电式混合动力电动汽车(PHEVs)
hybrid electric vehicles(HEVs)	混合动力电动汽车(HEVs)
fuel-cell electric vehicles(FCEVs)	燃料电池电动汽车(FCEVs)
regenerative braking	再生制动
battery packs	电池组
fuel efficiency	燃油经济性
mechanical coupling	机械联轴器，机械耦合，机械联接
planetary gear	行星齿轮

NOTES TO THE TEXT

[1] BEVs, also known as pure electric or full electric vehicles, are powered by an electric motor and do not employ an internal combustion engine.

句中 also known as pure electric or full electric vehicles 是 BEVs 的后置定语，用来解释说明 BEVs。本句可以译为："BEV 又被称为纯电动汽车或全电动汽车，它们由电动机驱动，不使用内燃机。"

[2] As a result, the main advantage of PHEVs is employing both engines types, which helps the consumers overcome range anxiety.

句中 which 引导非限制性定语从句，修饰前文的 employing both engines types。本句可以译为："因此，PHEV 的主要优势是采用两种发动机类型，这有助于消费者克服续航里程不够的焦虑。"

[3] A mild hybrid, also called a micro-hybrid, usually uses a 42-volt electrical motor and battery package (36-volt batteries, 42-volt charging) and is not capable of using the electric motor to propel the vehicle on its own without help from the internal combustion engine.

整句是一个并列句，它的两个分句共用主语。本句可以译为："轻度混合动力也称为微混合动力，它通常使用 42 伏电机和电池组(36 伏电池，42 伏充电)，并且在没有内燃机帮助的情况下，仅使用电机是无法驱动车辆行驶的。"

EXERCISES

I. Answer the following questions:

1. How are electric vehicles classified?
2. What are employed by PHEVs?

II. Translate the following paragraphs into Chinese:

1. The propulsion system in FCEVs is more efficient than those in the conventional ICEVs(internal combustion engine vehicles), and they do not emit any pollutants. FCEVs can be fueled within 10 minutes and they can drive up to 300 miles.

2. Unlike BEVs and PHEVs, the FCEVs do not use power grid to charge their batteries. Also, their onboard batteries are fairly small in size compared to those of BEVs, PHEVs, and HEVs. The disadvantages of FCEVs included having limited networks of hydrogen fueling stations, and the technology being still in its infancy stages.

3. Parallel hybrid drive. A mechanical gearbox is required. Both drives are connected to the mechanical gearbox, and only one electric machine is necessary.

TEXT B Autonomous Vehicles

Autonomous driving started in the 1980s. Today, some aspects of these early achievements have reached series production in the form of driver assistance systems for cars. Lane detection is used to facilitate lane departure warnings(LDWs) for the driver and to augment the drivers heading control in lane keeping assist systems (LKAS). The detection and tracking of vehicles driving ahead is used in adaptive cruise control systems (ACC) to keep a safe and comfortable distance.[1] More recently, pre-crash systems emerged that trigger full braking power to lessen damage if a driver reacts too slowly.

Meanwhile, the attention of research in autonomous vehicles has switched its focus from the well-structured environments encountered on highways as studied in the beginning to more unstructured environments, like urban traffic or off-road scenarios.[2]

Three elements are common to all autonomous ground vehicles: sensors to perceive the environment and the own movement, on-board computers, and actuators for vehicle control. Fig. 14-7 shows the LIDARs, cameras and Global Positioning System (GPS) antennas used on three vehicles of the DARPA Urban Challenge teams.

For environment perception, both image-based sensors like monocular and stereo cameras(monochrome and color), and range sensing devices like RADAR and LIDAR are used. The high-definition Velodyne LIDAR with a 360°, 3-D view and rich point cloud was designed especially for autonomous vehicles and is used in many systems. RADAR sensors are additionally able to determine the object's relative velocity directly.

To estimate the vehicle's motion, measurements from odometry and inertial sensors are incorporated, supported mainly

Fig. 14-7 Three vehicles of the DARPA Urban Challenge teams

by global position measurements from GPS.

All distributed or centralized processing on board the vehicle has to be real-time capable. This is an important prerequisite for vehicle control algorithms and system safety checks.

Actuators are necessary for closing the control loop, e. g., for steering wheel, brake, or throttle control.

The ability to perceive the vehicle's local environment is one of the main challenges in the field of autonomous ground vehicles. Environmental conditions like lighting or colors are permanently changing, and there are a lot of static as well as dynamic objects in the scene to be taken into account.

As a prerequisite for the perception and control modules, a good estimation of the vehicle's motion is necessary. Especially when the vehicle is moving fast or on nonflat terrain, relevant rotation along the longitudinal and lateral axes occurs. Working with measurements which are not taken at one unique timestamp, it becomes important to compensate for the vehicle's ego-motion in all measurements. A reliable position estimation is also essential for trajectory control.

For a good estimation of the motion, all measurements regarding the own vehicle are incorporated. Typical measurements are velocity and steering angle from odometry and accelerations, angular rates, and attitude from inertial sensors.

The Velodyne LIDAR is ideally suited for detecting and tracking objects participating in urban traffic. [3]

An imprecise localization of an autonomous vehicle might result incatastrophic behavior. The vehicle could drive on the wrong side of the road, it could believe a goal position to be inside a large obstacle, or it might even expect pedestrians crossing the road to be on the sidewalk. It is well known that GPS signals get weak or corrupted in dense forests or "urban canyons".

In contrast, having a completely autonomous unmanned vehicle in real public traffic is still legally vague.[4] Who is accountable for accidents: the(not-driving) driver, or the car manufacturer? After lobbying from Google's driverless car project (Fig. 14-8), Nevada has passed first laws regarding autonomous vehicles in 2011, at least to facilitate research in this field.

It is very interesting to observe that even car manufacturers opposed to or at least not pushing autonomous vehicles in the past now investigate such systems, up to autonomous driving tests on public roads. So the field is gaining momentum, and it now seems more likely than just a couple of years ago that we will experience autonomously

Fig. 14-8 Google's driverless car

driving vehicles in everyday traffic within the next 10-15 years.

All in all, much more work is required until autonomous vehicles can safely and robustly participate in real-world urban traffic as well as in complex off-road scenarios.

NEW WORDS

autonomous	[ɔːˈtɔnəməs]	a. 自主的，有自主权的
augment	[ɔːgˈment]	v. 增加，提高，扩大；n. 增加，补充物
trigger	[ˈtrigə(r)]	n. 起因，触发器；v. 触发，开动
scenario	[səˈnɑːriəʊ]	n. 设想，方案，(电影或戏剧的)剧情梗概
antenna	[ænˈtenə]	n. 天线，触角，触须
high-definition	[ˌhaɪ ˌdefiˈniʃn]	a. 高分辨率的
longitudinal	[ˌlɔŋgiˈtjuːdinl]	a. 纵向的
lateral	[ˈlætərəl]	a. 横向的
catastrophic	[ˌkætəˈstrɔfik]	a. 灾难的，惨重的，结局悲惨的
momentum	[məˈmentəm]	n. 动力，势头，冲力，动量

PHRASES AND EXPRESSIONS

lane departure warnings(LDW)	车道偏离预警
lane keeping assist systems(LKAS)	车道保持辅助系统
adaptive cruise control systems(ACC)	自适应巡航控制系统
RADAR	导航雷达，雷达
LIDAR	激光雷达
image-based sensor	基于图像的传感器
point cloud	点云，三维点云，点云数据
relative velocity	相对速度
odometry	测距(程)法
timestamp	时间戳

NOTES TO THE TEXT

[1] The detection and tracking of vehicles driving ahead is used in adaptive cruise control systems(ACC) to keep a safe and comfortable distance.

句中 driving ahead 是现在分词构成的词组做后置定语，修饰 vehicles，表示"在前方行驶的车辆"。本句可以译为："自适应巡航控制系统(ACC)对前方行驶的车辆进行检测和跟踪，以保持安全舒适的行驶距离。"

[2] Meanwhile, the attention of research in autonomous vehicles has switched its focus from the well-structured environments encountered on highways as studied in the beginning to more unstructured environments, like urban traffic or off-road scenarios.

句中 encountered on highways 是过去分词短语构成的词组做后置定语，修饰 environments，表示"在高速公路上遇到的环境"。本句可以译为："与此同时，对自动驾驶汽车的研究重点已经从最初研究的高速公路上遇到的结构良好的环境转变为非结构的环境，如城市交通或越野场景。"

[3] The Velodyne LIDAR is ideally suited for detecting and tracking objects participating in urban traffic.

句中 participating in urban traffic 是现在分词短语做后置定语，修饰 objects，表示"城市交通中的目标"。本句可以译为："威力登（Velodyne）激光雷达非常适合探测和跟踪城市交通中的目标。"

[4] In contrast, having a completely autonomous unmanned vehicle in real public traffic is still legally vague.

句中 having a completely autonomous unmanned vehicle in real public traffic 是动名词短语做主语。本句可以译为："相反，在现实的公共交通中拥有一辆完全自主的无人驾驶汽车在法律上仍然模糊不清。"

EXERCISES

I. Answer the following questions:

1. Which devices are used for environment perception?
2. Some typical measurements regarding the own vehicle are incorporated for a good estimation of the motion. What are they?

II. Translate the following paragraphs into Chinese:

1. Three elements are common to all autonomous ground vehicles: sensors to perceive the environment and the own movement, on-board computers, and actuators for vehicle control.

2. Actuators are necessary for closing the control loop, e.g., for steering wheel, brake, or throttle control.

3. An imprecise localization of an autonomous vehicle might result in catastrophic behavior. The vehicle could drive on the wrong side of the road, it could believe a goal position to be inside a large obstacle, or it might even expect pedestrians crossing the road to be on the sidewalk.

TEXT C Toyota Prius Hybrid Drive System

Principles of Operation

Toyota has produced the world's first mass produced hybrid automobile. The hybrid system is the wave of the future, and now there are more incentives to purchase one. Owners of the Prius or any other hybrid gas-and-electric vehicle, may be eligible for a federal income tax deduction. According to the Internal Revenue Service, hybrid vehicles qualify for a longstanding tax deduction that applies to vehicles powered by clean-burning fuels. The policy allows a one-time deduction which can be claimed by the consumer for the year the car was first put in use.[1]

In its simplest form, a hybrid system combines the best operating characteristics of an internal combustion engine and an electric motor. More sophisticated hybrid systems, such as the Toyota hybrid system, recover energy otherwise lost to heat in the brakes and use it to supplement the power of its fuel-burning engine. These sophisticated techniques allow the Toyota hybrid system to achieve superior fuel efficiency and a massive reduction in CO_2.

Upon its release in 2001, the Prius was selected as the world's best engineered passenger car. The car was chosen because it is the first hybrid vehicle that holds four to five people and their luggage. It is also one of the most economical and environmentally friendly vehicles available. In 2004 the second generation Prius won the prestigious Motor Trend Car of the Year Award.

The Toyota Hybrid System powertrain in the second generation (THS-II) Prius provides impressive EPA fuel economy numbers—60 mpg in city and 51 mpg in highway, and meets the AT-PZEV specifications.

The main components of the hybrid system are IC engine, motor generator 1(MG1), motor generator 2(MG2), planetary gear set, inverter, HV battery and HV ECU, see Fig. 14-9 and Fig. 14-10.

The 1NZ-FXE 1.5-liter gasoline engine employs VVT-i variable valve timing and ETCS-i electronic throttle control. Motor generator 1 (MG1) operates as the control element for the power splitting planetary gear set. It also supplies electrical power to drive motor generator 2(MG2). MG1 effectively controls the continuously variable transmission function of the transaxle and operates as the engine starter. MG2 is used for motive force

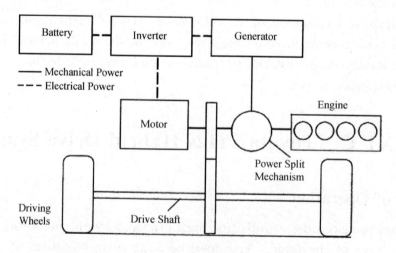

Fig. 14-9 Toyota hybrid drive system configuration

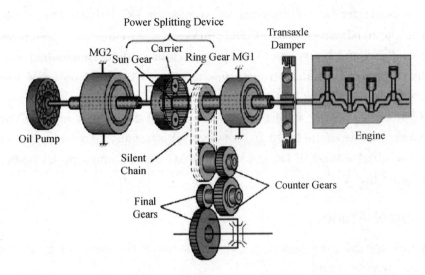

Fig. 14-10　The main components of Toyota Prius hybrid system

at low speeds and supplemental force at high speeds. It provides power assist to the engine output as needed and helps the vehicle achieve excellent dynamic performance. It also functions as a generator during regenerative braking.

The planetary gear unit is a power splitting device. MG1 is connected to the sun gear, MG2 is connected to the ring gear and the engine output shaft is connected to the planet carrier. These components are used to combine power delivery from the engine and MG2 and to recover energy to the HV battery. Current between MG1, MG2 and the HV battery is controlled by the inverter. The inverter converts high-voltage battery DC to AC power and it rectifies high-voltage AC from MG1 and MG2 to recharge the high-voltage battery.

The battery stores power recovered by MG2 during regenerative braking and power generated by MG1. The battery supplies power to the electric motor when starting off or when additional power is required.

When starting off and traveling at low speeds, MG2 provides the primary motive force. The engine may start immediately if the HV battery state-of-charge(SOC) is low. As speed increases above 15 to 20 mph the engine will start.

When driving under normal conditions the engine's energy is divided into two paths; a portion drives the wheels and a portion drives MG1 to produce electricity. The HV ECU controls the energy distribution ratio for maximum efficiency.

During full acceleration power generated by the engine and MG1 is supplemented by power from the HV battery. Engine torque combined with MG2 torque delivers the power required to accelerate the vehicle.

During deceleration or braking the wheels drive MG2. MG2 acts as a generator for regenerative power recovery. The recovered energy from braking is stored in the HV battery pack.

The inverter converts the high voltage direct current of the HV battery into three-phase alternating current of MG1 and MG2.

The boost converter boosts the nominal voltage of DC 201.6V that is output by the HV battery to the maximum voltage of DC 500V.

On the '04 Prius and later, the THS-II generator outputs at nominal voltage of DC 201.6V. The converter is used to transform the voltage from DC 201.6V to DC 12V in order to recharge the auxiliary battery.

An A/C inverter, which supplies power for driving the electric inverter compressor of the A/C system, has been included in the inverter assembly. This inverter converts the HV battery's nominal voltage of DC 201.6V into AC 201.6V and supplies power to operate the compressor of the A/C system.

Hybrid Control Modes

The hybrid system uses various modes to achieve the most efficient operation in response to the driving conditions.

Starting Out

When starting out under light load and light throttle only MG2 turns to provide power. The engine does not run and the vehicle runs on electric power only. MG1 rotates backwards and just idles; it does not generate electricity.

Normal Driving

Above approximately 14 mph during normal low-speed driving the engine runs and provides power. MG2 turns and runs as a motor and provides an electric assist. MG1 is turned in the same direction by the engine as a generator and provides electricity for MG2.

Deceleration and Braking

As soon as the accelerator pedal is released by the driver, MG2 becomes a generator. MG2 is turned by the drive wheels and generates electricity to recharge the HV battery. This process is called regenerative braking. As the vehicle decelerates, the engine stops running and MG1 turns backwards to maintain the gear ratio.

When the brake pedal is depressed most of the initial braking force comes from regenerative braking and the force required to turn MG2 as a generator. The hydraulic brakes provide more stopping power as the vehicle slows.

Reverse

When the vehicle moves in reverse, MG2 turns in reverse as an electric motor. The engine does not run. MG1 turns in the forward direction and just idles; it does not generate electricity.

Diagnostic Trouble Codes

DTC P3120 HV—Transaxle Malfunction ('04 & later Prius)

The HV ECU checks the energy balance and detects an abnormality if the magnetism in the motor or generator greatly decreases.

DTC P3125—Converter & Inverter Assembly Malfunction

If the vehicle is being driven with a DC-to-DC converter malfunction, the voltage of the auxiliary battery will drop and it will be impossible to continue driving. Therefore, the HV ECU checks the operation of the DC-to-DC converter and provides a warning to the driver if a malfunction is detected. DTC P3125 will be stored.

DTC P3000—HV Battery Malfunction

The HV ECU warns the driver and performs the fail-safe control when an abnormal signal is received from the battery ECU.

DTC P3009—Insulation Leak Detected

DTC P3009 sets when there is a leak in the high-voltage system insulation, which may seriously harm the human body. (Insulation resistance of the power cable is 100 k ohms or less.) If no defect is identified at inspection, entry of foreign matter or water into the battery assembly or converter and inverter assembly may be the possible cause. Use a Megger Tester to measure the insulation resistance between the power cable and body ground.

DTC P3115—System Main Relay Malfunction

The HV ECU checks that the system main relay (No. 1, No. 2, No. 3) is operating normally and detects a malfunction. Information Codes 224 – 229 may be present. Refer to the Repair Manual for each description.

Safety Precaution

Repairs performed incorrectly on the hybrid control system could cause electrical shock, leakage or explosion. Be sure to perform the following procedures:
- Remove the key from the ignition. If the vehicle is equipped with a smart key, turn the smart key system OFF.
- Disconnect the negative(-) terminal cable from the auxiliary battery.
- Wear insulated gloves.
- Remove the service plug and do not make any repairs for five minutes.

In order for your insulated gloves to provide proper protection, the insulating surface must be intact. To check the integrity of the glove's surface, blow air into the glove and fold the base of the glove over to seal the air inside. Then slowly roll the base of the glove towards the fingers.
- If the glove holds pressure, its insulating properties are intact.
- If there is an air leak, high voltage electricity can find its way back through that same hole and into your body! Discard the glove and start over until you have a pair of intact gloves that can fully protect you from the vehicle's high voltage circuits.

Due to circuit resistance, it takes at least five minutes before the high voltage is discharged from the inverter circuit. Even after five minutes have passed the following safety precautions should be observed:

- Before touching a high voltage cable or any other cable that you cannot identify, use the tester to confirm that the voltage in the cable is 12V or less.
- After removing the service plug, cover the plug connector using rubber or vinyl tape.
- After removing a high voltage cable, be sure to cover the terminal using rubber or vinyl tape.
- Use insulated tools when available.
- Do not leave tools or parts(bolts, nuts, etc.)inside the cabin.
- Do not wear metallic objects. (A metallic object may cause a short circuit.)

After disabling the vehicle, power is maintained for 90 seconds in the SRS system and five minutes in the high voltage electrical system. If either of the disable steps above cannot be performed, proceed with caution as there is no assurance that the high voltage electrical system, SRS, or fuel pump are disabled. Never cut orange high voltage power cables or open high voltage components.

NEW WORDS

incentive	[in'sentiv]	n.	鼓励，刺激；a. 激励的
eligible	['elidʒbl]	a.	符合条件的，合格的
deduction	[di'dʌkʃən]	n.	减除，扣除，减除额
longstanding	['lɔŋ'stændiŋ]	a.	长时间的
one-time	['wɔntaim]	a.	从前的，一度的
massive	['mæsiv]	a.	大量的，大规模的，大块的
prestigious	[ˌpres'ti:dʒəs]	a.	享有美誉的，声望很高的
abnormality	[ˌæbnɔ:'mæliti]	n.	变态，异常
fail-safe	['feilseif]	a.	故障保险(的)，失效保护
intact	[in'tækt]	a.	完整无缺的，完好的
revenue	['revinju:]	n.	收入，国家的收入，税收

PHRASES AND EXPRESSIONS

income tax	所得税
Internal Revenue Service	美国国内税务局
qualify for	有……资格
regenerative braking	再生制动
power splitting	功率分流
boost converter	升压变压器
electrical shock	电击
service plug	维修插头

| vinyl tape | 聚氯乙烯绝缘胶带 |
| with caution | 谨慎，留心 |

NOTES TO THE TEXT

[1] The policy allows a one-time deduction which can be claimed by the consumer for the year the car was first put in use.

这项政策还允许消费者在车辆初次投入使用的那一年申请给予一次性减税。

EXERCISES

I. Answer the following questions:
1. List the main components of the Toyota hybrid system?
2. What are the functions of MG1?
3. What are the functions of MG2?
4. What is the difference between the functions of inverter and boost converter?

II. Briefly describe Toyota Prius hybrid control modes.

Related Terms

LEV	低排放车辆
ULEV	极低排放车辆
SULEV	超极低排放车辆
PZEV	部分时间零排放车辆
AT PZEV	先进技术部分时间零排放车辆
ZEV	零排放车辆

Translation Techniques(14)——论文摘要翻译

1. 论文摘要翻译范例

例1：

汽车线控驱动技术的发展

【摘要】电子技术和控制理论的飞速发展为进一步改善车辆动力学特性及提高主动安全性提供了有效途径，例如已经广泛应用的各种底盘控制技术。综述了汽车线控驱动技术的发展现状和相关技术，着重介绍了线控转向、线控制动、线控节气门等系统的结构、组成、工作原理和性能特点，并讨论了线控驱动的集成化和相关技术要求。

Development of the Drive-By-Wire Technology

【Abstract】Rapid development of electronic technology and control theory provides an effective way for further improvement of vehicle dynamic characteristics and active safety, for example, the various widely used chassis control technology. Development of the vehicle drive-by-wire technology and relative technology are summarized, and structure, working principle, performance and features of steer-by-wire, brake-by-wire, by-wire acceleration pedal are emphatically introduced, and integration of by-wire drive and relative technology requirements are discussed.

例 2:

汽油车进、排气系统降低噪声研究

【摘要】提出了一种汽油车进、排气系统降低噪声方法,并基于 Helmholtz 共振原理,利用三维 CAD 软件 Pro/E 设计了进气谐振消声器。利用 GT-power 软件建立了整车、发动机、进气谐振器、排气消声器的联合模型。根据发动机工作过程,对排气消声器进行了改进设计。试验结果表明,采用进气谐振器和改进后的排气消声器,能够降低汽车加速行驶车外噪声,且基本保持汽车输出功率不变。

Research on Noise-Reduction of Gasoline Vehicle Intake and Exhaust System

【Abstract】A noise-reduction method of gasoline vehicle intake and exhaust system was brought up. Based on Helmholtz resonance principle, intake resonator was designed by means of Pro/E software of CAD in this paper. The combination model of complete vehicle, engine, intake resonator and exhaust muffler was established by using GT—power software. Based on engine working process, the improving design of exhaust muffler was developed. The test result shows that the outer acceleration noise could be reduced by applying intake resonator and redesigned exhaust muffler, and the output power of vehicle was proved to remain stable.

例 3:

高燃油经济性高性能四气门稀燃发动机的研制

【摘要】降低油耗对汽车制造厂家非常重要。稀薄燃烧作为一种有希望改善燃油经济性的方法,正在得到各种各样的研究组织和汽车制造厂家的研究,并且迄今为止,已见有若干稀燃技术研究成果的报道。

对一种四气门稀燃发动机的研制作了介绍,特别是介绍了燃烧的改进、发动机管理系统的研制和实验结果的获取。

讨论的主题有:(1)使用一种专门设计的可变气门定时与升程机构,改善部分负荷条件下制动比油耗以及利用优化的涡流比和可变涡流系统来获取高输出功率;(2)空燃比控制系统的研制;(3)整车燃油经济性的改善;(4)满足 NO_x 排放标准的方法。

The Development of a High Fuel Economy and High Performance Four-Valve Lean Burn Engine

【Abstract】The reduction of fuel consumption is of great importance to automobile manufacturers. As a prospective means to achieve fuel economy, lean burn is being investigated at various research organizations and automobile manufacturers and a number of studies on lean burn technology have been reported to this date.

This paper describes the development of a four valve lean burn engine; especially the improvement of the combustion, the development of an engine management system, and the achievement of vehicle test results.

Major themes discussed in this paper are(1) the improvement of brake-specific fuel consumption under partial load conditions and the achievement of high output power by adopting an optimized swirl ratio and a variable swirl system with a specially designed variable valve timing and lift mechanism, (2) the development of an air-fuel ratio control system, (3) the improvement of fuel economy as a vehicle and(4) an approach to satisfy the NO_x emission standard.

例4：

用于轿车的电动混合动力系统

【摘要】介绍了各种混合动力系统的结构，讨论了它们用于轿车的优点和缺点，特别介绍了串联混合动力、并联混合动力、增加转矩和速度的混合动力、单轴混合动力和双轴混合动力。

大众-奥迪集团已经开发了装备有适合于各种应用场合的混合动力装置的不同车辆。介绍了这些车辆，并给出了有关能耗、排放和运行性能的试验结果。总之，对不同情况下的市场机遇的某些问题还有待进一步考察。

Electric Hybrid Drive Systems for Passenger Cars

【Abstract】Various hybrid drive configurations are described and their advantages and disadvantages for application in passenger cars are discussed; specially, these are the series hybrid, the parallel hybrid, hybrid drives with added torque and speed, single and two-shaft hybrids.

The Volkswagen and Audi group has developed different vehicles with hybrid drive for various applications. These vehicles are described and test results are presented on their energy consumption, emissions and driving performance. In conclusion, some considerations are pursued concerning their chances on the market in different scenarios.

2. 论文英文摘要翻译注意事项

从上述5例摘要可以看出，英文摘要具有广泛使用被动句、时态多用一般现在时、句子结构紧凑等主要特点。在英语摘要的编写或翻译中，应注意以下几点。

(1)对摘要内容的一般要求

1)摘要一般应包含研究对象(目的)、研究方法(所用的设备、材料)、结果与结论。

2)摘要要尽量简短，尽可能删掉课题研究的背景信息，不能出现图表参数。

3)摘要中出现的数据应该是最重要、最关键的数据。

4)摘要不能对原文进行补充和修改，文摘中的内容应在正文中出现，并且是正文的要点。

5)摘要中的缩写名称在第一次出现时要有全称。

6)英文摘要一般以100~150个英文单词为宜。

(2)时态以一般现在时为主

在英文摘要中，以一般现在时为主，也使用一般过去时和现在完成时。

一般现在时用于描述通过科学实验取得的研究结果、结论，揭示自然界的客观规律；一般过去时用于描述对在一定范围内所观察到的自然现象的规律性认识，这种认识也许有一定的局限性；现在完成时用来表明过程的延续性。

概括起来，阐明要论述的主题，可用现在时；叙述实验方法与过程，应用过去时；描写实验前已完成的动作(过去的过去)，用过去完成时；说明实验结果，可用现在时(表示客观真理)或现在完成时(已取得的阶段性成果)。

(3)语态以被动语态居多

英文摘要主动语态偶有出现并有增长的趋势，但目前，仍以被动语态居多。这种语态可以避免提及有关的执行者，使行文显得客观。同时，被动语态的句子在结构上有较大的调节余地，有利于采用必要的修辞手段、扩展名词短语、扩大句子的信息量，有利于突出重要的概念、问题、事实、结论等，产生语义鲜明突出的效果。

(4)注意中英文的语言习惯不同

在翻译时，不应该简单地以中文的自然句为单位来逐字逐句地翻译，而应围绕文摘的各项内容来推敲用词和选用恰当的句子结构。

UNIT 15　DEVELOPMENT AND DESIGN OF ELECTRIC VEHICLES

TEXT A　Development of New Battery Electric Vehicles

A new platform for battery electric vehicles is a vehicle platform that uses new technologies and designs to conceive, develop, and produce a dedicated application of electric architecture. Although each automotive company has its own focus on the electric vehicle development stage, their project development thinking and approach are very similar. As shown in Fig. 15-1, the vehicle development process includes the entire process from project initiation to Standard Operation Procedure(SOP), which is divided into six stages: market positioning stage, project initiation stage, scheme and styling stage, detailed design stage, product validation stage and mass production preparation stage.

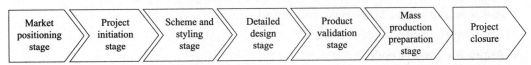

Fig. 15-1　New product development process framework

Generally speaking, in a complete set of positive electric vehicle development process, the common points of main work in each stage are as follows:

1. Market positioning stage

The stage is the market positioning stage, which analyzes national policies, infrastructure, market and customer needs, competitive situation, and combines with the vehicle company's own capabilities and strategies to develop and depict a preliminary vehicle solution to beat competitors in the target market, and evaluate and revise based on historical data and experience.[1]

1) In this stage, the range and energy consumption index of the model should be planned.

2) The degree of perfect energy replenishment facilities in the target area needs to be considered in the configuration planning to determine whether the vehicle can be configured for battery swap, DC charging, etc.

3) To clarify the business model of the application for the target customer group, and accordingly plan the functional configuration and range target of battery electric vehicles.

4) When designing for time-share rental market demand, the installation interface of

anti-theft and robbery alarm, third-party driving record and remote control interface should be reserved; when electric commercial vehicles are applied to buses and group customers, attention should be paid to consider the passenger capacity demand in the vehicle layout stage and design the range according to the driving distance.

5) Project positioning based on the established advanced competitive models in the current market is an important part of the work in this stage. Current market models with certain sales volume have been recognized by the market in terms of policy compliance, convenience of energy replenishment, and business model, which are of important reference value.

2. Project initiation stage

The objective of this stage is to clarify the achievability of the vehicle concept, the reasonableness of the investment, and the feasibility of various plans, to sort out all work objectives, programs and plans for the entire development cycle, and to confirm the project management baseline.

In this stage, the automotive companies need to review whether the current spectrum of products is ready to enter the pre-project validation stage, consider its necessity in terms of product strategy and company objectives, and make a decision on whether to start the project study. The key control activities required during this stage are as follows:

1) Approve the initial project life cycle and product positioning.
2) Approve the initial body type and brand.
3) Approve the initial business plan.
4) Apply for project code.
5) Approve the initial target market and major competitor products.
6) Approve initial project work plan, cost estimates and resource requirements.
7) Approve the proposed candidates for project director and project preparation work team.

3. Scheme and styling stage

In this stage, the concept design is used to revise and finalize the executability of the program for the styling, structure, process, technology, and quality of the vehicle and components, as well as the degree of theoretical achievability and risk. The vehicle concept design includes styling design, architecture design, general layout design, vehicle matching simulation, the first batch of FP Car(Function Prototype Car-1, a prototype to support the initial verification and calibration work of electric vehicle electric drive system) trial production, and finally freeze the data. Electric vehicles are equipped with more high-voltage and low-voltage components. When determining the overall scheme, special consideration needs to be given to the layout of the traction battery, drive motor, electric air conditioning system and the resulting impact on the vehicle layout. In addition, the main work of the design of the vehicle's high-voltage and low-voltage electrical systems is also completed at this stage.

4. Detailed design stage

In this stage, the second batch of FP Car(Function Prototype Car-2, a prototype car to support further design and verification of the vehicle/system solution, including the vehicle layout, electrical principle, electric drive system matching, electric auxiliary system and joint verification of the vehicle communication) is firstly carried out for trial production.

On this basis, engineering data and components design need to be completed, and then the company will conduct trial production to complete structural and functional verification and then conduct the first batch of EP Car(Engineering Prototype Car-1, a prototype car that combines the progress of components design for the full optimization of the vehicle design scheme, which meets the requirements of the vehicle and components design specifications and the technical conditions of the vehicle product, and carries out components commissioning, etc.) trial production, and finally complete engineering data release and mold opening instructions release.

This stage of work is to clarify that the drawing structure of the product is verified, the drawings and technical agreements have been determined and meet the requirements of the supplier and the process department for the design and manufacture of the tooling, and the key attributes are initially verified to meet the targets or to be less risky.[2]

Electric vehicles are equipped with "big three electric" including traction battery, electric motor and electric control system, and "small three electric" including electric brake, electric steering, electric air conditioning and other unique components and systems. This requires that in the detailed design stage, in addition to the traditional materials, functions, dimensions and other aspects of verification and confirmation, but also the need for high-voltage, low-voltage related to the design, analysis and approval of the electrical performance. In addition, according to *the Interim Measures for the Management of New Energy Vehicle Traction Battery Recycling*, the power battery system needs to reserve an interface for the gradual use or recycling of the vehicle after its end-of-life during the design stage.

5. Product validation stage

The main work of this stage content is to carry out mold manufacturing, OTS(hard molded components) production, regulatory certification, and tooling validation. In this stage, the second stage of EP Car(Engineering Prototype Car-2, prototype car for fine debugging of components, announcement regulation verification, etc.) trial production and PPV Car(Production Process Validation Car, prototype car for final assembly sequence verification, production line process verification, etc.) small batch assembly verification will be carried out, and product promotion and marketing planning will be initiated.

In this stage, the companies need to clarify that the structure, performance, quality, reliability and cost of the product have met the project objectives and that the production line, tooling, apparatus and equipment have been verified and are ready to determine if the vehicle is ready for mass production.[3] In the product validation stage, electric vehicles place more emphasis on vehicle functionality and reliability performance based on the vehicle network, as they carry more electrical components compared to traditional fuel vehicles. In addition, due to the structural specificity of electric vehicles, regulatory certification and access is also a top priority in the product certification stage.

6. Mass production preparation stage

The stage is the mass production preparation stage, the main work content is to carry out production line verification, tooling acceptance, production training, sales training, market promotion program implementation and market readiness check, verify the components manufacturers' climbing ability and components production consistency ability. This stage is completed by the production of PP Car (Pre-Pilot Car, a prototype car assembled on the production line using tooling components according to the process requirements for final verification and approval of the product and/or process) and P Car (Pilot Car, a prototype car mainly used to verify the quality of components provided in bulk under fully tooled and process conditions), and finally clarifies that project goals are met, market readiness is checked, and products are ready for mass production and sales. Electric vehicles are basically similar to conventional fuel vehicles in the preparation stage for mass production.

NEW WORDS

conceive	[kən'siːv]	v. 想出（主意、计划等）；想象；构想；设想
dedicated	['dedikeitid]	a. 专门的，专用的
infrastructure	['infrəstrʌktʃə(r)]	n. 基础设施，基础建设
depict	[di'pikt]	vt. 描绘；描述
replenishment	[ri'pleniʃmənt]	n. 补充；充满
interface	['intəfeis]	n. （人机）界面；接口；接口程序
feasibility	[ˌfiːzə'biliti]	n. 可行性；可能性
approve	[ə'pruːv]	v. 批准；赞成；同意；通过
revise	[ri'vaiz]	v. 修改；改变（意见或计划）
clarification	[ˌklærəfi'keiʃn]	n. 说（阐）明；解释

PHRASES AND EXPRESSIONS

electric architecture	电气化架构
Standard Operation Procedure (SOP)	标准操作（作业）程序（SOP）
energy consumption index	能耗指标
anti-theft and robbery alarm	防盗和防抢劫报警器
trial production	试生产
traction battery	动力电池

production line 生产线
tooling acceptance 工装验收

NOTES TO THE TEXT

[1] The stage is the market positioning stage, which analyzes national policies, infrastructure, market and customer needs, competitive situation, and combines with the vehicle company's own capabilities and strategies to develop and depict a preliminary vehicle solution to beat competitors in the target market, and evaluate and revise based on historical data and experience.

句中 which 引导非限制性定语从句，修饰 market positioning stage, based on historical data and experience 为状语，意为"依据历史数据和经验"。本句可以译为："该阶段为市场定位阶段，分析国家政策、基础设施、市场和客户需求、竞争形势，并结合汽车公司自身能力和战略，来开发和描绘出初步的车辆解决方案，在目标市场击败竞争对手，并依据历史数据和经验进行评估和修订。"

[2] This stage of work is to clarify that the drawing structure of the product is verified, the drawings and technical agreements have been determined and meet the requirements of the supplier and the process department for the design and manufacture of the tooling, and the key attributes are initially verified to meet the targets or to be less risky.

句中 that 引导宾语从句，作为 clarify 的宾语。本句可以译为："本阶段的工作是为了明确产品的图纸结构已得到校验，图纸和技术协议已确定，并满足供应商和工艺部门对工装设计和制造的要求，关键属性已初步验证以满足目标或降低风险。"

[3] In this stage, the companies need to clarify that the structure, performance, quality, reliability and cost of the product have met the project objectives and that the production line, tooling, apparatus and equipment have been verified and are ready to determine if the vehicle is ready for mass production.

句中 that 引导宾语从句。本句可以译为："此阶段需明确产品的结构、性能、品质、可靠性和成本已达到项目目标，生产线、工装、器具和设备已验证并准备就绪，以确定车辆是否可以批量生产。"

EXERCISES

I. *Answer the following questions:*
  1. What are the battery electric vehicles for new-product development process framework?
  2. What is the main work content of mass production preparation stage?

II. *Translate the following paragraphs into Chinese:*
  1. The degree of perfect energy replenishment facilities in the target area needs to be considered in the configuration planning to determine whether the vehicle can be configured for battery swap, DC charging, etc.

2. When determining the overall scheme, special consideration needs to be given to the layout of the traction battery, drive motor, electric air conditioning system and the resulting impact on the vehicle layout.

3. In this stage, the second batch of FP Car(Function Prototype Car-2, a prototype car to support further design and verification of the vehicle/system solution, including the vehicle layout, electrical principle, electric drive system matching, electric auxiliary system and joint verification of the vehicle communication) is firstly carried out for trial production.

TEXT B Layout Design of Battery Electric Commercial Vehicles

Compared with battery electric passenger vehicles, the layout space of battery electric commercial vehicles is more generous. This section will briefly discuss the principles and main contents of the vehicle layout of battery electric commercial vehicles.

The vehicle layout of battery electric commercial vehicles should meet the requirements of safety, environmental protection and related regulations and international practices, as well as the corresponding functional and performance requirements. The overall balance of the vehicle is the basis of the vehicle layout, the design should put the use performance in the first place, and then consider the problem in the order of manufacturing, maintenance and appearance, so that the vehicle is easy to use, easy to repair, easy to build and good to look at. The vehicle layout should be coordinated and fit with the shape idea. Battery electric commercial vehicles should focus on the performance of high-voltage parts such as waterproof, dustproof and fireproof, in line with the style and requirements of the shape, and fully consider the assembly requirements of the body and chassis and high-voltage parts.

The high-voltage parts of battery electric commercial vehicles mainly consist of electric drive system, energy storage device, electric accessories, electric control unit, receiving device and other related high-voltage parts. The safe operation for the vehicle is ensured through the electric control unit between each system.

Power battery pack and other energy storage devices according to market demand mainly have bottom middle section plus rear section and top plus bottom rear section layout form: bottom should be fully considered energy storage device heat dissipation, insulation needs and anti-collision requirements, top energy storage device should increase the corresponding protective cover.

Electric accessories, electric control unit is mainly concentrated in the vehicle under the last row of seats and the rear high-voltage parts compartment, the electric control unit and the rear surround should ensure a certain safety distance.

If there is a receiving device, the receiving device is generally arranged on the roof of the vehicle.

The design of low-floor or low-entry battery electric bus should comply with the national standard. The layout of the vehicle high-voltage parts should ensure the width and slope of the channel between the wheel covers, the height of the one step from the ground and the height of the carriage and other overall space design requirements.

Among them, the requirements for the width between the front wheel covers are as follows.

For the length of less than or equal to 9m low-floor, low-entry bus, the width of the channel between the front wheel cover is greater than or equal to 550mm.

For the length of more than 9m low-floor bus, the width of the channel between the front wheel cover is greater than or equal to 800mm.

For the length of more than 9m low-entry bus, the width of the channel between the front wheel cover is greater than or equal to 600mm.

The width of the channel between the rear wheel covers is greater than or equal to 500mm; the width of the channel between the wheel covers should be measured in the range from the floor surface to 1800mm above. When the vehicle is in normal driving quality and the body lifting system is not working, the channel's longitudinal slope should not exceed 8% and the transverse slope should not exceed 5%.

Level-one tread height from the ground should be measured when the body is in normal driving quality and placed on a flat horizontal surface, the specific requirements are as follows.

The level-one tread height from the ground of the bus with low floor should be less than or equal to 360mm.

The level-one tread height from the ground of the low-entry bus with air suspension should be less than or equal to 360mm, and the level-one tread height from the ground with mechanical suspension should be less than or equal to 380mm.

The cabin height requirements for Low-floor or low-entry bus are shown in Table 15-1. Low floor area refers to a single floor channel area without treads.

Table 15-1 the cabin height requirements for low-floor or low-entry bus

Classification		Cabin height requirement /mm
Single-decker bus	Vehicle length ≤9m	≥ 2000
	Vehicle length >9m	≥ 2200
Double-decker bus	Lower: low-floor area	≥ 1800
	Upper: low-floor area	≥ 1680

Generally, the power battery pack of low-floor battery electric vehicle is arranged at the bottom of the rear section and the bottom space under the seat or on the roof, the electric drive system is arranged at the bottom of the rear section, and the electric control parts of the vehicle are arranged in the rear high-voltage electrical parts compartment.

The electric drive axle scheme is adopted for battery electric cargo vehicles. The power battery pack can be arranged in the middle of the two longitudinal beams or on both sides of the chassis and the rear of the cab. The layout of the power battery pack should meet the requirements of the top loading space, avoid the moving parts on the vehicle chassis and consider the distribution of the vehicle's center of gravity and the load distribution of the vehicle. In addition, reliable mechanical and electrical connections need to be provided between the power battery pack and the vehicle, and heat dissipation and insulation needs should be fully considered. The outline dimensions, axle loads and mass limits of cargo vehicles should conform to the requirements of the national standard.

NEW WORDS

generous	['dʒenərəs]	a. 慷慨的；丰富的；充足的
functional	['fʌŋkʃənl]	a. 实用的；功能的；机能的
longitudinal	[ˌlɔŋgi'tjuːdinl]	a. 纵的；纵向的；纵观的；经度的
transverse	['trænzvɜːs]	a. 横(向)的
decker	['dekə(r)]	n. 层

PHRASES AND EXPRESSIONS

high-voltage part	高压部件
electric accessories	电器附件
power battery pack	动力电池组
anti-collision requirement	防撞要求
the height of the carriage	车厢高度
axle load	轴重

EXERCISES

I. Answer the following questions:

1. What are the requirements for the vehicle layout of battery electric commercial vehicles?

2. Where is the electric drive system for typical layout of high-voltage parts of low-floor battery electric vehicles arranged at?

II. Translate the following paragraphs into Chinese:

1. The vehicle layout of battery electric commercial vehicles should meet the requirements of safety, environmental protection and related regulations and international practices, as well as the corresponding functional and performance requirements.

2. Electric accessories, electric control unit is mainly concentrated in the vehicle under

the last row of seats and the rear high-voltage parts compartment, the electric control unit and the rear surround should ensure a certain safety distance.

3. In addition, reliable mechanical and electrical connections need to be provided between the power battery pack and the vehicle, and heat dissipation and insulation needs should be fully considered.

TEXT C Optimal Configuration Selection Principle for Hybrid Drive Systems

The basic approach of optimum configuration selection is as follows: obtaining the basic parameters and basic performance indexes of the vehicle, preliminarily selecting several commonly-applied configurations for further optimum selection according to the application conditions, and then finalizing the satisfactory configuration based on the optimum configuration selection method.[1]

The basic process of optimum configuration selection of hybrid electric vehicles is shown in Fig. 15-2.

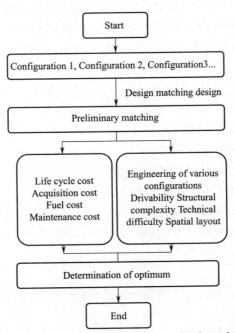

Fig. 15-2 Process of optimum configuration selection of hybrid system

Provided that the vehicle parameters and basic performance indexes are the same, subject several typical hybrid system configurations to preliminary matching to obtain the preliminary matching results of each configuration. Then, based on the preliminary matching results and in consideration of the life cycle cost and engineering difficulty of each hybrid system configuration, the optimum configuration is selected.

1. Preliminary matching of configurations

Though the configurations of hybrid system are different from each other in structure and layout, their matching approaches are basically similar. In most cases, the matching is performed in the order of "total power → engine power → power, speed and torque of motor → energy, power and capacity of traction battery" based on the power transmission characteristics and internal energy flow relation.

(1) Calculation of total power of hybrid system

Generally, the total power required by a hybrid vehicle mainly includes the power at maximum vehicle speed(P_{max1}), the power at maximum grade ability(P_{max2}), the power for acceleration(P_{max3}) and the power for speed following in drive cycle(P_{max4}). The required total power(P_{max}) is to be calculated according to Formula(15-1).

$$P_{max} \geqslant \max(P_{max1}, P_{max2}, P_{max3}, P_{max4}) \tag{15-1}$$

(2) Type selection of engine

According to the operating characteristics of the engine and the motor(i. e. the engine has a large moment of inertia and a slow response, while the motor has a fast response), it is required to make the engine provide steady state power with slow change, while the motor provide peak power with instantaneous change. The steady state power includes the power at cruise speed P_{e1} and the continuous climbing power P_{e2}.

For driving at cruising speed, the required engine power is to be calculated as Formula (15-2).

$$P_{e1} = \frac{v_x}{3600\eta_{tr}}\left(mgf_r + \frac{C_D A v_x^2}{21.15}\right) \tag{15-2}$$

Where, v_x— cruise speed(km/h);

m— vehicle mass(kg);

g— gravitational acceleration(m/s^2);

C_D— coefficient of air resistance;

A— windward area(m^2).

The engine power required for continuous climbing is to be calculated as Formula (15-3).

$$P_{e2} = \frac{v_{ic}}{3600\eta_t}\left(mgf_r\cos\alpha + mg\sin\alpha + \frac{C_D A v_{ic}^2}{21.15}\right) \tag{15-3}$$

Where, $\alpha = \arctan(i/100)$;

v_{ic}— climbing speed(km/h).

The engine power should at least meet the power requirements determined above, as shown in Formula(15-4).

$$P_e \geqslant \max(P_{e1}, P_{e2}) \tag{15-4}$$

(3) Type selection of motor

As the applicable working conditions of motors in different configurations are different, their matching process involves certain differences. For motors of parallel P2 configuration, switching series-parallel configuration and planetary series-parallel configuration, the specific selection requirements are as follows.

1) Parallel P2 configuration. In this configuration, the motor provides rated power during pure electric driving mode, and provides instantaneous peak power when driving resistance increases or rapid acceleration is required. The maximum speed of motor shall meet the limit speed requirement of vehicle.

2) Switching series-parallel configuration. In this configuration, as the engine is disabled from operation when the vehicle speed is low, the main clutch must stay disengaged, and the main motor is required to work for driving alone. The auxiliary motor mainly starts and shuts down the engine, and can serve as an auxiliary driving source when a higher torque/power is required.

3) Planetary series-parallel configuration. A planetary series-parallel hybrid system allows for decoupling of engine speed, torque and road load to control the engine to follow the optimal curve as desired, and thus, the two motors can realize such functions as engine speed decoupling and torque peak shaving.

(4) Type selection of traction battery

As the auxiliary energy source of hybrid electric vehicles, the traction battery is required to fast respond to the power demand from the motor during driving to provide driving energy or store the energy recovered during regenerative braking.[2] Therefore, the traction battery should meet the power requirements of the power system, and should have sufficient capacity to meet the all-electric range requirement of the hybrid electric vehicles.

The power level of the traction battery is related to the motor(i. e. the output power of the traction battery should be such that a balance is realized between the system circuits). The charge/discharge current of the traction battery is somehow limited, as a too high charge/discharge current will cause temperature rise and thereby shorten the service life of the traction battery. The charge/discharge current of the traction battery is related to its capacity, and the maximum current is generally limited to $3 \sim 5C$(C is the capacity of the traction battery).

The energy of the traction battery pack is mainly to meet the range index of the vehicle. Generally, the constant velocity method is used to calculate the required energy of a traction battery, as shown in Formula(15-5).

$$E_b = \frac{\frac{sP_b}{v} + E_{eacc}}{\zeta_{soc}} \qquad (15\text{-}5)$$

Where, E_b — energy of traction battery required for a range s (kW·h);

v — vehicle speed(km/h);

E_{eacc} — power consumption of electric accessories(kW·h);

ζ_{soc} — the depth of discharge of the traction battery, for example, for a discharge from 100% to 20%, the depth of discharge is 80%, and 100% discharge of rated capacity is not allowed;

s — required range(km);

P_b — output power of traction battery at the current vehicle speed.

The relation between the capacity and energy of the traction battery is as follows(15-6).

$$C = 1000 \frac{E_b}{U_b} \qquad (15\text{-}6)$$

Where, C — capacity of traction battery(Ah);

U_b — average operating voltage of traction battery(V).

The capacity selection of a traction battery is closely related to the rated voltage of electrical system. When the power is too high and the selected rated voltage of the electrical system is too low, it suggests that the capacity of the traction battery is too high, which makes the charge/discharge current too high, and will pose safety risk to the hybrid system and great challenges to the motor control unit.[3]

The voltage level of power battery shall be reasonably selected according to the requirements of national standards.

2. Comprehensive optimum configuration selection

The optimum configuration selection of hybrid system is based on the matching results and in consideration of the life cycle cost and engineering difficulty of each configuration.

(1) Life cycle cost of each configuration

The life cycle cost mainly includes acquisition cost, fuel cost and maintenance cost, among which, the acquisition cost mainly refers to the cost caused by the configuration difference between the hybrid electric vehicle and the traditional power-driven vehicle; the fuel cost refers to the cost for use of fuel and electric energy during the operation of the hybrid electric vehicle. The life cycle cost is calculated as shown in Formula(15-7).

$$C_{back} = C_{gz} + C_{ry} + C_{wx} \qquad (15\text{-}7)$$

Where, C_{back} — life cycle cost;

C_{gz} — acquisition cost;

C_{ry} — fuel cost;

C_{wx} — maintenance cost.

1) Acquisition cost of each configuration. The acquisition cost of each configuration is to be estimated. The motor system is mainly composed of a motor and a motor control unit, and its cost function is based on the mass production condition(Equation15-8).

$$C_{motor} = c + dP_{mpeak} \qquad (15\text{-}8)$$

Where, c, d — fitting functions, which are obtained from the relation between the price of the motor and its control unit and the power;

P_{mpeak} — peak power of motor(kW);

C_{motor} — cost of motor. The traction battery and other components can be evaluated according to market investigation or experience.

2) Fuel cost of each configuration. The fuel cost of each configuration can be represented as follows(Equation 15-9).

$$C_{ry} = \text{Day} \frac{\text{fuel}(L - L_1)}{100 P_{rfuel} + E_{bat} P_{rele}} \tag{15-9}$$

Where, Day — the average annual operation days of buses(excluding maintenance days);
L — mileage covered per day(km);
L_1 — all-electric mileage covered per day(km);
fuel — fuel consumption per 100 km(L/100km);
P_{rfuel} — diesel price(dollar/L);
E_{bat} — energy of traction battery(kWh) required for pure electric driving;
P_{rele} — electricity price(dollar/kWh).

3) Maintenance cost of each configuration. The maintenance cost of each configuration can be estimated according to market investigation and experience.

4) Sensitivity analysis. The life cycle cost is affected by the change of fuel price and acquisition cost. To improve the predication accuracy of the life cycle cost of the hybrid system configuration, it is necessary to consider the influence of the factors mentioned above and carry out individual factor sensitivity analysis, mainly including change of fuel price, change of acquisition cost and change of maintenance cost.

(2) Engineering difficulty of each configuration

The engineering comparison and analysis of configurations can be carried out from the aspects of comprehensive performance, structural complexity, technical difficulty and spatial layout. Each evaluation index is scored, and the total score of each configuration is calculated. The comparison of total score reflects in essence the comparison of engineering difficulty of each configuration.

NEW WORDS

configuration [kənˌfigəˈreiʃn] n. 配置；结构
sensitivity [ˌsensəˈtivəti] n. 敏感；灵敏性

PHRASES AND EXPRESSIONS

cruise speed 巡航速度
gravitational acceleration 重力加速度
windward area 迎风面积

regenerative braking	再生制动；反馈制动
life cycle cost	全寿命周期成本
acquisition cost	购置成本

NOTES TO THE TEXT

[1] The basic approach of optimum configuration selection is as follows: obtaining the basic parameters and basic performance indexes of the vehicle, preliminarily selecting several commonly-applied configurations for further optimum selection according to the application conditions, and then finalizing the satisfactory configuration based on the optimum configuration selection method.

句中 obtaining、selecting 和 finalizing 是并列的三个短语。本句可以译为："优化配置选择的基本方法如下：获取车辆的基本参数和基本性能指标，根据应用条件，初步选择几种常用配置，为进一步的优化选择，然后根据最优配置选择方法确定满意的配置。"

[2] As the auxiliary energy source of hybrid electric vehicles, the traction battery is required to fast respond to the power demand from the motor during driving to provide driving energy or store the energy recovered during regenerative braking.

句中 recovered during regenerative braking 作后置定语，修饰 energy，表示"再生制动时回收的能量"。本句可以译为："作为混合动力电动汽车的辅助能源，在汽车行驶过程中，动力电池能快速响应电机的功率需求，来提供驱动汽车的能量或储存再生制动时回收的能量。"

[3] When the power is too high and the selected rated voltage of the electrical system is too low, it suggests that the capacity of the traction battery is too high, which makes the charge/discharge current too high, and will pose safety risk to the hybrid system and great challenges to the motor control unit.

it suggests that 中的 it 指代前面 When 引导时间状语从句的含义，that…control unit 作 suggest 的宾语从句，在此从句中，Which…control unit 为非限制性定语从句，Which 指代 the capacity of the traction battery is too high，pose risk to 表示"对……构成安全隐患"。本句可以译为："当功率过高并且电气系统选择的额定电压过低时，表明动力电池的容量过高，使充/放电电流过高，会对混合动力系统构成安全隐患，并对电机控制单元构成极大挑战。"

EXERCISES

I. Answer the following questions:

1. What is the basic approach of optimum configuration selection?
2. What is the formula for engine power required for continuous climbing?

II. Translate the following paragraphs into Chinese:

1. Then, based on the preliminary matching results and in consideration of the life

cycle cost and engineering difficulty of each hybrid system configuration, the optimum configuration is selected.

2. As the applicable working conditions of motors in different configurations are different, their matching process involves certain differences.

3. In this configuration, as the engine is disabled from operation when the vehicle speed is low, the main clutch must stay disengaged, and the main motor is required to work for driving alone.

4. The life cycle cost mainly includes acquisition cost, fuel cost and maintenance cost, among which, the acquisition cost mainly refers to the cost caused by the configuration difference between the hybrid electric vehicle and the traditional power-driven vehicle; the fuel cost refers to the cost for use of fuel and electric energy during the operation of the hybrid electric vehicle.

REFERENCES

[1] MARTIN W Stockel, Martin T Stockel & Chris Johanson. Auto Fundamentals[M]. Tinley Park, Illinois: The Goodheart-willcox Company, Inc. 1994: 44-47, 408-412, 463-464.

[2] MARK Ryan, John H Haynes. L'INCOLN Rear-wheel Drive Models Automotive Repair Manual[M]. Newbury Park, California: Haynes North America, Inc. 1996: 9-4~9-9.

[3] 陈焕江, 徐双英. 交通运输专业英语[M]. 北京: 机械工业出版社, 2002: 1-4.

[4] 黄韶炯, 栾志强. 汽车专业英语[M]. 北京: 人民交通出版社, 2005: 15-16.

[5] 傅晓玲, 尚媛媛, 等. 英汉互译高级教程[M]. 广州: 中山大学出版社, 2004: 125-128.

[6] 许建平. 英汉互译实践与技巧[M]. 2版. 北京: 清华大学出版社, 2003: 32-35.

[7] 卢红梅. 大学英汉汉英翻译教程[M]. 北京: 科学出版社, 2006: 92-94.

[8] 李俊玲, 罗永革. 汽车工程专业英语[M]. 北京: 机械工业出版社, 2005: 42.

[9] THOMSON D L. Advanced Engine Performance [M]. Independence, KY: Delmar Learning, 2004: 53-61.

[10] CHARLES O Probst. BOSCH Fuel Injection & Engine Management[M]. Cambridge, Massachusetts: Robert Bentley. 1991: 4-7, 30-39.

[11] TOM Denton. Automotive Electrical and Electronic Systems[M]. Burlington: Elsevier Butterworth-Heinemann, 2004: 251-255.

[12] Toyota Technical Training. Toyota Hybrid System Diagnosis-Course 072. [EB/OL]. (2014-11-4) [2015-8-1]. http: //autoshop101. com.

[13] FRED Bordoff. Emission Control System. [EB/OL]. (2011-8-21) [2015-8-1]. http: //www. familycar. com.

[14] Lexus Technical Training. Traction Control System. [EB/OL]. (2013-1-21) [2015-7-15]. http: //autoshop101. com.

[15] KARIM Nice. How Fuel Cells Work. [EB/OL]. (2011-1-19) [2015-7-1]. http: //auto. Howstuffworks. com.

[16] KARIM Nice. How Turbochargers Work. [EB/OL]. (2008-8-1) [2015-8-15]. http: //auto. Howstuffworks. com.

[17] SCHNUBEL, M. Classroom Manual for Advanced Engine Performance[M]. Boston: Thomson Delmar Learning, 2006:119-123, 176-182.

[18] 宗长富, 刘凯. 汽车线控驱动技术的发展[J]. 汽车技术, 2006(3): 1-5.

[19] 葛蕴珊, 谭建伟, 姜磊, 等. 汽油车进排气系统降低噪声研究[J]. 汽车技术, 2006(11): 9-13.

[20] 赵萱, 郑仰成. 科技英语翻译[M]. 北京: 外语教学与研究出版社, 2006: 296-302.

[21] Takefuml Hosaka, Minoru Hamazaki. Development of the Valve Timing and Lift(VTEC)Engine for the Honda NSX[J]. SAE TRANSACTIONS, Journal of Engines. 1991, 100: 1-5.

[22] WILBERFORCE TABBI, EL-HASSAN ZAKI, KHATIB FN, et al. Development of Electric Cars and Fuel Cell Hydrogen Electric Cars [J]. Oxford: International Journal of Hydrogen Energy, 2017, 42(40): 5695-5734.

[23] Masahiko Miyaki, Hideya Fujisawa, Akiro Masuda. Development of New Electrically Controlled Fuel Injection System ECD-U2 for Diesel Engines[J]. SAE TRANSACTIONS, Journal of Engines. 1991, 100:312-328.

[24] HARALD Naunheimer, BERND Bertsche, JOACHIM Ryborz, etal. Automotive Transmissions[M]. 2 ed. Berlin:Springer, 2011: 169-173, 208-209.

[25] RICHARD, F. Modern Automotive Technology[M]. Berlin: VERLAG EUROPA-LEHRMITTEL, 2006: 239-240, 280-281, 374-375.

[26] 宋进桂, 徐永亮, 等. 新能源汽车专业英语[M]. 北京：机械工业出版社, 2020: 050-051.

[27] Luettel T, Himmelsbach M, Wuensche H J. Autonomous ground vehicles—concepts and a path to the future [J]. Proceedings of the IEEE, 2012, 100(13): 1831-1839.

[28] SCHWEITZER M, UNTERHOLZNER A, WUENSCHE H J. Real-time visual odometry for ground moving robots using GPUs [J]. Computer Vision Theory & Applications, 2010: 20-27.

[29] MOORE M M, LU B. Autonomous vehicles for personal transport: A technology assessment [J/OL]. (2011-7-16) [2021-6-1]. http://ssrn.com/paper=1865047.

[30] 孙逢春, 林程, 等. 电动汽车工程手册 第一卷 纯电动汽车整车设计[M]. 北京：机械工业出版社, 2019.

[31] 孙逢春, 何洪文, 等. 电动汽车工程手册 第二卷 混合动力电动汽车整车设计[M]. 北京：机械工业出版社, 2019.

[32] 孙逢春, 章桐, 等. 电动汽车工程手册 第三卷 燃料电池电动汽车整车设计[M]. 北京：机械工业出版社, 2019.